CW00675754

The Humanist World of Renaissance Florence

This book offers a major contribution for understanding the spread and appeal of the humanist movement in Renaissance Florence. Investigating the connections among the individuals who were part of the humanist movement, Brian Jeffrey Maxson reconstructs the networks that bound them together. Overturning the problematic categorization of humanists as either professionals or amateurs, a distinction based on economics and the production of original works in Latin, he offers a new way of understanding how the humanist movement could incorporate so many who were illiterate in Latin, but who nonetheless were responsible for an important intellectual and cultural paradigm shift. The book demonstrates the massive appeal of the humanist movement across socioeconomic and political groups and argues that the movement became so successful and so widespread because by the 1420s–30s the demands of common rituals began requiring humanist speeches. Over time, deep humanist learning became more valuable in the marketplace of social capital, which raised the status of the most learned humanists and helped disseminate humanist ideas beyond Florence.

Brian Jeffrey Maxson is an assistant professor of history at East Tennessee State University. His research focuses on the cultural and political history of late medieval and Renaissance Europe. His articles have appeared in *Renaissance Studies* and *I Tatti Studies*, among other journals. He has held fellowships from the Fulbright and Dolores Zohrab Liebmann Foundations and has given invited lectures at the University of Oxford and the Ludwig Maximilians Universität in Munich.

The Humanist World of Renaissance Florence

BRIAN JEFFREY MAXSON

East Tennessee State University

CAMBRIDGE
UNIVERSITY PRESS

CAMBRIDGE
UNIVERSITY PRESS

32 Avenue of the Americas, New York, NY 10013–2473, USA

Cambridge University Press is part of the University of Cambridge.

It furthers the University's mission by disseminating knowledge in the pursuit of education, learning, and research at the highest international levels of excellence.

www.cambridge.org
Information on this title: www.cambridge.org/9781107043916

© Brian Jeffrey Maxson 2014

First published 2014

Printed in the United States of America

A catalog record for this publication is available from the British Library.

Library of Congress Cataloging in Publication Data
Maxson, Brian, 1978–
The humanist world of Renaissance Florence / Brian Maxson, East Tennessee State University.
pages cm
Includes bibliographical references and index.
ISBN 978-1-107-04391-6 (hardback : alk. paper) ISBN 978-1-107-61964-7
1. Humanism – Italy – Florence – History.   2. Renaissance – Italy –
Florence.   3. Florence (Italy) – History – 1421–1737   1. Title.
DG737.55M39   2014
945'.51105–dc23   2013027341

ISBN 978-1-107-04391-6 Hardback

To Jennifer and Alex

Contents

Acknowledgments

The research and writing of this book have benefited from the generosity of numerous agencies and universities. My thanks to Northwestern University, which made graduate education possible to a first-generation college graduate from a working-class background. The J. William Fulbright Foundation funded a year of research in Italy. The Dolores Zohrab Liebmann Foundation provided a year of uninterrupted time to write my dissertation. The Office of Research and Sponsored Programs, the School of Graduate Studies, and the History Department at East Tennessee State University all provided funds for long and short trips to Italy to revise and finish this book.

Over the past decade I have incurred more debts to scholars than is possible to list. I would like to thank a few rather than try and inevitably fail to list them all. Chris Celenza and Stuart Lingo introduced me to the Italian Renaissance and the possibility of graduate school. At Northwestern my graduate cohort taught me how to read an academic book, analyze the past, and say what I mean. My thanks especially to Nic Baker, Beth Condie-Pugh, Suzanne Lavere, Elise Lipkowitz, Peter Mazur, and Christopher Sparshott. Among the faculty, Richard Kieckhefer, Marco Ruffini, and Ethan Shagan offered support at critical times. Ed Muir was unfailing in his encouragement and a model adviser. Thanks, Ed, you are the best. Since defending my dissertation my academic debts have grown exponentially. I would like to thank Oren Margolis and Ron Witt in particular, as well as the two anonymous readers for Cambridge University Press. The staffs of all the libraries in which I have worked on this project have shown saintly patience with me, especially the Archivio di Stato, the Biblioteca Nazionale Centrale, and the Biblioteca dell'Istituto Nazionale di

Studi sul Rinascimento in Florence, as well as the Interlibrary Loan Department at East Tennessee State University, who are truly miracle workers.

My thanks also to my colleagues and students in the History Department at East Tennessee State University. Mickey Braswell, Emmett Essin, Steve Fritz, Mel Page, Dale Royalty, and Dale Schmitt kept me sane and caffeinated as I adjusted to life as an assistant professor. Andrew Slap read drafts of proposals and applications far outside his specialty and offered invaluable feedback. Victoria Meyer, John Rankin, and Kanisorn Wongsrichanalai provided implicit and explicit encouragement. John Greenlee offered indispensable editing advice. I am most grateful to work in such a congenial and supportive department situated in such a beautiful place.

Above all else I thank my family, whose support has been unflinching. I wish that my grandmother, Ruth Schmidt, great-uncle, Conover Wilkinson, and brother, Ronald Paul Maxson, had lived to see this project completed. My in-laws, Jim, Annette, Chad, and Missy Murray, all have tolerated my eccentricities with humor and welcomed me into their family with warmth. For twenty years Jeff McClintic has been my brother in all but blood – thank you for helping me learn to conquer my fears and believe in myself. For nearly as long, Jason Sieggreen has provided a model for what a good friend is supposed to be – thank you for keeping in touch and inspiring me to treat people better. My parents, Ron and Cathy, could not have provided a more loving home or been better parents. My daughter Alex was born in the midst of this project and brought new meaning to the word "joy." Regarding my wife, Jennifer, words simply fail me. I love you and thank you, here, there, and everywhere.

Introduction

A Social Conception of the Humanist Movement

From limited origins in thirteenth-century Padua the humanist studies of a handful of men and women exploded into a cultural and educational movement that reached across Europe and lasted for centuries. Writers like Petrarch, Bruni, and Erasmus became famous for their unparalleled mastery of the languages and writings of the ancient world. The humanists offered Europe a new focus for study, new approach to problems, and new style in which people could express themselves. But humanist studies and writings did more than change the way a few intellectuals discussed esoteric questions or alter the costume in which they dressed their words. Humanism introduced fundamental changes to the ways people viewed the world and interacted with one another. Humanism reintroduced the texts to the West that made possible the voyages of exploration, the Protestant Reformations, and the scientific revolution. Humanist innovations lie at the foundation of countless modern academic disciplines, including history, for which fifteenth-century humanist historians developed philological and evidentiary techniques that continue to inform historical research.

The humanists' focus on the lives of people in and outside the forum underlay their success. From the most basic perspective, humanists sought to inspire moral virtue in their contemporaries by encouraging the study of ethics, the emulation or avoidance of examples from history – and to a lesser extent literature – and a firm knowledge of the grammatical and rhetorical tools necessary to move others to their opinion of the morally correct point of view. Theoretically, political men and women, teachers, businesspeople, members of the church, and anyone else with the means to acquire humanist training could integrate their learning in their political, business, social, and all other dealings with people. Individuals could and were encouraged to raise their status through their learned pursuits. Meanwhile, the study and scrutiny of classical texts shattered the shackles of antiquity and allowed new paradigms to enter European thought and action. Natural scientists, political thinkers, and others used their humanist studies to surpass their classical predecessors and forge new paths across disciplines.

From the thirteenth through the seventeenth centuries, humanists wrote hundreds of treatises in a Latin that strived to be as classical as possible, a style now called "neo-Latin." They penned these works because the humanists believed classical Latin was the key to better rhetorical persuasion. Only recently have scholars truly turned their attention to editing and translating these texts, a large number of which survive unedited from the European Renaissance. Like the humanist book hunters whom they study, these modern scholars have striven to find, edit, and translate this important body of literature, effectively introducing it to English readers and reintroducing it to Latin ones. This admirable task has dominated the history of humanism for the past decade.

Consequently, scholars of humanism have focused their debates on the nuances and contradictions inherent in these humanist texts, especially the characteristics that distinguish humanism from earlier and later developments in intellectual history. Four major interpretations have proven particularly influential in the historiography. Ronald Witt argued that the style of humanist Latin set humanists apart from previous thinkers and authors. This style gradually moved across literary genres and culminated in changes in oratory in the early fifteenth century.[1] Paul Oskar Kristeller argued that humanists focused on the five subjects of the *studia humanitatis* – history, poetry, grammar, rhetoric, and moral philosophy. He famously contrasted the thought and writings of the humanists with those of more traditional philosophical movements.[2] Hans Baron pointed to the ideal of the active life, particularly in the context of a republic, as the defining aspect of humanist thought.[3] Eugenio Garin focused on the philosophical writings of the humanists and argued that they shared an advocacy for the active life and a rudimentary form of historicism.[4]

Fifteenth-century humanist authors often encompassed aspects of all four of these definitions. Both Witt and Kristeller most closely adhered to the concerns of the humanists themselves. Humanist writers appraised the Latin style of their peers and expected eloquence along classical, often Ciceronian lines. Moreover, most original humanist texts in Latin pertain to the subjects of the *studia humanitatis*. Certainly, Kristeller's definition, or categorization, as Christopher Celenza has argued, may be too stringent.[5] For example, Leonardo Bruni spent much of his career translating philosophical works by Aristotle and Plato that fell well outside the five subjects of the *studia humanitatis*. Yet, Kristeller himself was willing to accept a mixture of interests within a single individual, as shown in his discussion of the metaphysical and theological thought of Marsilio Ficino while also acknowledging his literary and stylistic concerns.[6]

Hans Baron and Eugenio Garin also focused on important aspects of humanist writings. The "Baron Thesis" argued that the year of crisis in 1402 dramatically shifted the content of literary works in Florence. After that year writers moved away from advocating a contemplative, apolitical life and began urging citizens to active lives dedicated to the defense of republican liberty. Baron's dating, causation, and arguments about republican sincerity probably are not correct.[7] However, most scholars have continued to accept that many fifteenth-century humanists in Florence advocated the ideal of the active life of a citizen.[8] Margery Ganz, Arthur Field, Mark Jurdjevic, and others have convincingly argued that this ideal of "civic humanism" continued even after many Florentine intellectuals began focusing on metaphysical questions.[9] As Eugenio Garin pointed out, much of the most innovative metaphysical speculation by humanist authors pertained to the place of man in the cosmos. Certainly, many humanists strayed from this line, never advocated it, or focused on religious matters, but Garin's broader points about historicism and his diachronic approach to intellectual history remain valid.[10] Taken together, these four definitions provide a good sense of the means and focus of cultural expression by fifteenth-century humanist authors.[11] They also shift the focus of humanist studies overwhelmingly to the writings and original ideas of the most exceptional humanists.

The arguments of this book uphold the importance of making humanist texts available to a broader readership even as it pushes all historians to expand the scope of their inquiries to include the learned pursuits of individuals outside the core group of well-known humanists and their works. Even a cursory glance through Paul Oskar Kristeller's *Iter Italicum*, a massively impressive finding guide to humanist texts, reveals that the "lost continent" of Renaissance Latin literature is enormous, but a deeper analysis reveals something additional.[12] The number of different humanist authors writing original Latin works at any given time was actually quite small. In the end, an exhaustive search would turn up maybe thirty humanist authors in fifteenth-century Florence writing Latin works, and far fewer major writers. A couple dozen authors were a drop in the bucket in a city with hundreds of patrician families, each with myriad distinct familial branches, and tens of thousands of other inhabitants. This was the situation in Florence, the city that enjoyed a peninsula-wide reputation as the center of humanist studies. How did so few people launch such a widespread movement? Put another way, if the humanist movement in Florence encompassed so few writers, how could it possibly have had the influence that later scholars have quite rightly attributed to it? Frankly, if so few people actually inhabited the lost continent of literature, why should most historians of Renaissance Italy and Europe bother to study the growing number of handsome editions and thoughtful translations of humanist works?

The answer to all of these questions lies in the thousands of active participants in the humanist movement who studied classical and humanist texts but who themselves were not part of its core members of prolific writers, brilliant classical scholars, and prominent patrons. The humanist movement during the Italian Renaissance included these outstanding individuals, but it also included less prominent patrons, less talented orators, less learned classicists, Latin-illiterate readers of humanist and classical works in vernacular translations, and everything in between. Men and women from across this range of humanist interests and abilities crowded bookshops and participated in discussion groups about classical and humanist texts and ideas. They differed in the degree of their interests and influence, but not in kind from their more learned contemporaries. The men and women outside the core group of humanists served as the primary audience for humanist and classical books. Most of them possessed more social status than the fraction of the movement made up of its most dominant players. In fact, the large group of so-called amateur humanists, scattered as they were across the spectrum of humanist interests and abilities, were often the only individuals in cities like Florence who possessed enough social status to fulfill the common refrain in humanist writings to combine learning with the active citizen life successfully. By the 1420s at the latest, this literary suggestion had turned into a practical necessity because most rituals during the Renaissance, in and outside Florence, required displays of humanist learning from participants.

Traditionally, scholars have focused on the most prolific humanist writers and relied on the terms "amateur" and "professional" whenever they have needed to discuss any other members of the humanist movement. However, such categories are misleading for understanding the primary distinctions among Renaissance humanists. More than fifty years ago, Lauro Martines rightly pointed out the problems with this distinction, even declaring that he discussed the matter with no less than Paul Oskar Kristeller.[13] Martines defined professionals and amateurs, stating, "The professional presumably counted on his humanistic culture for his livelihood, the amateur did not."[14] Martines's fine study went on to establish the then-novel claim that very few humanists were wandering scholars who used letters for subsistence and languished outside the halls of political power. Rather, humanists were members of wealthy and powerful political groups within Florentine society. Rarely was money the key distinction between admirers of the classics.[15] Therefore, it is problematic to distinguish among them using economic criteria.

Two examples reveal Martines's general problems with the professional and amateur dichotomy. In the 1440s and 1450s, Giannozzo Manetti was the most famed orator on the Italian peninsula. His diplomatic speeches attracted hundreds of people and his works and teachings inspired the thought of a generation. In many ways, he served as a temporal intermediary, carrying the torch of Florentine humanism from Leonardo Bruni, whose works he consciously emulated and shamelessly plagiarized, to Donato Acciaiuoli, the leading student of Giovanni Argyropoulos at the Florentine Academy in the 1450s.[16] By any standard, Giannozzo Manetti was one of the most important humanists in Florence in the latter 1440s and early 1450s. However, by economic standards Manetti was an amateur because most of his income derived from the silk trade.[17]

Meanwhile, Griso Griselli was a professional humanist because his income depended on his humanist studies. Born in 1424, Griselli served as Manetti's secretary on an important diplomatic mission to Venice in 1448. Griselli left a long and detailed diary of Manetti's activities in Venice, his interactions with the Venetian government, and his correspondence with Florence. By 1454 Griselli was registering acts as a notary in Florence: Manetti, who was by then in voluntary exile, served as his first client.[18] He corresponded with the learned humanist Donato Acciaiuoli and was one of many participants in a learned discussion with Manetti in Venice in 1448.[19] Griselli procured numerous important notarial positions before he died in 1497.[20] There is no doubt that Griselli pursued humanist studies, particularly in his youth. However, there is also no doubt that he enjoyed far less prominence and influence than his esteemed friend Giannozzo Manetti. The fact that Griselli earned his living with his pen made him, by economic standards, a professional humanist. Yet, to call a person of Manetti's stature an amateur by comparison with the professional Griselli seems to prioritize the origins of a person's paycheck falsely over an individual's impact on the humanist movement. The baggage of the word "amateur" insinuates that Manetti, a man whom both his contemporaries and modern scholars point to as one of the most outstanding humanists in the years following Leonardo Bruni's death, was somehow less serious, less influential, and less learned than his professional contemporaries.

Despite Martines's reservations, historians have continued to use the terms "professional" and "amateur" whenever less prominent humanists enter a study. In fact, Martines himself retained the categories while changing their meaning for his study. Martines argued that a distinction should be made between individuals who devoted their spare moments to humanist study and those who worked at it more often: The most serious humanists were professionals; the less dedicated were amateurs.[21] In practice, Martines avoided the problem by studying distinctions between social groups rather than differences between individual humanists. He argued that categories like professional and amateur were not useful for his project because he was concerned with the relationship between humanists and Florentine society. Indeed, Martines claimed that "stressing differences between the two [types of humanists] would have blurred the very thing we were after – the connection, if one there was, between humanism and the social groups which enjoyed power and prestige."[22] Moreover, distinctions between professionals and amateurs "would have produced generalizations about the connections between humanism and *individuals*, even if individuals with different kinds of professional or business interests, and nothing about the connection between humanism and those groups in society which exercise power, determine or direct values, and are hence the chief agencies of change in history."[23] In short, Martines avoided the question of the efficacy of the terms "amateur" and "professional" because distinguishing between types of humanists was unnecessary to make the type of claims argued in his book.

Over the past fifty years most historians have retained the professional and amateur dichotomy. In general, intellectual historians have avoided the problem by focusing on the original writings of the most prolific humanist writers, men whose key position in the humanist movement can be little doubted and thus for whom the terms are unnecessary. Meanwhile, humanism is so rarely a major topic in the work of other historians that, again, the issue does not usually arise. When it does, "amateur" is applied. The absence of humanism from much Renaissance scholarship is undoubtedly a by-product of the lack of dialogue between intellectual and social historians of the Italian Renaissance more generally.[24] Yet these historiographical trends have also been shaped by the four major, current definitions of Renaissance humanism. Each of these current definitions accepts that humanism became a broad cultural movement, but each one also overwhelmingly focuses on common themes across original humanist works in Latin, whether the focus is Latin style, common content, or disciplinary focus.

Yet, Latin writers were rare in the humanist movement, as this study shows for Florence and as Margaret King pointed out more than twenty-five years ago for Venice.[25] Most participants in the humanist movement were content to read the writings of others, especially classical authors; translate humanist and especially classical works; correspond with friends and acquaintances about their studies; and develop spoken eloquence in both Latin and the vernacular. In fact, scholars have long struggled with individuals who were clearly considered as central humanists in the fifteenth century, but who have left little literary production to merit this distinction. The most famous example is Niccolò Niccoli, who shunned writing original works because he believed he could never equal the ancients. Palla di Nofri Strozzi was another key figure who failed to pen original treatises. Carlo Marsuppini was a university professor and chancellor of Florence after Leonardo Bruni, but his handful of surviving writings was a fraction of the dozens of works by his prolific predecessor. Less learned and less famous men like Piero de' Pazzi, Marco Parenti, and Giuliano Davanzati – none of whom wrote anything in terms of original Latin works – were welcomed into learned discussions, were praised for their learning, and actively pursued books of interests to more well-known humanists. Such men were far more typical of the individuals involved in the humanist movement than their colleagues who were busy penning original works, but a conception of the humanist movement based primarily on original writings in Latin struggles to incorporate them into it.

Additionally, a focus on the original Latin writings of the few prolific humanist writers overshadows other important aspects of the humanist movement. Specific social and political contexts shaped humanist works collectively to a greater extent than most movements in intellectual history. Humanist writers tied their works to specific events or patrons, and the constraints of these contexts or the specific social and political goals of an author frequently overshadowed any desire to create new ideas in the abstract. In short, humanists were usually interested in making practical arguments in a classical way for a present problem rather than creating original metaphysical ideas for posterity. Studying the ideas in these texts through philology or primarily in the context of other texts can offer interesting and important insights into the history of ideas, but it also causes the texts to lose much of their original significance, authorial intention, and layers of meaning.[26] Moreover, the vernacular played a far more prominent role in the humanist movement than a focus on original texts in Latin allows. Many humanist writers, such as Leonardo Bruni and Giannozzo Manetti, wrote texts in both the vernacular and Latin. Certainly, they sometimes distinguished between their "light" works in the vernacular and their "serious" works in Latin, but they nevertheless applied their overriding interest in antiquity and classical style to both cases.[27] Angelo Mazzocco has demonstrated that fifteenth-century humanists held a variety of opinions about the validity of Italian as a learned language. Far from holding the vernacular in universal disdain, Italian humanist writers varied in the value they attached to works written in the vernacular.[28]

Finally, a focus on the original Latin writings of the humanists unintentionally downplays the role of the humanist movement in Renaissance society. The humanist movement becomes populated by a handful of elite men and sometimes women who wrote books read by a few like-minded individuals with the desire and/or the ability to read Latin. Yet, this view could not be further from the truth. Humanism and the people interested in it saturated the society of the Renaissance. To cite but a few examples, states exchanged letters in humanist Latin.[29] The rituals that filled Florentine city squares typically featured at least one humanist performance, often at the tensest moments for the city's diverse onlookers.[30] Humanist studies produced changes in the language of artistic appreciation, effectively altering the way people viewed art and the world around them. This new framework, in turn, shaped the artistic tastes of the men and women responsible for the art that still enables Florence to enjoy a cultural reputation beyond the moderate size of the modern city.[31] Increasingly over the fifteenth century, Florentines presented themselves as versed in the classics in order to maintain and earn capital for themselves, their families, and their city. By the mid-fifteenth century at the latest, large numbers of Florentines had been educated according to humanist-style curricula, were hiring humanist tutors for their children, were learning and imitating classical rhetorical techniques, were copying and reading humanist texts, and were commissioning works of cultural production inspired by their studies.[32] As many as two-thirds of Florentines in 1427 were literate, at least in the vernacular.[33] Certainly, not all of these individuals were capable of or interested in reading an Italian or Latin version of a classical or humanist text. Enough of them were interested, however, to support the hire of the Greeks Manuel Chrysoloras and Giovanni Argyropoulos at the

Florentine university, to enable Leonardo Bruni and other humanist writers to become very wealthy men, and to produce and consume the thousands of surviving copies of orations, original humanist works, books by classical authors, and translations of such authors that still stuff the special collections of European libraries.[34]

In order to examine the full breadth of the humanist movement, this book adopts a new approach to studying the learned interests of the Florentines. At the onset, a version of the broad conception of humanism proposed several years ago by Kenneth Gouwens has been adopted to help define humanism itself. Gouwens suggested that "humanism is best conceived not as the narrowly defined *studia humanitatis* of Kristeller but as the cultural context (or, discursive field) with which exceptionally visible figures such as Petrarch and Raphael operated."[35] This book breaks somewhat from Gouwens and argues that the term "humanism" should retain its somewhat narrow focus pertaining to the study of a particular Latin style, unique approach to philosophical questions, focus on the application of learning in the active life, and/or specific range of relevant subjects (as Witt, Garin, Baron, and/or Kristeller, respectively, argued). The terms "humanist learning" and "humanism" have been used interchangeably throughout this book with this definition in mind. The term "humanist movement," by contrast, should describe Gouwens's broad cultural context that developed around humanism as well as the people operating within this context. Involvement in the humanist movement can be traced through a number of evidentiary sources that link individuals to an interest in the classical world. These "learned connections" are discussed in detail in Chapter 1. This book focuses on the humanist movement rather than on humanism proper. In doing so, the book shifts scholarly focus away from the ideas in humanist texts and the specific characteristics that distinguished them from nonhumanist texts – accepting that such foci and distinctions remain important for other studies – and squarely onto the task of analyzing the individuals who were responsible for the movement's success: The individuals who made up the vast ranks of the humanist movement in the broader social and political world of fifteenth-century Florence.

This book also offers two essential categories to describe individuals who made up the humanist movement and their vast range of interests, abilities, and influence. People at the core of the humanist movement formed more and stronger connections to other people based on shared humanist interests. They read more classical and humanist books. Almost all of them knew Latin. Usually, but not always, these core humanists were also the writers of original humanist texts. Because of this connection to original works, these core humanists are called "literary" humanists throughout this book. Typically, but not always, literary humanists were members of new families and possessed a correspondingly moderate level of political and social status. Leonardo Bruni provides one good example of a literary humanist. Bruni was a parvenu to Florence and possessed hundreds of learned connections, as witnessed through his surviving epistles, evidence from his original works, readers and owners of copies of his works, and other archival sources. Giannozzo Manetti and Marsilio Ficino also serve as standard examples of literary humanists, although Manetti was from an older family than either Bruni or Ficino. In addition to these prolific writers, some literary humanists wrote few if any original works, but their importance to the humanist movement and interest in humanism warrant their place in this category. Niccolò Niccoli, Palla di Nofri Strozzi, and Carlo Marsuppini, mentioned previously, serve as three good examples of literary humanists who produced few original literary compositions. Literary humanists were the people with the deepest humanist learning, and they made up a tiny fraction of the humanist movement. They were unlike other humanists because of their greater role and skill in humanist letters, as witnessed through their original works, patronage, prolific correspondence with others, or occasionally the sheer weight of contemporary opinion on their learning.

All of the remaining individuals who participated in the humanist movement are called "social" humanists in this study. This term derives from the fact that only a few of them wrote original treatises in Latin or the vernacular. Therefore, their participation in the humanist movement must be traced through other means. These individuals formed fewer and weaker learned connections than literary humanists. They read fewer books. They varied from people fluent in Latin to people who could only read the vernacular. They read the works of humanist and classical authors in Latin or the vernacular. Some of them even translated Latin books into other languages. Many social humanists were patricians and thus have left piles of documentation on various aspects of their lives. Usually they carried a degree of social and political status far outweighing their position in the humanist movement. Other social humanists lacked family names and have left little evidence of any aspects of their lives, beyond a note naming them as the owner of a humanist text. The category "social" humanist encompasses individuals from a range of backgrounds with an enormous variation of skill levels, influence, and interest in humanism. Simply put, a social humanist was anybody for whom a convincing argument can be made that s/he had an interest in the writings and studies of individuals more engaged in the study of classical languages, the classical world, and its thought, literature, ruins, and rhetoric. Throughout this book, the term "humanist" without a qualifying adjective refers to all literary and social humanists collectively. Chapter 2 of this study demonstrates the range of learned interests possessed by social humanists, while Chapter 3 investigates the economic, social, and political backgrounds of individuals within the category.

For the sake of clarity, a number of other points should be made about what the categories "literary" and "social" are not. First, the humanist movement encompassed a broad, fluid spectrum of learned interests and abilities. The categories "social" and "literary" humanists have been adopted to distinguish two of the most distinct parts of this spectrum, namely, its most outstanding participants, from everybody else. However, these categories should themselves be conceived of as having fluid rather than fixed boundaries. Roberto Rossi, for example, was an enormously influential teacher in late fourteenth- and early fifteenth-century Florence with numerous and strong learned connections. Yet, he also wrote very little in terms of original literature and his learning seems to have been held in high, but not the highest esteem by his contemporaries. A case could be made for him to fit best in either group. To acknowledge gray areas such as these, an attempt has also been made throughout this study to point to areas in which the categories of "social" and "literary" risk oversimplification or fixing a false dichotomy upon a fluid situation. Second, the terms "literary" and "social" potentially suggest that literary humanists were not social and social humanists wrote nothing. All literary humanists participated in the same social networks and structures as the social humanists. Their placement in the literary rather than social category is not intended to exclude them from the society in which they lived. Additionally, some social humanists have left a small number of surviving Latin or Italian orations and letters as well as a handful of original treatises, although the number and significance of these objects pale in comparison with the output of most literary humanists. The term "social" reflects that the social humanists usually participated in the humanist movement through means other than original literary output. In other words, the terms "social" and "literary" describe what the case was typically, but not absolutely. Additionally, those categories are not meant as other designations for participants in the active versus contemplative life. Most social and literary humanists were involved in their communities, and most of them discussed in this book were involved in politics. Their differing degrees of learning,

social, and political status determined the roles they filled in their respective societies.

This investigation of the connections between individuals in the humanist movement contrasts with the group approach adopted by Lauro
Martines in his groundbreaking *The Social World of the Florentine
Humanists*. Martines's methodology of positioning prominent Florentine
humanists in groups worked well for establishing his claim that the main
Florentine humanists were part of the ruling class of the city. Yet, as he
himself pointed out, studies interested in other questions about the humanist movement need distinctions not present in his study.[36] In particular,
distinctions are necessary to move beyond the general link between the
humanist movement and the Florentine patriciate and to explain how and
why, exactly, humanism spread from a tiny group of core individuals into
a huge cultural movement. Distinctions are also necessary to get at the
crucial variations in learning among Florentine patricians as well as variations in the economic, political, and social status of humanists. Many
humanists were in the ruling class, but they were not the *same* as the ruling
class of Florence. It is precisely the variations among, and the particular
social circumstances of, individuals that shaped the function, participation, and spread of the humanist movement in Renaissance Florence. In
short, whereas Lauro Martines sought to establish that all individuals
associated with humanism were from the ruling class, this book argues
that thousands of individuals in and outside the political, social, and
economic elite were active members of the humanist movement.[37]

The focus of this book on individual connections fits into broader
historiographical trends that have developed since Martines wrote his
brilliant book. In politics, revisionist historians have pointed to decisions
and connections between individuals as the primary units for historical
analysis. The historiography on seventeenth-century England and the
British Isles provides a particularly good example of the revisionists'
emphasis on individuals, rather than groups, as primary historical agents,
as well as other characteristics common to revisionist historiography, such
as short-term causal agents and the role of chance in determining historical
outcomes.[38] In Italy, and Florence in particular, historians have demonstrated that complicated individual, familial, and neighborhood relationships formed the basis for the political and social life of the city.[39] On these
other subjects, scholars have debated whether individual relationships
coalesced around nuclear or extended families in Renaissance Florence.[40]
They have argued that individuals and their families gradually expanded
their geographical focus from local neighborhoods to citywide networks

over the course of the fifteenth century.[41] Yet, relationships based upon or shaped by shared learned interests have been absent from these analyses. Like every other aspect of Florentine society, the humanist movement was shaped by individual connections; these connections were often determined by familial and neighborhood relationships; and these learned relationships combined to make up the broader humanist movement. As shown in the next chapter, the study of learned connections can add insights and further complexity to these other types of social bonds more familiar to historians.

An analysis of learned connections in Renaissance Florence enables new insights into questions about the roles of humanism in Florence, the extent of humanist learning among the Florentine population, the shape and spread of the humanist movement, the reasons behind its appeal, and the investigation of individual social humanists. Scholars have investigated these questions separately but have yet to attempt a sustained synthetic analysis of them. Lauro Martines's *The Social World of the Florentine Humanists*, published in 1963, remains the last word on most social and political questions about all Florentine humanists. Although Martines pointed to the central role of the social humanists in the humanist movement, the vast majority of Martines's text focuses on the most famous literary humanists, such as Salutati, Bruni, Niccoli, and Manetti, while an appendix provides brief biographical profiles of dozens of typically less learned men.[42] In addition to Martines, scholars such as Mario Cosenza, Arthur Field, James Hankins, Jonathan Davies, Arnaldo della Torre, Emilio Santini, Armando Verde, Antonio Manfredi, and others have added basic information about the lives and studies of individual social humanists.[43] These Anglo and Italian studies shed welcome light on the social humanists and reflect painstaking, meticulous, and admirable research. However, such studies often leave scholars with raw information about the social humanists, but little interpretive framework, little sense as to why the learning of these social humanists mattered, or why humanist studies appealed to so many people.

A second group of historians have looked at the spread of humanist learning among the broader Florentine population. Several scholars, such as Anthony F. D'Elia, John McManamon, and Alison Brown, have examined the ideas in humanist texts and speculated that these ideas must have spread to an unspecified audience.[44] These fine studies clearly show an attempt by writers and speakers to broaden the appeal of humanism and indicate that a potential audience existed for it. But to whom, exactly, did humanism appeal and why? The chapters of this book add faces to humanist audiences and expand the numbers of people who could be expected to "get" humanist performances and read humanist books. Another group of scholars, led by Christian Bec and John Najemy, have shown the presence of humanism in ordinary writings of wealthy Florentines.[45] Najemy's arguments that Florentine humanists addressed their ideas to the Florentine *popolo* – the newer and sometimes less prosperous of the two social groups within the Florentine elite – have proven particularly influential. Najemy contended that the ideology of civic humanism promoted a political situation in which the *popolo* accepted the potential, but not the reality, of holding premier political offices and thus a resigned subjugation to their social betters. This book diverges from Najemy's arguments by viewing humanism less as a program aimed at one social group and more as a movement that possessed an audience across the Florentine population: It appealed to Florentines throughout the patriciate, *grandi*, as well as *popoli* and found a home even among Florentines with less socioeconomic wealth. More broadly, the focus of this book on prosopography, the history of the book, the history of ritual, and the Florentine social world diverges from the more intellectual historical approach of Bec and Najemy. Nevertheless, the arguments in this study uphold the findings of both scholars about the permeation of humanist studies among large numbers of Florentines even as it attempts to take this argument further and explain why this was the case, a topic touched upon by yet another group of scholars.

A third group of historians have examined the function of humanism in Florentine society and suggested some hypotheses behind its popularity. In addition to more specialized studies by Riccardo Fubini, Gary Ianziti, Sharon Strocchia, Mark Jurdjevic, and Stephen Milner, Ronald Witt has offered tentative hypotheses for the appeal of humanism to Florentines. [46] In a 1990 article, Witt explicitly linked the success of humanist educational curricula in Florence to the increased number of oratorical situations in communal politics. Witt focused particularly on diplomacy, demonstrating the vast increase in diplomatic commissions around the turn of Quattrocento. According to Witt, Florentine patricians needed a humanist education in order to meet the oratorical demands of Florentine political positions, particularly diplomatic ones.[47] Witt's magisterial *In the Footsteps of the Ancients* expanded these ideas regarding the relationships among humanism, diplomacy, and patricians. Witt suggested that the humanist education received by patricians influenced the content but not the style of their orations in the early fifteenth century. Over time, the Florentine patricians "made humanist education essential training for the upper classes in urban centers throughout Italy."[48] As in his earlier article, Witt contended that the oratory of a few Florentines was influenced by humanism in the late fourteenth and early fifteenth centuries before, eventually, a larger group of patricians incorporated some humanist elements into their own orations or at least possessed enough Latin to understand somebody else's speech.[49] In the 1420s, Leonardo Bruni was the first person to adopt humanist forms in the vernacular oratory available to most Florentine patricians.[50] Aside from his treatment of Leonardo Bruni, Witt focused primarily on the origin and development of humanism in the 1200s and 1300s. Consequently, questions of who exactly these patricians were and systematic evidence for their interests in humanism lay outside the temporal range of Witt's groundbreaking book.

Finally, the foundation for widespread humanist interests in fifteenth-century Florence was closely connected with the formal educational system, a topic exhaustively studied by Robert Black over the past several decades.[51] Black has convincingly demonstrated that primary education in early fifteenth-century Florence focused more on training businessmen than Latin scholars. Consequently, Black maintains that few Florentine patricians became "active participants" in the humanist movement, which Black defines as composing original Latin works.[52] This situation contrasted with the schools in greater Tuscany, where humanist educational changes were present much earlier than in Florence itself. As a result, Black argues that humanism was only weakly present in Florence before about 1470, at which point it greatly expanded its reach and became an attribute used to distinguish the members of the Florentine elite from lower social groups.[53] Black's conclusions are based on comprehensive, careful research, and this book agrees with many of his general conclusions, while disagreeing on some particulars. Using a broader definition to determine active participation in the humanist movement, this study argues for a much stronger presence of humanism in Florence before 1470. Black's research helps explain why the humanist movement in Florence focused on reading and orating, rather than writing original treatises: namely, that few social humanists possessed the educational background to pen Ciceronian Latin prose, even had they wanted to do so. Later chapters will add other reasons behind this focus. This book upholds Black's argument that the number of humanists in Florence expanded after 1470 and that the key reason behind this expansion was inexorably linked to issues of social status. However, here this association is viewed as an opportunity available to Florentines from many walks of life to obtain a crucial marker of elite status, rather than an exclusionary aspect of class.

Building on the research and arguments of these scholars, this monograph offers a new interpretation of the appeal and spread of the humanist movement while shifting its historical focus squarely onto the social humanists. Most individuals involved in the humanist movement in fifteenth-century Florence were social humanists. Their large numbers suggest that learned men and women viewed ephemeral oratorical performances as the key expression of a person's learning, rather than the modern academic focus on publishing original texts. The Florentine ruling groups possessed individuals who were interested in humanism to one degree or another and other individuals who were not. Whole branches of elite families cultivated humanist letters, while other branches left no evidence that they had anybody interested in humanism. Beyond patricians, nonelite individuals participated in the humanist movement, albeit with less surviving evidence to document their learned pursuits. As Ronald Witt argued, the oratorical demands of politics go a long way to explain the appeal of humanism to Florentine patricians; this book uses a case study of diplomatic ritual to add solid evidence to Witt's hypothesis. However, it also nuances and expands Witt's claims by showing that humanist performances served quite specific purposes in common rituals in Renaissance Florence. The arguments presented here agree with Lauro Martines that social rather than literary humanists were responsible for integrating humanist forms in most political situations. The analysis takes this line further by examining the social forces and many of the individuals who made this the case.

The book makes these points across seven chapters through a variety of published and unpublished evidentiary sources. The first three chapters examine the learned connections linking people to the humanist movement. The first chapter provides a foundation for locating these learned connections between people before examining how these connections intersected with other types of social relationships more familiar to modern historians. Chapter 2 traces the learned connections of roughly a hundred Florentines, ranging from literary humanists to weak social humanists. Chapter 3 looks at the variation in social, political, and economic status among people with clear connections to the humanist movement in fifteenth-century Florence. The evidence for these chapters is taken from an analysis of hundreds of letters, evidence of book ownership drawn from manuscripts as well as archival and library inventories, and extensive reading of hyperspecialized biographical and textual studies on Renaissance Florentines. The final four chapters offer a case study of diplomatic oratory and ritual to argue that the demands of ritual were primarily responsible for the spread of humanist learning to these broad sections of the Florentine population as well as the focus of humanists on reading and speaking rather than writing. Chapter 4 argues that diplomatic oratory served as a cultural gift from one state to another. The chapter uses descriptions of diplomatic rituals and a close reading of surviving diplomatic commissions as an evidentiary basis as well as the work of Pierre Bourdieu and Marcel Mauss as a theoretical framework. Chapter 5 uses a database of more than twenty-two hundred diplomatic positions to argue that only certain social humanists possessed the necessary mixture of humanist skills and social attributes to negotiate the gift exchanges in diplomatic rituals successfully. This database was built through the surviving books of fifteenth-century diplomatic commissions and electoral records. The final two chapters examine the integration of humanism into Florentine diplomacy and the humanist learning among Florentine diplomats. These chapters argue that, as the humanist movement increased in size, the prestige attached to humanist learning also increased over the course of the fifteenth century. The increased prestige attached to extraordinary humanist learning helps explain the further explosion of the humanist movement after the 1470s, in and outside Florence. Through these arguments, this monograph seeks to establish a new synthetic paradigm for understanding the humanist movement during the Italian Renaissance.

I

Learned Connections and the Humanist Movement

Poggio Bracciolini wrote to his friend Niccolò Niccoli in Florence on June 12, 1425, "You know that Bartholomeus de Bardis, a man very devoted to you and, what I consider most important, interested in our work but hemmed in by a host of business responsibilities, can satisfy his desire for study all too little."[1] Poggio stated that Bardi wanted Niccoli to buy him a few classical books: copies of Suetonius, Terence, and Quintius Curtius. Poggio concluded: "Add anything that seems good to you; for Bartholomeus is rich and wants books. So do our errand and do not put if off; let the price be what seems best to you."[2] Although employed in Rome as a banker for the Medici, the Florentine Bartolomeo Bardi epitomized the social humanist in fifteenth-century Florence.[3] According to Poggio, Bardi had the desire and the money to pursue humanist studies, but he had limited free time. Thus, he wrote nothing of his own, befriended Poggio to help him with his studies, and read books of interest to literary humanists like Poggio and Niccolò Niccoli. He also undoubtedly discussed these books with other people.

The clustering of literary humanists in Rome in the summer of 1426 provided an opportunity for one such discussion. Bardi, Leonardo Bruni, Poggio, Cosimo de' Medici, Francesco Barbaro, and others may have been present at such gatherings. Bruni had arrived in the Eternal City as a Florentine diplomat to negotiate territorial disputes with the pope in early June of 1426. The head Florentine governmental bodies at the time, its Signoria and the Dieci di Balìa, instructed Bruni and his colleague Francesco Tornabuoni to work with Bardi when dealing with the pope.[4] Bruni and Bardi already knew each other, as in 1424 Poggio had mentioned Bardi in a letter to Bruni describing a social gathering.[5] Beyond the connections between Bruni and Bardi, Poggio obviously knew both men and was also present in Rome during the same summer.[6] Cosimo de' Medici's employment of Bardi has been mentioned, and Cosimo's friendship with Poggio is well known. Cosimo's connections to Leonardo Bruni at this time were also strong, as evidenced from Bruni's dedication of his translation of Pseudo-Plato's *Epistles* in 1426 to him and by Bruni's investments in the Medici bank in 1427.[7] Cosimo carried a book to Rome in April or May of 1426, although it is unclear how long he stayed in the city.[8] Also in Rome at the same time was the Greek diplomat Andreas Chrysoberges, to negotiate the arrival of the Greeks for a council of reunion. Perhaps this Greek sought out Barbaro and Bruni – both accomplished Greek scholars – as well as their learned friends.[9]

Further evidence suggests that learned discussions between these men were likely in the summer of 1426. The presence of the Venetian patrician and literary humanist Francesco Barbaro in Rome in the same circles as Bardi during the summer of 1426 – Barbaro and Andrea Mauroceno were the Venetian diplomats with whom the Florentine Signoria charged their own diplomats Bruni and Tornabuoni to work closely – added another person with deep humanist interest to the mix.[10] Florentines abroad dined together and their discussions sometimes turned to humanist subjects. For example, Giannozzo Manetti dined with multiple Florentines one night on his mission to Venice in 1448 and they discussed a wide range of topics, including Boccaccio's *Decameron*.[11] Ultimately, whether Bardi discussed learned matters with these men in 1426 or not, he seems to have enjoyed the books that Niccoli selected for him. In September of 1425, he was looking for another book, this time Cicero's *On Duties*.[12] Bardi, in fact, continues to appear in reference to books, humanism, and humanists in Poggio's correspondence until Bardi's death in 1429.[13] It is therefore surprising that a list of books that he owned upon his death included only a copy of Vergil and several unspecified grammar books.[14]

Bardi was a social humanist because he possessed documentable connections to humanism but was by no means a central member of the humanist movement. His modest but real position in the movement is revealed through his learned connections. Bardi's scholarly friends and acquaintances included Niccolò Niccoli and Poggio Bracciolini. He also, more than likely, formed connections with Leonardo Bruni, Francesco Barbaro, and Cosimo de' Medici as well as, perhaps, Francesco Tornabuoni, Andrea Mauroceno, and Andreas Chrysoberges. Bardi's books too point to humanist interests: Quintius Curtius's *History of Alexander the Great*, Suetonius's *The Twelve Caesars*, Cicero's *On*

Duties, Vergil's *Aeneid*, and an unspecified work by Terence were at one point or another associated with Bardi. Bardi's connections to these works and these people were not particularly strong: He seems to have been close to Poggio but not the others, he died with only a copy of Vergil, and he has left no direct evidence that he actually read any of these texts. Bardi's small number of relatively weak learned connections to people and books sharply contrasts with the hundreds of strong connections typical of a literary humanist like Leonardo Bruni or Francesco Barbaro. As will be shown in later chapters, however, Bardi possessed far stronger connections to the humanist movement than many other social humanists.

People formed learned connections with each other through shared humanist interests that are traceable through a number of historical sources. Latin and vernacular epistolary exchanges provide the most obvious evidence for those connections. Letters written in humanist Latin, regardless of content, establish a learned connection between individuals. Latin letters about literary matters reflect an even stronger connection between the sender and the epistolary recipient. Letters in the vernacular that pertain to humanism also establish learned connections. References to third parties in such letters can also be evidence for such connections, albeit to varying degrees dependent on each reference. As shown in Chapter 2, the learned connections formed by the Florentine patrician Matteo Strozzi are revealed through all of these particular types of evidentiary sources.

Obviously, not all vernacular letters between individuals provide evidence of shared humanist interests. Vernacular letters about economic, political, or other topics do not reveal a learned connection. Even literary humanists wrote and received vernacular letters that may not establish learned connections. For example, the literary humanist Leonardo Bruni wrote a letter to Luca di Maso degli Albizzi while Luca was a diplomat to the pope in Bologna. Luca is most famous today as the brother of Rinaldo degli Albizzi, who oversaw the exile of Cosimo de' Medici in 1433 and then, less than a year later, himself fled Florence under his own sentence of exile. The relationship between Luca and his brother was so bad by 1434 that Luca actually took up arms against Rinaldo in support of the Medici.[15] By October 1436, the Medici regime trusted Luca enough to send him as a diplomat to Pope Eugenius IV, then in Bologna.[16] The trust was well placed. On November 26, 1436, the Otto di Custodia, a powerful governmental body entrusted with the security of the Medici's regime in the 1430s, wrote a response to an earlier letter from their diplomat.[17] In that letter, Luca had stated that a priest had arrived from Ancona and approached him. The priest wanted to serve as a diplomat for Rinaldo, his son Maso, and another exiled Florentine patrician, Biagio Guasconi. The priest also had a letter for Luca. Luca rejected the letter and the diplomat, sent the priest away, and informed the Florentines. The Otto stated that they appreciated Luca's actions and did not doubt his loyalty to the regime. That said, they asked Luca to get the letter if the priest returned or happened still to be in town. If that seemed morally objectionable to Luca, they asked him to find somebody else trustworthy to do it.[18]

Bruni's letter to Luca arrived several months later, on February 5, while Luca was still a diplomat to the pope. In a very short vernacular epistle, Bruni responded to a previous letter from Luca and offered advice on obtaining license to return to Florence.[19] The lack of cultural resonances or references in the letter provides no evidence of a learned connection between Luca and Bruni. However, it may provide supplementary evidence for other documents pointing to a potential learned connection. Luca learned Latin and possibly some Greek from Roberto Rossi and Poggio Bracciolini, both acquaintances of Bruni.[20] Like Bruni, Luca was interested in humanist studies. Before his falling out with his brother, Luca wrote Rinaldo a letter in which he cited Cicero in Latin.[21] Luca hired a grammar tutor, who used classical texts favored by humanist teachers, to instruct his children.[22] At least one of these sons, also named Luca, maintained an interest in the humanist movement later in life, as shown by Vespasiano da Bisticci's dedication of some of his famous *Lives* to him.[23] Further connections between the elder Luca and humanism may still be found in his voluminous autograph correspondences and notebooks from his extensive diplomatic career.[24] As later chapters argue, this extensive diplomatic career itself suggests Luca's participation in the humanist movement. This body of evidence combines with the familiar tone of Bruni's letter to suggest that Bruni and Luca may have shared a weak learned connection, despite the political content and plain vernacular style of the epistle.

Other sources point to learned connections between people. The interlocutors in humanist dialogues provide evidence for a learned connection between the author of the dialogue and the people whom the dialogue pretends to represent. Whether or not the interlocutors said the things described by the author or even whether the dialogue happened at all, these dialogues at least pretend to relate an actual conversation. Therefore, authors assumed that their audience was willing to accept the possibility that these particular interlocutors met together and held a discussion about humanism.

The examples of Leonardo Bruni's famous *Dialogues* and Giannozzo Manetti's *Dialogue at a Banquet* demonstrate these points. Bruni penned his two *Dialogues* as one coherent work based on Cicero's *On the Orator* in the first decade of the fifteenth century and scholars have debated the political ideas contained in it for more than fifty years.[25] For the purposes of this chapter it is enough to note the individuals depicted in the two books of the text. In the first book, Leonardo Bruni, Niccolò Niccoli, and Roberto Rossi visited Coluccio Salutati. The men discussed the new learning as well as Dante, Petrarch, and Boccaccio. In the second book, Bruni, Niccoli, Rossi, and Salutati were joined by Piero Sermini, who was chancellor of the Guelf Party and then later chancellor of the Florentine Republic itself.[26] Whether or not these learned discussions actually occurred, scholars can assume that Bruni's readers accepted the possibility that Bruni, Niccoli, Rossi, Salutati, and Sermini could hold a discussion about vernacular and classical letters at one of their homes. Each of them, consequently, can be linked to the humanist movement through Bruni's *Dialogues*.

Similarly, Giannozzo Manetti's *Dialogue at a Banquet* reveals a snapshot of intersecting learned connections of several Florentines, but in this case the men were far less renowned for their knowledge of humanism. For Manetti's *Dialogue*, scholars even know for certain that Manetti hosted a dinner party in Venice on the night that the dialogue supposedly took place.[27] In attendance were Manetti himself, his son Bernardo, and Giovanfrancesco Manetti – a converted Jew who lived in Manetti's house – as well as Manetti's secretary on the diplomatic mission, Griso Griselli. Florentine businessmen were in abundance. Alessandro Martelli, director of the Medici bank in Venice, was there. His colleague Pigello Portinari, who was entrusted with the Milanese branch of the Medici bank in 1452, was too. Carlo Bardi, Sinibaldo Donati, and Michele Rondinelli, from whom a learned letter on moral philosophy survives, were undoubtedly merchants abroad, and they also attended the event. Gabriele Belli, also present, knew Hebrew and was a convert from Judaism.[28] Unfortunately, no contextual evidence has been located for the final two attendees, Tommaso Ringadori and Nerozzo Neri.[29] Nevertheless, as with Bruni's *Dialogues*, whether or not these men actually discussed Boccaccio and other topics, the purported dialogue was at the very least a believable fiction for readers, such as the work's dedicatee Donato Acciaiuoli.[30]

Attendance at other ephemeral learned discussions establishes a learned connection. Arnaldo della Torre used reports of these oral discussions as evidence for humanist learning among members of these discussion groups, and thus a single example derived from his study will suffice here.[31] Della Torre cited an anecdote told by Vespasiano da Bisticci that the Florentine patrician Franco Sacchetti held discussions at his house twice a year to which he invited ten or twelve "learned gentlemen" for two or three days. In attendance were Giovanni Argyropoulos, Pandolfo Pandolfini, Alamanno Rinuccini, Marco Parenti, Domenico di Carlo Pandolfini, Piero Acciaiuoli, Donato Acciaiuoli, Carlo d' Antonio di Silvestro, Pierfilippo Pandolfini, Banco Casavecchia, and Vespasiano da Bisticci.[32] Despite the fact that the content of these discussions has disappeared from the historical record, della Torre rightly used Vespasiano's claim that they were all learned men to tie them to the humanist movement. Corroborating evidence for their humanist interests, discussed later in this chapter and in Chapter 2, confirms their involvement.

Teachers and informal lecturers as well as their students and audiences formed learned connections. Indeed, many individuals first encountered humanism through pedagogical relationships. Robert Black has carefully listed the public and private teachers in fifteenth-century Florence and analyzed their teaching methods.[33] Although humanist teachers should always be considered as strong members of the humanist movement, scholars should include their students with caution. Simply receiving a humanist education demonstrates only the weakest involvement in the movement because tutoring involved a passive relationship: A teacher was chosen, usually by a parent, for a person, usually a child. Students who lack any corroborating evidence for their interests in humanism should be considered on the outer fringes of the humanist movement. They certainly established learned connections among themselves and their teachers and fellow students, but they were far less involved in the movement than their contemporaries who were applying their training in practical situations, discussing humanist ideas in discussion groups, poring over classical texts late into the night, or even staining their fingers from ink spilled while penning original humanist treatises.

Bonds of literary patronage reveal learned connections between the patron and the author or translator. Individuals who provided patronage to others or received unsolicited dedications from authors and translators formed learned connections. Dedications of humanist treatises and translations often suggest an attempt by the author or translator to secure patronage. It was the classic gift, an offer of a literary work with the expectation of reciprocity in the form of monetary, social, or political reward.[34] It betrays an assumption by the author or translator that the dedicatee was familiar enough with the humanist movement to appreciate and accept the gift. Sometimes dedicatees received works with genuine intellectual interest; sometimes they only wished to appear to be patrons and friends of learned men and women. Regardless of the motivation behind the patronage, dedicatees were involved with the humanist movement to the point that they knew the rules of the game well enough to appreciate the gesture. In fact, many patrons played a crucial role in shaping humanist studies, in ways similar to the long acknowledged mutual role of patrons and artists in the creation of paintings, sculptures, and other artistic media in Renaissance Europe.[35]

Because of this critical role, the most influential of these patrons should be considered among the literary humanists. For example, the mercenary captain and patron of the arts Federico da Montefeltro desired a new copy of Aristotle's *Politics* for his growing library in Urbino. He wrote to the famous bookseller Vespasiano da Bisticci for a recommendation for a suitable translator. Vespasiano recommended his longtime friend Donato Acciaiuoli, who took on and completed the task.[36] Federico did not himself translate the book, but he influenced the humanist movement by choosing, seeking out, and paying for a translation of a particular work that would then become available to other people. Similarly, Cosimo de' Medici famously asked Marsilio Ficino to set aside his translations of Plato and focus on the works of Hermes Trismegistus.[37] Cosimo's patronage actively shaped the range of texts and ideas available to all participants of the humanist movement, particularly, in the case of Hermes Trismegistus, those who could not read Greek.

In other examples, patrons influenced the humanist movement by potentially inspiring translations of certain books, as shown by the case of the dedicatees chosen by Lapo da Castiglionchio the younger. Lapo may have translated specific *Lives* of Plutarch in order to send them to specific patrons whose lives mirrored the ones described in the ancient biography. Lapo sent his translation of Plutarch's *Life of Themistocles* to Cosimo de' Medici in 1435, one year after Cosimo's triumphant return to Florence had forced Francesco Filelfo and his student Lapo to flee the city. The dedication was rife with parallels. Like Cosimo, Themistocles had endured exile. As Lapo hoped Cosimo would, Themistocles had permitted the return of a political enemy.[38] Two years later, Lapo selected Plutarch's *Life of Artaxerxes* and dedicated it to Humphrey, duke of Gloucester. Once again, the translated biography mirrored the dedicatee's own life. In this case, both Artaxerxes and Humphrey were non-Italians, full of military virtue, who underwent difficulties in their marriages.[39] Lapo dedicated a similar "parallel life" to Cardinal Giuliano Cesarini the next year as Lapo continued to search for a stable patron, a quest cut short by his death from plague in 1438.[40]

Writers also molded the content of their original texts for the particular cultural and political contexts of their patrons. The Florentine government indirectly paid for Leonardo Bruni's *History of the Florentine People*, solemnized its narrative in public ritual, and guarded its copy of the text in the Signoria's chapel, nestled deep within the crenulated walls of the Palazzo Vecchio. In return, Bruni argued that Florence was heir to the expansive territory of the Roman Republic and that it was free from all European overlords – past or present – especially the Holy Roman Emperor and the French House of Anjou.[41] A change in the political situation and dedicatee changed the official version of Florentine history. In 1461, Donato Acciaiuoli accompanied three Florentine diplomats to France to congratulate the new king, Louis XI. Despite firsthand knowledge of Bruni's *History* – even copying Bruni's text verbatim at points – Acciaiuoli revived the story of Charlemagne's refoundation of Florence, calling it an event "in the place of the highest glory" for the city.[42] Acciaiuoli's actions enabled the Florentine state to reinforce the ancient diplomatic connections between Florence and France. The story allowed the city to urge French kings toward acts favorable to the republic by suggesting that they follow the example of their illustrious ancestors. Like Bruni's, Acciaiuoli's narrative was solemnized through its presentation as a gift from Florence to the new king of France in a diplomatic ritual, despite the fact that it flatly contradicted Bruni's official version of the Florentine past solemnized decades previously.[43] In both cases, humanist writers shaped the content of their work for its dedicatee or its explicit patron much as visual artists shaped the style and content of their works for patrons.

Learned connections were only one of the bonds that people formed in the social world of Renaissance Florence, and these connections supplemented, complemented, as well as contradicted other types of relationships. Learned connections, for example, supported the strength of nuclear familial units in fifteenth-century Florence in that humanist interests seem to have passed down through generations of familial branches, especially from fathers to favored sons. Many members of the Guicciardini family participated in the humanist movement during the fifteenth century, but the evidence suggests that these men clustered in the most politically active branch over several generations. Beginning in the late fourteenth century Luigi Guicciardini had a relationship with the literary humanist Luigi Marsili; however, details on this learned connection are sparse.[44]

Luigi's oldest son, Piero, maintained these weak connections to the humanist movement. Piero was a close friend of the social humanist Matteo Strozzi, a man discussed in some detail in the next chapter. The two men were so close, in fact, that Piero signed many of his letters to Matteo with the word *amico* rather than his name. All of these letters are in the vernacular and all seem to lack explicit references to humanism.[45] Piero may have avoided such references in these letters, but his learned connections to other people suggest that he and Matteo may also have possessed a learned connection. Leonardo Bruni discussed the Venetian Marco Dandolo with Piero in 1428.[46] Several years prior, Piero had made the comment, perhaps for the first time, that Giangaleazzo Visconti considered the public letters of Coluccio Salutati to be more valuable than five hundred lances.[47] Piero may have been friends with literary and social humanists and appreciated the political power of their studies, but he himself struggled to write in Latin. A fragmented book of diplomatic letters from 1427 and 1428 – the same time that Piero is known to have held a conversation with Bruni – suggests Piero's difficulties with that language. Throughout the book, Piero's distinct hand appears in the vernacular letters to the Florentine government. By contrast, also throughout the book, Latin letters appear in a different hand but are, nevertheless, signed by Piero. On one occasion, a vernacular letter ends with the explicit statement that Piero wrote the letter in his own hand and sent it to the Dieci di Balìa. The Latin letter on the same page simply states that it was sent to the Dieci, without any comment on who wrote it.[48]

The learned connections of men from this branch of the Guicciardini family grew stronger with Piero's sons, Luigi di Piero and Jacopo di Piero. Luigi in particular was a solid member of the humanist movement. The literary humanist Matteo Palmieri described Luigi as one of the most outstanding youths in Florence in the late 1430s and included him in his dialogue *On Civic Life*, along with Agnolo Pandolfini and Franco Sacchetti.[49] The prominent social humanist Niccolò della Luna, a man discussed in the next chapter, counted Luigi as one of his learned friends. Luigi, in fact, helped Niccolò della Luna and Matteo Strozzi exchange an unknown book transcribed by Benedetto Strozzi.[50] By the 1470s, Luigi was capable of giving a "worthy and impromptu response" to a Latin oration, which meant he could speak in elegant, impromptu Latin, a skill that even the literary humanist Carlo Marsuppini may have lacked.[51] At least two of Luigi's manuscripts still survive, a copy of Bruni's *On the Italian War against the Goths* and a book containing rhetorical works of Cicero.[52]

Luigi's brother, Jacopo, was also involved in the humanist movement, but not nearly to the degree of his learned fraternal kinsman. Francesco Guicciardini described Jacopo as "lacking letters," but Francesco's statement was not entirely correct.[53] Jacopo received at least two literary dedications, a vernacular work from Marsilio Ficino and a Latin work from Lorenzo Cyathas.[54] More tenuously, the social humanist and exile Jacopo d' Agnolo Acciaiuoli asked the social humanist and exile Dietisalvi Neroni to recommend him to Jacopo Guicciardini when Guicciardini was in Naples as a diplomat.[55] The attempts of two exiled men to ingratiate themselves to a powerful partisan of the Medici family are not noteworthy for establishing learned connections in and of themselves; however, the connections between Jacopo Acciaiuoli and Dietisalvi Neroni with humanists in Naples, discussed in the next chapter, may add a learned dimension to the relationship. Jacopo Guicciardini's extensive career as a diplomat to powerful Italian states also suggests some knowledge of humanist rhetoric and some oratorical ability, as, perhaps, do a series of vernacular letters to Jacopo from Bartolomeo Scala.[56]

Strong connections to the humanist movement continued over the next two generations. Jacopo's son, Piero, was a student of Marsilio Ficino.[57] Additionally, Ficino wrote a letter to him in 1476 and dedicated his *Apology* to Piero, as well as to Piero del Nero and Piero Soderini.[58] Ficino penned his *Apology* in 1489 in order to secure aid from prominent Florentines after the publication of his *Three Books on Life*. In this bizarre book, Ficino offered advice on maintaining a person's health, including prescriptions to drink an "ounce or two" of blood from the left arm of a "willing, healthy, happy, and temperate" youth as a morbid fountain of youth.[59] Ficino suggested that the blood should be drunk with an equal amount of wine and sugar when "hungry and thirsty and when the Moon is waxing."[60] If a person had difficulty digesting raw blood, then s/he could sweeten it with sugar and still gain the same benefits.[61] In his *Apology*, Ficino was not concerned about blood sucking, but rather was worried that his avocation of magic, images, and astrology in the book would lead to attacks against him.[62] Thus, Ficino called upon Piero Guicciardini to defend him against critics by reminding those "intellectual busy bodies" that the book was discussing magic only "in the course of an interpretation of Plotinus."[63] Additionally, Ficino urged Guicciardini to argue that Ficino only discussed good, natural magic and wrote nothing about the wicked demonic variety.[64] Beyond this relationship with Ficino, Piero Guicciardini's own words reveal his interest in humanism. In January of 1485, Guicciardini delivered an *Exhortation to Justice*, undoubtedly on the occasion of his election as one of the Sixteen Standard Bearers – a powerful advisory body to the Florentine Signoria - in late December of 1484. In the midst of the speech, he cited Aristotle, Thomas Aquinas, Plato, and examples from classical Roman history.[65] Piero Guicciardini passed his humanist interest down to his son, Francesco di Piero Guicciardini, who, together with Niccolò Machavelli, famously produced new methods for studying history and politics.

Several prominent patrician families likewise transmitted humanist learning along patrilineal lines of distinct familial branches. Since most of these figures appear elsewhere in this study, the analysis here can be quite brief. The Strozzi family possessed numerous branches that passed on humanist learning, including Palla di Nofri to his sons Lorenzo, Nofri, and Bartolomeo; Matteo to his son Filippo; and Benedetto to his son Piero. The Medici family featured Cosimo, who passed his interests down to his sons Giovanni and Piero, who in turn passed them down to Lorenzo the Magnificent. Agnolo Acciaiuoli handed off the family's learned torch to his son Jacopo. Gino Capponi passed his weak humanist interests on to his son Neri. Marco Parenti shared his learned pursuits with his son Piero. Lorenzo Ridolfi and his son Antonio likewise had humanist interests.

Other branches of these families seem to have taken a less active role in the humanist movement, suggesting, in terms of learned interests, the coherence of nuclear familial units in Renaissance Florence. Giovanni di Francesco Guicciardini was the namesake of his grandfather. The grandfather, Giovanni di Luigi, along with Palla di Nofri Strozzi, failed to provide troops in support of Rinaldo degli Albizzi in 1434. According to Machiavelli, the elder Giovanni claimed that he was doing enough to support Rinaldo by preventing Giovanni's brother, Piero, from coming forth with substantial aid for Cosimo de' Medici.[66] The elder Giovanni has not been linked to the humanist movement, but his grandson and namesake owned a vernacular miscellany in 1467. The miscellany contained several examples of vernacular oratory by Leonardo Bruni, Giannozzo Manetti, Stefano Porcari, and Francesco Filelfo. It also had vernacular versions of speeches recorded in Sallust's *War against Catiline*.[67] No evidence has been found to link any other member of this branch of the Guicciardini family to the humanist movement.[68] Bernadetto de' Medici was a ubiquitous Florentine diplomat, especially to Naples, in the 1440s and 1450s. He brought the artist Andrea del Castagno to Florence and promoted Andrea's artistic career.[69] This evidence suggests some oratorical skill and some cultural inclinations, but his humanist interests were a shadow of the major branch of his family, dominated by Cosimo, Piero, and then Lorenzo, who lived just south of Bernadetto down the modern Via Cavour.[70] Beyond Giovanni and Bernadetto, Chapters 6 and 7 of this study introduce hundreds of Florentines from prominent families who have yet to be linked to the humanist movement. More research will undoubtedly add learned connections to some of these individuals, but certainly not all or even most of them. In short, families possessed branches that cultivated humanist studies in earnest, branches that possessed almost random individuals who possessed learned connections, and branches that apparently lacked any involvement in the humanist movement at all. The relationship between humanism and the Florentine ruling groups was, in short, partially shaped by familial bonds.

Learned connections also intersected with neighborhood bonds. Giuliano Davazanti was a successful lawyer and diplomat in the middle years of the fifteenth century. He is perhaps most famous today for delivering a short panegyric written by Leonardo Bruni to the recent conqueror of Naples, King Alfonso of Aragon. On that occasion Giuliano faced a daunting task: Florence had supported the king's Angevin enemies in the recent war and had even housed the defeated Renè of Anjou within their city. The pope – also living in Florence in 1442 – invested Renè as the true king of Naples after Renè arrived in Florence.[71] Nevertheless, Giuliano arrived in Alfonso's court months later professing the undying affection of the Florentines to Alfonso because of their ancient friendship. When Giuliano was not lying to powerful princes about the warmth of Florentine good wishes he lived west and a bit south of what is now the Piazza della Repubblica.[72] There, Giuliano wrote two short, autograph Latin letters to Matteo Strozzi, a man who lived so close to him that it is puzzling why Giuliano wrote to his neighbor rather than walking across the square and simply knocking on his door. In the two letters, Davanzati requested books from his neighbor, especially Cicero's *Phillipics*.[73] The proximity of their homes explains the existence of a learned connection between the two men, a learned connection that could be cultivated and used to strengthen other kinds of bonds at other times.

Across town and not long after Davanzati was seeking his neighbor's books, in the neighborhood around the Florentine Badia and Bargello, neighborhoods again shaped learned connections. Vespasiano da Bisticci's bookshop dominated the humanist scene in this part of town. Scholars have long debated the specific location of this store along the Via del Proconsolo in Florence. In 1968, Giuseppe Cagni published a photograph of a leather shop with classical decorations around its door at the southeast corner of the Via dei Pandolfini.[74] He argued that the decorations were probably installed to commemorate the illustrious past history of the building as the former home of Vespasiano's bookstore.[75] The decorations are in fact from a much later period, but, unfortunately, the popular myth propagated by the classical decorations is probably incorrect.[76] The bookstore almost certainly stood at the corner of the Via del Proconsolo and the Via Ghibellina, as of 2010 the site of a *gelateria* without any classically inspired decorations. The site of the modern ice cream parlor corresponds with fifteenth-century accounts that the bookstore was across from the Bargello, then the Palace of the Podestà, whereas the site of the former leather store with the neoclassical door does not.[77]

Less than a block from Vespasiano's bookstore lived the Pandolfini family, many of whom shared learned connections with Vespasiano and other learned men in the neighborhood. The true patriarch of the family was Agnolo Pandolfini, who lived about a block away from Vespasiano's bookstore. Buried in an extant tomb in San Martino a Gangalandi in Signa, Agnolo Pandolfini was a powerful and controversial patrician in the early fifteenth century.[78] The Florentine Signoria sent him as a diplomat to the bellicose King Ladislaus in Naples in 1413, even though factions in Florence could not agree on whether the proper course was continued war or the conclusion of a peace. Agnolo chose peace. Upon his return north, a friend stopped him to warn him that groups in the city were displeased with his actions and sought revenge. Agnolo purportedly shrugged off the warning, entered the city, and did not come to harm.[79]

What was less controversial was Agnolo's acknowledged strong position in the humanist movement. Vespasiano da Bisticci, his neighbor, claimed that Agnolo was learned in Latin as well as natural and moral philosophy. For Vespasiano, Agnolo's learning was particularly noteworthy because so few of Pandolfini's contemporaries possessed such learning, an exaggerated statement designed to praise Agnolo and one that reflects the explosion of humanist learning in the generations between Agnolo's death and the penning of Vespasiano's biography.[80] Giannozzo Manetti praised Agnolo's eloquence and memory, among other attributes, in a funeral oration written for Agnolo's son, Giannozzo.[81] Agnolo's learned reputation endured enough through the centuries that he could pass as the author of Leon Battista Alberti's *On the Family*.[82]

Vespasiano also recorded that Leonardo Bruni, a man who lived about two blocks to the south, sent unpublished works to Agnolo to gauge their merit.[83] A vernacular letter survives in which Bruni advised Agnolo to protest Agnolo's election as a diplomat because of his extreme age.[84]

Agnolo Pandolfini was not the only man whose learned connection with Bruni could be attributed to geographical proximity; Bruni's connections to the Castellani family – Bruni's neighbors and in-laws – are discussed later. Additionally, Bruni was a friend of Filippo di Ugolino Pieruzzi, who may not have traced his lineage to Bruni's neighbors, the Peruzzi, but who was active in the Badia, which was not far from Bruni's house.[85] Bruni also lived near the Cocchi-Donati family, a member of whom later translated Bruni's Latin version of St. Basil's *Letter to the Youth*.[86] Finally, Bruni lived next door to a member of the Panzano family, which was a splinter branch of the Ricasoli family, and Bruni dedicated his *Introduction to Moral Philosophy* to Galeotto Ricasoli.[87]

Humanist interests among the Pandolfini were skewed to one specific patrilineage. Agnolo Pandolfini had two sons, Carlo and Giannozzo. Carlo has left no evidence for learned interests beyond his extensive diplomatic career. Giannozzo's connections were also weak, but he has left a handful of tantalizing pieces of evidence for humanist interests beyond his own extensive diplomatic career.[88] Vespasiano da Bisticci requested that Giannozzo Manetti write a funeral oration for Giannozzo Pandolfini, a request that was undoubtedly inspired by Vespasiano's friendship with Pandolfini's sons and the proximity of their homes.[89] Additionally, Giannozzo Pandolfini was buried in the Badia in a simple tomb, but one with classical elements constructed by the workshop of Bernardo Rossellino.[90] The contrast between the learned interests of Carlo and Giannozzo grew stronger with their male offspring.

Each of Giannozzo's five sons has left evidence of learned connections, especially to their neighbor Vespasiano da Bisticci. The eldest, Pandolfo Pandolfini, received consolatory letters from Giannozzo Manetti, Donato and Piero Acciaiuoli, and Alamanno Rinuccini upon the death of his father, Giannozzo.[91] Vespasiano attested to Pandolfo's learning, which an undated *Exhortation to Justice* delivered by Pandolfo confirms.[92] In the midst of his discussion of justice, Pandolfo sneaked in quotations from Aristotle, Augustine, Plato, Seneca, Cicero, and others.[93] Pandolfo's brother, Pierfilippo, was no less learned. Pierfilippo amassed a large library and received a Latin letter from Ficino.[94] Latin letters by him to Florentines, such as Donato Acciaiuoli, and non-Florentines, such as Bartolomeo Platina, survive from 1459 and 1460.[95] Two decades later, on March 1, 1480, Alamanno Rinuccini requested that Francesco Filelfo send his greetings to Pierfilippo: Rinuccini assumed the two men were visiting one another, given that Pierfilippo was very learned, Filelfo loved learned men, and both Pierfilippo and Filelfo were then in Milan.[96] In the same year, conversations with Filelfo inspired Pierfilippo to order his agent Bartolomeo Cederini to hunt for learned books in a cupboard back in Florence.[97] Another brother, Niccolò, was also part of the humanist movement. Niccolò became Bishop of Pistoia in 1475 and was a notorious collector of benefices.[98] He even bought himself a cardinal's hat in 1517 from Leo X for 20,000 ducats.[99] Years previously, Donato Acciaiuoli described Niccolò – along with his four brothers – as learned, and Alamanno Rinuccini wrote two letters in humanist Latin to Niccolò.[100] He was also among the many members of the Pandolfini family to receive literary dedications from Vespasiano da Bisticci.[101]

Giannozzo's other two sons have left additional evidence of their learning. Jacopo Pandolfini appeared in a tale spun by Angelo Poliziano. Poliziano recalled that one day, Giovanni Argyropoulos returned to Florence from Rome without the beard he had formerly worn. Jacopo, wishing to show that Argyropoulos would not remain in Florence permanently, stated that Argyropoulos had not stayed when he had a beard; who thought he would remain without one?[102] Sometime after this remark, in 1472 Jacopo purchased the Palazzo Carducci – now known as the Palazzo Pandolfini – outside Florence.[103] Within its walls, Andrea del Castagno had painted his fresco cycle of famous men, which contained images of Petrarch, Boccaccio, Pippo Spano, Farinata degli Uberti, and others in the mid-fifteenth century.[104] The whole room, in fact, may have been inspired by humanist writings of Alamanno Rinuccini.[105] Shortly afterward in 1475, Jacopo Pandolfini purchased "two painted papers" from Vespasiano.[106] Jacopo's money for these endeavors was in part from business dealings in the Iberian peninsula, which historians know about because Donato Acciaiuoli wrote a letter on behalf of Vespasiano da Bisticci to send to the Spaniard Alfonso de Palencia, a letter that Jacopo carried.[107] Giannozzo's last son, Priore, often accompanied his brother Niccolò and Vespasiano da Bisticci to visit the social humanist Filippo di Ugolino Pieruzzi.[108] The offspring of these men and their wives were still in the neighborhood near Vespasiano's bookstore in the early sixteenth century, as evidenced by two sixteenth-century doorway inscriptions and classical decorations commemorating their presence. The classical decoration of a second story door in a building is partially visible from the road, roughly a dozen meters east of the Via del Proconsolo on the north side of the Via dei Pandolfini. The other classical inscription in the building is easily viewed from the interior courtyard.[109]

The propensity toward humanist learning among Agnolo's son Giannozzo and his offspring sharply contrasts with the lack of surviving information to link Giannozzo's brother Carlo and his sons to the humanist movement. Carlo himself has left little indication of any interest. He had four legitimate sons and one illegitimate: Domenico, Bartolomeo, Meglio, Alessandro, and Giuliano. Of these men, Domenico possessed by far the most and strongest learned connections. Donato Acciaiuoli wrote a Latin letter to Domenico and Domenico was one of the men invited to Franco Sacchetti's learned discussions.[110] Two other brothers left very weak evidence of potential humanist interests. Bartolomeo is known to have carried a letter between Filelfo and Alamanno Rinuccini in late February 1485.[111] Alessandro Pandolfini has yet to be linked to the humanist movement, but his son Pierfilippo may have possessed learned interests in the early sixteenth century.[112] Neither Meglio nor Giuliano has left even this smattering of evidence of humanist interests.

The correlative links between neighborhoods and learned connections should not be overstated. Members of the Pandolfini family had strong learned connections with Alamanno Rinuccini and Donato Acciaiuoli, neither of whom lived nearby. The surviving Palazzo Rinuccini is some distance away and across the river, although in 1427 all of the Rinuccini family declared the Bue neighborhood of the Santa Croce quarter as their home, the same quarter as Agnolo Pandolfini's home.[113] By contrast, Donato Acciaiuoli probably lived on the other side of town, either near his Acciaiuoli and Strozzi relatives or perhaps on the south side of the river near the traditional dwellings of the Brancacci, the family of his stepfather.[114] Either way, the learned connections of Donato and the Pandolfini had little to do with geographical proximity: The Acciaiuoli, Strozzi, and Brancacci all lived across town from the Pandolfini, Vespasiano, and their neighborhood.

Thus, learned connections could follow neighborhood bonds, but they also could ignore them. Giannozzo Manetti formed strong learned connections with members of the Pandolfini family as well as many of their friends including Donato and Piero Acciaiuoli, Alamanno Rinuccini, and Vespasiano da Bisticci. Yet, Manetti lived across the river from the Pandolfini and far from the neighborhood around Vespasiano's bookshop.[115] According to Leonardo Bruni, Coluccio Salutati fondly remembered walking across the city to visit the monk Luigi Marsili at his cell to talk about humanism. Salutati recalled that a bridge encountered on the walk marked the latest moment he could still think of a topic for discussion.[116] Coexisting with the pull of neighborhoods on the formation of learned connections, it seems that certain people or places – like Marsili's cell, the classrooms of exceptional teachers, or Vespasiano's bookshop – drew people from across the city and beyond.

Learned connections could also contrast with political allegiances. The group of Pandolfini family homes shared a block with the large Palazzo Pazzi. Agnolo Pandolfini's home, in fact, shared a wall with the Pazzi family. This proximity explains the marriage of Priore Pandolfini to Piero de' Pazzi's daughter, Elisabetta.[117] It also explains a Latin letter sent from Pierfilippo Pandolfini to Renato de' Pazzi, Piero de' Pazzi's son.[118] Nevertheless, the families were diametrically opposed, politically speaking, by the 1460s and 1470s. The Pazzi family attempted a violent overthrow of Lorenzo de' Medici and his brother Giuliano's regime in 1478. Through the 1460s and 1470s, the Pazzi resented Medici rule and cultivated French Angevin connections as a means of increasing their power and wealth and challenging Medici supremacy in Florence. The family was so close to the Angevins, in fact, that Piero's son was named Renato after his godfather, Renè of Anjou.[119] The Pandolfini family, by contrast, was a newer family in Florentine politics and depended in large part on the Medici for their prominent political position in the city.[120] The Pandolfini family also cultivated international ties to strengthen their family's domestic position. In this case, Pandolfo Pandolfini was so close to the bastard Aragonese house in Naples that he named his son Ferrante after his son's godfather, Ferrante, king of Naples.[121] Ferrante fought a long war against the Angevins in and over the Kingdom of Naples. Ultimately, Renato de' Pazzi was implicated in the Pazzi Conspiracy and executed.[122] Conversely, Pierfilippo Pandolfini was so close to Lorenzo de' Medici that one observer called him the most prominent man in the city.[123] As the crowds shouted for blood at the Palazzo Pazzi in April 1478, next door did Pierfilippo mourn the imminent doom of his former learned friend?

The Pazzi and Pandolfini provide but one example of the muddied relationship between learned connections and political alliances in Renaissance Florence. Arthur Field has argued that differences of opinion over literary matters may have followed political lines, a point that deserves future research.[124] In the meantime, Francesco Filelfo provides one example of fairly consistent relations, in that he famously quarreled with intellectuals associated with the Medici in Florence and cultivated ties, learned and otherwise, with their political opponents.[125] However, other examples were less straightforward. Giannozzo Manetti gave lectures on Aristotle's *Ethics* in 1430–1431 to a room full of Florentine patricians. The learned connections of each of these men will be discussed in the next chapter; for now it is enough to examine the politics of each of the students and the teacher of the class: In addition to Manetti, the known participants were Agnolo Acciaiuoli, Alessandro Arrighi, Antonio Barbadori, Benedetto Strozzi, Marcello Strozzi, Matteo Strozzi, and Palla Strozzi. Of these seven individuals, Matteo Strozzi and Palla Strozzi were exiled after 1434. Both the Barbadori family and the Strozzi family more generally had people exiled or otherwise punished in 1434.[126] The Arrighi family do not seem to have had members explicitly exiled or punished after the return of the Medici in 1434, but their familial political status was destroyed, as demonstrated by their failure to return a man to the Signoria before the end of the fifteenth century.[127]

By contrast, Agnolo Acciaiuoli and Giannozzo Manetti both rose to political prominence in the Medici regime in the 1430s and 1440s.[128] Agnolo's loyalty seems to have been unquestioned until the latter 1450s and 1460s. Manetti similarly was successful in Cosimo de' Medici's Florence until the early 1450s.[129] His extraordinary wealth and role as major creditor of the Florentine state combined with his unparalleled eloquence to make him an important player in Florentine politics in the 1430s, 1440s, and early 1450s.[130] Competition for political offices with Luca Pitti rather than philosophical disagreements about the value of republicanism probably led to the ruinous taxation that forced Manetti to flee the city in 1453, although he was never officially exiled.[131] Thus, Medici allies and enemies met together in Manetti's classroom in 1430–1431. Apparently, at times learned connections transcended political enmities, and at times learned connections were too important to overlook. Giannozzo Manetti, eventually, was censured by the Florentine Republic for his dedication of his *On the Dignity of Man* to Alfonso of Aragon in the midst of a war between Florence and Naples.[132] After the Pazzi Conspiracy, Marsilio Ficino wondered whether his learned connections with exiled and executed participants in the conspiracy would lead to his own demise or whether his social and learned connections with the Medici family would overcome them.[133]

Humanist learning and learned connections also made other types of social bonds possible. By the 1420s and 1430s humanist learning was beginning to enhance the social status and wealth of individuals who otherwise would have been excluded from the seats of power. Patricians who married their sons and daughters with these figures must have taken into account not only the wealth and familial ancestry of the potential partner, but also their reputation for humanist studies. For example, the wealthy immigrant Leonardo Bruni married his son Donato into the

Castellani family. The Castellani were an ancient family whose members enjoyed exceptional political prominence in Florence in the decades prior to the Medici restoration in 1434.[134] Even lesser branches of such a family would have looked to prominent Florentine lineages for marital matches; yet, in 1431 Donato di Leonardo Bruni married Alessandra di Michele Castellani. Bruni's extraordinary wealth made him a potential match for the Castellani.[135] Meanwhile, his learned connections with Matteo di Michele Castellani made him a familiar presence among Castellani family members. In 1421, Bruni wrote to Bartolomeo d'Arezzo and mentioned a discussion with Matteo Castellani about appointments to the Florentine Studio.[136] On this or some other occasion, perhaps Bruni and Castellani discussed Prosperus, Statius, or Cicero's *On Friendship*, all of which Matteo owned at the time of his death in 1429.[137]

Bruni's learning and wealth made his son eligible for the marriage while the hard times of the Castellani and other sociopolitical forces opened the door for the match. Donato's bride was Alessandra, sister of Bruni's friend Matteo. She was also the daughter of Michele Castellani, who died in 1424. By 1427, the household of Michele's widow, Bartolommea, was approximately fifteen hundred florins in debt.[138] A marriage to Bruni promised financial assistance and a beginning, presumably, to the end of the family's financial troubles. Beyond financial need, several other factors made the match between a learned parvenu and a family of Florentine aristocrats possible. Bruni and the Castellani lived in the same basic area of Florence, in the quarter of Santa Croce.[139] In fact, Bruni lived beside the Peruzzi family, members of which frequently intermarried with the Castellani and lived just northwest of the Castellani's large riverside home.[140] Additionally, the Castellani were prominent players in the Guelf Party in Florence, an organization for which Bruni wrote speeches in the early fifteenth century and whose statutes he rewrote in 1420.[141] The death of Michele in 1424 also removed the primary male figure in the lineage, an absence that undoubtedly decreased the desirability of marriages to the dead father's daughters. Marco Parenti, for example, viewed the lack of a father and other male relatives as a detriment to the marital value of a girl from the Adimari family. He did, however, inform Filippo Strozzi, the potential groom, that the lack of male relatives would mean fewer people to bother with.[142]

Learned connections also opened new political doors for Leonardo Bruni and other humanists. Bruni was an immigrant to Florence in the 1420s with little claim to social status beyond his literary reputation and fabulous wealth. Lots of people had wealth in Renaissance Florence without also achieving great social status to accompany it. Consequently, Bruni was certainly a patrician, but he was not one of the elite group of patricians who filled *pratiche* – debates on pending political decisions attended by men invited by the Florentine government – in the Palazzo Vecchio or who dominated the city's most lucrative and powerful offices. Leonardo Bruni's low status among Florentine patricians in 1420 is revealed through an episode involving his election and rejection of a diplomatic mission to King Alfonso of Aragon in that year. The Florentine Signoria originally elected Leonardo Bruni along with Antonio da Panzano, a relative of Bruni's neighbor Luca da Panzano.[143] Eight days later, Bruni pled "impediments" before the Signoria and asked to be excused from the mission.[144] As later chapters argue, ordinarily the Florentine government replaced people who rejected diplomatic missions with people with similar rank and status. In Bruni's place, the Signoria elected the lawyer Jacopo Niccoli, Niccolò Niccoli's brother.[145] While different in many ways, Bruni and Niccoli shared a lack of political experience or status in Florence. Beyond his three-month stint as chancellor, Bruni had not held a political position in Florence by 1420. Similarly, Jacopo Niccoli's political career had been limited to a low-level voting position on the Council of the People.[146] As a parvenu, Bruni had moderate to low political status similar to that of members of the politically unambitious Niccoli family.[147]

Thus, it is surprising to find Bruni accompanying Francesco Tornabuoni as a Florentine diplomat to the pope in Rome in 1426. Diplomatic missions to powerful princes required Florentines with old family ancestries and powerful political presences at home, both of which Bruni lacked. Yet, in all other ways Bruni was the obvious choice to go to Rome to help negotiate peace among Florence, Venice, and Milan. He was experienced with the papal curia, had actually worked briefly under Martin V as a papal secretary, and was undoubtedly the Florentine with the best relations with the often-hostile pope.[148] Bruni needed a little help from his friends to help people see beyond his parvenu taint.

He received this help from the social humanist Nicola de' Medici. Nicola, possibly a student of Bruni's, was the Standard Bearer of Justice, that is the head of the Florentine government, when the papal diplomat Domenico Capranica arrived stating the pope's request for orators at the peace negotiations.[149] Nicola called a *pratica* and asked his colleagues their opinion of, among other things, sending diplomats to Rome to work for the recovery of lands lost in the Romagna, to follow the peace talks closely, to respond quickly to requests from the pope, and to report back to Florence regularly with news. Nicola was clear that the diplomats should not be charged with making peace at Rome because the Venetians, then allies of the Florentines, possessed that power through their treaty of alliance. According to Nicola, it would be a "diminishment of the city's honor" to charge the diplomats with a task that they could not actually conclude.[150] Leonardo Strozzi, a family with whom Bruni was well known and connected, concurred with Nicola that orators should be sent.[151] The record of the debate ends at that point and thus it is impossible to know for certain whether Nicola nominated Bruni, but it seems plausible that he at the very least supported Bruni's candidacy for the position. It also seems probable that Leonardo Strozzi and Bruni's friend Piero di Luigi Guicciardini, who was at that time a member of the Colleges – the two advisory bodies that advised the Signoria – supported Bruni's election. Bruni's learned connections to these men, and Nicola de' Medici in particular, opened a door for him into a prestigious political position that would have been locked to a man, even with his money, without his learned connections.

Learned connections also opened doors for people with greater social status. Courtiers abroad with knowledge of classical rhetoric possessed an advantage in courts where the ruler sought to project the appearance of being a friend to humanists. The experience of Giannozzo Manetti at the court of Alfonso the Magnanimous in Naples was one particularly prominent example. Manetti arrived in Naples in 1445 with only two diplomatic missions under his belt and no known connections with King Alfonso.[152] His reputation for learning, however, preceded him and was enhanced through his performances while in Naples. Upon his arrival, Manetti honored the wedding of Alfonso's son Ferrante through a glittering oration in praise of King Alfonso.[153] In the speech, Manetti used the prominent placement of Greek sources and historical figures to demonstrate his extraordinary erudition and thus flatter the king's own learning, who, Manetti implicitly suggested, could be expected to appreciate the learned references.[154] According to Vespasiano, Manetti's oration was so captivating that the king failed to shoo away a fly that landed on his highness's nose in the midst of Manetti's speech.[155] Incredible as it may seem, the fact that Manetti could tell this exact story in an oration to the same king on a different diplomatic mission years later suggests that Vespasiano was relating more or less an accurate tale, or at the very least a fiction that had worked its way into the historical memory of the king.[156] Vespasiano claimed that Manetti's success with his oration inspired fathers to educate their sons beyond basic business school ("beyond the abacus") because these fathers saw "how much honor to a city and to a family is a citizen like that."[157] In terms of Manetti himself and his diplomatic mission, Manetti's reputation for learning earned him special invitations to the royal court to engage in learned discussions and debates.[158] Such opportunities built relationships that made Manetti, along with Bernadetto de' Medici, Florence's diplomat of choice with Alfonso in the 1440s and early 1450s. Manetti's relationship with the king eventually led to Manetti's downfall in Florentine politics, but this relationship, ostensibly based on shared learned interests, also gained Manetti a position in Naples during his voluntary exile. Manetti's position reportedly paid a handsome salary and enabled him to pursue his learned studies free from the ennui of court, to which he was required to go only when asked.[159]

Learned connections, in conclusion, were an essential thread in the social fabric of Renaissance Florence. They shared a mutual relationship with other bonds that drew people together and drove them apart. Learned connections, potentially, made bonds formed in neighborhoods stronger. A published humanist dialogue featuring allied families in jovial conversation could not help but reinforce the image of solidarity among them, much as painting the coat of arms of an in-law on a bedroom wall, on a marriage chest, or on a wedding portrait permanently tied families together through visual imagery. Sharing humanist interests brought kinsman together in branches of families. They drew people together for business deals and marriages, some of which would have been impossible without the strong learned reputations that people like Poggio or Bruni brought to the table. As other kinds of social bonds, the importance of learned connections differed from individual to individual. Some people actively cultivated learned connections and used them to practical ends. Others created learned connections seemingly by accident, an unavoidable offshoot of living in a society so permeated with humanism. The next chapter provides examples of the range of strength and number of learned connections possessed by social humanists. Reconstructing these learned connections not only shows the range of interests and abilities possessed by the social humanists, but also puts faces in the crowds that flocked to humanist orations.

2

Literary and Social Humanists

Matteo Strozzi died in exile at a young age, leaving a young wife and even younger children to return to Florence, a city full of enemies responsible for driving out Matteo, his friendly kinsmen, and his political allies. Famously, Matteo's widowed wife, Alessandra, sent her sons to work with family members in Naples. There, she hoped that they would learn the mercantile trade, revive the economic fortunes of the Strozzi family, cultivate powerful patrons abroad, and bide their time for a triumphant return to Florence. Eventually they did triumph, if fleetingly, and the enormous Palazzo Strozzi stands testament to their success. Long before the construction of that magnificent palace Alessandra sent her sons dozens of fascinating letters, which historians have studied for their penetrating insights into the Florentine marriage market and the negotiation of a male dominated political sphere by an intelligent and strong-willed mother and widow. Alessandra's correspondence often mirrors and complements the savvy letters of her loyal son-in-law, Marco Parenti, letters that historians have also published and thoroughly analyzed. But, Marco and his mother-in-law were not the only people in this branch of this family to leave rich letters to posterity. The dead patriarch, Matteo Strozzi, has left hundreds of letters written to him by friends and clients throughout the latter 1420s and early 1430s. Ironically, in this case the rich white male has received far less attention than his wife or his much less influential son-in-law.

Matteo's letters provide evidence for many of his learned connections in the 1420s and early 1430s. He possessed far more and stronger learned connections than that left by Bartolomeo Bardi, the Medici banker who in the last chapter asked Poggio Bracciolini to find him books. Matteo still, however, had far fewer and weaker learned connections than literary humanists like Bruni, Manetti, and Poggio. Thus Matteo was a social humanist. He and similar people marked one end of the range of interests, influence, and abilities that encompassed the social humanist category. At the other end of the spectrum were individuals who read a handful of vernacular classical texts. This chapter provides examples of the wide range of learned interests and abilities of people in the humanist movement, ranging from the strongest literary humanists at one end to the weakest social humanists at the other. Admittedly, most of the individuals discussed here may be unfamiliar to all but a handful of Florentine specialists. Nevertheless, the following prosopographical analysis is essential to demonstrate the large number of learned connections intersecting across the Florentine social world and the corresponding large size of the humanist movement. This chapter, which documents a sampling of the learned connections of roughly a hundred Florentines, represents a fraction of the total evidence available for the humanist movement in Renaissance Florence. While the examples here are organized by proximity to the center of the humanist movement rather than chronology – and thus examples from different decades are sometimes discussed together – later chapters of this book offer a diachronic analysis of the spread and size of the humanist movement in fifteenth-century Florence.

The most prolific humanist writers in fifteenth-century Florence also had the most and strongest learned connections. These men have always fit snugly into scholarly conceptions of the humanist movement, and, therefore, they can be dealt with quickly here. In the 1380s the literary humanist and monk Luigi Marsili held learned discussions about humanism in his cell; decades later Coluccio Salutati still fondly remembered them.[1] Salutati himself picked up the humanist mantle in Florence from Marsili, as definitively shown in multiple studies by Ronald Witt.[2] Leonardo Bruni was a literary humanist by virtue of his innumerable learned connections, his prolific original writings, translations, and powerful political positions in Florence.[3] Bruni's contemporary Poggio Bracciolini spent most of his career away from Florence in the papal curia, but he maintained contact with Florentines through letters and investments and eventually he took over the Florentine chancery late in life.[4] The literary humanist Ambrogio Traversari also spent much of his career away from Florence as head of the Carmelite order, but before he left the city he led learned discussions in his cell at Santa Maria degli Angeli.[5] Like these two men, Francesco Filelfo, another literary humanist, kept in touch with many Florentine humanists after he fled the city.[6] Giannozzo Manetti left Florence after running afoul of the Medici regime, but prior to his self-imposed exile he was one of the leading humanists in the city from the latter 1440s through the early 1450s.[7] Manetti's deep learning and busy civic career made him an example for literary humanists of the next generation, particularly Donato Acciaiuoli. Acciaiuoli had many politically questionable friends in his early life before gaining Lorenzo de' Medici's trust in the late 1460s and early 1470s. He also was a gifted student of Giovanni Argyropoulos, wrote original humanist works, and has left a pile of autograph Latin letters for historians.[8] Marsilio Ficino was a prolific letter writer whose enormous number of learned connections ranged from the most cultivated individuals to the most superficial dilettantes.[9] The Florentine chancellor, Medici ally, and parvenu Bartolomeo Scala formed learned connections through his writings, correspondence, and position in the Florentine chancery from the 1460s through the 1490s.[10] These individuals – and others like them – were literary humanists because of their active pens, the strength and number of their learned connections, and the favorable opinions of their learning among their contemporaries and modern scholars.

The category of literary humanists was not limited to writers of Latin poetry and prose. Few writings survive from Niccolò Niccoli, but his efforts to promote humanist studies in Florence, his acquisition of his fabled library, as well as the opinion of his contemporaries clearly establish him as a leading figure.[11] Fifteenth-century sources likewise secure Palla di Nofri Strozzi a position at the center of the humanist movement in early fifteenth-century Florence, although Palla has left few original writings.[12] Carlo Marsuppini's reputation for learning earned him the position of Florentine chancellor after Leonardo Bruni died in 1444. Like Bruni, Marsuppini had a mastery of letters and service to the state that were immortalized in a beautiful tomb in Santa Croce; unlike the prolific Bruni, few original literary writings survive from Marsuppini's pen.[13] Key patrons were literary humanists by virtue of their support for humanist studies. For example, Cosimo de' Medici received dozens of translations and original works from famous and lesser-known humanist authors. His grandson, Lorenzo de' Medici, surpassed him in the number of literary works dedicated to him, even as his role as a patron of the visual arts remains debated by scholars.[14]

Finally, even individuals with questionable Latinity could be literary humanists. Vespasiano da Bisticci repeatedly contrasted his vernacular biographies of fifteenth-century figures with Latin lives of his subjects, beseeching others to translate and flesh out his meager notes.[15] Nevertheless, Vespasiano's promotion of humanism, his presence in learned discussions, the quality of his friends, and his reputation as a seller of humanist and classical books make a compelling case for his inclusion among the literary humanists whom he so admired. Among Vespasiano's learned connections was Giannozzo Manetti: Vespasiano accompanied Manetti's diplomatic entourage in 1447 to congratulate the new pope, Nicholas V.[16] Vespasiano and Manetti corresponded throughout the latter 1440s and continued their epistolary exchange even after Manetti left Florence for Naples and Rome in the 1450s.[17] Vespasiano was also close with Donato Acciaiuoli and his equally learned – albeit short-lived – brother Piero in the 1440s and 1450s, even taking refuge with them during an outbreak of plague in 1449.[18] Vespasiano was invited to the learned debates at the home of Franco Sacchetti and possessed strong learned connections with all five sons of the Florentine knight Giannozzo Pandolfini, as was described in the previous chapter.

Vespasiano also possessed learned connections with Jacopo Acciaiuoli, the little studied son of Agnolo Acciaiuoli, who joined his father in exile after their failed political coup in Florence in 1466. Jacopo, in fact, shared many of the same learned friends as Vespasiano. He wrote to the book-seller and asked him to send his greetings to all the members of their "*accademia*," which included Donato and Piero Acciaiuoli as well as Giovanni Argyropoulos.[19] A note from Giannozzo Manetti asked Vespasiano to send his greetings to the Acciaiuoli brothers as well as Jacopo Acciaiuoli.[20] Donato, in fact, corresponded directly with Jacopo in a surviving Latin letter, as did Bartolomeo Scala.[21] After his exile, Jacopo referred to Hannibal, Carthage, and Scipio in a vernacular letter written to the social humanist Dietisalvi Neroni in Naples.[22] Perhaps Jacopo participated in learned discussions with less learned Florentines too. In a letter of October 15, 1486, Jacopo advised Filippo Strozzi – Matteo Strozzi's son and a man with only modest humanist interests – that he was setting out for Hungary. In a tone of utter finality, Jacopo sighed that he did not know when he would return and begged Filippo, "When you find yourself with dear friends and relations, remember me."[23] Filippo did not have to cherish Jacopo's memory for long: On June 12, 1487, Jacopo again wrote to Filippo, stating that he was leaving the Italian peninsula. Once again, Jacopo was going to Hungary, this time with the son of the duke of Ferrara. Rather than the melodramatic melancholy of his previous request for Filippo to remember him when with friends, this time Jacopo simply wrote that he would be back in two months.[24]

Finally, Vespasiano's ownership and work in his bookshop, which served as a center for humanist studies in Florence during the mid-fifteenth century, further strengthened his position in the humanist movement.[25]

Customers, copyists, book buyers, and sellers all established weak and strong learned connections to Vespasiano, to which his familiarity with the learned men in his *Lives* attests. In addition, Vespasiano himself enjoyed a reputation for his ability to track down classical books.[26] This reputation, his learned connections, and his key role in providing texts to others suggest Vespasiano's central position in the humanist movement.

Less strong and less studied are the learned connections possessed by social humanists in fifteenth-century Florence. Some social humanists had so many connections to humanism that they clearly played a notable role in that movement, albeit on a lesser scale than men like Bruni, Ficino, Cosimo de' Medici, or Vespasiano da Bisticci. The impenetrable mysteries of chance have left historians with a large cache of Latin and Italian letters written to Matteo Strozzi dating from the 1420s until Matteo's exile by the Medici and their allies in 1434. Matteo has left little autograph or firsthand evidence to establish his involvement in the humanist movement. He compiled a large library and left a few Latin writings in his own small but elegant hand.[27] His learned presence is also gleaned from documents recorded during his time as an overseer for artistic projects for the Florentine Cathedral.[28]

This trickle of evidence from Matteo himself contrasts with the flood provided by the letters to him sent from others. As mentioned in the last chapter, Matteo's neighbor Giuliano Davanzati wrote to him requesting books. In another example, Biagio Guasconi corresponded with Matteo in Latin.[29] Years later, Biagio Guasconi joined Rinaldo degli Albizzi and his son to send a priest to Luca degli Albizzi while Luca was in Bologna as a diplomat. Guasconi also received the dedication of a book from Francesco Barbaro, in which Barbaro blasted Niccolò Niccoli.[30] This dedication complements political bonds: Guasconi was eventually exiled by the Medici and received a book criticizing a Medici partisan; however, it also contradicts them because Francesco Barbaro was a friend of Cosimo and especially his brother Lorenzo.[31] Matteo Strozzi served as an intermediary between Biago Guasconi and other humanists, as demonstrated by the copyist Benedetto Strozzi's request that Matteo recommend him to Guasconi.[32] Benedetto Strozzi himself has left further evidence of a learned connection to Matteo Strozzi. Benedetto concluded a vernacular letter to Matteo with two pained lines of Latin. With an obvious tone of exasperation, he declared that Matteo had written to him in Latin and requested that all future correspondence be in Italian.[33] An ironic request, given that Vespasiano da Bisticci described the impressive size of Benedetto's Latin library in his short biography of the man.[34]

Matteo Strozzi maintained learned connections with many other men who actively engaged in the humanist movement without writing original works. Matteo corresponded with the learned Florentine patrician Domenico Martelli and the learned copyist Mariotto Nori. While Domenico was a law student in Bologna, he sent Matteo Strozzi several Latin letters including one interesting exchange about a copy of Lactantius's *The Phoenix*. The work had just arrived in Bologna, and Domenico sent it along to Matteo, but the courtier Alessio di Bivignano failed to deliver it. Instead, the learned professor Luca di Guido Siciliano, who had been seized with love for Matteo after seeing the quality of Matteo's letters, copied the entire work and sent it to Domenico to send along again, which he did.[35] Years later, Domenico quoted Aristotle in a *pratica* held November 13, 1465.[36] By that date, Domenico had established connections with both Medici allies and their opponents. He had corresponded with Matteo, a man whom the Medici eventually exiled from Florence. Nevertheless, Cosimo de' Medici thought highly of Domenico. A friend wrote to Cosimo describing Domenico as "a fine and wise man, very tender and loving to his friends."[37] With this characterization, Domenico must have considered Piero di Cosimo de' Medici a friend: Domenico betrayed Francesco Neroni to Piero after Francesco invited Domenico to participate in the anti-Medici plot of 1466.[38]

Mariotto Nori was a copyist with many learned connections, including one to Matteo Strozzi. In a Latin letter, Nori asked Matteo to convey his greetings to Leonardo Bruni, Giannozzo Manetti, and Carlo Marsuppini.[39] Nori also received Latin letters from several literary humanists, including Ambrogio Traversari and Guarino Veronese.[40] Nori may have established his connection to Guarino Veronese through Antonio Corbinelli, a Florentine Greek scholar who donated his large library to the Badia and who wrote to Guarino on Nori's behalf.[41] Nori pursued this connection with Guarino further, studying under the famed teacher and transcribing copies of Justin in 1425 and Servius in 1427 for Guarino.[42] Additionally, Francesco del Benino wrote to Nori in Latin. Francesco himself was a man who received poetic lines from Francesco Filelfo and who was described by Vespasiano da Bisticci as learned and eloquent in the Latin language.[43] In an interesting bit of trivia, Vespasiano recorded that while Francesco was a most just judge, he was an enemy of game players and blasphemers. Francesco ordered corporal rather than monetary punishment because he sought to punish crimes in ways that transgressors would remember.[44] Perhaps Mariotto Nori, the copyist, also knew Vespasiano, the bookseller. After all, in 1427, Nori owed money to Piero

Bettuci.[45] Bettuci was the neighbor and partner of Michele di Giovanni Guarducci, who owned the bookshop later taken over by Vespasiano da Bisticci.[46]

Matteo Strozzi's attendance at readings of Aristotle under Giannozzo Manetti in 1430–1431 further expands Matteo's learned friends and acquaintances.[47] Manetti himself has left no surviving correspondence with Matteo, but he did write a letter of consolation to Matteo's widow, Alessandra, after the death of her son in 1459. Alessandra and Manetti were not close, as Alessandra despaired that she did not know how to respond to a letter from a man of such learning and stature. She told her son Filippo that she would delay sending a letter thanking Manetti, and, in the meantime, she requested that Filippo thank Manetti personally since Manetti was so fond of Filippo.[48] Manetti's letter has not survived but was undoubtedly heartfelt, given Manetti's own inconsolable grief at the loss of a child some two decades earlier.[49] Years before the death of either child, Matteo sat with several other Florentine patricians to hear Manetti talk about Aristotle. Perhaps Manetti spoke in Italian to accommodate Matteo's kinsman Benedetto, who, as noted previously, could read but struggled to write Latin and who was present.[50] Another member of the Strozzi with better Latin, Palla di Nofri, also attended the group. Manetti's audience had others whose presence places them within Matteo's cluster of learned connections.

Agnolo Acciaiuoli had several strong connections to the humanist movement and was present for Manetti's readings. Agnolo was knighted as a youth and exiled in 1433. In the years after his return to Florence in 1434, Agnolo entertained the emperor of Constantinople with the humanist Cyriac of Ancona and served as Florentine diplomat to Francesco Sforza, duke of Milan, even as he was taking Sforza's money to be a political adviser. Eventually, Agnolo died in exile from Florence, having rebelled against the Medici family and lost in 1466.[51] In terms of his learning, in 1436, Manetti dedicated his *On Secular and Pontifical Processions* – a description of the consecration of the Florentine cathedral by Eugenius IV – to Agnolo, who by that time was actually Manetti's brother-in-law.[52] Shortly after, in 1438, Agnolo appeared as an interlocutor in Manetti's *Consolatory Dialogue*, written after the death of one of Manetti's children.[53] Much later, in 1451, Manetti requested that Vespasiano da Bisticci recommend him to Agnolo.[54] Beyond his learned connections to Giannozzo Manetti, several other literary humanists acknowledged Agnolo's humanist learning. Francesco Barbaro, Francesco Filelfo, and Ambrogio Traversari wrote letters to Agnolo in humanist Latin.[55] Agnolo himself cited Matteo Palmieri's *On Civic Life* in a surviving letter.[56] In 1440, Leonardo Bruni dedicated his *Commentary on Xenophon's* Hellenica to Agnolo, his colleague on the Dieci di Balìa. Bruni's preface to the work suggests that the two had debated the wisdom of Bruni's caution in military affairs, a point of view that Bruni hoped Xenophon might defend.[57] Agnolo's sympathies with aggressive military policies coincided with his aggressive acquisition of books. In 1450, Francesco Filelfo wrote to Andrea Alamanni in Greek claiming that Agnolo had borrowed three books while Agnolo had been a diplomat in Milan. Rather than return them, Agnolo took them with him when he returned to Florence. Filelfo asked Alamanni to speak with Agnolo and procure their return.[58] Agnolo even took on the role of a teacher, instructing the learned brothers Donato and Piero Acciaiuoli in his house before sending them to other pedagogues.[59]

Matteo's three other classmates in Manetti's readings of Aristotle possessed weaker and fewer learned connections. One classmate, Antonio Barbadori, possessed a copy of Statius's book of Latin poems, the *Silvae*, in the mid-fifteenth century. The *Silvae* was one of numerous classical books rediscovered by Poggio Bracciolini beyond the Alps during the Council of Constance.[60] Throughout 1415, 1416, 1417, and the first part of 1418, Poggio, Bartolomeo da Montepulciano, and Cencio Rustici, all of whom had studied under Manuel Chrysoloras, as well as another Greek scholar, Sozomeno of Pistoia, braved bad roads, weather, and steep mountains to visit monasteries in search of manuscripts. The payoff was enormous. The learned friends found Quintilian's *Institutes of Oratory*, as well as works by Valerius Flaccus, Ammianus Marcellinus, and Lucretius; works by grammarians; commentaries; and others. In the fourth excursion from the council in search of books, Poggio discovered Statius's *Silvae*.[61] Poggio had the work copied and sent to Francesco Barbaro and Niccolò Niccoli in 1418.[62] His friend Bartolomeo da Montepulciano also took the book into Italy.[63] In Italy, Bartolomeo gave his copy of the book to Giovanni Barbadori, who in turn gave it to his son Antonio.[64] Antonio lent it to Carlo Marsuppini, before, finally, Francesco Filelfo inquired about the book in a letter to Antonio Barbadori in 1464.[65]

Also in attendance were Alessandro Arrighi, whose family would later be politically disgraced – though not exiled – after the return of the Medici in 1434, and another Strozzi kinsman, Marcello Strozzi. A Latin letter among Matteo's correspondence states that the sender, "Al. Arig." – clearly Alessandro Arrighi, was sending his copy of Aristotle's *Rhetoric*, translated by Filelfo, to Matteo, because the sender did not have time to read it.[66] Alessandro did find time to pass his humanist interests down to his son Simone, who copied an Italian version of Livy's fourth book between 1451 and 1452.[67] Finally, Marcello Strozzi, whom Vespasiano da Bisticci described as "learned," possessing a "good knowledge of Latin letters," and a "most religious man," was a classmate of Matteo.[68] Marcello may also have formed a learned connection with Leonardo Bruni, as both men were present in the papal curia in 1408. In fact, according to Bruni, only the departure of Pope Gregory XII's cardinals en masse in that year prevented the pope from sending the two men as diplomats together to Florence on a minor mission.[69] Marcello also received Latin letters from Ambrogio Traversari and associated with the humanist Leonardo di Piero Dati in Rome.[70] Leonardo di Piero Dati, not to be confused with Leonardo di Stagio Dati – the brother of the famous diarist Gregorio Dati – also wrote numerous letters to Matteo Strozzi from Rome during the 1430s, a highly volatile time in the Eternal City.[71]

A final handful of other patricians also formed learned connections with Matteo Strozzi. Matteo's relative Raimondo Mannelli asked Matteo repeatedly to recommend him to Leonardo Bruni. Mannelli had been a sea captain in the naval battle of Rapallo and wanted to ensure that Bruni had a detailed and eyewitness account of it for Bruni's *History of the Florentine People*. Therefore, Mannelli sent his own vernacular account of the battle to Matteo Strozzi for polishing before, he hoped, it would be forwarded to Bruni.[72] Last, Matteo shared a learned connection with Niccolò della Luna, who, in one letter, requested that Matteo use Luigi Guicciardini as an intermediary in a book exchange.[73] Niccolò della Luna has himself left significant evidence to reconstruct part of his learned connections, to which this chapter now turns.

Like his cousin Matteo, the social humanist Niccolò della Luna enjoyed a strong position in the humanist movement, but one less pronounced than that of the literary humanists.[74] Niccolò was born around 1410 into a wealthy mercantile family that reached its political height with the election of Francesco, Niccolò's father, to be Standard Bearer of Justice.[75] Francesco himself was not without cultural interests, as he worked with no less than Filippo Brunelleschi on the construction of the Ospedale degli Innocenti, Brunelleschi's first public building and one of his most famous.[76] In fact, the evidence suggests that Francesco della Luna fancied himself a bit of an architect. On at least two occasions during the building's construction he seems to have altered the designs to fit his own ideas, much to the chagrin of Brunelleschi, the architect's fifteenth-century biographer, and later historians.[77] Francesco's contemporaries were kinder in their appraisals and he received a lifetime appointment as an Overseer of the Ospedale – a body charged with overseeing the construction of the building – in 1433, the year of the Medici exile from Florence.[78] Both Francesco della Luna and the humanist Filippo di Ugolino Pieruzzi were stripped of their respective appointments in 1444.[79]

Although the Balìa – a political body used by the Medici to influence governmental decisions – contended that the removal of Francesco and Filippo from office was due to a general objection to lifetime appointments, the actual motivation was political. Other men served lifetime appointments after 1444 as Overseers of the Ospedale.[80] In addition, Vespasiano da Bisticci provides evidence for the political problems faced by Filippo di Ugolino in the 1430s: Around 1433, Filippo hid from political prosecution in the house of Gregorio Dati, who was his colleague on the Overseers.[81] The return of the Medici gave ephemeral hope to Filippo's position and, in 1438, he received his lifetime appointment to the Overseers of the Ospedale. Just six years later, in 1444, his lifetime appointment was revoked and he was sent into exile.[82] Likewise, Francesco della Luna was exiled from Florence in 1444, the same year his position as Overseer was revoked.[83] Unfortunately, Francesco's political hardship was passed down to his son, Niccolò, who also inherited his father's cultural interests.

Francesco's son Niccolò was a much stronger social humanist than his father. Although Niccolò did not attend Manetti's lectures on Aristotle, he did write to his cousin Matteo Strozzi in August 1430 to express envy over Matteo's attendance at the lectures.[84] By the following year, Niccolò had established a relationship with Francesco Filelfo, who dedicated a poem to Niccolò on October 7, 1431, and who, along with Carlo Marsuppini, was one of Niccolò's teachers.[85] A decade later, Niccolò participated in the vernacular poetry competition on the topic of friendship in 1441, an event organized by Leon Battista Alberti and paid for by Piero di Cosimo de' Medici.[86] By that point, the dominance of the Medici family had caused the political foundations of the della Luna family to crumble. In 1444, Niccolò complained to his learned friend Andrea Alamanni about his absence from political offices.[87] Niccolò, oppressed by taxes, his friends, his exile, and his father and brother having recently died, retired to a monastery in 1449. He died roughly a year later.[88]

In the decades prior to his death, Niccolò established learned connections to literary and social humanists alike. He shared many of the same friends as his first cousin and correspondent Matteo Strozzi. Like Matteo, Niccolò corresponded with Leonardo di Piero Dati, leaving extant letters from both sides of the correspondence, some of which have been published.[89] Matteo was a frequent correspondent with Piero Guicciardini, whereas Niccolò wrote letters to Piero's son Luigi.[90] In a letter to Lorenzo di Palla Strozzi, Niccolò referred to a Benedetto, a man who had apparently fallen off the wagon of virtue and letters and back into other pursuits, prompting Niccolò to quote Juvenal's second satire, "O nobles! Is it a censor or a soothsayer that we need?"[91] The identity of this Benedetto could very well have been the same Benedetto Strozzi who corresponded with Matteo Strozzi around the same time and with whom Matteo listened to Giannozzo Manetti speak on Aristotle.[92] Niccolò also shared learned connections with Nicola de' Medici, who was the son of a Strozzi matron.[93] Niccolò della Luna, in fact, dedicated two works to Nicola: his *Handbook of Golden Sayings and the Moral Life* and his *Song in Praise of that Most Eminent Light of the Church Jerome.*[94]

Niccolò della Luna's learned connections stretched deeper into the Strozzi family, especially to the children of Palla di Nofri Strozzi. Niccolò established learned connections with at least three of Palla's sons. Niccolò considered Bartolomeo di Palla Strozzi a learned friend. Although Bartolomeo received a humanist education and was the favorite son of his father, he died at a young age in 1426.[95] Lorenzo di Palla Strozzi, whose likeness can still be approximated from Gentile da Fabriano's *Three Magi*, received Latin letters from Niccolò.[96] In 1427, Leonardo Bruni had 1,000 florins in Lorenzo's bank.[97] Like his father, Palla, Lorenzo was "*litteratissimo,*" but also like his father, Lorenzo was exiled from Florence by the Medici.[98] Archival evidence suggests that Lorenzo was exiled from Florence in 1434, but Vespasiano da Bisticci claimed the sentence did not fall until 1438 and described the four years Lorenzo endured in Florence after the return of the Medici as similar to an "excommunicate."[99] Also according to Vespasiano, Lorenzo's wife, Alessandra Strozzi (Bardi), described Lorenzo's sentence of exile as "the worst evil I could have foreseen."[100] Lorenzo left Florence for Gubbio, where he took a position as guardian of a Florentine youth. Vespasiano claimed that this youth resented Lorenzo's attempts to curb his "evil ways" and consequently killed him in the streets.[101]

Niccolò wrote Latin letters to a third son of Palla, Nofri di Palla Strozzi.[102] Another Strozzi relative with potential connections with Bruni, Nofri wrote to Matteo Strozzi and mentioned one of Bruni's dialogues.[103] Like his father, Nofri was exiled from Florence by the Medici.[104] While in exile, he and another brother, Giovanfrancesco, received a consolatory letter from Francesco Filelfo after the death of their father.[105] In the 1450s, Nofri, then in Padua, prepared a map of the world and an illuminated copy of Ptolemy for René of Anjou. In addition, Nofri served as representative of Donatello while the artist dealt with Gattamelata's heirs and constructed the famous equestrian statue of that condottiere.[106]

Niccolò della Luna's presence in Filelfo's *Florentine Commentaries on Exile* reinforces the evidence for learned connections among Niccolò and several social and literary humanists. Niccolò's appearance in the dialogues is not surprising given his friendship with Francesco Filelfo and his political problems under the Medici in Florence.[107] In addition to Niccolò's connections to Palla di Nofri Strozzi and his son Nofri, Niccolò wrote a Latin letter to another discussant in this dialogue, Giannozzo Manetti. In the letter, Niccolò referred to another discussant, Leonardo Bruni, in familiar terms.[108] In a further letter, Niccolò wrote to Manetti to praise Manetti's funeral oration for Bruni.[109] Beyond their shared opposition to the Medici, no connection is known among Niccolò della Luna, Rinaldo degli Albizzi, and Ridolfo Peruzzi, other interlocutors in Filelfo's book. Both Albizzi and Peruzzi were powerful oligarchs and social humanists whose learned connections are discussed elsewhere in this study.[110] Similarly, as pointed out by Arthur Field, Poggio Bracciolini appeared in Filelfo's dialogue as a "buffoon" and has not been traced otherwise to Niccolò.[111] Regardless, readers of Filelfo's treatise could imagine these men getting together to discuss exile, and thus the interlocutors establish a probable learned connection to Niccolò. The diametrically opposed politics of some of the purported participants simply mirrored similar humanist discussions in Florence itself.

Finally, Niccolò maintained learned ties to at least one member of the Fortini, a family that was, like the della Luna, punished by the Medici in 1444. Ser Benedetto Fortini was the successor of Coluccio Salutati in the Florentine chancery. Benedetto died in 1406 and his passing was marked by a lavish state funeral.[112] Niccolò della Luna did not write to this man, but rather to a different, younger Benedetto Fortini, who was born in 1410.[113] This Benedetto was the son of Paolo Fortini, a man best known today as the oligarchic candidate whom Leonardo Bruni defeated to become chancellor of Florence in 1427.[114] Paolo's death in 1433 prevented any repercussions for his political allegiances in 1434, but Paolo's son Benedetto – Niccolò's learned friend – had no such luck and was exiled in 1444.[115]

Not all of Niccolò's learned connections were so politically problematic. After all, Niccolò shared learned interests with Luigi Guicciardini, whose family was among the chief supporters of the Medici family. Niccolò exchanged letters with another Medici ally, the young Alamanno

Rinuccini, whose political fallout with Lorenzo de' Medici happened years after Niccolò's death.[116] Additionally, Niccolò della Luna can be linked to three Medicians from modest familial backgrounds: Andrea Quaratesi, Matteo Palmieri, and Tommaso di Lorenzo Ceffi. Little is known about Andrea Quaratesi beyond that he studied under Filelfo, received a letter from Niccolò della Luna, and owned a copy of Vergil's *Ecologues* from his days as a schoolboy.[117] Niccolò's letter twice refers to a "*frater Giuliano,*" presumably Andrea's brother, who may have owned a book on John the Baptist and a vernacular translation of Aristotle.[118] Later members of the Quaratesi family are more familiar to scholars because Andrea's sixteenth-century namesake had his portrait drawn by none other than Michelangelo Buonarroti.[119] An even later member of the Quaratesi family bought the fifteenth-century Palazzo Pazzi and moved the family from their former stronghold in the *oltrarno*.[120] Another Medici ally and learned friend of Niccolò della Luna was the literary humanist Matteo Palmieri, who applied his humanist interests in Latin and vernacular writings.[121]

Finally, Niccolò della Luna received works from the Medici ally Tommaso di Lorenzo Ceffi, although these works may not survive for perusal by modern scholars.[122] Ceffi himself had the respect of other humanists such as the poet Cristoforo Landino and Leon Battista Alberti. Landino, a man most famous for his commentary and lectures on Dante, dedicated a poem to Ceffi in which he responded to poetic comments made by Ceffi about Landino's love interest, Xandra. In this raunchy poem, Landino claimed that Ceffi was mistaken in his accusations that Landino sought Xandra out of lust. He warned Ceffi to retract his critiques or he would tell the unpleasant truth about Ceffi's own love interest.[123] Ceffi's reputation as an overly harsh critic extended into the literary realm. In 1443, Leon Battista Alberti sent a copy of his treatise *On the Family* to Leonardo di Piero Dati and Ceffi for comments before the work's publication. The two men urged Alberti to amend the text, critiquing Alberti's style and frequency of quotation, particularly quotes from undisclosed authors.[124]

Later in the century, surviving Latin letters from the Florentine patrician Giovanbattista – also known as Giovanni or Giambattista – Ridolfi reveal many of his learned connections. These connections were fewer and less pronounced than those of Matteo Strozzi or Niccolò della Luna and thus Giovanbattista was further from the center of the humanist movement. Born in 1448, Giovanbattista became a powerful Florentine patrician in the latter fifteenth and early sixteenth centuries. He was a highly visible follower of Savonarola but managed to escape the friar's fall from power with minimal damage to his own political career. Ridolfi continued to influence Florentine politics under Piero Soderini, the Florentines' ephemeral experiment with a lifetime ruler. Giovanbattista was elected in Soderini's place, but he too was pushed out of the position by the Medici. Even under these new masters Ridolfi maintained his political prominence. Most notably, in 1513 he was sent as Florentine ambassador to the new pope, Leo X. Ridolfi, who died not long after in 1514.[125] Years before his death, before he followed Soderini as Standard Bearer, even before he became a follower of Savonarola, Giovanbattista was a patron of humanist studies. Most notably, in 1476, he, along with Girolamo Strozzi and Nicholas Jenson, was involved with the printing of 1,025 copies of Cristoforo Landino's Italian translation of Pliny's *Natural History* in Venice.[126]

In addition, letters in humanist Latin survive from Giovanbattista to Lorenzo the Magnificent, Jacopo Salviati, Alamanno Salviati, Bernardo Nerli, Bernardo Adimari, Giovan Vittorio Soderini, Francesco Diaccetto, Guglielmo Capponi, and Niccolò del Benino throughout the 1470s.[127] Most of these men maintained connections to the humanist movement beyond their Latin correspondence with Ridolfi. Lorenzo the Magnificent's critical role in the humanist movement needs no further elaboration here, but the learned interests of several of these other figures are less well known. The connections between the cousins Alamanno and Jacopo Salviati and Giovanbattista Ridolfi went beyond shared learned interests: Giovanbattista's bride, Cornelia, was Alamanno Salviati's sister.[128] Alamanno and Jacopo both enjoyed connections to Niccolò Machiavelli.[129] In particular, Jacopo Salviati assisted Machiavelli with tax problems in 1502 and Machiavelli dedicated his *First Decennale* to Alamanno Salviati in 1504. The men had a falling out and Machiavelli attempted to rupture the learned bond between him and Alamanno by removing the dedication from the 1506 edition of the work.[130]

Giovanbattista's other correspondents also possessed additional links to the humanist movement. Bernardo Nerli and his brother Neri paid for the first Greek edition of Homer to appear in Florence in the late 1480s. The edition even contained a letter in Latin from Bernardo to Piero de' Medici, son of Lorenzo the Magnificent.[131] Bernardo Adimari, a distant relative of a Buonaccorso Adimari who copied books by Bruni, received a Latin epigram from the poet Ugolino Verino.[132] Similarly, the lawyer Giovan Vittorio Soderini received a Latin poem from Naldo Naldi, as well as a letter from Marsilio Ficino.[133] Francesco Diaccetto was a pupil of Marsilio Ficino and was mentioned as a potential model for style in Baldassare Castiglione's *The Courtier*.[134] Guglielmo Capponi sought to learn Greek and was a correspondent of Alamanno Rinuccini.[135] Alamanno Donati dedicated a treatise to Guglielmo in which Guglielmo appeared as an interlocutor.[136] Finally, Niccolò del Benino received two letters from Marsilio Ficino.[137] All of these men in this chapter suggest a humanist movement open to a range of interests and abilities, rather than a small group of Latin writers. The ranks of the social humanists were vast, filled by individuals with deep humanist interests as well as dilettantes with other primary concerns.

Other social humanists have left less evidence of their learned connections, but nonetheless seem to have been actively engaged in the humanist movement. They may have been stronger humanists than Matteo Strozzi, Niccolò della Luna, and Giovanbattista Ridolfi, even if the evidence for their learning is scarcer. Roberto Rossi is a quintessential example of an individual who participated in the humanist movement in the fluid area where the categories of social and literary humanists overlap. In the late fourteenth century Rossi attended the discussions led by Luigi Marsili at Santo Spirito and then became one of Manuel Chrysoloras's first students of Greek.[138] Rossi put his training to use in original translations, learned discussions, and the classroom. Rossi's translation of Aristotle's *Posterior Analytics* survives, and it is likely that he translated other works, although it is far from certain how many or of what quality.[139] As noted in the last chapter, Rossi was prominent enough among humanists in early fifteenth-century Florence that Leonardo Bruni chose Rossi's home as the setting for the second day of his *Dialogues*, which established learned connections among Rossi, Bruni, Niccoli, Salutati, and Piero Sermini.[140] Another literary humanist, Guarino Veronese, dedicated his translation of Plutarch's *Life of Flaminius* to Rossi in 1411. In this case, Guarino may have sought to flatter Rossi by associating an ancient philhellene with a modern one.[141]

Even the meager amount of surviving evidence to link individuals to Rossi's classrooms suggests that he taught students with a diverse range of interests and ability in humanism. The literary humanist Cosimo de' Medici and the social humanists Luca degli Albizzi and Domenico Buoninsegni – a man discussed in the next chapter – attended class under Roberto Rossi.[142] Far fewer and weaker were the learned connections of another student, Bartolo Tedaldi.[143] Jonathan Davies has argued that the individuals who held the position of university official in Florence usually possessed humanist interests, and he cites the examples of Niccolò Niccoli,

Giannozzo Manetti, and others to prove this point. Bartolo Tedaldi was a university official from 1446 to 1447 and a student of Rossi's but has left no other evidence for his involvement in the humanist movement.[144] Alessandro Alessandri also attended Rossi's classroom.[145] Scholars still have a good idea of the likeness of Alessandro Alessandri and two of his sons because, sometime after 1450, Alessandro commissioned an altarpiece to St. Lawrence that contains portraits of Alessandro himself and his off-spring.[146] Alessandro's known learned connections are few, but Matteo Palmieri dedicated his *On Civic Life* to him. In fact, *On Civic Life* was a dialogue in which the interlocutors and dedication were undoubtedly shaped by neighborhoods: Palmieri, Alessandro, and the primary interlocutor in the treatise, Agnolo Pandolfini, all lived quite close to one another.[147]

Nicola de' Medici was another extremely prominent social humanist like Roberto Rossi, but one who has left even less documentation to explain his reputation among his contemporaries. Both Bruni and Poggio wrote letters to Nicola and his name appears several times in Poggio's correspondence to others.[148] In addition to writing to Nicola, Bruni dedicated his translation of Demosthenes' orations to him, and both Niccolò della Luna and Leonardo Dati also dedicated works to him.[149] Nicola's probable influence in securing Bruni's election as diplomat to Martin V in 1426, discussed in the last chapter, further connected Nicola to Bruni. In fact, Biondo Flavio contended that Bruni was actually Nicola's teacher.[150] Nicola's son, Carlo, seems to have continued to cultivate the learned connection established between his father and Leonardo Bruni. Whether he acquired his copy of Bruni's *On the First Punic War* from Bruni himself or not, Carlo may have translated the work from Latin into Italian.[151] A handful of surviving letters and references, a couple of dedications, a friendship with Leonardo Bruni, and a possible vernacular translation by his son hardly seem enough evidence to place Nicola de' Medici among or near the most active and influential participants in the humanist movement. Yet, Leon Battista Alberti claimed that Nicola was one of the most learned men in Tuscany.[152] Biondo Flavio grouped Nicola together with Leonardo Bruni, Roberto Rossi, Jacopo da Scarperia, and Poggio Bracciolini as "the most notable figures now winning themselves a reputation [in humanist studies]."[153] In this case, the strength of Nicola's reputation among his contemporaries suggests that his involvement in the humanist movement was far more extensive than the dearth of surviving evidence suggests.

The placement of other individuals firmly among the social humanists is much more clear-cut. These men were far from the center of the humanist movement dominated by men like Bruni and Manetti – examples of obvious literary humanists. The examples to follow were also further from the center than men like Roberto Rossi, Nicola de' Medici, Matteo Strozzi, and Niccolò della Luna, all of whom help demonstrate the fluid boundaries between literary and social humanists. By contrast, Palla di Palla Strozzi, also known as Palla Novello, was clearly a social humanist. He had the unfortunate fate of sharing his name with his more famous cousin, Palla di Nofri. Consequently, the two men are often confused in the historiography and primary sources addressed to "Palla Strozzi" occasionally are unclear as to which man they meant. Unlike his more famous cousin, Palla Novello was not exiled by the Medici in 1434, despite his political prominence. Palla Novello has left an enormous amount of fodder for historical studies, most of which relates to his career as a diplomat.[154] Palla housed the artist Gentile da Fabriano between 1420 and 1422 and lived across the piazza from the later site of the Palazzo Strozzi.[155] In addition to serving as landlord to a talented artist, Palla has left tantalizing glimpses into his humanist interests. In 1413, an unidentified "Marco of Pistoia" in Pisa wrote to Palla and referred to a transcription of the letters of Cicero.[156] From Palla's own hand, he has left an assortment of vernacular and Latin letters to various unidentified people and notable princes, as well as orations for various political occasions in and outside Florence.[157] Palla's only published letter is a Latin epistle to Leonardo Bruni dated 1410.[158]

Dietisalvi Neroni was another prominent Florentine patrician with well-developed humanist interests. As with other social humanists, historians can still glimpse Dietisalvi's face in fifteenth-century art, particularly in a surviving bust of him in which he wears classical garb.[159] Dietisalvi not only sought to project an artistic image of himself as a Roman patrician, he also collected an extensive library full of classical works, especially rhetorical handbooks and speeches by that most renowned Roman orator Cicero.[160] Perhaps Dietisalvi emulated or cited one or many of these works in his "*longa et optima*" oration in a *pratica* in June 1451, a speech that contrasted with Banco Bencivenni's "*brevibus verbis*" on the same day.[161] Perhaps it was similar in style to the "*longum sermonem*" in April by Girolamo Machiavelli, a man who was famously exiled after an attempted revolt against the Medici in 1458.[162] Whether or not Dietisalvi dipped into the texts in his library for his *pratica* oration, friends in Florence knew about his books. Maybe Franco Sacchetti desired Dietisalvi's copy of Plautus to prepare for the biannual meeting of learned men at his house. Perhaps Piero de' Medici wanted the same book because he had heard of the quality and humor of Plautus's plays. Regardless of their reasons, both men borrowed Dietisalvi's copy of the Roman playwright's work. Additionally, Dietisalvi assisted in the construction of Niccolò Niccoli's library at San Marco. He wrote a Latin letter to the learned lawyer Zenobi Guasconi, who performed a series of lectures on the *Decretals* at the University of Florence in 1431.[163] In another case of learned connections transcending political factions, Zenobi was a member of the Balìa that recalled Cosimo de' Medici in 1434. For his efforts, he was banned from political office for twenty years, although he continued to teach law at the Florentine Studio.[164] Dietisalvi, meanwhile, rose to prominence in Cosimo's Florence.

Dietisalvi's learned and other social connections extended into the neighborhood around Vespasiano's bookshop. In 1450, Giannozzo Manetti wrote to Vespasiano da Bisticci that he planned to meet with Dietisalvi. He asked Vespasiano to greet Dietisalvi on his behalf.[165] A year later, Manetti asked Vespasiano again to recommend him to Dietisalvi and this time added requests for a good word to Agnolo Acciaiuoli and greetings to Piero and Donato Acciaiuoli.[166] Other known social connections between Dietisalvi and members of this neighborhood might have also carried a learned connotation. The learned social humanist Pierfilippo Pandolfini worked at the bank of Dietisalvi's brother, Francesco Neroni, and eventually married Francesco's daughter.[167] Pandolfo, Pierfilippo's learned brother, sought to exploit this connection and asked Pierfilippo to speak well of him to Dietisalvi and Otto Niccolini.[168] Maybe Dietisalvi befriended Agnolo Acciaiuoli's son, Jacopo, in these circles. In 1470, four years after both Dietisalvi and Jacopo had been exiled from Florence, Jacopo wrote to Dietisalvi in Naples and asked him to greet the Neapolitan literary humanist Giovanni Pontano, members of the Neapolitan chancery, and "all our other most dear friends" in Naples.[169]

Piero de' Pazzi is a final example of a social humanist with about the same amount of involvement in the humanist movement as Palla Novello Strozzi or probably a little less than Dietisalvi Neroni. Piero seems to have enjoyed his youth until a fateful encounter with Niccolò Niccoli pushed him to more serious, learned pursuits. In particular, after a verbal scolding from Niccoli blasting his irresponsible youthful dalliances, Piero became renowned for his memorization of the *Aeneid* and various orations by Livy.[170] The anecdote of Niccoli's disgust at a man of Piero's station frittering away his time is well known, but what has previously gone unnoticed is the geographical context of the exchange. Niccoli attended learned discussions beside the modern Bargello; that undoubtedly means that these discussions occurred outside the area that became Vespasiano's bookstore.[171] It was presumably on a trip to one of these discussions or to Vespasiano's shop itself that the famous exchange took place. After all, Piero lived about a block north of the bookshop along the Via del Proconsolo.[172] Piero must have desired that his children not waste their youths on frivolities as he had so he hired Marsilio Ficino as a tutor for them.[173] Ficino, in turn, wrote to Piero in Latin.[174] A Latin translation of Lucian was even dedicated to Piero de' Pazzi.[175]

Piero shared learned connections with many of the students of Giovanni Argyropoulos, leading to some speculation that Piero himself studied under this Greek master.[176] The evidence for this point is inconclusive, but the correspondence of Donato Acciaiuoli, one of Argyropoulos's best students, links Piero de' Pazzi to Vespasiano da Bisticci, Carlo d' Antonio di Silvestro, Marco Parenti, Alamanno Rinuccini, and Banco Casavecchia.[177] It is not surprising that Piero established a learned connection with Vespasiano da Bisticci, given the proximity of their homes, or with the literary humanist Alamanno Rinuccini, who was extremely active in similar circles in the 1450s. The family name of Carlo d' Antonio di Silvestro has not been previously identified, but Carlo d' Antonio Serristori was the only active Florentine officeholder with the name "Carlo d' Antonio di Silvestro" during the 1440s, 1450s, and 1460s. Carlo d' Antonio di Silvestro Serristori was born in 1425 and in 1439 was first drawn for political office, a position that, obviously, his young age of fourteen prevented him from fulfilling. His extensive officeholding career began later in 1454.[178] Additionally, three wills survive from the man, two from 1485 and one from 1493.[179] Despite this probable identification, no additional information has been located in Carlo Serristori's wills or any other source to document his humanist interests.

Marco Parenti and Banco Casavecchia were also linked to Donato Acciaiuoli, Giovanni Argyropoulos, and Piero de' Pazzi. Marco Parenti has not traditionally been considered among the ranks of Florentine humanists, a conclusion based primarily on the absence of humanist forms and content in Marco's surviving vernacular letters and chronicle.[180] Yet, vernacular chronicles and letters often lacked overt humanist influences. As demonstrated later, Marco's son Piero was a translator of humanist works into the vernacular, but he also wrote a vernacular chronicle with only the most dubious influences from humanism. Palla di Nofri Strozzi has left countless written letters from his political career that lack humanist resonances. The evidence for Pandolfo

Pandolfini's position in the humanist movement is stronger than the case for Marco Parenti, but all of Pandolfo's surviving letters lack ostensible humanist influences. Pandolfo's letters, Leonardo Bruni's vernacular letter to Luca degli Albizzi, Marco Parenti's letters, Marco's chronicle, as well as that of his son were all examples of the written word that conformed to the generic rules of the fifteenth century. Sometimes humanism infiltrated these genres and sometimes it did not, but the presence or absence of humanism in such documents should not be taken as conclusive evidence for a person's exclusion from the humanist movement, particularly when contrary, compelling evidence exists. Such is the case of Marco Parenti. Francesco Filelfo, Donato Acciaiuoli, Alamanno Rinuccini, Cristoforo Landino, Vespasiano da Bisticci, and others complimented Marco's learning.[181] He was a guest for the learned discussions held at Franco Sacchetti's villa, discussed in the last chapter.[182] Marco's mother-in-law, the astute Alessandra Strozzi (Macinghi), described him as "studious."[183] If the definition of a humanist based on learned connections and the opinions of Marco's contemporaries – rather than original production in Latin – is adopted in this case, Marco Parenti seems quite similar to other social humanists discussed in this book.

Banco Casavecchia rounded out the students of Giovanni Argyropoulos linked to Piero de' Pazzi. In addition to his attendance at Argyropoulos's discussions, Banco corresponded with Donato Acciaiuoli and was praised for his learning by Francesco Filelfo and Vespasiano.[184] Filelfo, in fact, wrote a letter to Alamanno Rinuccini in which he requested that Alamanno send his greetings to Banco and Marco Parenti.[185] Banco Casavecchia's residence on the south side of the Arno enabled his descendants to cultivate ties with a later resident of the *oltrarno*, Niccolò Machiavelli.[186] In his will from November 1511, Machiavelli stipulated provisions for the distribution of his goods to his heirs in the event that he died before they turned eighteen years of age. Machiavelli declared that his widow, Marietta, should oversee his estate until his heirs came of age and that she should be in charge of appointing a guardian for the estate in the event of her own death. If she died without appointing somebody, then Francesco del Nero should take on the task. In the event that Francesco was dead, then Filippo Casavecchia, son of Banco, was to appoint a guardian for the estate.[187] Filippo, in fact, wrote to Machiavelli to discuss the topic of friendship, cited discourses on friendship, and referred to Roman history as evidence.[188]

Other Florentine patricians with humanist interests pursued their studies even less than Banco Casavecchia. These men were still social humanists, but the evidence for their humanist interests is weaker. Thus, they were located at increasing distance from the center of the humanist movement. Rinaldo degli Albizzi hired the learned Tommaso Parentucelli, later Pope Nicholas V, to tutor his children.[189] In a letter that contradicts or perhaps predates political factions, Leonardo Bruni wrote to Lorenzo de' Medici – Cosimo de' Medici's brother – stating that neither Lorenzo nor Rinaldo degli Albizzi should worry about his safety because the place where Bruni was staying was not dangerous.[190] Several manuscript witnesses also include that Bruni asked Lorenzo to send his greetings to Rinaldo.[191] In this example, Lorenzo and Bruni's shared learned connection, established through the Latin letter, as well as additional evidence for Lorenzo's humanist interests – such as the humanist letters sent to him by Francesco Barbaro – suggest that each of these men shared his humanist interests with Rinaldo degli Albizzi, and, consequently, Rinaldo himself should be included among the participants in the humanist movement.[192] Other evidence supports this argument. Bruni dedicated his treatise *On Knighthood* to Rinaldo.[193] A surviving letter in Latin exists from Rinaldo's pen, as does a copy of part of Francesco Filelfo's *Florentine Commentaries on Exile*.[194] Both Filelfo and Roberto Rossi wrote to Rinaldo in humanist Latin.[195] Yet, Rinaldo's humanist interests should not be overstated. Certainly, Rinaldo's remarkably extensive diplomatic career spanning the first third of the Quattrocento suggests knowledge of humanist rhetoric and oratorical skill. However, the enormous amount of documentation left by Rinaldo related to this diplomatic career has few overt traces of humanism.

Other men participated in the humanist movement even less. Countless letters survive to and from the immensely wealthy merchant Filippo di Matteo Strozzi, few of which contain direct evidence of Filippo's potential interests in humanism.[196] Nevertheless, like Rinaldo degli Albizzi, Filippo formed learned connections that suggest some involvement with humanism. Several learned men corresponded with him, albeit in Italian and without cultural allusions. The extensive correspondence of Marco Parenti to Filippo Strozzi is well known to scholars.[197] Donato Acciaiuoli wrote to Filippo while Donato was a diplomat in Rome in 1477.[198] Jacopo d' Agnolo Acciaiuoli wrote several letters to Filippo in the 1460s, 1470s, and again in the 1480s.[199] Alamanno Rinuccini wrote a vernacular letter to Filippo Strozzi on January 30, 1485.[200] The literary humanist Bernardo Rucellai corresponded with Filippo.[201] Additionally, Giannozzo Manetti associated with Filippo in Naples in the late 1450s, although no correspondence survives between the two men.[202] According to Filippo's son Lorenzo, the businesslike letters of his father hid the fact that Filippo was a "friend of learned men."[203]

Filippo's literary and artistic commissions further tied him to the humanist movement. In the early 1470s, Filippo sought out a copy of Bruni's *On the First Punic War* and a history of the world in the vernacular by Justin. In 1472 he acquired a copy of Biondo Flavio's highly influential *Italy Illustrated*, Matteo Palmieri's *On Civic Life*, and Petrarch's *The Triumphs*. In 1476, Filippo received his copy of the first Italian printed edition of Pliny's *Natural History*, an edition that he helped finance. In the same year, he bought a manuscript copy of Jacopo Bracciolini's Italian translation of Poggio's *History of the Florentine People* and helped finance the first printed Italian translation of the same work as well as Donato Acciaiuoli's Italian translation of Bruni's *History of the Florentine People*. Additionally in 1476 Filippo acquired numerous religious texts, a copy of the *Aeneid*, and Boccaccio's *The Crow*. Two years later he paid ten florins for two copies of Jacopo Bracciolini's *Commentary on the Triumph of Fame*, one of which Filippo hired a miniaturist to illuminate.[204] In 1484 Filippo sought a copy of Bartolomeo Scala's oration before Innocent VIII.[205] Like many educated fathers, Filippo sought to pass down humanism to his children and bought several classical books for his sons.[206] Additionally, he proclaimed his classical tastes – or at least his preference to appear to have classical tastes – through the style and content of his chapel in Santa Maria Novella: Each bright frescoed wall is packed with classical figures and allusions.[207] Filippo's artistic and literary commissions combine with his extensive connections with learned men to place him in the humanist movement. Nevertheless, Filippo's small number of learned references in his surviving correspondence and the lack of praise for his learning by his contemporaries suggest that he was far less interested in humanism than many of his peers.

Other examples of weak learned connections by Florentine patricians abound. Niccolò da Uzzano may have had a bust of himself carved in a classical style, possibly by Donatello himself.[208] He was one of the patricians in charge of overseeing the decoration of the doors of the Florentine Baptistery, and in this role he probably worked with Leonardo Bruni.[209] Pierfrancesco de' Medici, who may have provided a political alternative to the rule of his cousins over Florence, hired a young Bartolomeo Scala and requested books from Rome while Scala lived in his house.[210] Guglielmo Tanagli was a friend of Niccolò Niccoli and had a good humanist hand.[211] He collated an early fifteenth-century manuscript of Quintilian and cited Sallust in a *pratica* in 1458.[212] Otto Niccolini was a prominent diplomat and key member of the Medici inner ruling circle in the 1450s and 1460s.[213] He also participated in at least one learned discussion with Cosimo de' Medici and Giovanni Argyropoulos, in addition to receiving a Latin letter from Bartolomeo Scala as well as establishing learned connections with the literary humanists Benedetto Accolti and Marsilio Ficino.[214] Nevertheless, Niccolini left a will that listed his books, all of which pertained to the study of law, none of which pertained to the *studia humanitatis*.[215] Buonaccorso Pitti the elder served as an intermediary in a book exchange between Coluccio Salutati and the French court.[216] Pitti counted Roberto Rossi among his friends and Salutati called him "my brother."[217] Nevertheless, Pitti's well-known diary contains no traces of humanist interests. Finally, Bartolomeo di Niccolò Taldo Valori referred to ancient Rome in an otherwise plainly styled vernacular speech.[218] All of these people were Florentine patricians who participated in the humanist movement even as their primary interests clearly lay elsewhere. They were weaker social humanists and occupied a position distant from the center of the humanist movement. They formed learned connections, but on a much smaller scale than the literary humanists or the more prominent social humanists.

Social humanists varied in the strength of their humanist interests; they also varied in their social and political prominence. As the next chapter argues, humanists were from all corners of the Florentine patriciate and beyond, descending even onto the middle rungs of the Florentine social ladder. Humanists were often key political players – like most of the examples cited in this chapter – but they could also be men far removed from social and political prominence in the city. Whatever their background, few social humanists wrote original literary treatises and only some of them could speak or even read Latin. Nevertheless, they have left evidence of their interests in humanism through learned connections. The following chapter argues that the humanist movement and the learned connections that constituted it extended as far into the Florentine masses as the surviving historical documentation allows for inquiry.

3

The Social Origins of the Florentine Humanists

In the heart of Florence near Orsanmichele – the granary turned church adorned with classicized sculptures of the patron saints of the Florentine guilds – Niccolò Cieco and Michele del Giogante delighted onlookers with classically inspired performances in the Piazza di San Martino.[1] The two men lived together from 1435 and late in the same year collaborated on a memory treatise based on precepts outlined in Cicero's *On Oratory*, Quintilian's *Institutes of Oratory*, and Pseudo-Cicero's *Rhetoric to Herennius*.[2] Niccolò and Michele used these teachings to deliver public songs and performances portraying biblical stories, contemporary events, and the classical past.[3] Meanwhile, Sandro Lotteringhi, whose family maintained a low status in the Florentine patriciate and whose kinsman Lotteringo possessed about fifteen hundred florins in 1480, copied classical texts with Michele and Giovanni Matteo di Meglio.[4] In another text, Sandro commented on the types of temperance that Plato found pleasing, used secular political content from Valerius Maximus, copied excerpts from Brunetto Latini and Giovanni Villani, transcribed prayers and names of saints, and drew pictures of Greek crosses.[5]

Niccolò, Michele, and Sandro were but three examples of men with documentable connections to the humanist movement from the middling ranks of Florentine society. These individuals originated outside the meta-phorical halls of social and political power in Florence, yet, they revealed exactly the same kinds of intellectual interests as more influential literary and social humanists. They were often men of modest wealth: They were not individuals from the bottom rungs of the economic ladder of Florence – the learned pursuits of such people have been lost – but they were also not among the top taxpayers of the city. Most, though not all, of the men discussed in this chapter were lesser members of patriciate families, but humanists were also found among families from outside the enormous Florentine patrician group, the ranks of which included about a third of Florence's population.[6] The examples from the last chapter combined with this one again suggest that most humanists focused their studies on reading rather than writing. Moreover, the learned interests of the less socially, politically, and economically prominent social humanists are suggestive of the mass appeal of humanism. This chapter argues that the humanist movement was far more popular and open than has previously been appreciated by scholars; in fact, its very success hinged on its accessibility to a wide range of people.

Learned connections between texts and individuals suggest that Florentine humanists had an astonishing range of political, economic, and social backgrounds. At the most basic level, texts leave a record of the ideas and interests of their authors. Hence, an author who wrote in humanist Latin has obviously left strong firsthand evidence of his or her involvement in humanism. Yet, the authors of many vernacular works also betrayed their involvement through the content and style of their writings. For example, literary humanists penned works in the vernacular, such as Matteo Palmieri's *On Civic Life* or Leon Battista Alberti's *On the Family*. Particularly prominent social humanists also wrote vernacular works that were strongly influenced by humanism. For example, Domenico Buoninsegni used Latin versions of Leonardo Bruni's *History of the Florentine People* and *Commentary on His Own Times* to write his own vernacular history of Florence.[7] In Buoninsegni's case, his choice of sources was not particularly surprising: He himself was a student of Roberto Rossi and a collector of classical manuscripts.[8]

More surprising are the presence of humanist and classical sources in other vernacular works. The goldsmith Marco di Bartolommeo Rustici wrote a heavily illustrated vernacular work between 1441 and 1457 entitled *The Account of the Journey to the Holy Sepulchre*, a book famous today for its illustrations of Florentine churches.[9] In the midst of its copious sketches, Rustici's text betrays at least secondhand familiarity with the writings of Galen and Giovanni Villani. He was also aware of the arguments by Coluccio Salutati and Leonardo Bruni that veterans of Sulla, rather than Julius Caesar, had founded the city of Florence during the Roman Republic.[10] In addition, the book singles out Dante, Petrarch, Boccaccio, Salutati, Bruni, Carlo Marsuppini, and other figures as guardians whose learned words and auras protect the gates of Florence.[11] Palmieri, Alberti, Buoninsegni, and Rustici were all part of the same movement that instilled humanist ideas and forms into the vernacular texts so ably studied by both Christian Bec and John Najemy, as described in the Introduction.

Beyond original vernacular writings that reveal humanist influences, an active market for vernacular translations of classical and humanist works catered to individuals who clearly could neither read nor write Latin well, but who were interested in classical and humanist texts. The translators of these texts were often social humanists from the Florentine elite, but their activities suggest an attempt to engage elite and nonelite Florentines alike. Perhaps within the walls of his family's peculiar palace near Santa Croce, Giovanni Cocchi-Donati produced one of two existent translations of Leonardo Bruni's popular Latin version of St. Basil's *Letter to the Youth*.[12] Across the river and much farther south in the city lived the numerous branches of the Ridolfi family, including Antonio di Lorenzo Ridolfi, who produced another vernacular version of the same text.[13] Jacopo Bracciolini, the son of Poggio, was a prolific writer and translator, particularly of Latin works into the vernacular. He published an Italian version of his father's Latin *History of the Florentine People* in 1476, the same year that Donato Acciaiuoli published his Italian version of Leonardo's Bruni Latin book by the same name.[14] In addition, Jacopo made vernacular translations of his father's Latin version of Xenophon's *Cyropedia* and the classical historical work the *Augustan History*. He wrote an original biography of the merchant and war hero Pippo Spano in Latin, which was in turn translated into the vernacular by the Florentine Battista Fortini.[15] Eventually, Jacopo died hanging by the neck from a window of the Palazzo Vecchio for his involvement in the Pazzi Conspiracy in 1478.[16] It was Jacopo's second conspiracy against the Medici family and Lorenzo the Magnificent undoubtedly regretted halving the duration and fines imposed by Jacopo's sentence of exile issued in the 1460s.[17] No matter, Lorenzo's revenge was swift and final after the bloody events of that spring day in 1478. In a final example of vernacular translators, Piero Parenti is today most famous for his rich vernacular chronicle of Florentine events that covers the late fifteenth and early sixteenth centuries. But Piero also translated Leon Battista Alberti's famous eulogy for his dog as well as Donato Acciaiuoli's popular oration delivered before the new pope Sixtus IV in 1471.[18]

Texts also established learned connections with their readers and owners. A written text, once published and disseminated among readers and collectors, takes on a life of its own independent from its author. As such, texts spread humanism to new people irrespective of the presence or absence of a personal relationship between the author of the text and its readers and owners. The ownership of classical and humanist books reveals a strong humanist interest by the book's owner because the cost required to purchase such manuscripts was a bar against casual acquisition. For example, Vespasiano da Bisticci offered to sell a copy of Cicero's *On Duties* in Naples for five ducats, with the ducat being worth more or less the same as a florin. For buyers with somewhat more cash, he offered Bruni's Latin translation of Aristotle's *Ethics* for nine ducats, Valerius Maximus for eight ducats, or Cicero's *On Oratory* for around eight or nine ducats. For buyers with less money, he offered paper books for a little more than two florins each. Put another way: The sale of a copy of Valerius Maximus and Bruni's translation of Aristotle would pay Vespasiano's annual rent at his bookshop, which totaled fifteen florins, for a year with two florins left over. This hypothetical sale would also have been about one florin shy of the average cost of living in fifteenth-century Florence for a year.[19] Despite these high costs, the existence of hundreds of shops involved in one way or another with the book trade, many of which were in the same neighborhood as Vespasiano's store, attests to the interests of a literate population in books.[20] Printing eventually lowered the costs of book acquisition, but printing was not introduced to Florence until 1476, at the tail end of the temporal reaches of this study.[21] Book owners put in an extraordinary effort to obtain their learned object.

Actual records of book ownership suggest the wide range of social origins and political prominence among Florentine humanists. For example, Christian Bec reconstructed the possessions of Florentines who died intestate and whose heirs were too young to inherit their respective estates.[22] Since these estates often included books, Bec was able to produce the titles of many of the books present in the libraries of fifteenth-century Florentines. Combining a sample of these ownership records with Anthony Molho's detailed charts on the status of fifteenth-century Florentine families provides an idea of the social origins of the book owners. Molho listed hundreds of Florentine families that made up the Florentine patriciate in 1480 and categorized their respective influence and power into three groups, "high status," "status," and "low status."[23] The majority of owners of classical and humanist books were from high-status families – not surprisingly, given the overall skewing of the surviving evidence to this group – but with notable examples of individuals from status, low-status, and unlisted families.

High-status families were prominent among Christian Bec's lists of owners of surviving classical and humanist manuscripts. Niccolò

Guasconi was a powerful member of the Guelf Party throughout the fourteenth century. He was deprived of political office by the Ciompi government in Florence in 1379, but had vengeance on his enemies through his participation in the 1382 election of the Priors, a government that effectively ended the Florentine experiment with expanded popular rule. Subsequently, Guasconi enjoyed enormous political success over the next three decades until his death and burial in Santa Maria Novella in 1408.[24] Upon his death, Niccolò Guasconi owned a large library that included, among others, Cicero, Ovid, commentaries on Caesar and Juvenal, and several other books written in *"lettere antiche"*, a statement that may suggest the fonts preferred by humanists.[25]

Guglielmo di Francesco Tanagli, mentioned in the last chapter, was the most prominent, but not the only humanist in the high-status Tanagli family during the fifteenth century.[26] Guglielmo's distant relative Matteo di Bartolomeo owned copies of Sallust, Livy, Seneca, Boethius, Boccaccio, Dante, and others at the time of his death.[27] According to Marco Parenti, the Tanagli were "not a great family" and less noble than the Adimari family, but were still a family that was "old and of good stock."[28] The Tanagli were also a family nervous about making questionable political alliances, as shown by the heed they paid to the social humanist Antonio Ridolfi's advice not to marry another social humanist, the exiled Filippo di Matteo Strozzi.[29]

Other records of book ownership document the humanist interests of members of high-status families. Piero di Bartolomeo Ricci was a member of one such family.[30] In his *On the Family*, Leon Battista Alberti described the Ricci as a family on hard times.[31] Nevertheless, in 1484 Piero di Jacopo Guicciardini listed the Ricci family as being ancient and having a political role in the Florentine regime.[32] Around the same time, Piero Ricci was collating his manuscript of grammar exercises, biographical notes on ancient Roman statesmen, vernacular translations of classical letters, and vernacular and Latin letters by Michele and Ugolino Verino.[33] Piero's display of classical interests in this manuscript as well as his own literary output coincided with his reputation among learned men. Piero adopted the name "Crinito," supposedly because he hated his given name. He studied under Angelo Poliziano and published numerous books, most famously his *On Latin Poets* and *On Honest Instruction*.[34] Piero was a frequent participant in the learned discussions hosted by Bernardo Rucellai.[35] According to Paolo Giovio, Piero died young – he may have been forty at the time of his death – after a disagreement with a guest at Pietro Martelli's villa turned ugly. This unnamed guest threw cold water on Piero Crinito and he "struck by the insolence of the insult died a few days after."[36]

Patricians from less politically and socially prominent Florentine families also owned humanist or classical books. Jacopo Riccardi, for example, may have been unable to read Latin as his copies of Suetonius, Valerius Maximus, Seneca, Boethius, Vergil, Livy, and Sallust were all in Italian.[37] According to Anthony Molho, the Riccardi were a family with neither high nor low status, but rather possessed a more middling position in the Florentine patriciate.[38] In 1414, Jacopo married up by taking Bartolomea Bonciani – a member of a high-status family at the height of its financial power in the early fifteenth century and the sister of Jacopo's business partner – as his bride.[39] Jacopo lived in the same administrative neighborhood of Florence as the literary humanist Cosimo de' Medici and may have enjoyed that man's friendship.[40] Nevertheless, Jacopo was a new man from a new family who quickly accumulated an enormous fortune by the 1427 *catasto*. By 1457, the family had nearly lost it all, before beginning a slow financial recovery.[41] The Nobili family held a similar status position in Florence, and one of them, Niccolò di messer Guccio, owned more than thirty manuscripts in 1425, including works by Cicero, Sallust, Terence, Lucan, Boethius, Vergil, Juvenal, Statius, Terence, Livy, and others.[42] Niccolò's sons Mario, Paolo, and Antonio were notorious in Florence during the second half of the fifteenth century, but not for their learned interests. Between 1459 and 1494 all three brothers were routinely accused of sodomy before the city's Night Officers, although even their status in the city was enough to prevent convictions. Guccio, a fourth brother, even held a position among the Night Officers.[43]

Members from low-status families also owned books related to humanism. Sandro Lotteringhi was from a patrician family with low status, and he too has left evidence of his humanist interests.[44] Already by the mid-Trecento the Lotteringhi were tracing their lineage back to a certain Lotteringo.[45] They were prominent enough by the same period to appear in the *Decameron*. Boccaccio told the story of one Gianni Lotteringhi, who was a master weaver in the parish of San Pancrazio (a church today most famous for housing Leon Battista Alberti's Chapel of the Holy Sepulchre).[46] Boccaccio depicted Gianni as a simpleton whose wife, Monna Tessa, convinced him that her lover's tapping on the door was in fact a werewolf.[47] By the fifteenth century the Lotteringhi held little wealth or political power. The lineage had only two men pulled for the *tre maggiori* – the collective name for the Signoria and its Colleges – between the fourteenth and sixteenth centuries: Ugo Lotteringhi held numerous positions on the Sixteen Standard Bearers and Twelve Good Men between 1330 and 1340, while Piero Lotteringhi was pulled for a position on the Priors in 1450, but was too young to hold the office.[48] Piero claimed a modest wealth of 676 florins in 1427, while his relatives Lotteringo di Luca and Piero d'Antonio had slightly more, 874 florins.[49] Lotteringo was only twelve in 1427 and still alive to submit a *catasto* in 1480.[50] An ostensibly shrewd businessman, Lotteringo had doubled his fortune to 1,503 florins over the fifty-three-year period.[51] Where exactly Sandro Lotteringhi fits into this lackluster familial background is unclear, but what is clear is that Sandro Lotteringhi possessed a manuscript miscellany focused on civic texts, including common excerpts from Brunetto Latini and Giovanni Villani alongside a paraphrasing of a story from Valerius Maximus.[52] In addition, Sandro helped copy a manuscript containing Leonardo Dati's *The World*.[53] He copied along with Giovan Matteo di Meglio and Michele del Giogante a miscellany containing classical and contemporary selections on the theme of friendship.[54] Modest wealth and social standing combined with modest interests in humanism.

Multiple members of the low-status (but politically connected) Cocchi-Donati family pursued humanist interests and have left firsthand evidence of their studies. Donato Cocchi-Donati cited Sallust in a *pratica*, received a letter from Alammano Rinuccini in humanist Latin, and received an epitaph from Ugolino Verino.[55] Donato's second wife was Costanza, daughter of the social humanist Piero di Luigi Guicciardini, and the couple passed their humanist interests on to their son, Antonio Cocchi-Donati.[56] Antonio was a professor at the Florentine Studio from 1473. He corresponded with Marsilio Ficino and was Angelo Poliziano's professor of canon law.[57] The learned connections of Antonio's brother Giovanni (from the same mother but a different father) were much stronger. In addition to Giovanni Cocchi-Donati's translation of Leonardo Bruni's version of St. Basil, Giovanni has left prophecies, poems, and other writings. He was a student of Ficino and corresponded with other learned men.[58] A relative of the two brothers, Jacopo di Niccolò Cocchi-Donati, spent time in 1451 in jail (a year after he had served as Prior, in fact), where he copied an eclectic manuscript containing letters by Leonardo Bruni and translations by Ambrogio Traversari. He later added original religious poems and other secular works, including some short poems composed by Roberto Rossi for the Palazzo Vecchio.[59] Almost fifteen years later Jacopo attended and transcribed the Latin oration delivered by Donato Acciaiuoli in which Cosimo de' Medici was given the Augustan title *Pater Patriae*.[60] Ten years after that in 1475, Jacopo owned a book of the Virgin.[61]

Other owners' records in manuscripts provide evidence of humanist interests among Florentines even further down the social and political ladder, even among people outside the Florentine ruling families. The Teci were not among the leading families of Florence. Nevertheless, Piero Teci owned grammar books and works by Ovid and Aristotle in 1423.[62] Perhaps Piero's heirs, once they came of age, moved the books into their home adjacent to the artist Luca della Robbia's workshop. Particularly, Piero's heirs lived beside a shed containing animals for Luca's workshop in 1446.[63] In 1425 Tommaso di Bartolo di ser Tino owned two separate manuscripts of Cicero, as well as works by Boethius, Ovid, Terence, and others.[64] Two years later Tommaso's heirs Andrea and Lionardo filed a joint *catasto* return that declared their wealth to be 3,494 florins, making them the fifty-ninth richest household in the Santa Maria Novella quarter of Florence.[65] The sons of Niccolò di Guido della Foresta possessed some-what more wealth, 4,580 florins in their 1427 *catasto* filing, but a similar economic ranking as the sixty-first wealthiest household in the Santo Spirito quarter.[66] In 1426, Niccolò di Guido della Foresta owned a copy of Valerius Maximus.[67] Both the descendants of ser Tino and the della Foresta family were wealthy and included learned men but lacked more general social and political status in fifteenth-century Florence.

Additional little-known figures from lesser Florentine families have left evidence of their humanist interests through the books that they owned. Bartolomeo di Gabriello da Prato owned numerous volumes, including the letters of Seneca, Lucan, Horace, and Vergil, in 1450.[68] Bartolomeo's lack of a true surname makes further identification of this man difficult. Similarly, Pellegrino Vinaccesi is a shadowy figure who in 1451 possessed several religious books in addition to his copies of Aesop, Prosperus, Ovid, and Prudentius.[69] It is not clear where Pellegrino fit into the broader Vinaccesi lineage, which coupled its modest patrician wealth with a similar middling political status. Both Bartolomeo di Filippo Vinaccesi and Filippo di Niccoluccio Vinaccesi were wealthy in the 1427 *catasto*, but by no means among the upper echelons of even their quarter of the city. Bartolomeo possessed a total wealth of 3,800 florins, whereas Filippo possessed 2,255.[70] Such wealth made Bartolomeo the 88th highest taxpayer in the San Giovanni quarter in 1403, a position that dropped to 112th by 1427.[71] Filippo was not among the top 150 taxpayers in the San Giovanni Quarter in either 1403 or 1427.[72] The Vinaccesi in general enjoyed similarly modest political success. A Filippo di Niccoluccio was born in 1462 and was a member of the Priors, Twelve Good Men, and Sixteen Standard Bearers in the latter fifteenth and early sixteenth centuries. Niccolò di Filippo Vinaccesi was a member of the Priors in 1470, while Niccoluccio di Filippo was a member of the Twelve Good Men in 1473. Two other family members, neither of whom was Pellegrino, were drawn for but did not actually hold office.[73]

The borrowers of classical and/or humanist books also have left evidence for their interest in humanism and similarly had a range of economic, social, and political backgrounds. For example, a list of borrowed books from the mid-1450s exists in a recording of governmental *pratiche*, possibly by Poggio Bracciolini.[74] The list recorded loans to literary and social humanists alike. One borrower of the books was the literary humanist Vespasiano da Bisticci; Bernardo Nuti was another. Bernardo Nuti was from a family outside the ranks of the Florentine patriciate and earned his money in part as a schoolteacher.[75] Nevertheless, his learning was so well known that he was a candidate to succeed Carlo Marsuppini as a professor at the Florentine Academy. Marsuppini had been a jack-of-all-trades professor who covered most of the subjects relevant to the *studia humanitatis*. It was unclear who would succeed him upon his death in 1452; eventually the scope of the position was broken up and Nuti failed to net anything.[76] Nuti later worked in the Florentine chancery under Bartolomeo Scala alongside Scala's other assistants, the humanists Alessandro Braccesi, Niccolò Michelozzi, Francesco Gaddi, and Cristoforo Landino.[77] Cristoforo Landino, in fact, wrote several poems to his colleague Nuti.[78] Nuti himself translated Leonardo Bruni's Latin version of Aristotle's *Nicomachean Ethics* and Bruni's *On the Italian War against the Goths* into Italian.[79] The third borrower, Naldo Naldi, will be discussed along with some of his learned friends later in this chapter.

Finally, the copyists of classical and humanist books also revealed humanist interests. Secretaries and professional copyists established learned connections with their texts and these connections place them within the humanist movement. The role of secretaries in the humanist movement is well known and thus need not be elaborated on here. It is enough to state that secretaries across fifteenth-century Italy and even Europe had to master classical rhetorical forms in order to participate in the epistolary exchanges underlying Renaissance diplomacy.[80] Less studied are the copyists of humanist and classical books, men and women whose chosen patrons and chosen fonts – calligraphic forms developed by Niccolò Niccoli, Poggio Bracciolini, and others – reveal their involvement in the humanist movement.[81] In the early fifteenth century in particular the limited number of scribes with knowledge of the preferred new fonts were in high demand among humanists. Poggio Bracciolini, in fact, lamented that his apprentice in learning "a script which recalls antiquity and to which [Poggio] pushed [the scribe] with the greatest difficulty" frittered away his time, a statement suggesting the value and rarity of knowledge in preferred fonts during the early Quattrocento.[82] The fact that many literary humanists with the means to hire copyists nevertheless chose to copy their own books further suggests that skill in humanist fonts, especially in the first half of the fifteenth century, established a person as a participant in the humanist movement.[83]

Examples of learned scribes in Florence abound. As Albinia de la Mare has argued, most of these copyists were "men of substance or good family," but such men were also rarely part of the central political or social circles in Florence.[84] Antonio di Mario (died ca. 1461) was the second earliest scribe to have sold his abilities with humanist fonts to copy manuscripts. Antonio's earliest work appears in 1417, about seven years after the first professional humanist scribe, Giovanni Aretino.[85] Antonio followed Giovanni Aretino as the favored copyist of Niccolò Niccoli, Leonardo Bruni, Cosimo de' Medici, and other members of the Medici family.[86] Antonio frequently applied his skill with fonts to humanist and classical authors. Among humanist works, he made at least four copies of parts of Bruni's *History of the Florentine People*, four copies of Matteo Palmieri's *On the Times*, a manuscript full of Bruni's shorter works, a copy of Sozomeno of Pistoia's *Chronicle*, and translations of classical works made by Bruni and Ambrogio Traversari. Antonio's transcriptions of classical works were far more numerous, including works by Cicero, Aulus Gellius, Eusebius, Valerius Flaccus, Varro, Apuleius, and many others.[87]

Piero di Benedetto Strozzi was the son of the Benedetto who corresponded with Matteo Strozzi and Niccolò della Luna, copied manuscripts, and struggled to write in Latin. Piero grew up in close proximity to his father's learned friends and relatives, but the same upbringing also tied him to the political disadvantages reaped by the Strozzi in the latter 1430s and early 1440s.[88] Piero left Florence in the 1440s for school in Bologna, where he decided to become a priest. He obtained a benefice from Pope Nicholas V through the intervention of Giovanni di Cosimo de' Medici in 1447, a position that Piero held until 1491.[89] Piero was a favored copyist for Vespasiano da Bisticci for decades, and he frequently made lavishly decorated manuscripts that Vespasiano sent to secular rulers, nobles, and prominent churchmen throughout Europe.[90] Unlike his father, Piero was in total command of the Latin language and has left at least two original letters in Latin written in his own hand.[91] In addition, Piero copied works in Latin of Augustine, Diogenes Laertius, Seneca, Tacitus, Ptolemy, Plutarch, Aristotle, Pliny, Vergil, Cicero, Xenophon, and others.[92] Piero copied all the surviving books of Livy an astonishing four times.[93]

Piero; his father, Benedetto di Pieraccione Strozzi; and his brothers Pagholo and Francesco are not to be confused with other contemporaneous members of the Strozzi family with similar names and artistic as well as learned connections.[94] For example, Benedetto di Caroccio Strozzi was somewhat older and had at least three children, Antonio, a different Francesco, and Zanobi.[95] This Benedetto's sons joined Palla Novello and Marcello Strozzi as the principal Strozzi scions that supported the Medici in Florence between 1434 and the 1460s.[96] Benedetto's son Antonio was the first Strozzi admitted into the Priors, in 1450, after the return of Cosimo de' Medici in 1434.[97] He shared close connections with Alessandra Strozzi (Macinghi), even trading houses with the famous matriarch in the 1440s.[98] Within this house, Alessandra left some of her dead husband's Latin books for the new tenant.[99] Antonio also possessed learned connections with Carlo Marsuppini: Carlo wrote an Italian engraving for a stone to be part of a chapel. The stone was carved in Florence under the eye of Antonio, but intended for another Strozzi family member in Barcelona. The engraving read, "There is nobody in Italy today a better man than him," a phrase that Antonio thought would resonate with the learned but not other people.[100] Like his brother, Francesco Strozzi maintained a connection with Alessandra Strozzi (Macinghi) and her son Filippo Strozzi. Alessandra commented on how Francesco, for example, granted greater status to the new husband of the illegitimate daughter of Jacopo Strozzi – Filippo Strozzi's business associate – than she did, and thus she planned to follow Francesco's lead by honoring the man in the future.[101] Francesco also carried fennel to Filippo Strozzi by sea, a gift from Filippo's mother.[102] While not tied to the humanist movement, Francesco did serve as a member of the Opera del Duomo – the governing body that oversaw artistic projects on the cathedral – in the 1430s, including the period during which Paolo Uccello was commissioned to paint his famous equestrian fresco of the condottiere John Hawkwood.[103] The final brother, Zanobi, was a miniaturist of numerous religious books in mid-fifteenth-century Florence. A follower of Fra Angelico, Zanobi illustrated books for the Medici, Vespasiano da Bisticci's bookshop, and choir books for Santa Maria del Fiore.[104] All of these members of the Strozzi family were well off financially, but they were also people of middling political and social position in mid-fifteenth-century Florence. Most of them took part in the humanist movement.

Other scribes were even more learned but further from the center of political and social power in fifteenth-century Florence. Piero Cennini had a modest background but used his learning to associate with the leading men of Florence during the second half of the Quattrocento. Piero's father, Bernardo, was a goldsmith in the workshop of Lorenzo Ghiberti from the 1440s. From the 1450s Bernardo had a position with the Florentine mint, where he developed skills he would later apply to typesetting. Bernardo printed one of the first books in Florence, Servius's commentary on Vergil, accompanied a few months later by versions of Vergil's *Ecologues*, *Georgics*, and *Aeneid*.[105] Bernardo worked closely with his son Domenico on the job of printing the text, while a second son, Piero, prepared the editions for each text.[106]

Piero Cennini had far more involvement in the humanist movement than preparing an early printed text of Servius and Vergil's surviving works. While studying under Bernardo Nuti, Piero struck up a friendship with the Florentine humanist Bartolomeo Fonzio.[107] Consequently, Bartolomeo wrote numerous Latin letters to and on behalf of his friend, including repeated recommendations to Donato Acciaiuoli.[108] Other men wrote to or about Piero too, including Lorenzo de' Medici, Niccolò Michelozzi, Marsilio Ficino, and Alessandro Braccesi.[109] Latin letters from Piero to Florentine men also survive. For example, Piero corresponded in Latin with Pierfilippo Pandolfini (who also corresponded with Piero Cennini's friend Bartolomeo Fonzio) in 1483 and, in the same letter, praised the learning of the Florentine patrician Tommaso Ridolfi.[110] Piero's connections to the Ridolfi stretched back over a decade: Piero had served as a diplomatic secretary under the social humanist Antonio Ridolfi in 1469.[111] Piero also wrote a long Latin letter describing the Florentine Baptistery to the Neapolitan Pirrino Amerino.[112] Additionally, Piero was a prominent copyist of a large number of classical and humanist texts.[113] In at least four of these manuscripts Piero insisted that any remaining errors in his copies were not his fault, but rather reflected the poor quality of his exemplum for the text (in these cases a copy of Martial, Pseudo-Acron on Horace, the letters of Pliny, and the *On the Meaning of Words* of the humanist poet Maffeo Vegio). In three cases (the copies of Martial, Pseudo-Acron, Maffeo Vegio) Piero responded to potential critics of his edition, stating that anyone who did not believe the fault to lie with the exemplum was "spiteful," "doesn't have a heart," and "is mistaken because of spite and ignorance."[114]

Florentines across the spectrum of social status and political prominence bought, borrowed, and copied books. The wealthiest men in the city
became humanists, as did men from more middling wealth. The most
powerful men in Florentine politics studied humanism while men who
never sat on the *tre maggiori* did the same. People with surnames like
Guicciardini and Medici became humanists, as did people who lacked
surnames entirely. For all of these men the humanist movement appears
to have been about the study of texts and spoken eloquence, rather than the
creation of new Latin written works. More specifically, Florentine humanists focused their studies overwhelmingly on classical rather than contemporary writers. An analysis of a sampling of the contents of libraries
accumulated by fifteenth-century Florentines suggests that the libraries of
social and literary humanists alike focused on Roman and Greek works
rather than the works of more recent writers.[115]

Christian Bec's lists of libraries left by intestate Florentines suggest that,
in terms of nondevotional literature, classical works dominated libraries.
Between 1413 and 1453, no fifteenth-century authors appear in the libraries, compared with Donatus (twenty-six libraries), Ovid (nineteen libraries), Boethius (eighteen), Vergil (seventeen), Aesop (twelve), Cicero
(twelve), et cetera.[116] Between 1467 and 1520, the Italian poet Luigi
Pulci appeared in five libraries, Savonarola and Marsilio Ficino in three,
and Bartolomeo Fonzio in two. All of these contemporary works combined were less than the number of works by Cicero (eighteen), who was
also joined by Vergil (sixteen), Ovid (sixteen), Donatus (twelve), Livy
(nine), and others.[117]

These trends were the same in libraries of a social humanist, Dietisalvi
Neroni, and a literary humanist, Giannozzo Manetti. Dietisalvi did not
own a single book by a fifteenth-century humanist in his large library.
Instead, he possessed works by Seneca, Statius, Ovid, Cicero, Boethius,
Valerius Maximus, Juvenal, Priscian, Plautus, Vergil, and other classical
and patristic authors.[118] The large number of manuscripts formerly owned
by Giannozzo Manetti and now in the Vatican Library suggest that he, not
surprisingly, had a greater interest in the original writings of his humanist
contemporaries than Dietisalvi or than is revealed in the *pupilli* records.
Manetti possessed 18 books that he had personally authored, 4 books by
Bruni, 2 by Antonio Loschi, 2 by Matteo Palmieri, 1 by Biondo Flavio, 1 by
Giovanni Tortelli, 1 by George of Trebizond, 1 by Antonio Panormita, 1
by Paolo Vergerio, 1 by Vittorino da Feltre, and 1 by Lorenzo Valla, for a
total of 33 manuscripts out of 171 listed (19 percent). Two books by
Petrarch and 1 by Boccaccio could be added, for a total of 36 manuscripts

by contemporary or near-contemporary authors out of 171 listed (21 percent). However, this number is artificially high because of the large number of Manetti's copies of his own books (18). When these manuscripts are subtracted, the resulting number is 18 of 153 (11.7 percent). By comparison, Manetti owned 16 manuscripts of Cicero alone, many of which contained multiple works of Cicero under the same cover. Yet, the number of 18 may still be too high, as several of Manetti's books by contemporary authors were reference books or commentaries to supplement classical texts. He owned Tortelli's *Grammar Commentaries*, 2 manuscripts of *Commentaries on Cicero* by Antonio Loschi, George of Trebizond's *Books of Rhetoric*, Vittorino's work on Cicero's *Rhetoric*, and Valla's popular *On the Elegance of the Latin Language*. When these and the texts authored by Manetti are subtracted, the remaining number of original humanist works by fourteenth- and fifteenth-century authors is even less.[119] These points are not meant to detract from the quantity or the significance of the literature produced by fifteenth-century authors, but rather to suggest at least two conclusions. One, the humanist movement was more about reading and studying classical works than writing new ones. Studying the humanist movement exclusively or even primarily through the lens of original humanist works, therefore, leaves out an enormous part of the picture. Two, the libraries of Giannozzo Manetti, Dietisalvi Neroni, and the people in the *pupilli* records differed primarily in size rather than scope or focus. Participants in the humanist movement varied in their degree of interests in humanism rather than the general focus of their studies.

An examination of the owners and scribes of fifteenth-century manuscripts suggests similar conclusions. Like people, texts played both pivotal and fringe roles in the humanist movement. The strength and number of a text's learned connections are a good indicator of its significance – or lack thereof – in the humanist movement. With regard to texts, usually classical works by Cicero, Livy, and other popular classical authors possessed the most learned connections.[120] Original humanist texts and translations did coexist with classical works, and these fifteenth-century works varied in the size and significance of their respective learned connections.[121]

Some texts were disseminated widely among Renaissance Florentines and, thus, had a greater role in the humanist movement in the fifteenth century. For example, the surviving vernacular and Latin manuscripts, both full texts and fragments, of Leonardo Bruni's *On the First Punic War* created a large and partially reconstructible number of learned connections. Bruni's text survives in Latin in 134 manuscripts, Italian in 120,

French in 27, Catalan in 2, and Spanish in 1. At least one owner is known for 24 of the Latin manuscripts and 15 of the Italian manuscripts.[122] At least part of the name is known for the scribes who copied 25 of the Latin versions and 25 of the Italian versions. Whether the books were too expensive or a person was too cheap, many of these scribes copied the book themselves, a time-intensive and monotonous activity that demonstrates a significant interest in the book's content. Therefore, amateur – in the economic sense of the term – copyists established a learned connection with the books that they transcribed.

Keeping with the focus of this book, the analysis of the learned connections to this text will focus on fifteenth-century Florentines. Five owners of the Latin version of Bruni's text are known with absolute certainty to have been Florentines, four of whom lived during the fifteenth century. The fifth Florentine who owned a copy, the historian Benedetto Varchi, falls outside the scope of this study.[123] One fifteenth-century owner was Piero de' Medici, son of Cosimo and a literary humanist by virtue of his patronage.[124] Another literary humanist, Alamanno Rinuccini, also owned a copy of the book.[125] Rinuccini was a key student of Giovanni Argyropoulos and has left a copious record of his original works and translations to posterity.[126]

Two social humanists also owned a Latin copy of Bruni's *On the First Punic War*. Antonio di messer Giovanni, probably Antonio di messer Giovanni Canigiani, possessed a copy. Antonio Canigiani also had strong learned connections to both Cristoforo Landino and Marsilio Ficino.[127] A more prominent social humanist, Giorgio Antonio Vespucci, possessed a copy of Bruni's book in his large library.[128] Given that he was a monk at San Marco, it is not surprising that Vespucci tended to favor religious subjects in his studies, yet his possession of Bruni's book as well as a copy of Eusebius's *Chronicle* suggests that he also enjoyed histories.[129] Giorgio Antonio taught Latin to his far more famous nephew, Amerigo Vespucci, whose first name later labeled two continents.[130] In a letter to Piero Soderini, then head of the Florentine government, Amerigo reminisced about their shared school days learning grammar under Giorgio Antonio at San Marco. The letter cited both Petrarch and Pliny before moving on to describing his voyages across the sea.[131] Additionally, Giorgio Antonio corresponded with Marsilio Ficino and, in 1453, served as an intermediary for Donato Acciaiuoli to send a copy of Cicero's *On the Orator* to the learned Filippo di Ugolino Pieruzzi, a man who had worked in the Florentine chancery.[132]

The ownership of vernacular versions of *On the First Punic War* and its known Florentine scribes tie even more Florentines to the humanist movement. Maso, son of the social humanist Luca degli Albizzi, owned a vernacular copy of the *On the First Punic War* that he probably copied himself.[133] Other patricians from prominent Florentine families also had a copy. Bartolomeo Corbinelli has not left a long historical trail about his life, but he did participate in one of the great moments in Florentine history. In 1471, Bartolomeo was a member of the Opera del Duomo. Under his watch and that of his colleagues, the lantern was placed atop Brunelleschi's dome, completing the centuries-long ordeal to cap the greatest architectural marvel of its time – one that continues to dominate the Florentine cityscape.[134] The historical trail for Andrea da Verrazzano is even shorter than that of Corbinelli, concealing even whether the man who owned Bruni's book lived in the fifteenth or the sixteenth century.[135] An Alessandro da Verrazzano, however, was a scribe of classical and humanist books in the mid- and later fifteenth century.[136] In addition to these members of prominent familial lineages, Bartolomeo Belfrale owned a copy of Bruni's work. Belfrale's note in his copy lets posterity know that Iacopo di Francesco di Lorenzo di Niccolò da Soci di Casentino made the copy in the house of Bartolomeo's father, Domenico, located near Santa Trinità.[137] Carlo, son of Bruni's friend Nicola de' Medici, also made a vernacular copy and may have been personally responsible for translating it.[138] Giovanni da Stia was a notary who made two Latin copies of the book, not an overly surprising achievement given his prominence as a copyist of humanist texts.[139] Several other scribes with Florentine family names have left little information to document their lives. Zanobi Bartolini made an Italian copy of the work in 1464, a second copy of it a year later, and a vernacular copy of Josephus's *Judaic Wars* around the same time.[140] Filippo di Niccolò Frescobaldi made a vernacular copy of Bruni's history in 1454.[141] Buonaccorso Adimari copied vernacular versions of Bruni's *On the First Punic War, On the Italian War against the Goths*, and works of Cicero, and made two copies of Bernardo Nuti's vernacular translation of Bruni's version of Aristotle's *Nicomachean Ethics*, one in 1464 and one in 1467.[142] The Adimari were an impressive family, but in 1480 Buonaccorso was on the lower end of the 1,502 wealthiest families listed in the *catasto* and was the poorest head of household in the Adimari extended family.[143]

Collectively, the Florentines who established learned connections to the Latin or Italian version of Bruni's *On the First Punic War* reinforce the central points of this chapter. The owners of Bruni's book were not using it to write their own original humanist histories or Latin treatises of any kind. Of the fourteen fifteenth-century Florentines who owned or copied the work, only one of them, Alamanno Rinuccini, actively penned original works in Latin. Once again the evidence suggests that humanists usually focused on studying and reading, rather than writing original works. As Leonardo Bruni himself put it, "Most people are merely readers of works written by others and write nothing themselves."[144] Moreover, the humanist movement encompassed an astonishing range of individuals. Certainly, individuals from high-status families dominated the number of owners and copyists of Bruni's *On the First Punic War*. Nine of the fourteen Florentines connected to the book were from these families, including the Adimari, Albizzi, Canigiani, Corbinelli, Frescobaldi, Medici (two), Rinuccini, and Vespucci. Yet, the owners of Bruni's book were usually less prominent members of these families. Additionally, other individuals from less illustrious lineages had learned connections to Bruni's book. One person was from a family from the status category, the Bartolini. Although no one was from the families listed with low status, four individuals were members of families outside the lineages that constituted the Florentine patriciate, including the Belfrale, Casentino, Verrazzano, and Giovanni da Stia.[145]

Not only did humanist interests span at least the wealthier half of the Florentine population, it seems that shared learned pursuits enabled individuals to establish friendships irrespective of socioeconomic differences. For example, the learned friends of the humanist Naldo Naldi differed in their degrees of humanist interests and had a range of social and political backgrounds. Naldi was another figure who was interested in humanist letters but was from outside the core political and social families of Florence. The death of Naldi's father in 1447 or 1448 coupled with the theft of Naldi's remaining patrimony resulted in his declaration of bankruptcy in 1457 at the age of twenty-one. Naldi's financial difficulties did not stop him from producing Latin poems by the age of fifteen, possibly at the instigation of his humanist friend Alamanno Rinuccini. Sometime later Naldi appears to have begun tutoring and receiving more general patronage from wealthy families, including the Medici. By 1465, Naldi's humanist friend Niccolò Michelozzi described Naldi's leisured life in the country studying Priscian.[146] Around 1474 Naldi may have traveled to France, as his friend Alessandro Braccesi recommended him to a certain Gulielmus Franchus.[147] Shortly after, Naldi had a falling out with the chief citizen of Florence, Lorenzo de' Medici, and moved to Forlì around 1476. After Forlì, he lived in Venice and finally returned to Florence in 1480, perhaps through the intervention of Marsilio Ficino. Naldi moved between Florence and Venice in the 1480s and 1490s and continued to write poems until his death in 1513.[148] It is tantalizing, albeit speculative, to link Naldi's problems with Lorenzo de' Medici and his exodus from Florence in 1476 with Naldi's friend Alamanno Rinuccini, who experienced problems with the same man in the same year.[149] Contemporaries could even confuse the two men: Vespasiano da Bisticci wrongly attributed Rinuccini as the author of Naldo Naldi's extended Latin life of Giannozzo Manetti, another man who left Florence after encountering political problems.[150]

Naldo Naldi wrote numerous humanist works of poetry and prose in addition to establishing learned connections to literary and social humanists. For example, Naldi dedicated humanist poems to Lorenzo the Magnificent, Ugolino Verino, Amerigo Corsini, Renato de' Pazzi, Michele del Caccia, Piero del Nero, Giovanni Cavalcanti, and Marsilio Ficino.[151] All of these men, a mere sampling of Naldi's total learned friends, had varying degrees of interest in humanist letters. Lorenzo the Magnificent was a prolific patron of humanist letters and the leading citizen of Florence by the late 1460s. He was a rare combination of social status, political power, and deep humanist interests. Alamanno Rinuccini also coupled his illustrious ancestry with a wide reputation for humanist letters. Marsilio Ficino was the leading metaphysical philosopher of his day.

Amerigo Corsini, Ugolino Verino, and Alessandro Braccesi were all poets like their friend Naldo Naldi. Corsini's early poems are mostly lost, but his larger epic poem on Cosimo de' Medici survives, as do numerous classical and humanist manuscripts copied in his hand.[152] Bartolomeo Fonzio dedicated his collected letters to Corsini.[153] Ugolino Verino likewise enjoyed a strong position in the humanist movement and has left numerous prose and poetical works to posterity.[154] Finally, Alessandro Braccesi was a poet and frequent correspondent with several learned Florentines, although most of his surviving correspondence with major and minor historical figures, unfortunately, has yet to be collected and edited.[155]

The other dedicatees of Naldi's poems were learned men in their own right even as they varied in the strength of their humanist interests. Giovanni Cavalcanti was named the "hero" of Marsilio Ficino's famous gathering to celebrate Plato's birthday.[156] Cavalcanti was also a poet and a very close friend of Ficino, who featured him in many dialogues and wrote several affectionate letters to him.[157] Piero del Nero was close to Marsilio Ficino, who dedicated his *On the Christian Religion* to Piero and sought Piero's defense for his *Three Books on Life*. Piero even paid for the publication of Ficino's *Book on the Sun and Light*. Piero's library and letters have been lost, save for two surviving codices copied by Piero himself in 1478: a copy of Cicero's *Familiar Letters* and a book containing several minor philosophical works of Cicero.[158] Another of Naldi's dedicatees, Niccolò Michelozzi, has attracted the interest of several scholars, probably because he was the personal secretary of Lorenzo de' Medici and the son of the famous architect Michelozzo.[159] Niccolò corresponded with literary and social humanists alike, in Latin and Italian.[160] He copied classical books for himself and for his friends.[161] An eloquent Latin speech survives in which Niccolò seeks admission into the Guild of Judges and Notaries.[162] Paolo Viti has tracked down the individuals to whom Niccolò delivered this Latin oration, a group that included the social humanist Domenico Martelli.[163] Martelli and his colleagues were elected for a four-month term, and thus Niccolò's humanist speech may have been one of many that the group heard in September, October, November, and December of 1465.[164] The final two dedicatees of poems from Naldo Naldi were less involved in the humanist movement. Renato de' Pazzi received poems from Naldo Naldi and corresponded in Latin with his neighbor Pierfilippo Pandolfini. Michele del Caccia possessed no known learned connections other than the poem from Naldo Naldi.[165]

This sampling of individuals suggests the wide range of social, political, and learned characteristics of humanists connected to Naldo Naldi. Half of this sampling were patricians in wealthy and powerful families. The del Caccia, Cavalcanti, Corsini, Medici, Pazzi, and Rinuccini possessed high status in Florence according to Anthony Molho, while the del Nero possessed status and the Verino, Michelozzi, Ficino, Naldi, and Braccesi were not listed among Florentine patrician families.[166] Of the six individuals from high-status families, only Giovanni Cavalcanti and Lorenzo de' Medici were heads of households in 1457/8 or 1480 (and thus issued a *catasto* return in their own name).[167] It is unclear whether the Michele del Caccia connected to Naldo Naldi was Michele Salvatore del Caccia, who was the head of a household in 1480, or one of the three other men of the same name in Florence around the same time.[168] Regardless, of these twelve men, six of them were from the best lineages in Florence, but usually they were less prominent members of their families. The other six men, the other half, had less prominent Florentine lineages.

In fact, these learned friends of Naldo Naldi consisted primarily of individuals outside the more prominent political and social groups in the second half of the Quattrocento. Lorenzo the Magnificent, of course, was an exception. As later chapters argue, Florentines tended to select learned men from ancient political families to serve as diplomats abroad. Thus, the absence of Naldi's friends from diplomatic ranks is suggestive of their distances from the core political circles in Florence. Five of Naldi's friends were appointed as diplomats a total of twelve times before the end of 1494: Niccolò Michelozzi was a diplomat six times in the 1480s and early 1490s; Lorenzo de' Medici was a diplomat three times; Alamanno Rinuccini went to the pope on a single occasion; Piero del Nero served as a commissary in 1490; and Giovanni Cavalcanti was a diplomat to France in 1494.[169] The other seven individuals, including Naldi himself, never served as either a Florentine diplomat or a commissary.

The domestic political careers of these men also suggest their respective distances from the centers of political power. Lorenzo the Magnificent, again, was an exception. Other than Lorenzo, none of Naldi's learned friends were members of the Balìe of 1458, 1466, 1471, or 1480. None of them sat on the Council of Seventy – a political body with wide-ranging political authority tightly controlled by the Medici – in 1480 or 1489.[170] The individual political careers of these men were likewise lackluster: Most of them held some political offices, but infrequently, and none of them served as Standard Bearer of Justice. Beyond Lorenzo de' Medici, Giovanni Cavalcanti enjoyed the most political prominence by far. He was elected to the *tre maggiori* sixteen times including one election to be Standard Bearer of Justice. Unfortunately, youth prevented him from holding that high office. In fact, youth, tax problems, and other issues prevented Giovanni from holding eleven of these sixteen positions. Ultimately, he was in the highest offices a total of five times: once as a member of the Sixteen Standard Bearers, twice as a member of the Twelve Good Men, and twice as a Prior.[171] Amerigo Corsini was a member of the Priors three times and held positions in the Wool Guild, in addition to being elected to a handful of other positions from which he was disqualified.[172] It is unclear which Michele del Caccia was a friend of Naldo Naldi, although none of the three possibilities – Michele di Galeotto, Michele di Marco, or Michele di Michele – enjoyed a prominent political career. Michele di Galeotto was eligible only a single time to sit among the *tre maggiori*, while the other two Micheles were ineligible for all of their respective elections.[173]

Other friends held similarly few political positions. Piero del Nero's youth prevented him from holding five offices; absence prevented a sixth – he actually held only two positions on the Priors and one spot on the Sixteen Standard Bearers over a thirty-year period.[174] Alamanno Rinuccini held office twice, one time as Prior and one time as a member of the Twelve Good Men, and was ineligible for three other offices.[175] Alessandro Braccesi was the notary for several governmental bodies between the 1460s and 1490s, including for the Signoria in 1474.[176] Renato de' Pazzi failed to hold a major political office in Florence, although he was elected to both the Priors and the Twelve Good Men before he came of age.[177] Likewise, Niccolò Michelozzi was too young to be a Prior in 1467, while tax problems prevented him from later occupying a position in the Guild of Wine Merchants.[178] Neither Naldo Naldi himself nor Ugolino Verino held or was elected to hold a prominent political office in fifteenth-century Florence, although Verino served as a notary and secretary for different governmental bodies on several occasions.[179] Unlike the even split in status of the familial lineages among Naldi's learned friends, the same men were mostly minor political figures. Lorenzo de' Medici, Giovanni Cavalcanti, and possibly Niccolò Michelozzi were the only three from the group who routinely had a direct say in political operations.

The mixed political careers and social backgrounds of Naldi's friends are revealing for the nature of civic humanism – defined here as the application of humanism in a public or semipublic situation – in Renaissance Florence. John Najemy argued that humanism reinforced a political structure where the possibility of holding office rather than the reality of shared political power fashioned the political world. Naldi's friends were mostly members of families who could hold office, but these particular individuals largely did not. For them, appearance differed from reality just as Najemy's argument suggested it would. Yet, Najemy's arguments only explain why so many Florentines accepted a particular political power structure in Florence: Why did so many Florentines become interested in humanism in the first place? The next chapter argues that people cultivated humanist letters to acquire the rhetorical skills necessary to complete common social and political rituals. These occasions usually required at least a rudimentary knowledge of humanist rhetoric, and the humanist interests of Naldi's friends suggests that each of them could, at the very least, meet this demand if called upon to do so. And they were: Even their small number of political offices gave Naldi's friends a chance to show off their learned abilities. Other social humanists were not so lucky in politics, but they cultivated humanist letters for the potentiality of these or similar occasions. As they waited, they too could demonstrate their learning in the midst of other ordinary rituals involving the spoken word.

The argument that the preparations to meet the demands of social, religious, political, and diplomatic rituals – whether a person prepared for the potential or actually participated in the ritual – underlay the popularity and spread of Florentine humanism also explains why humanists focused so much more attention on studying the works of others than on creating original treatises. Rituals required an oral display of humanist rhetorical techniques, not the creation of an original treatise. In short, most humanists focused on reading rather than writing because the goal of their studies was spoken eloquence in ephemeral social and political situations. Therefore, the social humanists have left evidence for their learning in exactly the places it would be expected: letters, descriptions of the spoken word, and books that helped train eloquent men. Over time, orators became valued for their learning. Consequently, humanism itself gained value in the market of social status. Naldo Naldi's circle of learned friends would have been impossible without this development: Members of the Corsini, Medici, and other elite families valued humanist learning enough to associate themselves permanently with individuals who possessed far fewer marks of traditional social and political status than they did. By the 1430s, 1440s, and 1450s, the humanist movement and the broader social and political world began to feed off one another. People pursued humanist studies in order to successfully complete rituals. Their performances then enhanced their reputations for learning and eloquence. Subsequently, the more people who delivered humanist orations, the more difficult it became to deliver a speech deemed more exceptional than previous ones delivered on similar occasions. This development gradually increased the prestige attached to the best displays of humanist learning and the status of the best humanist orators. People, in turn, with or without real hope of becoming prominent Florentine patricians embraced humanism for the status that a learned reputation could gain them in their own communities. The result was that, as Robert Black has argued, by the 1470s humanist educational forms were widespread. Additionally, the ascendancy of humanist studies among Florentine patricians and the strong presence of such studies among more middling Florentines were complete. Ultimately, by 1484, the parvenu Bartolomeo Scala would be treated as the social better of individuals who possessed all the right familial, economic, social, and political criteria to be the cream of the Florentine patriciate crop, but these Florentine elites lacked Scala's well-established reputation for humanist letters. Humanism had created less an insular republic of letters and more a ladder against the wall of the Florentine social hierarchy.

4

The Humanist Demands of Ritual

The entrance of the soon-to-be-crowned Holy Roman Emperor, Frederick III, into Florence in 1452 began the same as most occasions involving the arrival of a foreign prince to the city, except for the rain. After traveling through the northern gate of Florence, it was undoubtedly a drenched procession that finally arrived at Frederick's quarters at Santa Maria Novella on the other side of town.[1] The next morning, the dried-off members of the Signoria and the Dieci di Balìa visited Frederick at the church and bestowed lavish gifts on him.[2] Preceding the gifts, Carlo Marsuppini offered prepared remarks in Latin that related the Florentines' joy at Frederick's arrival, their hopes for his reign, their offer of whatever aid they could give, and a request for forgiveness that their entrance ceremonies the day before were not up to Frederick's magnificence. The emperor gestured his approval and had his secretary, Aeneas Piccolomini, respond to Marsuppini, including a question that required an immediate answer.[3] The Signoria requested that Marsuppini respond, but Marsuppini was unable to do so. Again and again they asked, but Marsuppini could not offer an answer to Piccolomini's question in impromptu Latin. Facing a loss of honor, the Signoria turned to Giannozzo Manetti, a member of the Colleges. Manetti also declined, stating that it was Marsuppini who should speak.[4] With the Florentines facing dishonor, Manetti finally agreed to respond, and Vespasiano claimed that all *intendenti* agreed that Manetti's impromptu remarks were more elegant than the prepared ones by Marsuppini.[5] The Florentines rewarded Manetti's performance with an appointment to the Florentine entourage that escorted Frederick to Rome.[6]

In a similar story with a less happy ending, an imperial ambassador arrived before the Florentine Signoria, then consisting entirely of men who did not know Latin. The ambassador, an archbishop, spoke in Latin and the Florentine chancellor, as was customary, responded in Latin and told the archbishop the day that he should return for a response. The day arrived and so did the archbishop, but the chancellor was absent. The Standard Bearer of Justice was embarrassed, but he was unable to speak to the emperor's ambassador in Latin. Vespasiano da Bisticci related that the social humanist Filippo di Ugolino Pieruzzi lamented the shame that the exchange had brought upon the Signoria. Filippo claimed that he would have paid good money if the Standard Bearer of Justice could have been given just enough Latin for just long enough to respond to the visiting dignitary.[7] Vespasiano concluded the anecdote, writing, "Here it is shown how much honour and profit letters may bring, looking at the disgrace the Signoria suffered on this occasion."[8] The language was similar in Vespasiano's passage that had introduced the anecdote, "[Filippo] had great scorn of unlettered folk, especially if they should be in the service of the state."[9]

These two anecdotes reveal the essential role of humanist learning in the midst of rituals in Renaissance Florence. Both stories suggest that the Florentines placed an enormous amount of importance on the delivery and response of orations in political rituals. The ends were not practical. In the first example, Italians spoke with other Italians. In the second, Pieruzzi was ashamed because of the Signoria's loss of honor, not their inability to communicate political particulars. In these two cases, humanist oratory was an essential component in the gifts that surrounded the entrance of prominent rulers and their representatives into the city of Florence. As such, participants in the rituals were expected to possess enough humanist learning to carry the festivities to a satisfactory conclusion. Vespasiano's tale of the Signoria's inability to respond to the archbishop suggests that the ritual could break down. However, the fact that Vespasiano could still, in the latter fifteenth century, retell a tale by then decades old – Pieruzzi died in 1454 – suggests the scarcity of such failures.[10] The story warned Vespasiano's readers to remain diligent in their studies so that they could maintain the Florentines' honor if and when given the opportunity to do so.

And there were plenty of opportunities for them to do so: Oratory was ubiquitous in Renaissance Florence. Speeches accompanied the transfer of command of the Florentine armies to a mercenary captain. Six model speeches survive from five literary humanists – Leonardo Bruni, Giannozzo Manetti, Cristoforo Landino, Bartolomeo Scala, and Marcello Virgilio – speeches that other patricians could have emulated during what must have been a relatively common occurrence given the frequency of war in fifteenth-century Florence.[11] At the end of the war, the Florentine Republic sometimes honored victorious military leaders with extravagant ceremonies and elaborate orations. Bartolomeo Scala delivered one such speech to Federico da Montefeltro in 1472.[12] As in the anecdotes that began this chapter, members of the Florentine government responded to foreign leaders and ambassadors with speeches; numerous examples and summaries survive from social and literary humanists alike.[13] Visitors to the Signoria met them in their chambers within the Palazzo Vecchio while next door the writers in the Florentine chancery scripted letter after letter in humanist Latin.[14] Many meetings between Florentines and foreigners occurred in the Piazza della Signoria at the *ringhiera*, a raised platform on which the Signoria sat during public rituals and from which members of the Signoria or the Florentine chancellor addressed the Florentine public and visiting dignitaries.[15] Leonardo Bruni's selection of the Latin word *rostrum* to describe the *ringhiera* in his *History of the Florentine People* suggests the close connection between the platform and oratory, as politicians in ancient Rome used the *rostrum* to orate to the public.[16] Additionally, humanist orations resounded from the thick city walls when particularly prominent visitors reached the city gates to enter the city.[17]

Oratory was just as prominent in domestic settings for domestic audiences. Patricians debated the pros and cons of going to war in *pratiche*, which from the late fourteenth century contained speeches influenced by humanism.[18] These speeches turned large inner rooms of the Palazzo Vecchio into halls for oratorical exchange.[19] Vernacular orations accompanied the election of every new Signoria, six times a year. Fifteen days later a member of the Sixteen Standard Bearers delivered a vernacular *Exhortation to Justice*, which by law in 1415 had to contain references to sources drawn from religious, legal, or secular authorities.[20] Numerous orations survive from the most extravagant weddings and funerals of the period.[21] Individuals copied these speeches, not because they were the only such speeches delivered, but because they were considered potential models for orations delivered by other individuals at similar occasions.[22] Other weddings and funerals undoubtedly possessed similar performances that have been lost or were not written down. After all, wedding chests carried by hand in wedding processions through the Florentine streets mirrored classical epithalamia with their visual references to antiquity.[23] Learned patrons sponsored cultural performances such as the Certame Coronario, a poetry competition on the topic of friendship.[24] Confraternities featured learned orations and commissioned learned individuals to speak to them and/or write for them.[25] Popular poets referred to classical works or addressed topics from classical history.[26] Popular preachers like Giovanni Dominici and Bernadino da Siena disagreed on humanism and its potential for preaching.[27] Nevertheless, both men cultivated learned friendships, Dominici with Salutati, Bernardino with Giannozzo Manetti.[28] Leonardo Bruni may have disliked Dominici's politics and personal morals, but he did respect his eloquence.[29]

The necessity of humanist performances in a variety of social and political rituals and the sheer frequency of these rituals in Renaissance Florence explain why the humanist movement had so many participants and why they focused on reading rather than writing. So many Florentines studied humanism so that they could, as Vespasiano urged, maintain their personal honor as well as that of their city, should they be in a position to do so. Increasingly during the fifteenth century people cultivated humanist letters to prepare themselves for the speeches pivotal in ordinary and extraordinary rituals. The function of oratorical displays varied across different rituals, but oratory always occupied the pivotal moment, whatever the ceremony. To demonstrate the essential role of spoken eloquence in Renaissance ritual – as well as the complex relationship between ritual and oratory – the remainder of this chapter examines a case study of diplomacy. Humanist performances in diplomatic rituals served as a cultural gift from Florence to host rulers. Individuals who hoped to participate in these rituals had to possess the humanist learning necessary to complete the gift exchange successfully. Diplomatic ritual was but one revealing example of the function and necessity of humanist performances in practical situations, situations that ranged from appearing learned at a dinner party to participating in the elite ceremonies described in this chapter. At a dinner party, the stakes for humanist displays were personal and involved familial honor and status; in diplomacy, the stakes were peace or the disastrous bellicose consequences of failed diplomacy.

Scholars have long stressed the close relationship between humanism and diplomacy. In his famous book *The Civilization of the Renaissance in Italy*, Jacob Burckhardt argued that diplomacy was synonymous with oratory, the traditional purview of the humanists. He wrote, "It was not for nothing, in the first place, that the ambassadors from one state to another received the title of orators. Whatever else might be done in the way of secret negotiation, the envoy never failed to make a public appearance and deliver a public speech, under circumstances of the greatest possible pomp and ceremony."[30] Other scholars have assumed that humanism was important in diplomacy. Garrett Mattingly offered that humanist eloquence was a key characteristic in Renaissance diplomats and then made large claims for the impact of humanism on Renaissance diplomacy. In his book *Renaissance Diplomacy*, Mattingly argued that the humanist emphasis on oratory led states to focus more on diplomacy in early fifteenth-century Italy. This increased focus on oratory led to the Peace of Lodi and the origins of the resident ambassador.[31] Despite this alleged importance, Mattingly devoted little space in his monograph to humanism, a common trend in the historiography on Renaissance diplomacy to the present. For example, Donald Queller noted the increased importance of humanism in fifteenth-century diplomacy. Like Mattingly, Queller presented a handful of comments on the subject that played a minor role in his study of the origins and developments of different types of diplomatic representations.[32] Several other scholars have examined humanist diplomats to investigate the political particulars underlying their missions.[33] Most recently, diplomatic historians have produced fascinating results regarding the actual practice of Renaissance diplomacy, even as humanism has been largely absent from their fine studies.[34]

In diplomacy, oratory functioned as one of several gift offerings from Florentine diplomats to a host ruler during the rituals that surrounded the diplomats' entrance into the host ruler's presence. Only individuals capable of fulfilling the demands of all the gift exchanges in these rituals could serve as Florentine diplomats. The script for these rituals began with the social status of the individuals sent as diplomats. According to both Poggio Bracciolini and modern historians, wealth, familial ancestry, and a long tradition of officeholding determined social status in Florence.[35] When selecting from men of varying social status for diplomatic positions, the Florentine government had to weigh not only the status of the ruler at the diplomatic destination, but also the status level of the diplomats sent by other powers to the same ruler. In one striking example, the Florentines originally intended to send a man of high status to the mercenary captain Jacopo Piccinino. After discovering that Florence's ally Milan was sending a much less renowned man, the Florentine government immediately rescinded their own diplomat's election and elected a new diplomat with fewer credentials and lower status. Whether or not Piccinino or other rulers would have been offended or flattered by too prestigious a diplomat, the Florentines could not risk upstaging Milan.[36] Such worry about sending a person with the proper social status was a legitimate concern. Charles the Bold of Burgundy, for example, condemned the fact that the Neapolitans had selected a more prestigious diplomat for a mission to the king of France in 1474 than they had sent to him.[37] Pope Pius II recorded in his *Commentaries* that he had criticized the Holy Roman Emperor for sending diplomats to the Council of Mantua who possessed too little status.[38]

The Florentines gave an initial gift to a ruler by sending prestigious individuals to his/her presence. In this first gift exchange, the ruler and/or a group of prominent citizens greeted the diplomats outside the city walls. The distance from the city at which a ruler greeted visiting diplomats was a statement of the esteem in which the ruler held them and their home city. A greeting at a shorter or a farther distance from the city walls equated to the level of the gift of status that the host ruler offered to the diplomat. As the representative of the Florentine Republic abroad, the level of a diplomat's social status reflected on his city just as the ruler's treatment of him reflected on the relations between the regimes themselves.[39] In this way, the distance at which a ruler or his or her representatives met a diplomat became a gift of status from the host state to the diplomat's home state. Immediately after the entrance of the diplomats into the host city – or soon after if the time of day or some other contingency prohibited an immediate audience – the diplomats had their first meeting with the ruler. In this meeting, the head of the diplomatic mission presented the letters of credence to the ruler. At this point or in a private meeting a day or two later, a member of the diplomatic entourage delivered an oration. A good example of this sequence of events is taken from the Florentine mission to France in 1461/62. On December 23, the king of France himself met the diplomats about six miles outside Tours, an extraordinary gesture. He stated that he was leaving town for the *feste*, but wanted to greet the diplomats before he left. The diplomats waited until the king returned and were granted an audience on December 30.[40] At the meeting on the thirtieth the diplomats presented their letter of credence, and one of the Florentine orators, Filippo de' Medici, delivered their initial oration. Like the material gifts of money, jewels, precious metals, or cloths that the Florentines presented on subsequent days, Filippo's oration served as a cultural gift to express the goodwill of the diplomats' city toward the host ruler.

Richard Trexler described the role of material gifts in diplomacy in his fundamental work on Florentine ritual, *Public Life in Renaissance Florence*. Trexler argued that Florence attempted to establish a "personal identity" for gifts to rulers on each unique occasion.[41] The Florentines had to vary the gifts that it gave from ruler to ruler and even to the same ruler from mission to mission. Through varying the value of some kinds of gifts and the quality of the workmanship of other kinds of gifts, the Florentines demonstrated the importance of this particular mission at this particular moment to this particular ruler. To accomplish these ends, the Florentines allowed for gifts in diplomacy to exceed the limits imposed by statutory law. Host rulers, in turn, evaluated the gifts that they received from Florence and compared them with the gifts that they received from other foreign powers as well as previous missions from Florence. For Trexler, such gifts enhanced the city's reputation for wealth and generosity in the eyes of foreign powers.[42] Yet, humanism was noticeably absent from Trexler's description. The Florentines used humanist eloquence in exactly the same way as Trexler describes the use and purpose of material gifts. The value of cultural gifts, like those of status and material objects, varied from mission to mission. Since a cultural gift was an expected aspect of the ceremonies that opened diplomatic negotiations between states, Florentine diplomats needed to possess a degree of humanist learning in order to meet the gift-giving requirements of diplomatic ritual.

The cultural gift of humanist oratory differed from the use of other types of culture to express goodwill toward a ruler in a diplomatic setting. Richard Trexler has noted that paintings could be offered as a gift to visiting rulers to Florence, and Melissa Bullard has noted that Lorenzo the Magnificent used art and culture to establish an image of himself and Florence abroad.[43] Assuming that diplomats also offered this type of gift, the addition of an ancient sculpture or beautiful painting automatically established the individual identity of a mission. Oratory differed from art because, unlike art, orations appeared in every diplomatic mission in one form or another. Therefore, oratory was more like the gifts of status that began the entrance ritual of the diplomats. Every diplomat carried a certain level of status to which every host ruler reciprocated by greeting the diplomat at a certain distance from the city walls. Likewise, every diplomatic mission contained opening words and thus an implied statement from Florence regarding the importance of that particular mission and the quality of the host ruler. The city conveyed this message through the language of the diplomat's initial oration, his or her reputation for eloquence, and the content of the speech.

A cultural gift means the offering of culture, broadly defined, to demonstrate the goodwill and/or sincerity of the Florentines in a diplomatic setting. Marcel Mauss famously argued that a gift was both a mandatory and a voluntary action on the part of the giver. Situations required that individuals offer gifts under the acknowledged or unacknowledged façade of voluntary action. Similarly, the recipient of the gift ostensibly volunteered to receive it, but in actuality was required to accept the gift as well as reciprocate the gesture.[44] Pierre Bourdieu added to Mauss's conception of the gift and argued that gifts carried symbolic capital. David Swartz summarized this concept by stating that it was "a form of power that is not perceived as power but as legitimate demands for recognition, deference, obedience, or the services of others."[45]

Mauss's conception of the gift combined with Bourdieu's idea of symbolic capital describes the character and necessity of the cultural gift of humanist oratory in fifteenth-century diplomacy. The goal of oratory as a cultural gift was always to end the opening rituals of a diplomatic mission by earning a positive response from the host ruler. The fulfillment of these rituals required that the diplomats give such performances; nevertheless, panegyrics feigned voluntary praise of a ruler. These panegyrics created symbolic capital for the diplomats as well as Florence itself. This capital enhanced the reputation for learning of individual diplomats and the city of Florence as well as making rulers more amenable to Florentine demands. Diplomats reported to Florence that their oration had been a success by reporting on the honor that they had received at their reception. This honorable reception was the reciprocation of the host ruler of the Florentine cultural gift. The outcome of the successful reciprocation was the increase in symbolic capital for the diplomats, Florence, and the host ruler: The diplomats were capable of delivering an outstanding oration; the city of Florence was capable of sending such diplomats; and the ruler was capable of appreciating and reciprocating the gesture. An anecdote from Vespasiano da Bisticci demonstrates these arguments.

Giannozzo Manetti was upset. His friend, Vespasiano da Bisticci, could tell by the sudden change in Manetti's countenance that the pope's message had displeased Manetti, and, yet, Vespasiano was puzzled at his friend's reaction. The pope's messenger had announced a great honor for Florence and, still, Manetti was clearly unhappy. Vespasiano and Manetti were in Rome as part of the city's congratulatory mission to Tommaso Parentucelli, who had just been elected Pope Nicholas V.[46] The Florentines had enjoyed good relations with Nicholas's predecessor, Eugenius IV. After all, they had housed Eugenius in their city after he had fled angry mobs in Rome in 1434 and had hosted the pope's ecumenical council that briefly restored the Greek Church to the Latin fold in 1439, thanks in no small part to Medici money.[47] Despite these close relations, the election of Tommaso Parentucelli as pope promised an even better friendship between the papacy and Florence, as Tommaso was a Tuscan and had spent part of his younger days living and working in Florence.[48] The Florentines elected six diplomats, as was customary, from the city's most illustrious individuals to help get the diplomatic ball rolling in a favorable direction. They sent some of their most prominent citizens – Agnolo Acciaiuoli, Alessandro Alessandri, Neri Capponi, Piero de' Medici, Giovannozzo Pitti, and Giannozzo Manetti – on what was formally known as a mission to offer Florentine obedience to the new pope.[49] Vespasiano da Bisticci also, apparently, went along, although it is unclear in what specific capacity.[50] The diplomats expected to arrive in Rome and congratulate the pope in a private consistory, and then most of them would return home, leaving only two diplomats to negotiate political matters with the pope after the obedience had been offered.

It was after the diplomats had settled into their lodgings in Rome to await their audience with the pope that Manetti's mood so changed from jovial to concerned. The pope had decided to alter the location of the diplomat's audience from a private to a much larger public consistory. He sent a message to the Florentine diplomats stating his decision, and it was at that moment that Vespasiano watched his friend's face drop. Vespasiano asked Manetti why the pope's words did not please him. After all, a public consistory was an "extraordinary honor" because it was reserved for diplomats from the king and emperors.[51] The pope had even told Vespasiano personally that he wanted to "give the greatest honor to the Florentines" by granting them the type of audience previously reserved for diplomats from these two unique rulers.[52] The pope, Vespasiano, implied, was offering the Florentines a great gift and he could not understand why Manetti would be sorrowful at the gesture. Manetti's head turned to Vespasiano and replied that Vespasiano "ought not to be amazed, Manetti being at the court of Rome, where all the most important men are found in all of Christendom, more now than had been in a long time."[53] Manetti claimed that the "following morning he could earn little and lose so much, because many have spoken as well as he could or better."[54] He continued, "And if to my disgrace I should make a mistake, I lose the outcome of forty years of study, and where would this occur? In the first city of the Christians, where so much can be lost and little gained. Thus, you should not marvel that my mood has so changed."[55] He concluded that notable men, particularly cardinals, had come from "more than 150 miles, only to see and hear his opening oration."[56] For these reasons, Manetti was afraid.

Then as now, even the longest nights before the most stressful occasions do come to an end, and the following day the Florentine diplomats entered the public consistory. Manetti delivered a more-than-hour-long oration, which survives in numerous manuscript copies, but remains unedited.

Everybody in attendance was completely silent and fixed their full attention on Manetti. After he had concluded, presumably all eyes turned to the pope to hear his response. The pope too had been fixated by Manetti's enrapturing oratory, and he demonstrated his approval by responding to each point of the oration. Upon exiting the audience, all Florentine friends in Rome declared that the speech had won honor for the city of Florence that would spread throughout the Christian lands.[57]

Clearly, the author of this anecdote, Vespasiano da Bisticci, molded and embellished his tale, as usual, to beatify Giannozzo Manetti, despite Vespasiano's claims to have been an eyewitness to the events related. Above all, it is hard to reconcile Manetti's shock over the sudden change of venue for his speech with Manetti's comment that people had already converged upon Rome just to hear him speak. Nevertheless, even if Vespasiano shaped his narrative to heap praise upon Manetti and even if, as shown later, Vespasiano's usual villains, the Venetians, were not as incompetent as he made them out to be, Vespasiano conceived of the function of Manetti's oratory in terms of a gift exchange. The pope offered the initial gift to the Florentine diplomats by deciding to meet them in a public rather than private consistory. This news disturbed Manetti because he was now responsible for delivering an oration that was not only fitting of the pope's election, but also significant enough to serve as reciprocation for the pope's gift. Manetti feared that he was not up to the task and staked the efficacy of a lifetime of study on the gift exchange. Had he performed poorly or even delivered a typical oration, his studies would be for nothing. Yet, Manetti was successful and the pope demonstrated his approval of the oratorical performance by his point-by-point response, or, in other words, the pope reciprocated the Florentines' cultural gift.

Vespasiano's description of the diplomats' return to their lodging after their public consistory also reveal his conception of Manetti's speech as the focal point of a gift exchange. Vespasiano reiterated his description of the initial gift from the new pope Nicholas V. He wrote, "This act of speaking in the public consistory was the first the Florentines had ever done, because that place was reserved for audiences with diplomats from the king and from the emperors. The pope gave it to the Florentines in order to give them this honor."[58] Vespasiano then turned to detailing the tremendous success of Manetti's oratorical act of reciprocation. He wrote, "All others who have spoken there since have taken the structure of their own orations from Messer Giannozzo, being a new custom because the oration that day was so outstanding."[59] Moreover, the Venetian cardinals who heard the speech quickly wrote to Venice. They informed the Venetian government of Manetti's performance and sent a copy of the oration to them. The Venetians, consequently, added a member to their own diplomatic entourage to the pope and their diplomats "placed a few lines from Manetti's [oration] here and there" in their own speech.[60] They did this action because the Venetians wanted to emulate Manetti's successful gift offering.

Vespasiano then described the reward for the Florentines for their successful gift exchange with the pope. According to Manetti's colleague on the mission, Neri di Gino Capponi, the stakes for Manetti's cultural gift could not have been higher. Capponi declared to Manetti that, before the speech, he "had never considered the danger that confronted our city."[61] He narrated that Manetti had almost suffered an injury on the trip to Rome that would have prevented his presence at the opening ceremonies. Capponi asked, "If you had not been here, where would the honor of our city and of us have been?"[62] Nobody else in the entourage could have given the speech that Manetti had delivered. "For this reason, our country and we especially are in your debt."[63] When the diplomats exited onto the street, they could hardly walk through the throngs of people declaring the honor that Manetti's speech had won for the diplomats as well as Florence. Vespasiano concluded: "Consider everyone how much honor and glory the city of Florence had that morning, and by this is shown how much value a single man has for a republic. This undertaking was a greater honor for Manetti than being reappointed Captain of Pistoia."[64]

In this important narrative, Vespasiano repeatedly returned to the theme of the successful gift exchange between the pope and the Florentine ambassadors, particularly Giannozzo Manetti. The pope had honored the ambassadors through the location and type of audience granted to them. Manetti had reciprocated the gesture through his oratorical performance, or, rather, his cultural gift. Manetti's successful cultural gift earned a concrete reward: It established a new tradition of granting an audience in a public consistory rather than a private one, placing the Florentines on the same level as diplomats from the king and emperors. Neri di Gino Capponi tied the city's honor to Manetti's oration. According to Vespasiano, the crowds, pope, and cardinals could not have honored Manetti and his city more. Manetti's oration was so successful that the Venetians had to send home and add another member to their diplomatic entourage. This move ensured that they too could offer a cultural gift. According to Vespasiano, the honor of the city of Florence hinged upon the success of Manetti's cultural gift. The successful delivery of a cultural gift, in fact, meant more to the Florentine patrician Manetti than holding a political office, a bold statement given the all-encompassing importance of officeholding for many members of the Florentine patriciate.

Archival evidence corroborates Vespasiano's claims concerning the success of Manetti's orations and his conceptualization of them in terms of a gift exchange. In 1451, Giannozzo Manetti offered a cultural gift through his oration to the king of Naples. Manetti arrived in Naples to preserve the peace between the two Italian powers.[65] Toward this end Manetti sought to offer the king a cultural gift. Vespasiano da Bisticci claimed that he was successful, writing that "he recited a most worthy Latin oration *De pace observanda*. That morning he earned the greatest amount of honor, because all the ambassadors of all the powers of Italy were present in addition to his majesty the king."[66] King Alfonso reciprocated this gift by sending an eloquent diplomat of his own to Florence. The Florentine Signoria wrote to its diplomat Manetti on March 20 that, on the fourteenth, Alfonso's diplomat had arrived in Florence. This "most outstanding ambassador and poet gave and orated a most elegant oration in the presence of this Signoria, the Venetian ambassadors, and all the Colleges, plus many of our most esteemed citizens."[67] The Signoria then listed some particulars of the commission. They concluded, "You as a prudent man render in the name of this Signoria innumerable thanks to his majesty for having mandated such outstanding ambassadors and with such a humane commission."[68]

On April 3, the Florentines were still raving about the oratorical performance of the king's ambassador. They summarized their letter of the twentieth by stating that they did not doubt that Alfonso acted toward the end of "the true glory."[69] This opinion "has been confirmed and secured by his ambassadors, who expounded with such humanity the affection of this most serene king towards this Republic, to whom without a doubt one can say his majesty already has the minds of this our people. You, most prudent, with all your abilities and diligence engineer to preserve such benevolence."[70] This benevolence was the result of a successful exchange of cultural gifts. Manetti had offered an eloquent oration to King Alfonso. Alfonso had reciprocated with a diplomat who did the same thing in Florence. The Florentines expected Manetti to maintain the goodwill accomplished through the gift exchange using his "abilities" and "diligence."

Similar archival and literary evidence exists for Florentine diplomats other than Giannozzo Manetti. In 1408 Filippo Magalotti and his colleagues were charged with a delicate mission to King Ladislaus of Naples, who had just conquered Rome. The political purpose of the mission hinged on convincing the king that a defensive league between Florence and him was unnecessary. Should that fail, the ambassadors were to obtain clauses that exempted the pope, the emperor, and especially the king of France from the requirements of such a league. A combination of justifications for exempting these parties and sample responses to potential inquiries from the king take up the overwhelming majority of the commission.[71] One of Magalotti's colleagues on the mission, Jacopo Salviati, summed up his impression of the diplomats' major goals by stating that they had to convince the king not to enlarge his state further, to establish the long friendship between the two powers, and to find out whether the king planned to invade Tuscany.[72]

The portion of the commission pertaining to Magalotti's initial oration preceded the instructions for these political delicacies. The ambassadors were to present Florence as "true sons" of the king.[73] In fact, they were to tell the king "how we [the Florentines] have always been true sons and servants of the king's ancestors and of the king."[74] The ambassadors were to express the willingness of the Florentines to aid the king in anything "possible and honest."[75] The ambassadors were to respond as best as they could to any statements by the king on these matters. Magalotti turned these instructions into a panegyric of the king and his ancestors.[76] He followed the advice of Cicero and praised both external as well as internal characteristics of the king.[77] He implicitly praised the king's learning by citing several learned sources and expecting the king to appreciate these citations.[78] The instructions explicitly stated that this speech was to be separate from the subsequent political discussions: "After this speech either immediately or in that time that seems more useful" begin addressing the political particulars of the mission.[79] Ostensibly following his instructions, Magalotti's speech twice referred to the later discussions in which the ambassadors would address the particulars with the king.[80] Through these statements, he was able to give the appearance of drawing a stark division between the opening oration and the subsequent negotiations. By drawing such a distinction, Magalotti appeared to focus exclusively on praising the king.

Magalotti's diplomatic colleague on the mission, Jacopo Salviati, himself noted that the function of Magalotti's speech was donative rather than political:

The next morning we all went together to see and state our commission [to the king]; the first time that we spoke [to him], Messer Filippo Magalotti spoke for us in the palace of the pope at Saint Peter's. The king had many notable barons and knights with him for the purpose of display. Every man thought that the said Messer Filippo spoke as well and notably as was done long ago. It is true that his speech was not of substantive things, but pertained to the recommendations [and] the offerings, which are used in the beginning [of missions]. Moreover, he demonstrated how consistent and long the friendship had always been between the king's ancestors and our people. In concluding, Magalotti stated that those other more secret parts [of the commission] would be stated to the king at his wish.[81]

Salviati commented on the quality of the audience that witnessed Magalotti's oratorical performance. The impressive crowd was evidence of the king's initial gesture. Magalotti, in turn, delivered an oration whose quality rivaled that of the ancients. Salviati's comment, "It is true that his speech was not of substantive things," implied the epideictic rather than deliberative structure of Magalotti's oration. Salviati's words reveal that he viewed the oration as serving a different purpose than the more substantive words to be spoken in future meetings with the king. This function was to demonstrate Florentine goodwill before the impressive audience of the speech. In other words, Magalotti's speech served as a cultural gift.

A mission from Florence to Naples in 1477 provides a final example. In 1477, King Ferrante of Naples married for the second time. Despite tensions between the Florentines and the king, political units within the king's diplomatic circle had to send ambassadors to congratulate the newlyweds.[82] The Florentine diplomats Bongianni Gianfigliazzi and Pierfilippo Pandolfini were given detailed instructions for their opening oration as well as the political negotiations that were to occur on subsequent days. Gianfigliazzi and Pandolfini's commission stressed that they were to speak only of the wedding in their opening oration. Next, they were to "proceed in honoring the celebration, accommodating yourselves to the time and ambiance of the occasion."[83] At the appropriate time and place, the ambassadors were to present the commune's gift, "ornamenting it with the words that seem best to you."[84] They were to stress that the gift could not equal the goodwill shown to Florence by the king. However, the Florentines hoped that it would at least show their "well wishes" toward him.[85] The speech instructions concluded with the statement "In your first audience, you will not speak other than in general [terms, namely that] the primary reason for your arrival [is] for the wedding."[86]

Both the Florentine diplomats and the king himself attest to the success of the diplomats' gift offerings. The speaker, Pierfilippo Pandolfini, separated his opening oration from the later political negotiations by stating, "There are some other things, most serene king, which our governors mandated [us] to tell your majesty separately, which we will explain in detail at a time granted to us at your majesty's convenience."[87] As already seen in Magalotti's speech in 1408, these words or minor variations of them were a common method that Florentine diplomats used to declare the end of their donative initial orations. Such statements separated the purpose of the opening oration from the political discussions on subsequent days. The Florentine orators to Naples in 1477 went beyond this basic statement to make more explicit that the function of their oration was to serve as a cultural gift. They told the king, "Moreover, in order that we attest to the benevolence and devotion of the Florentine people towards your regal majesty on this nuptial celebration not only by our presence and our oration, we offer a certain small gift to the new queen, as we think will not be scorned."[88] In addition to their status and cultural gift, the orators presented something tangible.

The archival documents related to the mission in 1477 also attest to the gift-giving function of the diplomat's opening oration. The Florentine Signoria wrote to their diplomats and summarized the diplomats' own description of their initial meeting. The letter recalled the diplomats' description of "the majesty of the king, of the honor given to you at your entrance, as you wrote on the thirtieth, as well as the pleasing audience and of the demonstrations of affection made to you, as you wrote on the thirty-first."[89] The king himself wrote to Florence to thank the Signoria for their cultural gift as well as the other offerings from the diplomats during the opening reception. He stated:

We saw and received gladly the legates that you sent to honor our wedding. Indeed, their arrival in the ongoing nuptials was most joyful, and the gift that they gave to us in your name was most boundlessly pleasing. We receive it, done with the best intentions, as if from you, whom we know are most affectionate to us. Therefore, we give thanks to you for the orators sent, for the gift, and for the outward signs of your so great affection and benevolence towards us. We, remembering them in the future, promise to return the favor when future custom demands.[90]

The king thanked the Florentines for three gifts. He thanked them for the material gift ("the gift"), the status of the ambassadors ("those ambassadors sent"), and the cultural gift, the oration ("the outward signs of your so great affection and benevolence"). He even promised to reciprocate these gestures at a future time.

As with gifts of status and material gifts, the Florentines had to vary the quality of the cultural gifts that they offered to different rulers. While each diplomatic mission featured a cultural gift, only certain rulers and circumstances called for the most elaborate ones. Typically, orations delivered on these most demanding occasions are the examples that have survived in the historical record. These occasions included missions with unusually high political stakes, such as missions to make peace or war that fit with Florentine interests at the time. More commonly, these missions included all diplomats sent to a handful of powerful rulers. For Florence, this list always included the emperor, the pope, and the king of France, and sometimes included the duke of Milan, the king of Naples and, rarely, Venice. The missions also included ceremonial occasions such as weddings, the accession of new rulers, greeting rulers who passed through their territory, and celebrations for newly victorious rulers.[91] By contrast, most missions to small Italian powers as well as powerful republics required diplomats to reiterate the information in their commission in the vernacular.[92]

This distinction in language for different missions and even different parts of the same mission served a practical as well as ceremonial purpose. Diplomatic missions to minor powers typically were shorter and involved fewer meetings between the diplomats and the host ruler. For example, in October of 1458 the Signoria instructed their ambassador Bernardo Buongirolamo to meet with Jacopo Piccinino, declare his commission, and return to their presence without awaiting further letters from them.[93] Even missions to major powers could be very brief. Agnolo Acciaiuoli and Jacopo Guicciardini were instructed to leave the papal court for Naples, declare their commission to the king, and then to return to Rome as quickly as possible.[94] On these occasions, the vernacular was a language that all present in the audience understood. Therefore, its use guaranteed that all members of the diplomats' audience could follow their political arguments; that the diplomats could begin political negotiations immediately; and that they could keep the diplomatic exchange short. However, the use of language on these short minor missions differed from that on most missions to major rulers. Diplomatic ritual required a Latin panegyric on these more demanding occasions. By curtailing the use of Latin to panegyrical opening speeches, diplomats did not have to worry about Latin-illiterate rulers missing a piece of information crucial for the ensuing political negotiations – for less learned rulers, the fulfillment of the ritual by speaking words in the prestigious language of Latin was a gift in and of itself.[95] The ritual was fulfilled so long as a ruler's advisers assured their master of the quality of the cultural gift. Negotiations could then commence in the vernacular. In short, throughout the fifteenth century, Florentine diplomats varied the quality of their opening orations depending on the occasion and the ruler to whom they spoke. Through enhanced eloquence on special missions or to certain rulers, the diplomats offered a gesture of extraordinary esteem to the host ruler from the Florentines.

The instructions for diplomatic orations suggest that the quality of diplomatic oratory varied by destination and situation and that this differentiation continued throughout the fifteenth century. From at least the fourteenth century, the Florentine chancellor differentiated among missions by varying the detail of his instructions for these orations. In the late fourteenth century, instructions for minor missions were short. For example, in 1375, the Signoria sent an ambassador to Siena with the instructions to greet the Sienese rulers as "affectionately as you are able and in the usual way."[96] Later fourteenth-century examples retained this brevity. An ambassador to Lucca in the summer of 1398 – more than twenty years later – was to greet the Lucchese "affectionately."[97] Instructions to a diplomat to Faenza from the same summer used the identical word *affectuosamente* to describe the type of greeting the ambassador was to offer Astore, the ruler of that city.[98] By contrast to these minor players in Italian politics, instructions for the orations before the pope often contained more detail. For example, a mission by top ambassadors to the pope in Rome in 1399 contained long and detailed instructions for their first oration. On this occasion, the ambassadors were to stress the ancient Guelf ties of Florence. They were also to recommend King Ladislaus to his holiness.[99] Another similar example occurred in a commission of ambassadors to the pope in 1401.[100] Such detailed instructions served to remind orators to deliver more elaborate opening orations and to help them construct their performances. The orators needed to display the goodwill of the Florentines on such missions in a way that was unnecessary on missions to lesser powers or less pressing circumstances. They did this through their personal status, material gifts from Florence, and the quality of their oratory.

The diplomatic commissions covering the 1410s and early 1420s suggest an increase in the attention paid to rhetoric during those years and continued differentiation among different types of missions. As in the late fourteenth century, many missions to the pope or important missions to other rulers contained long instructions for the initial oration.[101] The key difference between the later fourteenth century and the 1410s and 1420s was the increased detail given to less prominent missions. In 1414, diplomats to Bologna were told, "You will greet and comfort [the rulers] with an abundance of agreeable and commodious words."[102] In 1418, an ambassador to Mantua was told to greet the ruler "affectionately" but additionally to greet him as a "brother and friend."[103] A diplomat to

Ferrara was instructed to "greet and comfort [the marquis of Ferrara] on behalf of our Signoria as a most singular and good brother and friend and offer to him generally those words and means required among good friends and brothers."[104] In 1421, a diplomat to Faenza was to "greet and comfort" the rulers "most affectionately," but again instructions added another phrase, as "our intimate and most singular friends."[105] In 1424, a diplomat to Siena was told to use "those effective and hot words that you know to be desirous and useful for the occasion."[106]

The increasing presence of humanism in oratory during the fifteenth century raised the stakes for opening diplomatic orations to all powers. Consequently, the Florentine chancellors Leonardo Bruni and Carlo Marsuppini standardized and elongated the instructions for opening orations. Under Bruni (chancellor, 1427–1444), even missions to middling powers began to include longer speech instructions. For example, the commission to ambassadors to Siena in 1428 began, "First, express the customary greetings and comforts, as if to our good, true, and closest older brothers, with those sweet and extensive words that seem appropriate to your prudence."[107] In 1431, a commission for ambassadors to Perugia similarly instructed, "First, arriving at Perugia, offer the greetings and comforts to those Signor Priors as true and good brothers and most flawless friends of our community, as is the tradition, and as you know well to do by your prudence."[108]

Carlo Marsuppini (chancellor, 1444–1453) maintained Bruni's trend toward prolixity. For example, in 1447, Marsuppini instructed the Florentine ambassador to Faenza:

When the time will be made available, present first your letter of credence with the owed and suitable reverences. On behalf of this Signoria, greet and comfort with words friendly, honorable, and full of affection, making broad and general gestures; demonstrating to him that neither tongue nor mind nor your actions would be sufficient to be able to express how much affection and love this Signoria and all this people have towards him.[109]

A year later in 1448, he informed the Florentine ambassador to Francesco Sforza:

When the time will be appropriate, present first the letter of credence with the obligatory and accustomed reverences on behalf of this Signoria. Comfort and greet his excellence with words that are affectionate, honorable, and full of singular affection, making broad gestures to him in general, with those words that seem to your prudence to be commodious to the time, the material, and the person whom you represent and similarly the person before whom you speak.[110]

The similar wording from commission to commission suggests that the ritual requirements were the same for these two missions. The increased verbosity in the instructions suggests that, overall, more attention was paid to opening orations in 1450 than in the 1390s.

Yet, even as the instructions for opening orations became increasingly prolix and uniform, particular powers or special occasions continued to require more elaborate oratorical performances. Consequently, the instructions for such missions provided diplomats with more detailed guidelines. In 1447, the Florentines sent a congratulatory mission to the new pope Nicholas V. The contrast between these instructions and the guidelines Marsuppini provided to the diplomats to Francesco Sforza or Faenza affirms the differences in oratory used for different missions. To illustrate these differences, the instructions for the opening oration are quoted in full.

When the time will be given to you, present yourselves in the presence of the most Holy Father and make the owed reverences and ceremonies. Present your letter of credence, first kissing the said letter as is custom. Congratulate and celebrate his blessedness with words ample, grand, honorable, and full of devotion and filial affection regarding the happy accession of his blessedness, demonstrating the immense happiness and rejoicing that this Signoria and all this people and patricians have had because of the election of this holy and highest pastor. There is not anyone who ever remembers news so happy having come to our city, news from which all the city and every person in it universally takes immense joy and incredible happiness. This should not surprise anyone because all Christians considered most lofty God to have foretold of a successor of Peter and a governor in whom would be the most excellent virtue, most admirable learning, the highest fatherly charity and love towards all faithful people. Deservedly, one ought to rejoice and praise God for an accession of this type. If for anyone this rejoicing was fitting, it was a necessary and owed duty for our city, which loves, observes, and holds his blessedness in the highest honor, reverence, and devotion, and which felt in the past and hopes in the present to be loved and cherished by him. But it is not your intention to seem to offer an account of the happiness and joy or of the singular devotion and reverence of this people towards his holiness because neither your talent nor eloquence nor any abundance or river of ornate words would be enough to be able to declare those things fully. In this first meeting, use words necessary, sonorous, and fitting to demonstrate how much joy and happiness have been taken by all because of such an accession. At your first meeting there extend in your congratulations as much as your prudence judges to be useful and make the owed recommendation of all of us – our citizens, merchants, and prelates – and after you make those offerings include at the end that at another time when you are in the presence of his blessedness at his feet you will address some other things that have been commissioned to you.[111]

The greater importance of the occasion necessitated a far more elaborate oratorical performance from the Florentine diplomats to the pope. Thus, the chancellor provided more guidelines for the orator to follow so that he could offer a successful cultural gift.

By the latter 1450s, the assumption that diplomats on missions with particularly significant ceremonial components would offer a cultural gift had become so established that instructions from one ceremonial occasion to the next became identical. For example, the long instructions from the Florentine Signoria to Antonio Pierozzi for his congratulatory speech to the pope in 1458 were identical to those suggestions given to Filippo de' Medici on the same type of occasion in 1464.[112] The fact that both Pierozzi and Filippo were archbishops even allowed Benedetto Accolti, the author of both commissions, to maintain the same phrasing for the individualized addresses that conclude both sets of speech instructions.[113] Accolti was able to cut and paste these passages from one mission to the next because the ritual and the expectations for it were the same on both missions. This ritual began with the social status of the Florentine diplomats and ended with the presentation of the cultural gift. The outstanding personnel of both missions, each featuring the city's most powerful citizens from the oldest families, accomplished the former. The latter demand required a humanist oration, but beyond these basics, the specifics were left up to the individual orator.

As the fifteenth century progressed and resident ambassadors became increasingly common, the instructions for most missions significantly reduced the section devoted to opening orations. Replacing one resident ambassador with another simply changed the face of Florence's representative abroad. These events required much simpler ritualized actions, such as presenting the host ruler with a revised letter of credence. For example, in 1488 Pierfilippo Pandolfini went to Milan to replace the Florentine ambassador Piero Alamanni. In contrast to the prolix speech instructions given to the temporary ambassadors of the past, Pierfilippo's commission is concise. It instructed him to approach the duke with Florence's old ambassador, Piero Alamanni; then "you will say that you have been mandated by us, seeming to us that it was necessary to make this demonstration on the transition to our new ambassador to his excellent Signor and for no other reason," followed by a brief description of the political particulars underlying Pandolfini's mission.[114] Gone are the instructions about greetings, gesticulations, and the type of words to use. Instead, the new diplomat appeared with the old diplomat as a symbolic transfer of power from one representative to another. In this web of permanent diplomatic representation, it would seem that humanist orations became increasingly limited to missions explicitly to offer congratulations to rulers or to participate in other major ceremonial events. Yet, such missions continued, and, judging by the survival of sixteenth-century diplomatic orations, the cultural gift remained a component of Renaissance diplomacy into the 1490s and beyond.[115]

This exchange of symbolic gifts supports the findings of Edward Muir on the importance of other aspects of diplomatic gift exchanges. Muir related the stakes involved in the gift exchanges of these occasions. He described these ceremonies as forming a "ritual defense" around a city.[116] Like crenulated walls, these ritual defenses protected a city from the potentially harmful presence of a powerful foreigner or his or her representative. Hostile outsiders could become a rallying point for disfranchised insiders seeking to return to power.[117] By closely following rigid ceremonies that included several exchanges of symbolic, material, and cultural gifts, both parties made an implicit pledge to respect one another's security. As such, all behaviors and words in the ceremonies marking the entrance of diplomats into a foreign space were monitored for deviations from the standard script. Deviations to do less than expected could carry insults, but other variations that exceeded normal behavior demonstrated to a host ruler the extraordinary goodwill of a diplomat and the city that he represented. Although Muir does not discuss the role of oratory and humanism in these rituals, humanist orations occupied the climactic moment in the rituals that separated the formal entrance of a diplomat from the more specific political negotiations that followed.

The Florentine government itself recognized the importance of the cultural gift. Florentine patricians consulted handbooks that instructed them on the correct way to greet different rulers and the types of orations to perform in their presence.[118] They copied examples of successful orations into miscellany books. In the latter part of the fifteenth century, the Florentine government also began participating in this practice. Secretaries in the Florentine chancery began taking greater care to record and even enhance the orations that were delivered in advisory council meetings as well as the exchanges between the Signoria and visiting diplomats.[119] Yet, beyond this, the government also began recording actual speeches. The Florentine herald Francesco Filarete recorded the oration delivered by the ambassador from Ferrara, Ludovico Carbone, in his official log of Florentine ceremonies.[120] Similarly, nestled within the summaries of verbal responses to visiting diplomats, secretaries in the Florentine chancery occasionally added descriptions of the ceremonies surrounding the diplomatic speeches.[121] In both contexts, future participants in the Florentine government were provided with a successful oration to consult for their own oratorical performances. Most striking of all, Bartolomeo Scala's assistant recorded the words that Scala uttered before Innocent VIII in 1484 into the book of Florentine diplomatic commissions kept by the Florentine Signoria.[122] As shown later, by the 1480s such books recorded elections, extensions of commissions, and the commissions themselves. They also contained a record for future Florentines of an example of a successful cultural gift.

Humanist performances were a frequent and essential aspect of social, religious, and political rituals in Renaissance Florence. While the specific function of a humanist performance varied from ritual to ritual, context to context, its presence required potential speakers at the very least to dabble in humanist letters. In the case study of diplomacy offered in this chapter, these performances served as a cultural gift. Without humanist learning, an individual could not successfully offer one of the at least three gifts (status, cultural, and material) from Florentine diplomats to a ruler. Therefore, the Florentine government sent men who possessed enough humanist learning to negotiate these rituals. This identification of the necessity of humanist oratory in rituals offers an explanation for why so many people cultivated humanist studies and why they focused on reading the works of others rather than writing their own treatises. Florentines needed humanism to meet the demands of rituals. People who wanted the social status possessed by successful speakers likewise had to cultivate humanist letters.

As the next chapter argues, however, the cultivation of letters could only open so many doors for people in the fifteenth century. Humanist learning was but one of the attributes necessary to participate in rituals. Continuing the case study of diplomacy, it is clear that Florence sent men from its oldest and most powerful families as diplomats: since most literary humanists were parvenus, the men at the core of the humanist movement typically were excluded from diplomatic positions. By contrast, domestic rituals and the written word – under which a parvenu author disappeared beneath the typical anonymity of official dispatches – were more open to people from a broader range of backgrounds. In short, humanist training was only one of the characteristics that defined a person's status and permitted participation in social and political rituals. The differences among various rituals meant a range of opportunities existed where people could expect or hope to use their humanist training. As the next chapter shows, diplomatic rituals had extraordinary social and learned demands, but other occasions were more open to a broader range of people. The demands of the ritual world and the desires, often only marginally fulfilled, of individuals in the social world drove the spread of the humanist movement throughout the Florentine patriciate as well as the broader Florentine population.

5

Civic Failure of the Literary Humanists or Literary Failure of the Civic Humanists?

Jacob Burckhardt famously propagated a view of the Italian Renaissance in which the modern individual was born of the fifteenth-century Italian genius. Burckhardt envisioned a secular society where genius broke down the feudal hierarchies of the medieval world and men and women, in fact, were near-equals.[1] Humanism was a point of ambivalence for Burckhardt: Humanist writings and techniques contributed to Burckhardt's vision of the modern world, but humanists also prized Latin, much to the chagrin of a man who believed the national genius could only be expressed in the vernacular.[2] Nevertheless, for Burckhardt humanism took part in the protomodern social leveling in Renaissance Italy. With his usual evocative imagery, Burckhardt described the meritocracy of learning brought about by humanism. "Many of the social hours," he wrote, "which are now filled with music were then given to Latin or Italian oratory, with results which every reader can imagine. The social position of the speaker was a matter of perfect indifference; what was desired was simply the most cultivated humanistic talent."[3] Unlike the rejection by historians of Burckhardt's comments on gender equality, recent experts on humanism have upheld Burckhardt's comments on the selection of Renaissance orators.[4]

As is so often the case, Burckhardt was a little bit right and a little bit wrong in his assessment. He was right that brilliant humanists were sought out for their pens and their verbal proficiency. Some humanists enjoyed remarkable careers because of their ability with words. Lauro Martines demonstrated the political success of Coluccio Salutati and his sons, Roberto Rossi, Niccolò Niccoli, Leonardo Bruni, Giannozzo Manetti, and Matteo Palmieri in the period before 1460.[5] A handful of these men – especially Giannozzo Manetti and Matteo Palmieri – held the respect of learned men and women and filled political offices in and outside Florence.[6] Other literary humanists were most prominent, politically speaking, in the Florentine chancery, where Salutati, Bruni, Carlo Marsuppini, Poggio Bracciolini, Benedetto Accolti, and Bartolomeo Scala served as just the most famous examples.[7]

These literary humanists wrote more than just letters and commissions for the Florentine government: They were also expected to pen original treatises for fairly specific political situations. For example, Bruni blurred the boundaries between the public and the private through his dedication of his *On the Italian War against the Goths* to Alfonso of Aragon after that king defeated René of Anjou and entered Naples in 1442. Bruni's dedication closely followed the departure of Renè, Alfonso's defeated enemy, from Florence and shortly preceded the official congratulatory mission sent from Florence to Alfonso. The work was technically a private dedication, but Bruni's prominent public position and its timing suggest something more than a gift from one learned man to another.[8] Benedetto Accolti wrote his history of the First Crusade as propaganda for Florentine crusading efforts in the 1460s.[9] Once again, neither the Florentine government nor its ruling family the Medici officially served as patron for the work (although it was dedicated to Piero di Cosimo de' Medici), but the content of the treatise as well as Accolti's position as chancellor of Florence made the work's political message clear enough.[10] Much humanist literature was produced within this gray area between the private and public, and in these cases, the familial background of the author was, as Burckhardt claimed, largely irrelevant. What mattered were the eloquence of the work and its ability to persuade others to the professed point of view.

Yet, more broadly Burckhardt's argument collapses under the weight of a closer inspection into the political careers of several notable Florentine literary humanists, most of whom failed to hold political office outside the chancery. Of the ten humanists given ample treatment in Martines's study of officeholding, seven of them held few political positions outside the chancery. Coluccio Salutati was an immigrant and exclusively Florentine chancellor, although his sons enjoyed more wide-ranging, if ephemeral, political success.[11] Roberto Rossi was from a magnate family, meaning that he was legally prohibited from most offices, including all important positions on the *tre maggiori*. Consequently, as Lauro Martines eloquently wrote, "Four notable administrative posts and three terms in the Council of the Commune – this was the sum of Roberto de' Rossi's record in office. It was not impressive."[12] Niccolò Niccoli followed suit. Despite the fact that the Niccoli, unlike the Rossi, were not legally barred from any political offices, Niccolò as well as his five brothers enjoyed lackluster political careers. Niccolò served on the Council of the People in the 1390s and early 1400s. He also held a handful of budgetary and university posts later in life. Niccolò's brothers each served as a Florentine diplomat one or two times on minor missions. The Niccoli, Niccolò included, seemed to have shunned political offices of all kinds, content with other pursuits.[13]

Other literary humanists also stayed away from political offices.[14] Lauro Martines pointed to a "political vendetta" against the Rinuccini family lasting from the 1380s until the mid-fifteenth century as the reason why Cino Rinuccini did not hold political office.[15] This argument is supported through an examination of the Rinuccini men who served on the *tre maggiori* in Florence. As a family, the Rinuccini possessed prominent officeholders before the 1380s and then again after the 1440s.[16] Cino himself worked in only a handful of positions on the Guild Consul and in the Florentine legislative councils.[17] Poggio Bracciolini enjoyed a lifetime of patronage at the papal and other courts in Europe. In Florence he only held a position as Prior in 1455, and his offspring similarly enjoyed little political officeholding success.[18] Carlo Marsuppini was a wide-ranging professor and a highly sought after secretary. In addition to his unanimous vote to succeed Leonardo Bruni as Florentine chancellor, the duke of Milan sought Marsuppini's services and he was appointed an honorary papal secretary.[19] In terms of political offices, Marsuppini never sat on the *tre maggiori*, although two of Carlo's sons, Cornelio and Cristofano, each served a single time as a member of the Sixteen Standard Bearers long after Carlo's death.[20] It is not surprising that Leon Battista Alberti also failed to hold political office in Florence, given his status as a bastard son and his frequent absences from Florence.[21]

The extensive political careers of Leonardo Bruni, Giannozzo Manetti, and Matteo Palmieri made them the three exceptions to this trend. Bruni served as a Florentine diplomat and held positions in the Lawyers' Guild. Most strikingly, Bruni began a political career in the mid-1430s that belied his parvenu status. He was a member of the Priors in 1433, the Twelve Good Men in 1436, the Otto di Custodia in 1441, and numerous offices in between. Of particular note he served as a member of the Dieci di Balìa, an appointed body with full governmental authority when it was sitting. Whether ceremonial or not, Bruni's presence on this body is a conclusive indicator of his position in Florentine political circles by the end of his life.[22] Giannozzo Manetti likewise enjoyed particular political prominence. Starting in 1429 – but with a hiatus from 1429 to 1435 – Manetti held nearly continuous political positions. He was a member of the Twelve

Good Men, the Sixteen Standard Bearers, the Sea Councils, the Night Officers, a Podestà, a frequent diplomat, one of the Dieci di Balìa, as well as holder of other positions. Manetti lacked only a stint as Standard Bearer of Justice to complete his illustrious political career.[23] Finally, Matteo Palmieri enjoyed a wide-ranging political career, despite his humble origins.[24] Unlike Manetti, Palmieri managed to secure a term as Standard Bearer of Justice in 1453, the same year that Manetti left Florence in voluntary exile.[25] Additionally, Palmieri was a member of the Priors, Twelve Good Men, Sixteen Standard Bearers, Dieci di Balìa, Otto di Custodia and held prominent guild positions as well as diplomatic and administrative posts outside Florence.[26]

Despite the success of Bruni, Manetti, and Palmieri, most individuals at the center of the humanist movement either avoided or were excluded from political offices outside the chancery. Literary and prominent social humanists continued to fill chancery roles throughout the fifteenth century, but outside this role they were so absent after midcentury that historians used to argue that the new encounter with Plato shifted their intellectual outlook to accept the contemplative life.[27] Similarly, Robert Black has pointed out that Florence avoided sending members of their chancery on diplomatic missions during the latter fifteenth century.[28] Secretarial positions possessed power in their own right, but they were also roles in which the Florentines could employ men without traditional markers of social status. In this regard, Burckhardt was wrong. The social position of individuals determined where and in what capacity people filled political offices. Since humanist orations often accompanied a political office, social position largely determined the identity of speakers. Most of the time, literary humanists were also parvenus to Florentine society, and, thus, they simply did not make the cut.

The pivotal contribution of the social humanists to European history was that some social humanists possessed the social and learned criteria necessary to apply their humanist studies in rituals while the rest of them appreciated the humanist performances. In a movement focused on spoken oratory, a select group of social humanists were the most prestigious speakers, prestigious because they combined social status with eloquence in a way that most literary humanists simply could not match. The remainder of this chapter again turns to Florentine diplomacy to argue these points, not because most Florentines could expect to become diplomats, not even because most social humanists could expect to fill these prestigious positions, but because diplomatic rituals clearly demonstrate the learned as well as social demands on speakers on specific ritualized occasions. Although participants in all rituals had to possess a mixture of learned and social characteristics, potential diplomats faced a particularly daunting set of requirements. They had to be learned: Not only did diplomatic rituals always include a cultural gift, but subsequent diplomatic negotiations required individuals who could use their rhetorical abilities to drive the best bargain for Florence. Potential diplomats also had to be social heavyweights: As this chapter shows, ambassadors routinely were members of the oldest political families in Florence. These social and learned demands prevented the participation of all but the rarest of literary humanists. Instead, key social humanists from illustrious backgrounds actualized the civic humanist ideal in diplomatic settings. They, in turn, inspired others to seek similar success through humanist studies. Consequently, they played a crucial role in ensuring that the humanist movement would not be limited to a handful of scholars interested in modeling original texts on classical exempla.

A close examination of the diplomats sent on missions by the Florentine government during the fifteenth century reveals that the city repeatedly passed over literary humanists to fill diplomatic positions, despite the extreme oratorical demands on diplomats. The Florentines appointed at least 2,266 diplomatic and commissarial positions between 1394 and 1494. Like all historical beginning and end dates, 1394 and 1494 are somewhat arbitrary choices. The year 1394 was selected to coincide with the beginning of the Legazioni e Commissarie archival series in the Florentine State Archive, which holds the vast majority of surviving Florentine diplomatic commissions from the fifteenth century. The year 1494 coincides with the invasion of the French and the temporary ousting of Medici rule in Florence. The number of 2,266 was taken from a database constructed for this project that compiled individuals appointed in diplomatic commissions drawn from the archival series of all of the major relevant governmental bodies, the Signoria, Dieci di Balìa, and Otto di Pratica, as well as additional surviving diplomatic records from the late fourteenth and fifteenth centuries encountered during the research for this project.[29]

The construction of this database involved distinguishing among the diplomatic powers of different governmental bodies in Florence as well as locating as many diplomatic commissions as possible. The Signoria ultimately possessed the power to appoint Florentine diplomats during the fifteenth century; however, the situation inevitably grew more complicated. In practice, the Signoria, Dieci di Balìa, and after 1480 the Otto di Pratica appointed most diplomats. In addition, governmental bodies such as the Otto di Custodia and the Sea Councils (Consoli del Mare) occasionally possessed the authority to do so.[30] The theoretical boundaries between the powers of each of these bodies frequently blurred. For example, when sitting, both the Dieci di Balìa and the Signoria sent out diplomats. The Signoria sent men to major and middling powers in Italy while the Dieci typically sent commissaries to minor Italian powers and cities in and around Tuscany. Nevertheless, in 1452 both the Signoria and the Dieci sent diplomats to the visiting Emperor Frederick III.[31] In 1453, the Dieci sent diplomats to Milan and King Renè of Anjou, while the Signoria sent diplomats to the same rulers later in the same year.[32] The Dieci di Balìa was legally prohibited from sending diplomats to the emperor and the pope without the express consent of the Signoria (although it occasionally ignored this prohibition).[33] Consequently, the Signoria sometimes issued commissions to diplomats to the pope or the emperor and these diplomats directed almost all of their correspondence to the Dieci. The Signoria sent Leonardo Bruni and Francesco Tornabuoni to the pope in 1426, but Bruni and Tornabuoni corresponded mostly with the Dieci in a series of unpublished letters.[34] At times, diplomacy revealed the lack of cohesion among the organs of the Florentine state. For example, the Florentine Signoria and the Wool Guild each sent a representative to the pope to argue opposing sides of the question of the status of the San Lorenzo Chapter in Florence in relation to the Florentine Cathedral.[35] In another odd example, the diplomat Rinaldo degli Albizzi received a commission from the Signoria in which he was warned that neither Chancellor Coluccio Salutati nor the Dieci di Balìa should find out about it.[36]

Despite this ambiguity of power sharing, the Signoria, the Dieci di Balìa, and the Otto di Pratica have each left series of diplomatic documents in the Florentine State Archive. Two series in particular are useful for each body, the Legazioni e Commissarie and the Missive. In theory, the Legazioni series contains commissions and letters to diplomats while the Missive series contain letters to foreign rulers. However, mistakes in categorization exist: ASF Sig. Miss. I 28, 29, 31, and 37 are all letters to ambassadors rather than to rulers. Their content places them securely among the files typical of the ASF Sig. Leg. ASF Sig. Miss. I 38 contains letters sent by the Dieci di Balìa to both ambassadors and rulers and thus it more accurately fits among the fragmentary files of the Dieci. Leg. series. Dieci. Miss. 2 provides another rare example of letters from the Dieci to its diplomats. In addition, two books and a fragment of a third survive that record the elections of diplomats by the Signoria between 1408 and 1458.[37] Rather than being lost, it is probable that election books of this nature after 1458 never existed. After 1458, secretaries in the Florentine chancery seem to have stopped keeping separate books for this information and began incorporating it into the same books that contained diplomatic commissions.[38] The database includes all of the commissions in these series and has been supplemented with about seventy-five positions drawn from additional primary, secondary, and archival sources.[39]

The database contains most Florentine diplomats and their missions, but it is not completely comprehensive. Gaps in the archival records, particularly for the Dieci di Balìa, are the most glaring absence.[40] These gaps have been especially detrimental in locating all or even most commissarial positions appointed during the century. Further diplomats and commissaries could be added to the database through systematic research into period chronicles, payment records, personal record books, and other references in scattered archival series. For example, the payments from the Florentine government to Leonardo Bruni while Bruni was a diplomat for the Signoria to Rome in 1426 and to Forlì during the same year, probably for the Dieci di Balìa, are nestled in the enormous volumes of the Dieci di Balìa, *Debitori e creditori* series.[41] Systematic analysis of such sources would undoubtedly yield additional names for the database, but probably not enough to alter the conclusions of this study based upon the database. Decisions for inclusion or exclusion had to be made in situations where letters exist from Florentine governmental bodies to individuals abroad whose status is not explicitly mentioned. Similarly, the election books do not always mention whether a particular diplomat ever actually left Florence (if not, the mission was probably cancelled, postponed, or the diplomat silently replaced).

The database has also excluded some individuals. Florence used unofficial diplomats, most often to places generally outside the Florentine political sphere, such as Buda, but also to more common destinations like Naples.[42] The Medici, particularly after the 1450s, created a personal diplomacy alongside the official Florentine diplomatic channels. They used individuals besides the official Florentine diplomats, had Florentine diplomats send them their own letters, or had the diplomats send them the same letters before the diplomats corresponded with the Florentine government.[43] The database does not include these unofficial diplomats because their presence, however essential for understanding the narratives of politics, patronage, and power in and outside the city, was much less important in terms of the intellectual demands of diplomatic rituals, a prosopography of Florentine officeholders, and the relationship of humanist interests with other types of social characteristics among these officeholders. For these reasons, the database is not exhaustive; however, its size should prevent the inclusion of more commissaries and a handful of official diplomats from altering the relevant conclusions of this book based upon it.

The database reveals the paucity of literary humanists among Florentine diplomats. Of the 2,266 identified diplomatic and commissarial positions assigned by Florence between 1394 and 1494, 76 positions were occupied by literary humanists (3.4 percent). This number includes the missions of Palla di Nofri Strozzi (17), Donato Acciaiuoli (14), Giannozzo Manetti (12), Cosimo de' Medici (7), Matteo Palmieri (8), Bernardo Rucellai (6), Piero di Cosimo de' Medici (4), Lorenzo di Piero de' Medici (3), Leonardo Bruni (2), Bartolomeo Scala (2), and Alamanno Rinuccini (1). An argument could perhaps be made to include the missions of Gentile Becchi (4) and Agnolo Manetti (1) among this group. Yet, even with their addition, the number would increase to 81 of 2,266, or a mere 3.6 percent. Florence sent 17 men on 20 or more missions between 1394 and 1494, none of whom was a literary humanist. Expanding the number of missions to 10 or more broadens the group to include 58 Florentines, 3 of whom – Donato Acciaiuoli, Giannozzo Manetti, and Palla di Nofri Strozzi – were literary humanists (5 percent).[44] Thus, almost all diplomats and more than 96 percent of diplomatic positions were filled by individuals outside of the core members of the humanist movement. Put another way, in the century that witnessed the birth and flowering of civic humanism, the Florentines used a literary humanist to fill a political position with strenuous rhetorical demands about four out of every hundred times.

Aside from the notable exceptions of Palla di Nofri Strozzi, Giannozzo Manetti, Donato Acciaiuoli, and to a lesser extent Matteo Palmieri (who filled far fewer diplomatic positions), literary humanists were absent from the core group of Florentine diplomats.[45] Roberto Rossi's learning and influence placed him in the gray area between literary and social humanists, but Rossi lacked even a single diplomatic commission. Poggio Bracciolini and Leonardo Bruni spent large portions of their respective careers away from Florence in the papal curia. Poggio never served as a Florentine diplomat and Bruni's lackluster diplomatic career (one declined mission in 1420, two missions completed in 1426) contrasted with the prestige of his domestic offices.[46] Niccolò Niccoli avoided all government offices, including diplomatic appointments.[47] Alamanno Rinuccini wrote his controversial political works after his short diplomatic career, encompassing a single mission to the pope in 1476.[48] Bartolomeo Scala was an official Florentine diplomat once in 1484, but he also served as a diplomatic representative for the Otto di Custodia on two separate occasions in

1479. On the first mission in 1479, Scala was sent to San Gimignano to rally the Florentine troops to defend the Florentine territory of Colle, a territory that included Scala's hometown of Colle di Val d'Elsa. On the second mission a month later Scala was charged to move the army to a new camp, an assignment that ultimately proved unsuccessful.[49] None of the core Florentine humanists Coluccio Salutati, Jacopo da Scarperia, Ambrogio Traversari, Cino Rinuccini, Carlo Marsuppini, Cristoforo Landino, Angelo Poliziano, Marsilio Ficino served as a Florentine diplomat.

Most literary humanists lacked the familial prestige, antiquity, and/or legal status necessary to hold diplomatic positions. More than any other criteria, familial antiquity was the most common characteristic possessed by Florence's core diplomatic group. In particular, these diplomats shared a long familial history of serving in the *tre maggiori*, the three major political bodies in the Florentine Republic. Election of a family into the *tre maggiori* was *the* primary requirement for entrance into the Florentine ruling patriciate. Fourteen of the seventeen individuals (82 percent) who served as diplomats twenty or more times between 1394 and 1494 were members of families who had held offices in the *tre maggiori* by 1326. Two of the three others were former magnates or offshoots of magnate families, the Popoleschi (from the Tornaquinci family) and the Gianfigliazzi family.[50] Ten of the patricians among Florence's most prolific diplomats could boast an ancestor in the *tre maggiori* by the end of the thirteenth century.[51] The families of individuals who served as diplomats between ten and nineteen times reveal a similar pattern. Of the forty-one such individuals during this hundred-year period, thirty of them (73 percent) were in families represented in the *tre maggiori* in or before 1326.[52] If former magnates or new familial branches of magnate or other old families are included (the Adimari, Alessandri, Gianfigliazzi, Tornabuoni, and Vecchietti), then the number moves up to thirty-five of forty-one, or 85 percent.[53] An ancient familial history of officeholding in Florence trumped both a legal degree and a knighthood. Between 1394 and 1494, Florence sent fifty-eight diplomats on more than ten missions. Of these men, eight were lawyers.[54] Nine of these men started their diplomatic careers with knightly status and another sixteen were knighted during the course of their careers as a diplomat.[55] These figures suggest that a knighthood was a prize sought by diplomats rather than a prerequisite for a diplomatic career.

Throughout the first quarter of the fifteenth century, most of Florence's literary humanists lacked this ancient familial prestige or were from politically disenfranchised magnate families. Bruni, Poggio, and Marsuppini were immigrants to Florence.[56] Ambrogio Traversari was another newcomer to the city.[57] Coluccio Salutati gained Florentine citizenship for himself and his heirs only in 1400.[58] The Niccoli family had a longer history in Florence than these other families; however, the family had very limited participation in the commune's highest offices before the fifteenth century.[59] Roberto Rossi and Leon Battista Alberti were from old families; however, their status as a magnate and a member of the religious, respectively, prevented them from holding almost any government position, including diplomatic appointments.[60] As shown in the next chapter, by 1425 humanism had undoubtedly started to influence diplomatic oratory. However, by the same date, Florence had sent two literary humanists as diplomats, the humanist patron Cosimo de' Medici and Palla di Nofri Strozzi, a man who penned few original humanist works and who seems to have dedicated himself to translating Greek texts into Latin more after his exile to Padua than before he left Florence.[61]

The process of electing Florentine diplomats during the fifteenth century indicates that the exclusion of such men was intentional. Diplomatic positions differed from the most powerful domestic offices in Florence because diplomatic positions were picked whereas seats on the *tre maggiori* were theoretically selected by lot. These offices included the Standard Bearer of Justice (the official head of Florentine government), the Priors (eight men with powers just below that of the Standard Bearer), and their advisers (two bodies, the Twelve Good Men and the Sixteen Standard Bearers). By contrast, various Florentine governmental bodies picked particular individuals for particular diplomatic missions. A rigorous search in the Florentine archives for exact records that document the process of nominating diplomats during this period has turned up no concrete results. However, this process and the care put into it can be pieced together from other materials.

The decision to write a diplomatic commission and sometimes even the identity of the diplomat could be decided in a *pratica*. For example, the Florentine government held a *pratica* on May 13, 1448, to discuss whether Florence should make peace with Naples. Giovannozzo Pitti suggested that they make peace and send a diplomat to King Alfonso.[62] Giannozzo Manetti added that Florence send Bernadetto de' Medici, a man who had already been sent to the king in 1445, 1446, 1447, and who had not yet returned from a mission to Naples begun in February 1448.[63] Ultimately, on May 23, the Signoria sent a letter but no ambassador to Alfonso stating their desire for peace.[64] Bernadetto de' Medici did not go to Naples as

Manetti had suggested, but was rather assigned as a commissary with Neri Capponi.[65]

The Signoria and its Colleges could after decide among themselves to send a diplomat. Once this decision was made, these bodies created a list of potential individuals, most likely around ten, who were suited for the mission. For example, a seemingly unique archival record contains lists of the ten nominees for multiple diplomatic positions in 1500 and 1501. A mark was made to indicate the individual who eventually was selected to go.[66] Vespasiano da Bisticci suggests a similar scenario earlier in the fifteenth century. Vespasiano recorded that the Signoria needed to send a diplomat to Genoa. Many individuals were nominated for the mission, but the Signoria unanimously elected Giannozzo Manetti upon the urging of Leonardo Bruni.[67] After the Signoria and its Colleges voted on the individuals appointed for a mission, they informed the individual, who secured the position shortly after, and then provided that person with his commission at some point after that. The entire process could take a handful of days or much longer. For example, Luca di Maso degli Albizzi was elected on September 23, 1436, to go to the pope in Bologna. He received his commission several weeks later on October 16 and set out the same day.[68] By contrast, the following year Luca was elected as a diplomat to Venice on June 4, received his commission on June 9, and set out the same day.[69]

If that person presented adequate reasons to the Signoria and was excused from the appointment, the Signoria typically filled the vacancy with a person with similar social status and rank (*messer* or not). For example, Dietisalvi Neroni (prior to his knighthood) declined a mission to Venice in May 1445 with the pay of eight horses, presumably four florins per day, and a duration of sixty days. Franco Sacchetti, a man with similar social status who also lacked the title of *messer*, was elected to replace Dietisalvi with the same number of horses and probably pay, but for only forty days.[70] Whereas social status was an unofficial mark based on wealth, familial antiquity, and offices held, rank was a legal distinction between individuals who possessed an advanced degree or a knighthood (*messer* or *dominus*), and those who did not. This distinction, in fact, had ramifications for the pay provided to diplomats. Florentine law as of 1408 established that persons who had the rank of knight or who had completed a doctorate should be granted ten horses and no more than five florins a day. All others received no more than four florins a day and eight horses.[71] A law in 1430 changed many aspects governing the reimbursement and pay of diplomats in order to curtail abuses; however, the pay scale for doctors and knights versus all others remained the same.[72] The possession of the rank of *messer* could increase a person's status, although one could, of course, possess high status in the diplomatic world without also possessing an official title.

One potential explanation for the absence of literary humanists from among Florentine diplomats is that scholars have overemphasized the importance of oratory in diplomacy. Whether initial commissions, diplomatic dispatches, or final reports, virtually all correspondence between Florentine diplomats and their government lack ostentatious displays of humanist learning. The same records usually decline to mention specifics about the opening oration delivered on the mission, the occasion on which humanist rhetoric played its largest role. Instead, Florentine ambassadors described the political exchanges between them and their respective host rulers in plain language. They used phrases such as "we were given public audience" to describe their first meeting in the host space.[73] Diaries detailing the day-by-day activities of Florentine diplomats abroad say little about the initial oratorical performances of Florentine diplomats.[74] The descriptions of subsequent orations, responses to orations, and negotiations in diplomatic documents likewise provide frustratingly few pieces of evidence for humanist performances. Ermaolo Barbaro's famous treatise on the ambassador devoted little space to the opening oration. Barbaro stated simply that diplomats should be brief and stick to their commissions.[75] The relatively small number of surviving diplomatic orations by Florentine diplomats seems to suggest that few diplomatic occasions actually called for an elaborate oratorical performance.[76] As Ronald Witt has pointed out, most of these surviving oratorical examples by Florentine diplomats were from the pens of prominent literary humanists.[77] Perhaps only missions featuring these core humanists featured elaborate orations, whereas other missions did not.

The evidence suggests that this interpretation is unlikely. Rather, as the last chapter argued, humanist oratory was a common aspect of diplomatic missions even as literary humanists were usually absent from these occasions. Circumstantial evidence supports this point. References exist to eloquent orations that do not survive in the historical record. For example, one reference congratulates Otto Niccolini on a fine rhetorical performance at Siena.[78] Francesco Soderini was praised for a now-lost oration.[79] A monk wrote to Cosimo de' Medici requesting a copy of his oration before the pope.[80]

More solid evidence also suggests that the short repetitive statements used in archival documents to describe initial orations sometimes hid elaborate performances. Diplomats used the same cursory and standard language in their reports and dispatches to describe situations where a surviving humanist oration was delivered as they did to describe missions on which undoubtedly a couple of words of greeting followed by a short list of diplomatic demands sufficed. The earlier quote, "we were given public audience," describes a long-surviving humanist oration by Filippo de' Medici in 1461. Leonardo Bruni did not even mention the humanist oration that he delivered to Martin V in 1426. Instead, he stated simply, "We declared the reasons for our arrival to his holiness with many words and with the owed reverence," and then summarized the major points of his commission and the pope's response.[81]

Bruni's words masked an eloquent humanist oration that preceded the political negotiations. In 1426, Bruni spoke before Pope Martin V in Rome on a mission largely concerned with land disputes in the Romagna.[82] Bruni's opening speech said little ostensibly about these political matters and instead praised the pope by suggesting that he was the rebuilder of Rome and the papacy itself. After lauding the Holy See in general, Martin V as the sole possessor of the papacy, and Martin's glorious accomplishments in that role, Bruni turned to praise for the pope's efforts in Rome.[83] First, he praised the pope for making the roads to Rome safe again. Next, he lauded the pope's building efforts in Rome and church reforms.[84] Ostensibly, such praise fell into the category of external praise established in classical rhetorical handbooks.[85] Yet, Bruni's praise hid another layer.

Bruni structured his praise to present the pope as a second founder of the Roman Church. Previously, the roads to Rome "were traveled with extreme, mortal danger and the greatest fear."[86] They were full of "thieves."[87] The valleys and mountains offered "deathly fear to travelers."[88] These woods were a symbol of the problems and ruin of the church before the papacy of Martin V. Through Martin's restorative efforts, these same lands were peaceful and the trees and bushes, like those exhorted to praise the Lord in the Book of Isaiah, sing their praises for the pope.[89] Inside the city walls, the pope was a second founder of the church. Martin has refounded basilicas and temples in general. The only refurbished building that Bruni mentioned by name was the Lateran, the traditional home of the popes. As if restoring the home of the popes was not enough, the pope has rebuilt bridges, the Latin word for which, *pons*, is very similar to that of pope, *pontifex*.[90] Last, Martin has restored the ceremonies of the church to their original pristine state.[91] Rather than simply stating that the pope has restored the church and the papacy, Bruni has demonstrated his point through an elaborate metaphor. He concluded the oration by stating that the political matters could wait for another time.

Certainly, some diplomatic situations only featured a short list of demands rather than a Latin panegyric like Bruni's speech before Martin V. For example, Lorenzo Benvenuti went to Città di Castello in 1422 and described his initial meeting in similar language to Bruni and Filippo de' Medici: "[I] arrived at Castello, visited the Priors, [and] put forth the usual greetings, comforts, and offers."[92] Agnolo Spini's and Francesco Fioravanti's report on their mission to Siena in 1398 states simply that they went to Siena and were able to accomplish nothing.[93] Such missions undoubtedly required less of an opening oration than missions to more powerful rulers or for more critical diplomatic events. Different types of missions required variation in diplomatic oratorical styles. Language and rhetorical style were tied to diplomatic status and were tools that Florence used to make diplomatic statements. The importance of varying the status of the city's diplomats and their oratorical abilities from mission to mission was discussed at length in Chapter 4. For this section, it is enough to note that missions of low importance or to lesser powers had to feature less prominent diplomats and less eloquent performances in order to avoid offending more powerful states. Variance in the social quality of diplomats and the rhetorical quality of their words reflected on the status of both parties involved in the diplomatic exchange. Eloquent humanist orations for every mission would send the disastrous message that Florence viewed all rulers and diplomatic missions as equal. Nevertheless, important missions were a frequent event in the volatile world of fifteenth-century Italian diplomacy. Such missions required men with family backgrounds, political power, wealth, and learning.

When weighing such factors, the literary humanists in Florence simply did not make the cut. Certainly, as Lauro Martines has pointed out, virtually all literary humanists in Florence were wealthy.[94] However, as Robert Black indicates, most of these men were also immigrants.[95] As immigrants, they lacked the familial ancestries and tradition of political officeholding necessary for prominent diplomatic positions. The Florentine government, thus, employed them in more anonymous domestic positions, for instance, as secretaries, in which it could use their rhetorical training and ignore their backgrounds. While these humanist authors aided the state at home, social humanists incorporated humanist teachings into diplomatic oratory. Select social humanists consistently combined the necessary familial lineage with their learning to make them far stronger candidates for diplomatic positions than most literary humanists nearer the center of the humanist movement. Diplomatic ritual is but one revealing example of the complex calculation involved in the selection of eloquent men and women to speak on specific occasions.

The success of literary humanists in domestic positions compared to their general failure to penetrate diplomatic ranks points to a crucial difference between a speaker in a domestic setting and a diplomat abroad. Bruni and humanist parvenus wrote countless state letters to Florentine allies and enemies while they physically remained within Florence. In a domestic letter writing capacity, a writer's physical presence disappeared as his words became the utterances of the state. Similarly, individuals who spoke to diplomats or rulers within Florence became the voice of their social betters. A speech by Leonardo Bruni provides evidence for this claim. In his oration to the ambassadors of King Alfonso delivered in 1443, Bruni stated, "This is the response that is made to you on behalf of my magnificent Signoria, with the deliberation and consensus not only of this numerous multitude of outstanding citizens – whom you see to be present and in the audience – but also with the consensus and deliberation of all the city in which, you should understand, all our people are of one wish, consensus, and mind."[96] In this passage, Bruni made clear that his mouth uttered the words of the patricians present and even of the entire city. He reinforced his role as a mere conduit for their common decisions by drawing the attention of the king's ambassadors to the audience present.

The different role of a diplomat abroad usually prevented the physical presence of parvenus on diplomatic missions. A Florentine diplomat abroad was the embodiment of the Florentine regime. For example, a host ruler could select the city of Florence as a godparent for his or her child. A Florentine diplomat (or in this case technically a "proctor"), such as Maso degli Albizzi, performed the necessary ceremonies on behalf of the Florentine government.[97] As the regime personified, a diplomat could represent it in such rituals. However, again as the regime personified, a diplomat had status and shortcomings that were the same as his commissioner's strengths and weaknesses. Therefore, not only did sending diplomats with little social status and learning risk offending host rulers, such diplomats risked presenting Florence as a city of ignorant ruffians, void of established families and culture. In other words, a person in Florence spoke for the city whereas a person outside Florence spoke as the city. As such, a Florentine diplomat had to possess both familial antiquity and eloquent words. Consequently, domestic speaking events were more open to people from less illustrious backgrounds than occasions outside the city.

The differences between orations delivered on domestic and foreign occasions provide evidence for this point. As the last chapter argued, most orations by Florentine diplomats to host rulers functioned as a cultural gift. Rulers, diplomats, and outside observers all conceptualized these orations in gift-giving terms. As such, the orations almost always lacked overt political statements. Rather, diplomats abroad offered panegyrics to rulers and claimed that they would state their diplomatic commission at a later meeting. The next two chapters look at several examples of these speeches. Surviving orations delivered in domestic situations in Florence, by contrast, differed dramatically from these donative speeches in that they usually combined political responses and praise in the same oration. These domestic speeches were also often delivered by parvenus. These differences were possible because of the different function of domestic diplomatic orations. Unlike the mostly donative function that Florentine diplomats performed while abroad, orations delivered to visitors in Florence had a primarily political purpose: They were specifically to address questions and requests made by the visitors.

Although he was no parvenu, Palla di Nofri Strozzi delivered two surviving speeches that provide evidence for the political content and structure of domestic diplomatic orations. Palla di Nofri copied two orations that he delivered to visiting ambassadors in Florence in a diary he kept while serving on the Dieci di Balìa. Palla di Nofri delivered the first speech in unadorned Italian on June 29, 1423, to the archbishop of Genoa. The oration amounts to a partial list of the grievances held by Florence against the duke of Milan and a conclusion that the duke must retreat into his boundaries before negotiations between Florence and him would commence.[98] The oration lacks any embellishments of a classical structure, word arrangement, or source citation.

Palla di Nofri's second recorded oration marked a dramatic shift from this plain Italian speech. He delivered it to the ambassadors of the king of France on the next day, June 30, 1423.[99] First, Palla di Nofri delivered this oration in a classicized Latin; for example, note how Palla placed the finite verbs at the end of the following main and relative clauses: "*Et primo, cum debita reverentia salutationes tantae Maiestatis gratissimo animo susceperunt, tamquam a patre, protectore et benefactore huius civitatis cui se ac universam civitatem humiliter commandant.*"[100] Palla di Nofri also demonstrated his rhetorical care in constructing the sentences in his oration. For example, he uses alliteration in the repetition of the "c" sound at the end of the sentence (*civitatis, cui, ac, civitatem, commandant*). He used assonance by pairing the words "*protectore et benefactore.*" He joined two groups of polysyllabic words with similar sounds (*"patre, protectore, et benefactore huius civitatis"* and *"universam civitatem humiliter"*) with three short words (*"cui se ac"*). In the next sentence of the oration, Palla di Nofri used anaphora by beginning multiple clauses with the preposition "a" plus the name of a king: *"a Carolo Magno ... a Carolo primo ... a Carolo de Valosa ... a rege Roberto."*[101] However, alongside these rhetorical moves, Palla di Nofri's oration maintained the listlike structure used in his Italian oration from the previous day: He responded, point by point, to the visiting diplomats' requests. Palla's only use of history or a classical source occurred in his citation of the rebuilding of Florence by Charlemagne, a common trope in Florentine diplomatic relations with France.[102] In fact, rather than showing a knowledge of humanist writings, Palla's citation of this refoundation story was in direct contradiction of the arguments made by his friend Leonardo Bruni in the *History of the Florentine People*. In that work, Bruni had argued that this refoundation myth lacked evidence.[103] Palla's two orations suggest that domestic orations varied in structure and language from ruler to ruler, but maintained a primary focus on political matters and function of advancing political discussions.

An oration that Bruni – rather than a member of the Signoria, as was custom – delivered to diplomats from the king of Naples in 1443 also provides evidence for this point. After a lengthy introduction that praised King Alfonso and his treatment of the Florentines, Bruni entered into the political particulars of his response.[104] Alfonso's request that Florence cease aid to Francesco Sforza posed a problem to the republic: The king was asking the Florentines to choose between their honor toward Sforza and their love toward Alfonso.[105] Quoting Cicero, Bruni argued that honoring promises is the first rule of friendship. What person, let alone what city, was so vile to break such a rule?[106] The Florentines and King Alfonso, according to Bruni, were certainly not so treacherous. Next, Bruni related the narrative behind the creation of the league between Sforza and the Florentines.[107] He responded to two accusations stated by Alfonso's diplomats. First, the Neapolitan diplomats had claimed that the Florentines lacked papal consent to make promises to Sforza. Bruni claimed that they did, in fact, have papal approval. The Florentines did not have the papal bull as proof; however, they did have enough witnesses to meet the evidentiary standards of biblical law as outlined in Deuteronomy.[108] Second, the king's ambassadors had argued that Sforza lacked a claim to the Marche; thus the Florentines were not obligated to help him defend those lands. Bruni retorted that Sforza's land claims were irrelevant because the Florentines had promised their aid and must meet those promises.[109] Next, Bruni sought to assure the Neapolitan diplomats that the Florentines strove with all their actions to avoid offending King Alfonso. He referred to the recent league between Florence and Genoa and the Florentines' insistence that any defensive pact between the two cities not include attacks by Alfonso.[110] Bruni concluded that Alfonso's familial line and the Florentines had enjoyed good relations since the thirteenth century. The Florentines' honor obligated them to help Sforza, but they maintained their devotion to King Alfonso.[111]

This political structure contrasted sharply with the oration Bruni delivered before Martin V in 1426, discussed previously, as well as speeches he wrote for diplomats speaking outside Florence. For example, Bruni wrote an oration in 1438 to accompany the Florentine diplomats Giuliano Davanzati, Carlo Federighi, and Bernardo Giugni, who were sent to congratulate the newly elected Holy Roman Emperor in 1438.[112] Like Bruni's oration to Martin V in 1426, Bruni's oration to the emperor in 1438 focused on elaborate praise rather than politics. In the 1438 oration, Bruni attempted to portray the new emperor as Christ himself. Bruni began with a quote from Matthew, "We see His star in the east and we come to adore Him."[113] Through this quotation, Bruni changed the setting of the diplomatic audience from diplomats visiting a ruler, to the three wise men – not coincidently the number of Florentine ambassadors on the mission – visiting the Son of God.[114] Just as the wise men, the Florentine diplomats traveled to pay homage and offer gifts. Next, Bruni attempted to prove that his comparison was justified, stating, "Not without probable reason is this parallel made between the imperial dignity and a star shining in the sky."[115] A series of comparisons meant to prove this statement follow, climaxing with an eschatological quotation from Vergil, "Lest you think that all these things were now newly discovered by me, hear what Vergil, most learned of the poets, says: Behold the star of Dionysian Caesar appeared ‖ because of which the fields were rejoicing with crops ‖ and the grape was ripening on the sunny hills."[116] Bruni argued that this quotation showed Vergil's wish that the emperor would provide "tranquility and peace."[117] This interpretation continues the metaphor of the emperor as Christ. Like God in Isaiah 9:5–7, the emperor will be the "Prince of Peace."

The oration continued along the same lines. As if Christ had returned from the dead, the entire world experienced more joy at the emperor's accession than at that of any past ruler. He will bring peace to the Christians and war to the infidels. Bruni argued that the emperor's virtues –

"trust," "moderation," "strength," "clemency," "incorruptible justice," "admirable wisdom," and "the highest intelligence" – have warranted such hopes in "the states and peoples."[118] These virtues once again echo Isaiah, this time chapter 11 verses 1–5. In these eschatological passages, the virtues attributed to the emperor parallel those attributed to the prophesied Messiah, particularly "wisdom," "intelligence," "strength," "justice," and "trust."[119] Bruni concluded the oration by reminding the emperor of the donative purpose of the oration. The Florentines had already sent letters congratulating the emperor; "nevertheless, through live addresses too the city wished to express its congratulations more fully through our diplomats and, with them present, to rejoice with your most sublime highness on account of your happy accession."[120] The gift drew to a close: "Certainly, most serene prince, we have some things to discuss separately, which we will present more fully to your majesty when the time and place will be given."[121]

The records of speeches delivered by the Signoria to visiting diplomats also suggest that domestic diplomatic orations served a largely political rather than donative purpose. From 1458 through the 1490s, the Florentine chancellor recorded orations that visiting diplomats delivered before the Signoria and the response by the Signoria or occasionally the chancellor to these diplomats.[122] Like the orations by Bruni and Strozzi, all of these speeches focus on political matters, with words of greeting and praise preempting the political statements in each orator's speech. On a handful of occasions, visiting diplomats delivered panegyrics that ended by requesting a further audience to discuss more particular matters. On such occasions, a member of the Florentine Signoria or the chancellor approved the request with brief words. The subsequent political oration of the visiting diplomats is then provided.[123]

Finally, the practice of literary humanists writing orations for Florentine diplomats to deliver abroad also suggests the differences between domestic and foreign oratorical occasions. Some particularly delicate diplomatic missions required orations, the content of which was beyond the skill of the diplomats chosen. In such cases, literary humanists wrote the words that social humanists spoke. This practice seems to have begun at least by the chancellorship of Leonardo Bruni and continued throughout the fifteenth century. Bruni wrote no fewer than three orations for diplomatic missions in which he himself did not participate. In 1432, he wrote the oration that Biagio Guasconi delivered before the king of the Romans shortly before Sigismondo's coronation at Rome.[124] In 1438, Bruni wrote the oration that Giuliano Davanzati, Carlo Federighi, or Bernardo

Giugni delivered before the newly elected Emperor Albrecht III. Finally, Bruni wrote the oration that Giuliano Davanzati delivered to congratulate King Alfonso of Aragon on his conquest of Naples in 1442.[125] Each of these situations required cultural gifts to express the goodwill of the Florentines. Yet, like most literary humanists, Bruni lacked the familial and political background necessary to serve as a diplomat on these missions himself.

The practice of Florentine diplomats delivering orations written by their more learned peers continued after the chancellorship of Leonardo Bruni. In August 1465, Jacopo Guicciardini and Pandolfo Pandolfini delivered the words of Bartolomeo Scala before King Ferrante.[126] As with the example of Bruni, Scala, the son of a miller, lacked the familial ancestry necessary for Florentine diplomats on such an important occasion. Guicciardini and Pandolfini, by contrast, possessed the social backgrounds that Scala lacked.[127] In a final example, Pierfilippo Pandolfini delivered an oration written by the literary humanist Alamanno Rinuccini for a mission in 1477.[128] Rinuccini himself possessed an old family and outstanding learning, but he had recently lost the favor of Lorenzo de' Medici. This loss of trust excluded him from Florentine diplomatic positions after 1476.[129] Whether Pandolfini asked his friend Rinuccini, Rinuccini volunteered, or the Florentine government demanded, the act of having a literary humanist supply an opening oration points to the importance of the cultural gift and ensured its success on this occasion. It is unclear whether the king knew that Rinuccini had written the oration delivered before him or whether he just assumed it was the work of Pandolfini. Either way, literary and social humanists worked together to offer the king the most eloquent words that the city had to offer.

In domestic situations, parvenu humanists achieved success at integrating their learning into political situations. The most illustrious literary humanists dominated important and influential positions in the Florentine chancery. In the presence of their social betters their words lost their parvenu taint and became the eloquent voice of the Florentine regime. Their opportunities in domestic settings suggest that other Florentines could also complete domestic rituals with learned performances, even without high levels of traditional status. Yet, humanist parvenus, no matter how eloquent, lacked the familial antiquity in Florence to speak as the city abroad and rarely filled the most illustrious political offices in or outside Florence. As such, the words and figures of literary humanists like Bruni, Poggio, and Marsuppini existed mostly in the background of Renaissance politics. It was social humanists – particularly a select group of them who combined their learning with ancient familial histories – who were largely responsible for the integration of humanism into the most prestigious and most visible venues of the civic world. Certainly, most of these individuals wrote nothing in terms of original treatises or dialogues. In addition, the category of the social humanists, designed to focus on learned rather than social status, encompasses an enormous range of social backgrounds among its members. Many social humanists too lacked the familial background in Florence necessary to serve as Florentine diplomats or in other high-ranking positions.

Select social humanists possessed both the learned connections to suggest an active interest in humanism and the social status to integrate this learning into all types of situations. Their success combined with the performances of less illustrious – socially speaking – literary and social humanists in domestic settings to expand the humanist movement from an isolated curiosity of a few intellectuals into a broader cultural phenomenon. This chapter has focused on diplomacy, but its conclusions can be carefully applied to all ritualized occasions that featured an oratorical performance. The world of ritual dictated the selection of humanists and the success of oratorical performances; the success of learned men and women in rituals inspired other people, even less socially prominent ones, to emulate their humanist interests. The next chapter turns away from the synchronic analysis described over the last several chapters to a diachronic narrative detailing the infiltration of humanism into Florentine rituals. The process began in earnest by the mid-1420s, was complete by the 1450s, and was driven by the social humanists. As shown later, the infiltration and then permeation of humanist performances in rituals had enormous ramifications for the social world of the Florentine humanists.

6

The Rise of the Social Humanists, 1400–1455

In 1450, Poggio Bracciolini told a tale of Perugian diplomats to Pope Urban V supposedly from the 1360s.[1] Poggio did not provide the reason behind the mission, stating only that the Perugians sent three men to discuss unspecified matters with the pope. As the three diplomats traveled, one member of the group occupied his time writing and memorizing a long oration to be delivered upon their arrival in the pope's presence. When the long journey to Avignon ended, the diplomats discovered that the pope was very sick. However, according to Poggio, "wishing not to keep them longer in suspense, [the pope] ordered them to be introduced, with the previous request that they should speak but few words."[2] The diplomat charged with delivering the oration, however, "took no heed of [the pope's] sickly state nor of his keeping his bed, but was so verbose that the Holy Father gave frequent signs of fatigue whilst hearing him out."[3] The sick pope endured and when the man finally stopped talking, the pope asked the other two diplomats the reason for their arrival. "One of [the other ambassadors], who had escaped neither his colleague's silliness nor the Pontiff's weariness, at once replied: "Most Holy Father, we have express orders that if you do not immediately comply with our demands, we are not to leave your presence until our friend here has delivered his speech to you a second time."[4] The pope laughed and ordered that the wishes of the Perugians be fulfilled.

Whatever the tale's accuracy, the story suggests that elaborate opening orations were common by 1450 at the latest. The Perugian diplomat expected to deliver a long speech when he entered the pope's presence and the pope hoped to avoid this formality because of his illness. The story also indicates that diplomats walked a fine line with their orations. In this story, the Perugian speaker was unable to see that the pope's sickness changed the terms of the ritual of reception. Poggio did not criticize the man for delivering a long oration; Poggio was critical that the orator delivered it when the pope was sick. The implication is that a diplomat in such a situation should have asked the pope for a later meeting after the illness had subsided for the offering of the cultural gift. Only a witty remark saved the diplomats from their colleague's carelessness and the impending wrath of the pope.[5] In short, diplomats needed rhetorical skill to offer cultural gifts, but they also needed the astuteness to mold their gifts to specific circumstances.

By the time Poggio was writing his anecdote, a cultural gift to major political rulers and occasionally some minor ones required a humanist oration. In fact, by the 1420s social humanists and their humanist rhetoric had infiltrated diplomatic oratory. By 1455 the ubiquity of humanist orations began to increase the status of individuals who could deliver, not just a fine humanist oration, but an exceptional one. The learning of these men began to overshadow their other social deficiencies. The test case of diplomacy, thus, adds a diachronic element to the major arguments offered in this book. The humanist movement was vast by at least the latter 1420s. Most humanists were readers rather than writers so that they could focus on preparing themselves for public and private oratorical performances in social, religious, or political rituals. Some Florentines had a real chance of using their learning in practice; some of them only dreamed of the chance: Their social status and the demands of the specific ritual determined their success. Diplomacy suggests that, as more people pursued humanist letters, the prestige attached to a learned reputation increased and fundamentally altered the way people could increase their social and political status in Renaissance Florence. To make these changes, humanism first had to dominate ritualized performances, a story told in this chapter.

Ronald Witt has observed the limited inroads of humanism in oratory in the latter half of the fourteenth century. Witt argued that three Florentine rhetoricians – Cino Rinuccini, Luigi di Teri di Nello Gianfigliazzi, and Lapo da Castiglionchio – were instrumental in changing styles of oratory in that period. The evidence for the influence of these men on diplomatic oratory is varied. Witt argued that "the speeches of [Cino] Rinuccini himself probably come closest to representing the best of humanist efforts at composing speeches in Florence in the late fourteenth century."[6] Moreover, Witt convincingly demonstrated that Rinuccini focused on classical elements in his pedagogical orations; however, Rinuccini has left no evidence that he ever served as a diplomat. The evidence for Luigi Gianfigliazzi's influence on diplomatic oratory is inconclusive. Witt argued that Gianfigliazzi, who was frequently employed as a diplomat, wrote a summary of Cicero's *On Invention* and Pseudo-Cicero's *Rhetoric for Herennius*. However, as Witt pointed out, Gianfigliazzi has not left any examples of his oratory for historians to analyze. The fact that Gianfigliazzi's scholarship on Cicero lacks novel elements may suggest that he continued to prefer traditional oratorical forms.[7]

By contrast, the three surviving diplomatic orations by Petrarch's friend Lapo da Castiglionchio to the pope in Avignon in 1366 suggest that Lapo had begun to implement humanist rhetoric into diplomatic oratory. Witt argued that certain aspects of these orations fit into the medieval *ars dictaminis* tradition. In particular, he pointed to Lapo's use of abstract nouns and set phrases as evidence of the continuation of tradition in Lapo's oratory. However, Witt also pointed out that the orations made the first use of ekphrasis since antiquity. They also, according to Witt, did not display an overt concern for *cursus* (the prose meter underlying the *ars dictaminis* tradition).[8] Moreover, Lapo was well aware of classical standards for oratorical structure and scattered references to classical history, biblical history, and Roman topography throughout his orations.[9]

The oratory and learned connections of men such as Filippo Corsini, Filippo Magalotti, Lorenzo Ridolfi, and Rinaldo Gianfigliazzi suggest that at least a handful of Florentine patricians were continuing Lapo's innovations by the late 1390s and early 1400s. The evidence for the role of Corsini and Gianfigliazzi is found in their extensive diplomatic careers and surviving summaries of their domestic oratory. Gene Brucker has described the integration of humanism into the domestic orations of these two men: "Citizens who met in the *pratiche* became accustomed to speeches larded with quotations from classical authors, or references to Roman history."[10] According to Brucker, it was not only patricians like Agnolo Pandolfini or Roberto Rossi who used this style of oratory. In fact, "the lawyer Filippo Corsini and the knight Rinaldo Gianfigliazzi were its most active promoters."[11] Corsini favored Livy and cited Sallust, whereas Gianfigliazzi used evidence from Seneca to prove his points. Brucker likewise related how Lorenzo Ridolfi incorporated classical history into his domestic oratory. Ridolfi attempted to warn the Florentines that "Rome was the greatest power in the world and then declined almost to nothing on account of her quarrels, and we are not greater than the Romans once were."[12]

Although examples of diplomatic oratory are scanty for these men, Corsini, Gianfigliazzi, and Ridolfi all had ample opportunities to give humanist-styled orations. Between 1394 and 1415, Rinaldo Gianfigliazzi went on fourteen diplomatic embassies, including missions to the pope, emperor, and Florence's key ally during many of these years, Bologna.[13] Filippo Corsini's mission total was sixteen, to rulers including the pope, the emperor, and the king of France.[14] Between 1395 and 1436, Lorenzo Ridolfi was a diplomat twenty-seven times.[15] Moreover, he has left a Latin oration delivered before the pope in 1392 that reflects Ciceronian influences in addition to a manuscript with letters to Coluccio Salutati and other works on rhetoric.[16] A fourth member of this group, Filippo Magalotti, has also left evidence of his integration of humanism in his long diplomatic career. Magalotti was a diplomat twenty-one times between 1396 and 1408.[17] Although Brucker did not mention Magalotti's name among those individuals who sprinkled their domestic oratory with classical allusions, Magalotti has left historians a diplomatic oration that provides evidence of his humanist learning.

In 1408, the social humanist Filippo Magalotti delivered an oration to King Ladislaus of Naples, the recent conqueror of Rome.[18] Magalotti's commission dealt primarily with reasons to reject an offer of an alliance with the king. Magalotti devoted most of his oration to laying the foundation for this argument. Thus, the speech contained a strong, albeit implied, political component. Magalotti argued that Ladislaus should abandon his plans to expand his sphere of influence by devouring the papal state. Magalotti presented the long tradition of Ladislaus's ancestors of protecting the papacy as evidence. He also argued for the close ties between Florence and the king, a point made by stressing the common Guelf orientation of both powers. Magalotti stressed the bonds between Florence and the House of Anjou, of which King Ladislaus was a member. After establishing these long and close relations, Magalotti began his conclusion by restating the response of the Florentine Signoria to the ambassadors sent by the king: The Florentine ancestors and the progenitors of the king had never been in a league and the Florentines did not see a reason to break this tradition. Magalotti's oration thus subtly introduced Florence's political position and key arguments, even as it served as a cultural gift designed to flatter the powerful conqueror of Rome.[19]

Magalotti's oration served a ceremonial role as a cultural gift. As shown in Chapter 4, his colleague Jacopo Salviati, in fact, went so far as to claim the speech lacked "substantive things." The first half of Magalotti's oration patched together short Italian phrases with long Latin quotations.

Magalotti referred to biblical, classical, and humanist sources, including Boccaccio, Vergil, Jeremiah, Cicero (twice), Seneca, Petrarch, Samuel, Daniel, Dante, Jerome, Job, Peter, Aristotle, Deuteronomy, Psalms (four times) and Didymus of Alexandria. Biblical authors in this list are clearly the most abundant; however, these biblical quotations are often shorter than Magalotti's secular references.[20] Moreover, Magalotti incorporated his classical and humanist citations into the most noticeable parts of the oration. In the exordium, he jammed quotations from Boccaccio's *On Famous Women* and citations from Vergil, Cicero, a quote from Seneca about Cicero, Petrarch, and again Cicero.[21] Similarly, Magalotti concluded his oration with a quotation from "Didymus of Alexandria" about the art of rhetoric; this citation (four lines) actually takes up more space in Magalotti's conclusion than the orator's good wishes and hopes for the king's long reign (three lines).[22]

Magalotti juxtaposed learned citations with statements bemoaning his lack of oratorical abilities in order to disprove his feigned modesty and emphasize his rhetorical skill. He began his oration by making his audience aware that he knew of the importance of rhetoric in his oratorical presentation. "My heart is scared and trembles, thinking on the glorious ancestors of your serenity, knowing of the little talent, less ability and even less practice [that I possess in the art of speaking]. [These things occur] to such an extent that those members that nourish, rule, and perform [all] fall back to the heart's aid, as to their source, abandoning the tongue to the activity of speaking."[23] Magalotti immediately attempted to disprove these assertions by displaying his learning with quotations from Isaiah and Boccaccio.[24] After several more quotations designed to praise various aspects of the king, Magalotti returned to self-deprecation, this time stating that his small reputation makes it "frightening" to speak before the king and "so many notable barons, princes, and gentlemen."[25] Once again, Magalotti distilled his own argument by citing a learned source, this time Petrarch.[26] Magalotti drew attention to his lack of rhetorical abilities again soon after, evoking "divine aid" to "give a correct speech to me" and begging the king to forgive "the imperfection of my speech," a statement that he follows with a quote from First Samuel.[27] Magalotti concluded the oration with more self-deprecation, stating that he was well aware that his oration fell far short of meeting the importance of the material or the "dignity" of its authors.[28] He followed this statement with a quotation from Didymus of Alexandria.[29]

The style of the oration further demonstrates Magalotti's rhetorical care in preparing it. Magalotti used long sentences and rearranged his words for better rhetorical effect. The oration, for example, begins with the gerund *"chonsiderando."*[30] The following example has been left in Italian to highlight Magalotti's word order and overflowing use of subordinate clauses. Conjunctions and finite verbs have been underlined.

Avendo a parlare nel chospetto della gloriosa eccelsitudine e della mirabile profondita dintellecto della vostra serenita e chosi mangnificha esistenza di tanti notabili baroni principi esingnori dove per la excelentia della molte chose mangnifichamente trattate e per la profonda aquita dingengnio etiandio quantunque ongni adorno dire e di pocha reputatione veramente ispaventato e attonito piu mimaravilglio cheio nonmi confido di parlare.[31]

This run-on sentence with its multiple conjunctions and delayed placement of finite verbs conformed to the long sentences and word arrangement of Ciceronian prose, which also favored long sentences, subordinate clauses, and a flexible word order. Magalotti was offering a cultural gift through a classicized vernacular speech.

While Magalotti and company began citing more classical sources and structuring their orations along classical precepts, the majority of Florence's top diplomats between 1405 and 1425 probably rejected their innovations. During these two decades, eleven individuals participated in ten or more diplomatic missions. Direct evidence or the learned connections that would suggest the ability to use humanist rhetoric in diplomatic oratory were lacking in six of these diplomats: Bartolomeo Popoleschi, Jacopo Gianfigliazzi, Vieri Guadagni, Jacopo Salviati, Cristofano Spini, and Marsilio Vecchietti. Four of the five men with learned connections have already been discussed in this study: Rinaldo degli Albizzi, Niccolò da Uzzano, Matteo Castellani, and Lorenzo Ridolfi. Gino Capponi, the final member of this core diplomatic group between 1405 and 1425, also was involved in the humanist movement. Gino enjoyed a significant bump in status after the conquest of Pisa in 1406. He was a member of the Dieci di Balìa that oversaw the final brutal months of this war. The Florentines burned the countryside around Pisa, prevented the importation of food, and killed anyone caught attempting to take grain into the city. On October 9, 1406, Gino along with Bartolomeo Corbinelli rode into the formerly great city and provided some food to the surviving Pisans.[32] In addition to being a powerful patrician, Gino Capponi penned a history of the revolt of the Ciompi. In the work, Gino interspersed traditional chronicle elements like lists of Florentine Priors with more classical elements such as orations. He also emulated the Roman historian Sallust by focusing on a specific, defined event.[33]

Yet, even those figures with learned connections seem to have had limited interests in the new learning. Classical quotations and overt stylistic influences are few in the voluminous collection of letters written to and from Rinaldo degli Albizzi during his diplomatic career.[34] Gino Capponi's history writing is in Italian and contains many of the traditional aspects of the old chronicle tradition.[35] The surviving political verses of Niccolò da Uzzano likewise fit into late medieval Florentine traditions.[36] Even the man with the strongest learned connections in this group – Lorenzo Ridolfi – possessed a questionable degree of interest in the new learning. In his biography of Ridolfi, Vespasiano da Bisticci portrayed him as a deeply religious man, a "profound scholar in sacred learning," and a collector of the letters of St. Jerome, rather than a man learned in ancient Greek and Roman letters.[37] Ridolfi referred to classical Roman authors in his *Treatise on Usury;* however, his reliance on scholastic sources in the treatise eclipsed these few classical references.[38] The economic hardship and long familial history of the Castellani family made a perfect match for the rich and ambitious parvenu Leonardo Bruni – although shared learned connections between Bruni and Matteo Castellani certainly helped. In fact, the marginal learned connections of these five men – with the possible exceptions of Lorenzo Ridolfi and Matteo Castellani – made them most similar to a man like Buonaccorso Pitti – who frequently undertook diplomatic missions at the turn of the fifteenth century and was at the fringes of the humanist movement – than to Pitti's friend the literary humanist Coluccio Salutati.[39]

Other specific factors, in fact, better explain the diplomatic prominence of these men during these years. The political reputation of several of these men undoubtedly was both a precursor and a product of their diplomatic careers. Niccolò da Uzzano and then Rinaldo degli Albizzi were leading men of the Florentine state during the first third of the Quattrocento.[40] Cristofano Spini's political prominence earned him a state funeral in 1414.[41] Jacopo di Giovanni Gianfigliazzi served on the Signoria seventeen times between 1394 and 1434.[42] Matteo Castellani was likewise a leading member of the Florentine government.[43] Vieri Guadagni seems to have cultivated ties with foreign leaders. In 1406, a Sienese ambassador mentioned him as a man with whom he had conversed in Florence.[44] Later, Bartolomeo Cossa formerly Pope John XXIII, named Guadagni along with three other powerful Florentines (Bartolomeo Valori, Niccolò da Uzzano, and Giovanni di Bicci de' Medici) as executors of his will.[45]

Factors in addition to learning explain the presence of the other men in this group as well. While certainly a powerful man in politics, Lorenzo

Ridolfi was especially suited for diplomatic concerns related to the church. The commission behind Filippo Magalotti's oration in 1408, in fact, singled out Lorenzo Ridolfi to handle such affairs.[46] Legal factors were the most significant qualities for Bartolomeo Popoleschi. Popoleschi was one of the city's most distinguished lawyers in the early fifteenth century, a man who was especially well suited for political negotiations.[47] Several of the rest of the men in this core group were repeatedly selected for commissarial posts and/or diplomatic posts near war zones. Gino Capponi's notes on the conquest of Pisa (the focus of at least four of his diplomatic/commissarial missions) formed the basis of both Neri di Gino Capponi's Italian and Matteo Palmieri's Latin histories of these events.[48] Jacopo Salviati was a member of one of the core families in Florence and specialized in military matters.[49] Six of Marsilio Vecchietti's ten missions were commissioned by the Dieci di Balìa, a government body usually concerned with war.[50]

Other evidence suggests that the integration of humanist forms and content into diplomatic oratory was incomplete before the mid-1420s. Each of the six men Florence sent on its congratulatory mission to Martin V in 1418 had only limited connections with humanism and more compelling reasons than his learning to be present on the mission. Rinaldo degli Albizzi and Bartolomeo Valori were two of Florence's most powerful citizens. In this role, Albizzi took the lead in speaking to the pope on behalf of the diplomats.[51] Valori referred to ancient Rome a single time in an otherwise traditional vernacular oration delivered in Florence in the 1410s.[52] He was asked to remain after Albizzi left, presumably to fill the same role as Albizzi had.[53] Although this mission was Ridolfo Peruzzi's first, Machiavelli described him as one of the leading figures of the anti-Medicean party.[54] Peruzzi's learned connections were limited to a role in Francesco Filelfo's *Florentine Commentaries on Exile* and business dealings with Carlo Marsuppini and Niccolò Niccoli.[55] Marcello Strozzi's expertise at matters of the church best explains his presence on this mission.[56] Likewise, Lorenzo Ridolfi probably was present explicitly to deal with church matters, as Rinaldo degli Albizzi recorded that Ridolfi spoke for the ambassadors to the pope about the future council and the pope's plans to go to Florence.[57] The fact that the Florentine government asked Marcello Strozzi to remain after Ridolfi had left suggests their similar role on the mission.[58]

The sixth member of the mission, Leonardo di Stagio Dati, was assigned to head it and single-handedly offers evidence for the mixture of weak learned connections alongside strong political reasons in Florentine core diplomats before the mid-1420s. Dati is today most famous for being one of the individuals who presided over the trial of John Hus at the Council of Constance, for commissioning his tomb marker in Santa Maria Novella from Lorenzo Ghiberti, and for being the brother of the now-famous Florentine diarist Gregorio Dati.[59] On the one hand, strong evidence points to Dati's religious and diplomatic prominence as the key factors behind his selection. Leonardo Dati was a Dominican friar like Martin V, a similarity that the Florentines seem to have valued in its initial missions to that pope. For example, two and a half months after Martin V's election the Florentines initially sent a Dominican friar, Jacopo da Rieti, to congratulate him on his election as pope at the Council of Constance.[60] Moreover, Dati had the experience and confidence of both Martin V and the Florentines from at least 1418. In fact, Dati had been Florence's diplomat to the Council of Constance.[61] The instructions to Dati and his colleagues for the mission in 1418 state that it was Leonardo Dati himself, serving as Pope Martin V's ambassador, who had informed Florence of Martin's accession.[62] In later years, Leonardo Dati maintained a strong professional relationship with Martin V, even serving as a spokesman for the pope at the Council of Pavia/Siena in 1423/24.[63]

On the other hand, Dati's learning extended beyond his doctorate in theology to include humanist interests. For example, his treatise on the decadence of the Dominicans, in the words of one historian, demonstrates "great rhetorical knowledge."[64] Dati delivered countless sermons at the Councils of Pisa and Constance and undoubtedly the Council of Pavia/Siena.[65] He may have written a learned work, *The World*, on geography and astronomy.[66] Moreover, Dati was charged with delivering the ambassadors' initial oration on the mission in 1418. Dati's oration to Martin V does not survive; however, Filippo Rinuccini testified to its success:

We found the said Pope Martin at Milan, and there the first visitation was made and it lasted around one hour. Never before had a similar oration been heard. There were perhaps a hundred inkwells to write the oration while he was saying it. He made the greatest honor for himself and for Florence.[67]

Rinuccini's testimony is especially valuable because he was a youth accompanying the mission and thus most likely an eyewitness.[68]

Although Dati's oration to Martin V is lost, sermons that Dati delivered at the Council of Constance suggest that his oratorical style combined traditional and humanist oratorical concerns. In these sermons, Dati attempted to play with his word order.[69] However, Dati rarely mentioned classical sources. He made a reference to the early church father

Maximus.[70] He made a vague statement citing "the old canons."[71] In one sermon, Dati referred to two ancient Greeks, Anacharsis and Socrates, and cited Seneca twice.[72] Such citations indicate Dati's awareness of the power that such authorities could give his oratory. However, all four of these references probably arose secondhand from the popular *Bundle of Flowers* (*Manipulus Florum*), a medieval collection of sayings.[73] Moreover, Dati's references to scholastic works were much more prolific in his sermons.[74] Other council participants at Constance were more overtly referring to humanist sources. For example, an anonymous oration cited Petrarch and the Roman architect Vitruvius.[75] Taken together, this evidence suggests that Dati was a learned theologian who dabbled in humanism rather than being one of the core members of the humanist movement.

An anonymous Florentine oration delivered before Pope Martin V from the 1410s also suggests the preliminary nature of humanist infiltration into Florentine diplomatic oratory between 1405 and 1425. The oration has two major parts. The first part states how the new pope will drive out the church's past problems; the second focuses on Pope Martin's election. This content suggests the date of the late 1410s.[76] The orator stresses on more than one occasion that Martin is the only pope – not surprising, given the recent problems of the Great Schism. The orator uses these two sections to express his two major ideas: the orator's joy and hope at the pope's election and his pledge of servitude to the one true pope. The orator concludes with a recommendation of himself and his colleagues to the pope. This content was far from the praise of deeds, attributes, and virtues recommended for a classical panegyric. The oration also lacks a strong classical organization. Instead, the orator states the situation (here the joy at the election of the pope) and follows it with the purpose of the mission (here to offer the orator's "*servitutem*"). The oration does not include a clear conclusion.

Yet, the oration does contain numerous examples of the influence of classical rhetoric on diplomatic oratory. It lacks explicit quotations from classical authors, but it may begin with a veiled allusion to Cicero's *Letters to Friends*. The anonymous oration began, "*Posteaquam te, pater sanctissime, in pontificatum apostolice sedis dei aspiratu electum audivimus, tanta sumus affecti letitia, ut illam disserere nunquam posse despiciemus.*" Cicero's letter began with an identical use of vocabulary, "*Maxime sum laetitia affectus, cum audivi consulem te factum esse.*"[77] This excerpt from this anonymous oration also reflects its complicated arrangement of words, with the finite verb "*audivimus*" appearing long after its accusative pronoun "*te*" and the construction of the "*tanta . . . letitia*" clause, a clause that begins and ends with alliterative "t" sounds. The following sentence provides examples of several other rhetorical moves made by the speaker: *"qualem profecto desiderabat et qualem egebat ecclesia pastorem habet, et Columna comperta est qua ad ipsam erigendam constituendam atque firmandam melior nulla desideretur et expectetur."*[78] In this sentence, the orator has jammed alliteration (*"Columna comperta"*), anaphora (*"qualem ... qualem ..."*), assonance (both *"erigendam constituendam atque firmandam"* and *"desideretur et expectetur"*), and prolepsis (*"qualem ... desiderabat,"* *"qualem egebat,"* and *"pastorem habet"*). The orator also achieves a nice aural effect through his clause balancing. Such attention to rhetorical detail points to an individual well versed in classical rhetoric as its author. As a whole, this oration demonstrated a strong humanist influence, yet also suggests that more innovations were yet to come.

The presence of social and two literary humanists among Florentine diplomats up to 1425 similarly suggests that humanist oratory was just beginning to infiltrate diplomatic ranks in the first quarter of the fifteenth century. Both the literary humanists Cosimo de' Medici and Palla di Nofri Strozzi began their respective diplomatic careers prior to 1425.[79] Social humanists were more numerous. Matteo Strozzi was a diplomat once during these years.[80] Nicola de' Medici was a diplomat twice in the 1410s and early 1420s (1412 and 1422).[81] A young Agnolo Acciaiuoli was a diplomat to Naples in 1415, a precursor to his glorious future diplomatic career.[82] Piero di Luigi Guicciardini was a diplomat four times.[83] Leonardo Dati was a diplomat several times during the 1410s.[84] Luca di Maso degli Albizzi started his long diplomatic career in 1416 and served several times by 1425.[85] Giuliano Davanzati likewise rose to prominence as a diplomat by the mid-1420s.[86] The book owner Niccolò Nobili was a diplomat four times.[87] Palla Novello Strozzi also began his diplomatic career during these years.[88] Agnolo Pandolfini was frequently employed in Florentine diplomacy starting in 1403.[89] Buonaccorso Pitti went on seven diplomatic or commissarial missions by the end of the first quarter of the Quattrocento.[90]

At least six other social humanists can be added to these individuals. Felice Brancacci was the stepfather of the famous humanist Donato Acciaiuoli. He also oversaw the painting of the Brancacci chapel by Massaccio and had some interaction with Biondo Flavio in Rome.[91] Brancacci was a diplomat five times in these years, usually to minor Italian powers, but also once to Cairo on the inaugural voyage of the Florentine fleet of galleys from Livorno.[92] Salamone Strozzi declared bankruptcy along with several other Florentine patricians in late 1425.[93] His financial destitution, however, did not prevent him from serving as captain of the first fleet of galleys to sail from Florence to England around the same time, May 1425–February 1426.[94] Salamone also possessed a reputation for giving long domestic orations and served as a Florentine diplomat five times between 1406 and 1422.[95] The lawyer Piero Beccanugi was a diplomat and studied history. According to Gene Brucker, Beccanugi was the first Florentine patrician in a *pratica* to advise that "to administer public affairs intelligently, it is essential to look to the past [for guidance] to provide for the present and the future."[96] While a diplomat in Venice in 1431/2, Beccanugi also served as an intermediary for the Florentine Opera del Duomo to inquire about the artistic skill of Paolo Uccello.[97] Beccanugi was a diplomat twice during these years.[98] Francesco Soderini the elder, not to be confused with the cardinal active in the end of the fifteenth century, has left at least two elegant letters in Latin.[99] He appeared as an interlocutor in Francesco Filelfo's treatise on exile.[100] Soderini was a diplomat once in these years, particularly a mission to Toscanella in early 1419.[101] Galeotto Ricasoli was a diplomat a single time and the recipient of Leonardo Bruni's *Introduction to Moral Philosophy*.[102] The other individual, Lorenzo Benvenuti, was one of the rare social humanists who wrote an original Latin treatise as, in the early 1420s, Benvenuti penned a political treatise that lambasted Niccolò Niccoli.[103] Benvenuti also was a diplomat on three occasions.[104]

Undoubtedly, future research will yield additional learned connections among some of the other hundreds of men who filled the at least 693 diplomatic and commissarial positions appointed by Florence between 1405 and 1425. At present, a man with learned connections has been identified in 194 of these positions, or 28 percent. Additionally, the core Florentine diplomats from these early decades generally possessed only weak connections to the humanist movement while more learned social and literary humanists were rarely diplomats before 1425. The low number of social and literary humanists serving as diplomats and the general weakness of their learned connections sharply contrast with the results of the same inquiries into the men serving as Florentine diplomats between 1426 and 1435. By 1435, Florentine humanists filled twice as many of the total diplomatic positions, almost half, and these men were usually more involved in the humanist movement than their predecessors from the first quarter of the century.

That humanist oratory began to infiltrate diplomatic ritual by the latter fourteenth century and had a frequent presence in diplomacy by the latter 1420s supports the arguments of Ronald Witt about the spread of

humanism in Italy in the early 1400s. Like all gifts, humanist oratory
required a receptive audience to serve its donative purpose. Ronald Witt
has demonstrated that only in the 1420s had the humanist movement
infiltrated all the major political centers of Italy, by far the most common
destinations of Florentine diplomats. Witt's case study of the wandering
Augustinian friar Andrea Biglia in particular provides evidence that by the
late 1410s and 1420s, humanism had established a foothold in the Italian
diplomatic scene in general. Biglia spent periods of his life at Padua,
Florence, Bologna, Milan, Perugia, and Siena. Between 1423 and 1428
his oratorical reputation enticed the Milanese to request that he return to
his home city of Milan and deliver a humanist-styled funeral oration for
Giangaleazzo Visconti.[105] Even in a city without a strong domestic tradition of humanist-styled oratory, a value was placed on this type of rhetorical performance by the early 1420s.[106] By the latter 1420s at the latest,
therefore, Florentine diplomats bearing a humanist cultural gift could
expect a warm reception in Italian courts and government palaces.

By the mid-1420s and early 1430s the learned interests of Florence's
diplomats suggest that humanist oratory was common in opening diplomatic rituals. Between 1426 and 1435, 182 diplomatic and commissarial
positions have been identified. Thirteen individuals went on four or more
missions during this period. Eleven of these men participated in the humanist movement. Palla di Nofri Strozzi was the only literary humanist in the
group, but the strong social humanist Agnolo Pandolfini was also frequently engaged in diplomacy during this decade.[107] Men with more of a
middling interest in humanism were also a part of this group. Some of these
figures have already been encountered in this study, particularly
Alessandro Alessandri, Luca degli Albizzi, Rinaldo degli Albizzi, Felice
Brancacci, Piero di Luigi Guicciardini, Ridolfo Peruzzi, Francesco Soderini
the elder, and Marcello Strozzi.[108] One of the additional three men among
Florence's most prominent diplomats across these ten years also has left
evidence for his humanist interests. Neri di Gino Capponi inherited his
learned interests from his father. Neri delivered celebrated diplomatic
orations (none of which survive) and wrote a "humanist commentary,"
in the words of Eric Cochrane.[109] Capponi was also dedicated a history by
Matteo Palmieri.[110] Capponi's tomb – by Bernardo Rossellino – features
two classical putti holding his sculpted likeness, which may itself have been
inspired by Roman coins.[111] The only individuals with diplomatic activity
at this level during these years who have yet to be linked with humanist
learning were the powerful patrician Bernardo Guadagni and Astore
Gianni, a man who served alongside Rinaldo degli Albizzi in the disastrous

war against Lucca in the 1430. Machiavelli claimed that Astore rejected a proposal of submission from the people of Seravezza, a town north of Pisa near the coast. Instead, Astore pretended to accept their surrender, rounded up the men of the community in churches, and then ordered his soldiers to rape and plunder the town and countryside.[112]

Although varied, the learned connections of this group of prominent Florentine diplomats were stronger than those of the group of the most prominent diplomats between 1405 and 1425. For example, 84.6 percent of the individuals (eleven of thirteen) in this group were involved in the humanist movement, versus 45.4 percent (five of eleven) from the first quarter of the century. The learned interests, moreover, of Palla di Nofri Strozzi and Agnolo Pandolfini dwarfed those of men like Niccolò da Uzzano or Gino Capponi. Moreover, numerous other individuals with learned connections served as diplomats between one and three times between 1426 and 1435. These individuals included the literary humanists Leonardo Bruni, Cosimo de' Medici, and his brother Lorenzo, as well as the important social humanist Matteo Strozzi.[113] Diplomatic ranks also included other social humanists discussed earlier in this study, such as Piero Beccanugi, Matteo Castellani, Giuliano Davanzati, Biagio Guasconi, Zenobi Guasconi, Raimondo Mannelli, Lorenzo Ridolfi, Lorenzo di Palla Strozzi, and Palla Novello Strozzi, as well as additional figures.[114] For example, Francesco Alberti was a diplomat and participated in learned discussions with Leon Battista Alberti and Leonardo Dati, as well as Rossello Rosselli, Mariotto Davanzati, Anselmo Calderoni, and Giovanni Acquettini da Prato at the popular vernacular performances at San Martino.[115] Paolo Fortini was a diplomat and sired learned children, in addition to his position as Florentine chancellor between 1411 and 1427.[116] Nello Martini was a learned lawyer who suggested his knowledge of humanist rhetorical forms in a surviving diplomatic oration from 1425.[117] The learned connections of additional diplomats during these years will undoubtedly come to light in future studies; yet, even the present state of knowledge indicates that social or literary humanists occupied 103 of 181 (56.9 percent) missions between 1426 and 1435, roughly double the figures from the previous two decades.[118]

The personnel of Florence's obedience mission to Pope Eugenius IV in 1431 provide a final piece of evidence for the strong presence of humanism in diplomacy by the latter 1420s. All six of these individuals have left evidence of humanist interests and have already been introduced in this study: Palla di Nofri Strozzi, Giuliano Davanzati, Lorenzo di Giovanni de' Medici, Lorenzo Ridolfi, Ridolfo Peruzzi, and Zenobi Guasconi.[119]

Certainly, all of these men possessed political power and familial antiquity and these traits remained key factors underlying their diplomatic selection. Nevertheless, the strength of the connections formed by key Florentine diplomats to the humanist movement had greatly increased over the thirteen years since the obedience mission to Martin V.

This spread of humanism coincided with the growing consolidation of the Italian peninsula into a handful of major powers and this political consolidation increased the pressure on Florentine diplomats to offer high-quality cultural gifts. The fifteenth century was a time of increasing consolidation of territory from the hundreds of small Italian communes of the thirteenth and fourteenth centuries into far fewer territorial entities dominated by five major players. Through war and peaceful means, powerful political centers gobbled up minor powers on a rapid scale during the fourteenth and early fifteenth centuries. The expansion and greater centralization of territorial states like Florence, Venice, and Milan led to a decline in the number of diplomatic missions sent by Florence overall in the first half of the fifteenth century. This decline particularly affected the number of diplomats sent to minor Italian powers. Small Tuscan towns and minor Italian powers like Lucca witnessed the most significant decreases in the number of diplomatic missions to them from Florence.[120] According to the database of Florentine diplomats and their missions constructed for this project, missions to the minor Italian power Lucca declined steeply and did not recover after 1410, whereas missions to Venice gradually increased. Florence sent twenty-seven diplomatic missions to Lucca between 1400 and 1409, two missions between 1410 and 1419, six missions in the 1420s, two in the 1430s, and five in the 1440s. By contrast, Florence sent three missions to Venice between 1400 and 1409, seven between 1410 and 1419, twelve in the 1420s, twenty in the 1430s, and twenty-five in the 1440s.

Overall, more of Florence's diplomats went to major powers – missions that would require a strong cultural gift – in the decades leading up to the Peace of Lodi of 1454. Broadening the scope from just Lucca and Venice to contrast missions to major and minor powers more broadly reveals this trend. The pope, Milan, Venice, Naples, France, and the emperor made up the major powers in Florence's diplomatic circle by the mid-fifteenth century. The number of missions to these major powers dropped slightly before increasing again around midcentury. Florence sent sixty-four missions to these powers between 1400 and 1409, fifty-one between 1410 and 1419, forty-nine in the 1420s, fifty-seven in the 1430s, and sixty-one in the 1440s. By contrast, missions to minor powers dropped significantly over the same period. Florentine missions to all other places, including Bologna, Siena, Lucca, Ferrara, Genoa, all commissarial positions, minor Tuscan towns, and a negligible number of missions to major and minor rulers outside Florence's normal diplomatic orbit quickly declined from their peak number of 237 between 1400 and 1409, to 124 between 1410 and 1419, 125 in the 1420s, 104 in the 1430s, and 101 in the 1450s. In short, the number of missions to major powers maintained basically the same levels – in the first decade there were sixty-four missions; in the final decade analyzed there were sixty-one – even as this number made up a greater percentage of the whole. Meanwhile, missions to more minor players were cut more than half, from 237 in the first decade to 101 in the decade 1440–1449. Put another way, whereas between 1400 and 1409 missions to major powers made up about 21 percent of all missions, between 1440 and 1449 this number had almost doubled to 37.7 percent.

These statistics suggest that more and more Florentine diplomats accompanied missions requiring elaborate humanist displays of eloquence. As a vastly superior power, Florence undertook missions to its Tuscan neighbors that placed the onus of the diplomatic gift exchange squarely on the shoulders of these small towns. Florentine diplomats to minor powers gave shorter orations and carried fewer traditional marks of social status. At the beginning of the fifteenth century, when most missions were to minor powers and when humanism was just beginning to infiltrate polit-ical oratory, diplomatic ritual rarely required elaborate cultural gifts. Starting in the early 1400s, Florence's diplomatic missions gradually shifted to the powers that would eventually survive the hardening of the Italian state system in the 1450s and 1460s.[121] Such missions between powers of comparable status required stronger tangible and intangible gifts to effect a successful meeting between states. The decrease in diplo-matic missions in general meant fewer opportunities to leave an impression of the power and/or goodwill of the Florentine state. The diplomatic oration that dominated the ritualistic exchanges governing the entry of a diplomat into a host space made or broke this impression. This process of increased state expansion and centralization mirrored the increased inte-gration of humanism into diplomacy in the years leading up to the Peace of Lodi in 1454. The learned interests of Florentine diplomats sent between 1436 and 1455 suggest that this was the case.

By the latter 1430s, Florence's core diplomatic personnel possessed the ability to speak with humanist eloquence on their diplomatic missions. Between 1436 and 1455, eight of the nine individuals serving as Florentine diplomats ten or more times were connected to the humanist movement.

Many of these figures have already been encountered in this study. The literary humanist Giannozzo Manetti was a key Florentine diplomat during these years, filling at least twelve different diplomatic positions.[122] Manetti's surviving diplomatic orations from these years, in fact, constitute about half of all known surviving examples. Strong social humanists were also frequently sent as diplomats. Agnolo Acciaiuoli served on at least twenty-four missions.[123] Dietisalvi Neroni was a diplomat fourteen times.[124] Luca di Maso degli Albizzi was also a diplomat fourteen times.[125] Luigi Guicciardini served somewhat less, ten times.[126] Neri di Gino Capponi was a diplomat more, eighteen times.[127] To these men already addressed in this book, a new figure, Bernardo Giugni, can be added. Giugni was also a diplomat at this level of frequency.[128] He was buried in a humanist-styled tomb in the Florentine Badia.[129] Vespasiano da Bisticci attested to his good knowledge of Latin letters.[130] Marsilio Ficino sent a letter to him.[131] Much weaker evidence exists for another new figure, Giovannozzo Pitti. Pitti was repeatedly a diplomat during these years.[132] He argued in favor of the *studia humanitatis* in a debate about the Florentine Studio but has not left any other evidence for his humanist interests.[133] The ubiquitous diplomat Bernadetto de' Medici (twenty-four times) was the only man who served as a diplomat at least ten times during these years but who has not left any evidence for his humanist interests.[134] However, even Bernadetto was not totally divorced from Florentine culture as he appears to have been instrumental in drawing Andrea del Castagno to Florence and promoted his career as an artist.[135]

Social humanists also served as diplomats fewer than ten times between 1436 and 1455. Eighteen such individuals have been met earlier in this study: Alessandro Alessandri (nine missions), Piero Beccanugi (three), Donato Cocchi-Donati (seven), Giuliano Davanzati (eight), Piero Guicciardini (seven), Domenico Martelli (five), Cosimo de' Medici (two), Lorenzo di Giovanni de' Medici (six), Piero de' Medici (four), Otto Niccolini (eight), Matteo Palmieri (two), Giannozzo Pandolfini (eight), Piero de' Pazzi (one), Antonio Ridolfi (five), Lorenzo Ridolfi (one), Alamanno Salviati (seven), Marcello Strozzi (three), and Guglielmo Tanagli (six).[136] More diplomats during these two decades can be added to the humanist movement, and the evidence can be briefly summarized for each individual as follows: Giuliano Ridolfi – a diplomat six times – sent information about the Acciaiuoli brothers and Giovanni Argyropoulos to Alamanno Rinuccini.[137] Twice a diplomat, Antonio Pierozzi, the future San Antonino, has left two orations that betray humanist influences.[138] Giovanni di Cosimo de' Medici enjoyed humanist studies, possessed connections with numerous learned men, sought classical books, and was a diplomat three times.[139] Bernardo d' Alamanno de' Medici was a diplomat twice and delivered a sermon to the Compagnia de' Magi that possessed rhetorical flourishes.[140] Vespasiano da Bisticci attested to the learning of Franco Sacchetti, thrice a diplomat, in addition to the learned discussions held at Sacchetti's house discussed previously.[141]

The humanist interests of at least six other diplomats have been identified. Extraordinarily weak were the connections of Andrea de' Pazzi, who commissioned Filippo Brunelleschi to make the beautiful and classical Pazzi Chapel at Santa Croce and who owned the home in which a school textbook of Horace was copied, perhaps for his son Piero de' Pazzi.[142] Andrea de' Pazzi was a diplomat once during these decades.[143] Also weak were the connections of Bernardo Buongirolamo, who hired the learned tutor Piero di Domenico Domizi to teach Bernardo's son Giovanni in 1479. Already an experienced teacher, Domizi moved on from the Buongirolami to work for the city of Florence itself, before he was dismissed in 1486, probably because of his reputation as a pederast.[144] Prior to that date, Domizi often wrote Latin comedies for his pupils to perform publicly at the Church of Ognisanti and at the Palazzo Medici.[145] Niccolò di San Gimignano – diplomat once – copied texts in a humanistic hand and even translated St. Jerome's letters into Italian.[146] Two sons of Coluccio Salutati – Antonio and Leonardo – were each a diplomat during these years.[147] In a chapel designed by Andrea del Castagno, Orlando de' Medici was buried in a classical tomb made by Bernardo Rossellino. Orlando enjoyed an active diplomatic career of at least eight missions during these years.[148] Roberto Martelli – diplomat once during these years – was an intermediary between Cosimo de' Medici and Benozzo Gozzoli while Gozzoli created his famous *Procession of the Magi* for the Palazzo Medici.[149] Martelli was also a prominent patron of Donatello and the brother of the social humanist Domenico Martelli.[150] Other evidence points more explicitly to Martelli's interests in humanist letters: Roberto Martelli participated in a learned debate housed by the English protonotary Andrea Ols and also featuring Giannozzo Manetti, Carlo Marsuppini, and Matteo Palmieri.[151]

Other figures possessed suggestive connections, but the evidence is insufficient to link them conclusively to the humanist movement. One figure, Bertoldo Alberti, was a diplomat a single time during these years and received a recommendation to the governor of Bologna written by Leonardo Bruni himself. However, Bruni undoubtedly acted in an official capacity as chancellor and the recommendation should not in itself connect

Alberti with the famous humanist.[152] After negotiations fell through with his cousin, Lorenzo di Matteo Strozzi married Antonia, daughter of Francesco Baroncelli, in part upon the recommendation of Marco Parenti. No evidence suggests a learned connection between the negotiators of the marriage; rather, lofty social standing and physical appearance underlay the match.[153] Baroncelli was a diplomat once during these years.[154] Also a diplomat once, Nicola Capponi suggested that Benedetto Accolti receive a 150-florin raise in early 1461.[155] Capponi acted as a member of a *pratica* called to discuss the topic and thus there is no reason to assume a special connection between him and Accolti. Lodovico da Verrazzano – diplomat once – paid a notary in 1438 to create a copy of Boccaccio's *Decameron* for him, but whether Verrazzano read more widely or had learned interests beyond Boccaccio's bawdy tales is unknown.[156] Also suggestive but inconclusive is that Angelo della Stufa – a diplomat nine times – was cited as the oral source for a vernacular story written by Marabottino di Tuccio Manetti in the genre of the tales of Bocaccio's *Decameron*.[157] Niccolò Alessandri was a diplomat twice and served with Matteo Strozzi among the men in charge of artistic projects for the cathedral, but there is no further evidence to suggest he shared his brother Alessandro's humanist interests.[158] Alesso Pelli was also a diplomat twice. Pelli worked closely with Cosimo de' Medici, lived in his household, and has left vivid letters describing life in the Palazzo Medici, but there is no evidence that he shared his master's deep interest in humanism.[159] Antonio de' Pazzi associated with Poggio Bracciolini in England in the early fifteenth century, but it is unclear whether the men shared learned interests.[160] Pazzi was a diplomat once in 1448.[161] A Puccio Pucci received a letter from Bartolomeo Fonzio regarding the conspiracy of 1466 and its aftermath, but it was a different Puccio Pucci who was a diplomat at least twice in these years.[162] Future research may link these and other men active during this period to the humanist movement; nevertheless, even the present state of knowledge demonstrates the continued dominance of individuals with learned connections.[163] Altogether, individuals with humanist interests made up eight out of the nine people serving as a diplomat ten or more times between 1436 and 1455 (89 percent), twenty-one of twenty-eight of the people serving five or more times (75 percent) and filled 240 of 420 diplomatic positions (57.1 percent).

The personnel of the Florentine obedience mission in 1447 also point to the strong presence of humanism in Florentine diplomacy by midcentury. The Florentine mission to congratulate Pope Nicholas V in 1447 featured six individuals, all with learned connections: Agnolo Acciaiuoli, Alessandro

Alessandri, Neri Capponi, Giannozzo Manetti, Piero de' Medici, and Giovannozzo Pitti.[164] The man selected to give the obedience speech was Giannozzo Manetti, one of the leading humanists in Florence after the death of Leonardo Bruni. Manetti delivered a successful oration in classical Latin, with a classical structure and full of classical references and citations.[165] The tale of the hours leading up to the oration was included in Chapter 4 of this study, but here an examination of the oration itself can demonstrate the type of diplomatic oratory considered outstanding in the latter 1440s.

Manetti showered the new pope Nicholas V with praise fit for a king and built upon a strong classical, rhetorical foundation. Manetti stuck ostentatiously to a classical structure in his oration, using explicit statements to mark the transition from section to section. For example, he declared that although he wanted the oration to be brief, he had to declare the "division of the parts" for the sake of clarity.[166] Taking a cue from a diplomatic oration by Leonardo Bruni, Manetti drew a comparison between the announcement of the new pope in Florence and the star marking the birth of Christ in the Book of Matthew. Manetti included the standard account of Florentine support for papal causes over the past century and a half, recounting the stories of the Emperor Manfred, Charles of Anjou, and their descendants; however, he added a few twists designed to allude to his exceptional learning. Manetti cited "ancient histories, old annals, and chronicles" as the source for his historical references.[167] The fact that Nello Martini had used the exact same examples in a speech before the pope delivered in 1425 suggests that Manetti may have been exaggerating the range of his reading. Nevertheless, the phrase served to allude to Manetti's knowledge of these types of sources, rather than to footnote his actual research.[168] In another example, Manetti provided a long list of the Emperor Manfred's negative traits, which he concluded by alluding to his Greek learning: "Manfred, as the Greeks more elegantly and concisely call a person hostile to religion and without God, was an atheist."[169] In another display of learning, Manetti favorably compared Nicholas V to the more than 214 of his predecessors (he refrained from listing them all for the sake of time).[170] Just as at the time of the birth of Christ under Augustus or in the time of Numa Pompilius (second king of Rome) there will be peace. The name Nicholas itself, whether addressed from Greek or Latin etymology portends this peace.[171]

Manetti was also careful to introduce the political component of the Florentines' commission subtly in his opening oration. In addition to showing the pope that Florence had never received such good news as the announcement of the pope's election, Manetti and his colleagues were to discuss peace with the pope and the representatives of the king of Naples in subsequent audiences.[172] The instructions for the mission were explicit in its division between the initial cultural gift and the subsequent political negotiations. The commission's author gave long instructions for the first oration before stating, "Includ[e] at the end of your speech that another time when you are again at the feet of his holiness, you will speak of some other things that have been commissioned to you."[173] Manetti followed these instructions closely by ending his speech with a now-familiar statement alluding to later political negotiations.[174] However, he was also careful to hint at the political reasons underlying his mission. He argued that the announcement of the new pope was just like the star that marked the birth of the Prince of Peace. According to Manetti, like the Roman king Numa, the pope will usher in a new era of peace. Through these laudations focused on presenting the new pope as the person to bring peace to Europe, Manetti has previewed the later political particulars. Manetti was thus highlighting the gift-giving function of his oration by ostentatiously separating it from the mission's other concerns and simultaneously raising the political reasons underlying his mission.

Eight years later the obedience mission to the next pope, Pope Callixtus III, in 1455 was no less packed with humanists: Giovanni de' Medici, Otto Niccolini, Giannozzo Pandolfini, Antonio Pierozzi, and Antonio Ridolfi.[175] Not surprisingly, Antonio Pierozzi delivered an oration that was less classical in its content than Manetti's, but no less concerned with achieving rhetorical eloquence along humanist models. The expectation that Pierozzi would offer the new pope a cultural gift was the same as it had been for Manetti. In the words of Pierozzi's commission, his oration had to show the pope that "in our city, not even the oldest memories recall the arrival of news as happy as that of this election, and for this reason, unanimously, all of our city, old, young, and middle-aged, of every status and sex, have taken immeasurable joy and happiness because of it."[176] Pierozzi's oration had to prove to the pope that *this* obedience to *this* pope was more important to Florence than any previous one.

Toward this end, Antonio Pierozzi focused on combining displays of religious and secular learning in his opening oration. Such techniques enabled him to maintain the humanist style of his predecessors while differing from them in his choice of content. Whereas Manetti had given Greek sources a primary place in his oratory, Pierozzi saturated his speech with biblical references to Psalms, Genesis, Kings, Exodus, and Matthew among others.[177] Even Pierozzi's rare references to nonbiblical sources radically differed from Manetti's literary allusions. Rather than Plutarch or Demosthenes, parts of Pierozzi's oration are direct citations from medieval works such as Isidore of Seville's *Etymologies*, Bernard of Clairvaux's *On Consideration (De consideratione)*, and the *Donation of Constantine*.[178] Pierozzi referred four times to a line from Psalm 121, "I rejoice in those things that have been said to me."[179] Rather than a great classical figure, Pierozzi compared the new pope to the biblical figure Solomon.[180]

Pierozzi also used ancient history, a humanist subject, but added a distinct religious interpretation. Pierozzi related the entire history of the papacy as leading up to a great battle between a unified Italy under the pope and Emperor Mehmed, pawn of the Antichrist. After various ancient empires in the east, God had established Rome as the seat of the papacy and the empire. After the fall of Rome, God saved the church from the barbarian invasions. With God and Christ as instigators, Pope Nicholas V had brokered a peace to unite the peninsula. Pierozzi urged the pope to maintain this peace so that all of Italy could embark on a campaign against Mehmed and retake Constantinople.[181] Yet, Pierozzi's use of history turns his request into more than simply a desire for peace among Christians and war with the Turk. Following God's plan, Nicholas V had united Italy. The "Angel of Satan" threatened them.[182] Now, Pierozzi implicitly urged, was the time for Callixtus to begin the last battle between a united Christian front and the forces of the Antichrist.[183] This focus on the divine role of the pope in Armageddon highlighted Pierozzi's particular strengths. Attired in his simple religious garb, Pierozzi used religious content dressed in humanist words to offer a cultural gift.[184]

Even as Pierozzi's oration differed dramatically from Manetti's classical content and blatant classical structure, the saintly archbishop still adhered to a humanist oratorical style. For example, Pierozzi began his oration with the following long sentence, which has been left untranslated for the sake of stylistic analysis.

Beatissime pater & Domine, quia eum qui coram tua loquitur sanctitate commoveri contingit & tremere, tum propter celsitudinem throni tui, quo in humanis nullus est altior, tum propter intelligentiam tuam divino munere auream, utriusque iuris & sacrae sophiae notitia foecundam, nec non propter reverendissimos dominos cardinales, venerandosque antistites & doctores egregios adstantes vatiis scientiis refertos, mirandum non est, si nunc ego (cui nec sententiae suppetunt nec verba) quibus adiri debeat tanta maiestas, palleo & pene voce deficio.[185]

Pierozzi used anaphora by beginning three consecutive clauses with "*propter*." He used alliteration repeatedly with both "c" and "t" (for example,

commoveri contingit et tremere, tum propter celsitudinem throni tui). The
sentence begins with an example of prolepsis, with the accusative pronoun
eum appearing outside the *qui* clause in which it grammatically functions.
The word *quia* appears at the sentence's beginning, but explains the *si*
clause that does not appear until its final words. Such attention to rhetorical style suggests that, just like Manetti, Pierozzi sought to offer an oration
in a classical style.

Pierozzi's rearrangement of words in a direct citation provides further
striking evidence for his interest in creative word arrangements. Bernard of
Clairvaux had written (left in Latin for comparative purposes).

formam justitiae, sanctimoniae speculum, pietatis exemplar, assertorem veritatis,
fidei defensorem, doctorem gentium, Christianorum ducem, amicum Sponsi,
Sponsae paranymphum, cleri ordinatorem, pastorem plebium, magistrum insipientium, refugium oppressorum, pauperum advocatum, miserorum spem, tutorem
pupillorum, judicem viduarum, oculum caecorum, linguam mutorum, baculum
senum, ultorem scelerum, malorum metum, bonorum gloriam, virgam potentium,
malleum tyrannorum, regum patrem, legum moderatorem, canonum dispensatorem, sal terrae, orbis lumen, sacerdotem Altissimi, vicarium Christi, christum
Domini, postremo deum Pharaonis.[186]

Antonio Pierozzi inserted this quotation into his own speech with only
minor changes. For comparative purposes, the sections that differ from
Bernard's have been placed in bold. Passages that Pierozzi omitted have
been placed back into his text in brackets.

normam [sic] **fore** iustitiae, sanctimoniae speculum, pietatis **exemplum, veritatis
assertorem, defensorem fidei**, doctorem gentium, **ducem Christianorum**, amicum
sponsi, sponsae paranymphum, **ordinatorem cleri**, pastorem plebium, magistrum insipientium, **oppressorum refugium, advocatum pauperum, & spem
miserorum**, tutorem pupillorum, iudicem viduarum, oculum **coecorum** [sic],
**linguam mutorum, baculum senum, ultorem scelerum, metum malorum, gloriam
bonorum**, virgam potentium, malleum tyrannorum, **patrem regum moderatorem
legum**, canonum dispensatorem, [sal] **orbis terrae** lumen, [sacerdotem altissimi]
vicarium Christi, Christum Domini, Deum Pharaonis.[187]

To take just one example from Pierozzi's changes, in Bernard's phrase
*sanctimonie speculum pietatis exemplar assertorem veritatis fidei defen-
sorem fidei*, Pierozzi has changed *exemplar* to its synonym *exemplum*, a
change that allows for the removal of an "ar" sound and the continuation
of the "m" sound: *speculum ... exemplum ... assertorem defensorem ...*
and so on. Moreover, flipping *assertorem veritatis* and *fidei defensorem* to
veritatis assertorem and *defensorem fidei* likewise improves aural effect.
Compare the following: In the words from *speculum* to *defensorem*

Bernard's word order creates ending sounds with the following pattern: "um, is, ar, em, is, ei, em." However, Pierozzi's altered word order combined with his replacement of *exemplar* with *exemplum* achieves much greater assonant effect: (the same seven words) "um, is, um, is, em, em, ei."

By the mid-fifteenth century humanist oratory in diplomacy had become a common facet of a large number of diplomatic missions in and outside the Italian peninsula. Social humanists occupied more than half of all diplomatic appointments. The increasing political consolidation of the Italian peninsula meant fewer diplomatic positions overall, but a greater percentage of diplomats went to political centers with rulers expecting a cultural gift. Consequently, Florentine diplomats possessed humanist learning, just as individuals who dreamed of joining these ranks did. Diplomacy provides but one example of a phenomenon that extended, in one form or another, to rituals throughout Italian society and across the social, cultural, political, and religious worlds. The examination of the learned connections of Florentine diplomats suggests that humanism, largely through the efforts of the social humanists, infiltrated the ritual world of Renaissance Florence by the latter 1420s. By that time, Florentines studied the classical world to achieve spoken eloquence, an ephemeral performance lost as soon as the memory of the words faded from the minds of audience members.

Further political and diplomatic changes supplemented the ubiquity of humanist learning to bring about further changes after 1455. The changing political structure in Florence from an oligarchic republic to a principality in all but name under Lorenzo de' Medici caused changes in the key requirements in Florentine diplomats. As in the Milanese Duchy to the north, loyalty to the prince – or in Lorenzo's case, pseudoprince – became a prized quality in diplomats. Loyalty joined familial ancestry as a common trait among Florence's core diplomatic personnel. In a second development, the sheer number of humanists among Florentines and Italians more generally made bestowing an exceptional cultural gift, that is an oration perceived as being of higher quality than those delivered on previous occasions, more difficult than ever before. A typical humanist speech no longer sufficed to flatter rulers because humanist performances were no longer exceptional. Florentine diplomats needed something more. These two factors – the increasingly princely nature of Florence and the ubiquity of humanist learning – combined to open the door for individuals without traditional markers of social status to become prominent Florentine diplomats. Once the door was open, humanist eloquence became important and valuable enough to outweigh even other more traditional markers of social status in diplomatic gift exchanges. The case study of diplomacy reveals this development with some clarity, but there is every reason to suspect that other rituals, other examples, show the same exact rise in prestige attached to extraordinary humanist learning. Ultimately, the learned interests of the humanists – characterized by the cultivation of spoken eloquence through study and reading – changed the way that status was measured in Renaissance Florence.

7

Humanism as a Means to Social Status, 1456–1485

In late 1484 or early 1485 a secretary in the Florentine chancery, Filippo Redditi, transcribed a diplomatic speech into a book intended to record diplomatic commissions and correspondence.[1] Perhaps Redditi himself admired the Latin speech; after all, he was himself an able Latinist, as his surviving letters to Angelo Poliziano, Jacopo Salviati, Lorenzo de' Medici, Braccio Martelli, and Bernardo Rucellai attest.[2] That such a speech had been delivered was not unusual: By early 1485 Florentine diplomats always delivered a Latin oration to new popes. What was striking, how-ever, was the speaker whose words were recorded. Obedience missions to new popes always featured the most outstanding citizens in Florence; the individuals anointed with the task of the initial speech were no different. High-ranking church officials, leaders in the Florentine regime, men who combined deep humanist learning with ancient Florentine familial line-ages: These were the men chosen to speak on each of the seven Florentine obedience missions occurring between Pope Martin V and Pope Sixtus IV. That trend abruptly ended in 1484, when the literary humanist and son of a miller Bartolomeo Scala delivered the opening oration before the new pope, Innocent VIII. In a city that prized traditional marks of social status in its diplomats – ancient political, social, and economic standing – how was Scala's election possible? How could a parvenu not only be selected to speak on behalf of Florence before the new pope, but in fact receive a knighthood for his performance and witness six separate printings of the speech over the next five years?[3]

Scala's election and success embodied the rise in prestige attached to humanist learning and the changes in Florentine political culture over the course of the Quattrocento. Most Florentine diplomats by the 1430s and

1440s – let alone the 1480s – possessed the ability to offer a cultural gift in the form of humanist words. The demands of the cultural gift thus increased: A basic humanist oration was no longer an exceptional per-formance; it was what began all diplomatic missions to powerful states and rulers. In other words, it was the norm, and high-level ceremonial missions required far more than the average costumed words. People who could deliver these coveted performances – the most learned and talented of the literary humanists – were in short supply and thus the prestige attached to their humanist learning increased. Meanwhile, changes in the political culture of Florence also assisted parvenu humanists. Even as the Florentines continued to rely on individuals from the oldest families to fill the city's diplomatic ranks, cracks began to form in this tradition by midcentury. Italian monarchies tended to select their diplomats on the basis of personal loyalty, rather than familial antiquity, and Cosimo de' Medici and especially his grandson Lorenzo began to be seen as princely figures. By the 1480s, Lorenzo de' Medici was acting the part through his control of Florentine civic rituals and increasingly overt manipulation of Florentine offices. These developments enabled Bartolomeo Scala to ascend the social ladder and head the Florentine obedience mission in 1484/85.

By the 1480s Lorenzo the Magnificent was far more than the first among equals in Florence; he had become a quasi-princely figure over the city. Lorenzo was the third Medici to rule Florence in all but name, but his rule was more institutionalized, more overt, and more recognized than that of his father, Piero, or his grandfather, Cosimo. In part this was because Lorenzo was more secure in his position by the 1480s than either of his illustrious ancestors. Cosimo faced regular crises from 1434 until his death thirty years later. It was, after all, only in 1440 that Rinaldo degli Albizzi and his Milanese allies were decisively defeated on the battlefield. The year 1458 brought opposition from within in the form of Girolamo Machiavelli, and the Medici cracked down in response. Cosimo's beloved son Giovanni died young and thus his other son, Piero, rose to power after Cosimo's death in 1464. Key allies of Cosimo who had been content to maneuver in Cosimo's political shadow, men like Dietisalvi Neroni and Agnolo Acciaiuoli, desired sunlight of their own after Piero claimed suc-cession. Piero survived their rebellion, but not for long: By 1468 he was dead and his two sons, Giuliano and Lorenzo, were heads of the Medici family. Despite his wounds and the death of his brother, Lorenzo survived the famous Pazzi Conspiracy in 1478, an event still immortalized in graffiti – written during the fifteenth century itself or only later? – on the wall of the kitchen of the Palazzo Davanzati in Florence. Lorenzo used the event as an opportunity to make further institutional changes to the Florentine government, and these changes placed his regime on a stronger foundation than ever before.[4]

The rule of Lorenzo de' Medici in Florence had taken on monarchial qualities by the 1470s and 1480s and was viewed as such by outside observers. Even during the lifetime of Lorenzo's grandfather, Cosimo de' Medici, other rulers in Italy viewed the family as possessing princely power in Florence. Pius II noted that, after the summer of 1458, state decisions were made and debated at Cosimo's house. Both Pius II and Francesco Sforza made requests of Cosimo as if he were *signore* of Florence, only to be rebuffed by Cosimo's hollow protestation that he was but one man in a republic.[5] This image of Medici princes only grew under Lorenzo the Magnificent. Richard Trexler has argued that Florentine public rituals featured Lorenzo as a princely figure by the 1470s and until his death in 1492. In appearance, Lorenzo dressed as a citizen, but one followed by an armed retinue to distinguish himself from his comrades. Simultaneously, Lorenzo systematically attempted to remove opportunities for other families to gain honor in public settings, focusing rituals increasingly on his own person.[6] These changes extended beyond the political culture of Florence and its view from abroad; they also mirrored changes in the criteria for selecting diplomats.

Fifteenth-century Italian kingdoms used different criteria to pick their diplomats than the Florentines traditionally did. For example, Franca Leverotti has demonstrated that loyalty to Francesco Sforza was the primary characteristic of Milanese diplomats between 1450 and 1466.[7] The pope may also have viewed personal connections, together with ties between an individual and the diplomatic destination, as the key criteria among papal diplomats. In 1408, in fact, the pope selected Leonardo Bruni to serve as a diplomat to Florence; however, the mission never took place.[8] For Florence, Ricardo Fubini has convincingly demonstrated the transition from older marks of status to loyalty to the Medici, especially Lorenzo de' Medici, as the key criterion among Florentine diplomats by the latter half of the fifteenth century.[9] Fubini's arguments are compelling and fit into the broader changes in political culture in Florence, but they should not be overstated. Between 1456 and 1485 these Medici-approved individuals continued to be recruited from the same families.

Just as in previous decades, the most prominent Florentine diplomats between 1456 and 1485 were from the oldest political families in the city. This book has broken Florentine diplomatic positions into four groups –

1405–1425, 1426–1435, 1436–1455, and 1456–1485 – and identified the most prominent diplomats in each group. Of the eleven key diplomats between 1405 and 1425, seven individuals were members of families who entered the Signoria by 1317. Three of the remaining four individuals came from ancient magnate families, the Gianfigliazzi, Popoleschi, and the Vecchietti.[10] The remaining individual was Niccolò da Uzzano, an exception who rose to the heights of the Florentine Republic from an extremely wealthy, small, and new family in the Santo Spirito quarter of the city.[11] Between 1426 and 1435, of the thirteen individuals who went on four or more diplomatic missions, twelve were from families that met the same criteria for political antiquity, while the only remaining individual, Alessandro Alessandri, was from a family that had only recently split from the Albizzi. The next twenty years reveals the same consistent pattern: Nine individuals went on ten or more missions, all nine from lineages tracing their first entry into the Signoria back to 1306 or earlier. In the final group, ranging from 1456 to 1485, eight diplomats served on ten or more missions. Six of them had ancestors in the Signoria by 1302. Of the two remaining individuals Otto Niccolini could boast an ancestor in the Signoria by 1341 in addition to Otto's own prominent legal career.[12] The final individual, the lawyer Bernardo Buongirolamo, was a notable exception to this trend. Bernardo was neither derived from ancient Florentine familial stock (like most key diplomats) nor a factional leader in Florence (like Niccolò da Uzzano). Bernardo owed his success to his legal training and his position as a trusted ally of Lorenzo de' Medici.

Bernardo Buongirolamo embodied the slight but significant opportunities – for the purposes of this chapter particularly diplomatic opportunities – available to select new men in Lorenzo de' Medici's Florence. The Buongirolami emigrated from Gubbio in Umbria, and the first member of the family earned Florentine citizenship the same year as Leonardo Bruni, in 1416. Bernardo Buongirolamo was a diplomat from Florence at least fifteen times, despite also being the first Buongirolamo to enter the Florentine Signoria, in 1467.[13] Only two other individuals obtained premier diplomatic prominence between 1394 and 1484 and, like Bernardo, came from families entering the Signoria for the first time in the Quattrocento. One was Francesco Tornabuoni, a family offshoot of political magnates. The other man, however, was the lawyer Nello Martini, who was descended from a wealthy lineage in San Gimignano.[14] Nello benefited from entering Florentine politics at a time when lawyers from outside the city were more welcome than in later decades.[15] Bernardo became active in legal and political circles decades later than Nello

Martini, although still at a time more amenable to outsiders than in the final decades of the Quattrocento.[16] Both men became prominent diplomats. The least prestigious destination endured by Nello Martini during his diplomatic career between 1415 and 1429 was Genoa, while more commonly he was a diplomat to Milan, Naples, the pope, and the emperor.[17] Bernardo Buongirolamo, by contrast, seems to have risen through the diplomatic ranks. In 1467 he filled a mission explicitly calling for a man of "no great reputation," while years later he filled missions to major powers like Milan and the pope.[18] He must have owed at least part of his success to his own talents and abilities; however, at least one somewhat later Florentine, Francesco Guicciardini, blamed Lorenzo de' Medici for Bernardo's standing.[19] Ultimately, Bernardo Buongirolamo was unusual among Florence's premier diplomatic ranks, but like Nello Martini earlier in the century he used his legal background – supplemented by his relationship with Lorenzo de' Medici – to rise to political prominence.

What was unprecedented was the somewhat earlier diplomatic career of Matteo Palmieri, who was neither a lawyer nor descended from an ancient family. In the latter 1450s and 1460s, Matteo Palmieri was frequently a diplomat, despite the fact that he, in contrast to other fifteenth-century literary humanist diplomats like Cosimo de' Medici, Palla di Nofri Strozzi, Giannozzo Manetti, Alamanno Rinuccini, and Donato Acciaiuoli, had a modest Florentine ancestry. The Palmieri family first joined the Signoria in the early fifteenth century.[20] Moreover, Matteo's contemporaries varied when discussing his background, a difference of opinion that points to Matteo's lack of a solid social foundation. Vespasiano da Bisticci stated that he was "born of relatives of moderate condition, called the founder of his house, and earned nobility through his singular talents."[21] Alamanno Rinuccini in part disagreed, contending that Matteo was "born of good relatives, in fact, he possessed his original origins from certain German princes."[22] Matteo Palmieri's most recent biographer has investigated these and other pieces of evidence to conclude that his ancestors arrived in Florence and became part of the "upper-middle" rung of the Florentine social ladder before settling into the "merchant class."[23] Such was a comfortable enough position, but not the ranks from which the Florentines typically selected their more prominent diplomats. Despite his lack of the traditional marks of status so essential in the selection of Florentine diplomats, Matteo represented the city abroad repeatedly, oftentimes to prestigious destinations like the papal court in Rome. He was able to do this because of his humanist learning – greater than most and thus more rare and more valuable by the 1450s – and his close connections to the Medici family.

The Florentine government sent the parvenu Matteo Palmieri on several diplomatic missions, particularly ones critical to Medici interests. Matteo's position as *accoppiatore*, an office that was essential to the Medici control of Florence, demonstrates his perceived loyalty to the Medici, and his diplomatic career supports this assessment.[24] Matteo's first diplomatic mission occurred in the summer of 1452. Then, probably in response to King Alfonso's declaration of war against Florence, Matteo set off to Perugia to convince the Perugians not to assist King Alfonso.[25] This mission to a minor power called for a man of middling status, but one who could be trusted to toe the Medici line. As a diplomat he was a flop, but as a Medici toady he proved his worth. After his return, Matteo was elected as Standard Bearer of Justice and, not coincidently, during his term of office the Florentines renewed their Medici-based alliance with Milan against Naples and Venice.[26]

Afterward, Matteo Palmieri's missions were frequently to powerful princes on tricky political occasions. In 1455, Matteo was sent to Naples to present the peace accord between Florence and the king, and, along the way, he was to visit the newly elected pope, Callixtus III, in Rome.[27] Certainly, such a charge was a great honor, but this visit to the pope should not be overestimated: The Florentines frequently sent temporary ambassadors of low or middling status to prominent figures to inform them that more prestigious diplomats were on the way. Such had been the case for the election of Pope Martin V in late 1417. Two and a half months after that pope's election the Florentines elected the Dominican friar Jacopo da Rieti to congratulate the new pope as discreetly as possible at Constance.[28] The Florentines ordered Jacopo to meet the pope "in a cautious and secret way" so that "no one else" heard what he said to the pope.[29] Jacopo's commission then ordered him to give a congratulatory oration. The commission contained instructions to make certain that the pope knew about the celebrations in Florence accompanying Martin's election. The Florentines urged the pope to return to Rome and claimed that they had avoided sending an official congratulatory mission in order not to slow the pope's arrival. The pope dismissed Jacopo, called him to a private audience three days later, and assented to have the Florentines officially congratulate him upon his return to Italy.[30] The Florentines sent their official congratulations – featuring six prominent Florentines – late in 1418.[31]

Later diplomatic missions continued to reflect Matteo's trusted position among Medici clients. In May of 1466, Matteo was ostensibly elected to discuss merchant disputes with the pope, but in fact was elected to counter negative words spreading at the papal court about Piero de' Medici and his teetering political position in Florence, negative words that were beginning to push merchants to request payment on Piero's debts.[32] In early 1467, Matteo turned down a mission and was replaced by Luigi Guicciardini, a statement to the high status Matteo by then enjoyed.[33] The following year, he was charged with countering a peace plan put forth by the pope that would have called on Florence to help fund the condottiere Bartolomeo Colleoni, supposedly captain in the fight against the Turk, but in reality head of Venetian forces in Italy and friend of various Florentines exiled in 1466. After a little more than a month discussing the matter at Rome, Matteo returned to Florence, leaving Otto Niccolini to finish the negotiations.[34] Following another refused mission to Milan in 1468 (replaced this time with the Medicean parvenu Bernardo Buongirolamo), it was another five years before Matteo was elected for his final diplomatic mission, a charge in the spring of 1473 to discuss the renewal of the Italian League with Pope Sixtus IV. Sixtus, in fact, requested the exact same diplomats who had negotiated similar matters under his predecessor in 1468. While present, Matteo successfully put forward Lorenzo de' Medici's candidate for the Archbishopric of Florence and continued negotiations on the Italian League. Eventually Matteo left the matter unfinished for his replacement, the new archbishop of Florence, Rinaldo Orsini.[35]

A mission held between Matteo Palmieri's mission to the pope in 1466 and his rejection of the mission to Milan in 1467 illustrates his role and status among Florentine diplomats. On September 30, 1466, Florence sent diplomats to Bologna, Ferrara, the pope and Naples, and Venice and Milan, to reassure the major powers of Italy that Medici control over Florence was still secure after the failed coup in 1466. Matteo was selected to go to Bologna, indicating the esteem in which Piero de' Medici held him.[36] The fact that Matteo was involved in one of these missions at all suggests that he was a core, high-ranking Florentine diplomat. However, Bologna was undoubtedly the least prestigious of the missions, a fact that indicates Matteo's low status among this core. Moreover, Matteo Palmieri was repeatedly passed over for high-level ceremonial missions, such as the missions to greet the emperor in 1452 and 1468; the obedience missions of 1455, 1458, and 1464; and the congratulatory mission to the new king of France in 1461. Matteo's humanist learning and relationship with the Medici enabled him to overcome his modest background and break into the Florentine diplomatic core. The mission to Bologna suggests his position and status as a trusted Medicean lieutenant. It was an unprecedented accomplishment for a parvenu literary humanist, but it was a career of missions that emphasized Matteo's loyalty to the Medici rather than maximized his abilities as a humanist orator. Matteo's learning simply was not worth enough in the 1450s or 1460s to enable him to transcend his modest background and participate in the cultural gift exchanges at the heart of key ceremonial missions. Nevertheless, humanism in the 1450s and 60s was worth more in the market of social and political status than it had been thirty years earlier.

The contrast between the career of Matteo Palmieri and the diplomatic career of the only previous parvenu literary humanist to serve as a Florentine diplomat – Leonardo Bruni – suggests how far humanism had come from the 1420s to the 1460s. Bruni's diplomatic career had consisted of a rejected diplomatic election to Naples in 1420 and two completed diplomatic missions in 1426, one to Pope Martin V and one to the contested town of Forlì. Despite the ostensible prestige attached to the king of Naples and the pope, all of these missions required a diplomat of low status. As noted previously, in 1420 Bruni's relatively low social position is revealed through the man elected to replace him, Jacopo Niccoli. Similarly, missions to Forlì usually called for diplomats of lesser rank. What about the mission to the pope? In 1426, the Florentine government was looking for a diplomat who could send subtle, ambiguous messages to a pope renowned for his hostility to Florence. Leonardo Bruni fit the bill exactly, an observation probably made by friends in office who helped get him elected to the mission. In short, in 1426, it was not so much that Bruni's learning raised his status enough to serve as a Florentine diplomat as that his lack of traditional marks of status furthered Florentine diplomatic ends.

Bruni's papal mission fit into the context of the usual cycle of war and peace between Florence and Milan in the 1420s. After a brief peace in 1420, Milanese aggression toward Genoa sparked a new conflict between Florence and Milan in 1423.[37] After two years of fighting, the Florentines sent three of their most accomplished diplomats – Rinaldo degli Albizzi, the statesman Agnolo Pandolfini, and the lawyer Nello Martini – to Rome in 1425. These diplomats were initially charged with warming relations between Florence and the papacy; however, their commission eventually turned toward the negotiation of peace with Milan under papal auspices.[38] As the duplicitous Florentines negotiated peace, they also sent another experienced diplomat, Lorenzo Ridolfi, to Venice in order to entice La Serenissima into a league against the Milanese.[39] Both missions were successful, but to differing extents: The peace between Florence and

Milan lasted mere months, but the alliance between Florence and Venice lasted nearly three decades.⁴⁰

The hostilities between Florence and Milan focused on small towns in the Romagna. On May 14, 1423, the armies of Filippo Maria Visconti conquered Forlì. This conquest commenced the reengagement of hostilities between Milan and Florence. Eleven days after Visconti's conquest, the Florentines elected their war commission, the Dieci di Balìa. The Florentines suffered several military defeats to 1426.⁴¹ However, the diplomatic side of the conflict proceeded more favorably, as they reached an agreement to draw the duke of Savoy into the conflict. This treaty among Venice, Florence, and Savoy – eventually reached while Bruni was a diplomat in Rome – placed Milan in pincers between two enemies, Venice and Savoy.⁴² Meanwhile, two of the city's most prestigious diplomats – Rinaldo degli Albizzi and Nello Martini – were at the court of the Holy Roman Emperor in order to make a peace agreement between that ruler and Venice so that the Venetians could throw their full might against Visconti.⁴³ As the Florentines sought to strengthen and multiply their northern allies, the papal legate Domenico Capranica arrived in Florence requesting that they send diplomats to participate in peace talks in Rome under papal auspices.⁴⁴ Negotiations under Pope Martin V, a man notorious for his hostility toward the Florentines, were not an appealing invitation. Moreover, sending top diplomats to negotiate peace would violate the Florentine treaty of alliance with Venice as well as complicate their plans in Savoy and with the emperor. However, the Florentines could not reject the offer outright and thus risk pushing the pope further into the waiting arms of Visconti.

The Florentine government decided on subtlety in its diplomatic representation. Through the process described in Chapter 2, the Florentines elected the diplomatic novice and parvenu Bruni, whose strengths and weaknesses as a diplomat were well suited for this diplomatic mission. Bruni seems to have been especially suited to deal with the contentious issues of the Romagna, the issue that dominates the diplomatic letters between Florence and its ambassadors at Rome in the summer of 1426. In fact, after Bruni returned from his mission to the pope, the Florentines sent Bruni to Forlì to continue talks regarding this issue.⁴⁵ In particular, the lands under the control of Giovanni Gambacorta were a part of the dispute between Florence and Forlì.⁴⁶ Giovanni Gambacorta was a powerful Pisan patrician, but he was also the man bribed by the Florentines in 1406 to allow their conquest of Pisa.⁴⁷ He was also the grandfather of Alessandra Castellani, the future wife of Bruni's only son, Donato.⁴⁸ Therefore, Bruni was in charge of defending the claims of a man who five years later would join his extended family.

Moreover and most importantly, Bruni possessed strong and positive personal relations with Pope Martin V. Bruni himself provides a strong piece of evidence for his close ties with the pope. In his *Commentaries on His Own Times*, Bruni records a discussion he had with the pope before Martin left Florence. In this account, Bruni described the anger of the pope toward his treatment in Florence. Bruni worked and succeeded to some degree in pacifying the pope's wrath.[49] As recently as late 1420, Martin V had employed Bruni in the papal curia.[50] The fact that the Signoria elected Bruni as a diplomat in 1420 only after the pope had left the city is most likely not a coincidence: It probably reflects the importance of Bruni in the city as an intermediary between the papacy and the Florentine government.[51] Bruni continued to serve as an intermediary between the papacy and Florence after the 1420s; most notably, he served in this role during Eugenius IV's sojourns in Florence between 1434 and 1441, especially at the Council of Florence.[52] Bruni had dedicated his translation of Aristotle's *Ethics* to Martin V.[53] Poggio Bracciolini asked Bruni to write a letter to Martin V defending secretaries shortly after Bruni returned from his 1426 mission.[54] Finally, Bruni's career as a papal secretary undoubtedly made him more knowledgeable and more socially connected than most regarding the papal curia in general.

Yet, despite these strengths, Bruni brought comparatively low social status to the diplomatic table, as revealed through the quality of his replacement as diplomat in 1420. Bruni's low political status fit perfectly into the diplomatic goals of the Florentines for their mission to Martin V in 1426. His lack of diplomatic status enabled the Florentines to send a diplomat to the pope without estranging allies and potential allies in the north. At the same time, Bruni's close connections with the papacy, learning, and apparent knowledge of the disputes in the Romagna gave him an advantage once he arrived. As argued in Chapter 4, states observed and weighed the identity of diplomats from allies and enemies for clues as to their intentions and thoughts. In Bruni's case, the Florentines used him in a similar way to their use of celebrations at home. Richard Trexler has argued that, in terms of ritual celebrations at home aimed at a diplomatic purpose, "the most common response to complex diplomatic relations was neither silence or deceit, but ambiguity: carefully constructed, artful celebrations designed to maintain and augment friendships without estranging others."[55] Trexler offers the example of the celebration in Florence concerning Pope Julius II's defeat of the French, a Florentine ally, and conquest of Bologna. In its celebration, the Florentines performed the least amount of ritual celebration necessary to avoid offending the papacy. At the same time, the government ordered particular aspects of the procession to be suppressed in order to avoid offending the French.[56] In the same way, the Florentines attempted to send an ambiguous diplomatic message in the person of Leonardo Bruni, who lacked traditional diplomatic status but who took other strong attributes to the table.

Bruni himself hinted at this elaborate, subtle interplay of implicit statements embodied in his person. At the beginning of his opening speech before Martin V, Bruni was careful to hint at his expertise in diplomatic oratory, to remind his listeners that they were about to hear a new kind of oratorical performance – that is, an exceptional cultural gift – and at his close relationship with the pope. Bruni stated:

Those filling the office of legate who approach the apostolic and most holy See are accustomed, Blessed Father, to attempt with as much effort as they can through their mouth and words to raise this See up with the most exquisite praises. Yet, when I often present carefully and accurately heard them and would ponder on the one hand their language and on the other hand the greatness and majesty of this See, I always judged that their words were so deficient that the people praising their attempts all seemed absurd. Surely, it is clear that this opinion has some merit. Indeed, who in his right mind believes that he can assign with human words worthy praises to this See, the authority and power of which is not content with the lands or the extent of the seas, but rather it enters and transcends the heavens. What kind of person thinks that he can match the greatness of this See with confined sentences? Indeed, I think that the person who hopes to be able to do this does not recognize his own weakness. That person who dares an attempt is discovered to be imprudent. As is rightly said by philosophers, some things of quality are worthy of praise, others of veneration. Those things of praise fall into earthly esteem. However, those things of veneration are more heavenly and greater. Our praises seek to come near this latter type.[57]

By referring to his time in the curia ("I often present"), Bruni first transformed himself to become, not a Florentine diplomat from a parvenu family, but rather an old acquaintance of the pope deserving of an audience in his presence. Moreover, Bruni has reminded his audience of his expertise in diplomatic oratory by stating the innumerable times he has been a witness to such performances. Last, Bruni has informed his audience that he is offering a cultural gift: Previously, orators have foolishly focused on praising the pope. Bruni has chosen a new route, venerating that which words cannot possibly succeed in praising. It is fitting that the evidence for Bruni's new tactics is from unnamed *philosophis*, a reference to Plato, an author Bruni had a hand in reintroducing to the Latin West.[58] Bruni's

subtle reminders of his rhetorical skill made this move all the more powerful: Even the famed manipulator of words Leonardo Bruni was at a loss
when it comes to praising the Holy See.

After Bruni, it would be thirty years before the Florentines tried again to
use a parvenu literary humanist as a diplomat, and this time the diplomat,
Matteo Palmieri, was far more successful. Whereas Bruni's only major
diplomatic appointment emphasized his low social status, Matteo Palmieri
was repeatedly sent on key missions, including appointments reserved for
Florence's best. It was not that Matteo was more eloquent than Bruni:
There is no evidence that anybody considered Matteo Palmieri to be a
better orator than Leonardo Bruni. What had changed between the 1420s
and the 1450s were the sheer ubiquity of humanism and the political
culture of Florence itself. Humanism was worth more at the same time as
Florentines were willing to accept new markers of social and political
status. Nevertheless, the humanist learning of both Matteo and Bruni
was a secondary trait contributing to other social and political forces at
play. In both cases, both parvenu humanists remained on the outside
looking in on the missions featuring the strongest humanist component:
the ceremonial missions necessitating the strongest cultural gifts. Bruni's
learning and connections cracked the diplomatic door, Palmieri's opened it
further, but both men could only go so far.

Between 1456 and 1485 the increasing changes in political culture
combined with the continuing ubiquity of humanist learning among
Florentine diplomats to push the parvenu literary humanist Bartolomeo
Scala to new social and political heights. Throughout the growing percep-
tion that Cosimo and then Lorenzo de' Medici was the unofficial prince of
Florence, Florentines – for our purposes especially Florentine diplomats –
continued to cultivate humanist learning. In fact, once humanism established a foothold in diplomacy, it remained a consistent presence from the
latter 1420s until at least the 1480s. The percentage of diplomats who had
connections to the humanist movement and who filled three or more
missions in one of the following temporal blocks – 1426–1435, 1436–
1455, and 1456–1485 – actually remained basically the same throughout
the fifteenth century. Humanists made up fifteen of twenty-two (68.2
percent) of the individuals who were diplomats three or more times in
1426–1435; twenty-six of forty-two (62 percent) of such individuals in
1436–1455; and twenty-five of thirty-six (69.4 percent) in 1456–1485.
The number of three different missions was selected as the consistent point
below which the number of different individuals serving as diplomats
dramatically increases.

The learned interests of Florentine diplomats between 1456 and 1485 also suggest the ubiquity of humanists among Florentine diplomats. Between 1456 and 1485, all eight individuals filling more than ten diplomatic positions were literary or social humanists. Donato Acciaiuoli, Bernardo Buongirolamo, Jacopo Guicciardini, Luigi Guicciardini, Otto Niccolini, Pierfilippo Pandolfini, and Antonio di Lorenzo Ridolfi have all been discussed elsewhere in this study.[59] The remaining figure, Tommaso Soderini, became interested in humanist studies late in life and instilled this interest in his children, all of whom were active in the so-called Platonic Academy.[60] Perhaps Tommaso was encouraged in these endeavors by his business partner Matteo Palmieri, as the two men joined capital to invest in a business in the Old Market of Florence in 1451. Matteo and Tommaso were actually old friends by that point, and the friendship continued for at least a decade afterward.[61]

Dozens more individuals with learned connections served as Florentine diplomats fewer than ten times. Many of these figures have appeared elsewhere in this study, including (with number of missions in parentheses) Matteo Palmieri (five), Piero de' Pazzi (five), Bernardo Rucellai (five), Dietisalvi Neroni (four), Antonio Canigiani (three), Filippo de' Medici (three), Lorenzo di Piero de' Medici (three), Pierfrancesco de' Medici (three), Giuliano Ridolfi (three), Tommaso Ridolfi (three), Agnolo Acciaiuoli (two), Bernardo Giugni (two), Domenico Martelli (two), Niccolò Michelozzi (two), Pandolfo Pandolfini (two), Franco Sacchetti (two), Bartolomeo Scala (two), Piero Acciaiuoli (one), Maso di Luca degli Albizzi (one), Alessandro Alessandri (one), Piero de' Medici (one), Domenico Pandolfini (one), Antonio Pierozzi (one), and Alamanno Rinuccini (one).[62] Additional humanists can be added to these ranks. Luigi Alamanni was a member of Ficino's circle and served as a diplomat three times during these years.[63] Gentile Becchi was a tutor for the Medici family, writer of humanist Latin, and diplomat twice during these years.[64] Francesco Neroni received a dedication from Tommaso Benci for Benci's vernacular translation of Marsilio Ficino's version of Hermes Trismegistus's *Pimander* and was a diplomat once.[65] Francesco Dini printed a dispute between Lorenzo de' Medici and others about original sin and was a diplomat seven times.[66] Vespasiano da Bisticci claimed that Bartolomeo Fortini, twice a diplomat, had a good knowledge of Latin letters.[67] Francesco Gaddi was a friend of Bartolomeo Fonzio and Angelo Poliziano, was an assistant of Bartolomeo Scala in the Florentine chancery, and was a diplomat on three occasions.[68] Agnolo Manetti published an edition of his father's translations and was a diplomat once.[69] The Italian historian Arnaldo della Torre lists Niccolò Martelli, a diplomat once during these years, as another member of the so-called Platonic Academy.[70] After Martelli's death while serving on the Florentine galleys, Amerigo Corsini wrote a eulogy for him.[71] Marsilio Ficino included in his will that a Greek book of Plato should be given to Lorenzo di Pierfrancesco de' Medici, who was a diplomat twice.[72] Bernardo del Nero, diplomat twice, received dedications from Marsilio Ficino.[73]

These years included still other individuals with documented connections to humanist learning. Antonio da Ricavo wrote to Matteo Strozzi in Latin and was a diplomat four times during this period.[74] Francesco Soderini was praised for an eloquent oration delivered on a diplomatic mission and was a diplomat once during these years.[75] Paolo Soderini, in the words of della Torre, was "most dear" to Ficino and served on a single mission during these years.[76] Piero Capponi – diplomat three times before 1485 – appeared in a learned dialogue by Francesco Guicciardini and dabbled in humanism, according to a biographical sketch by Alison Brown.[77] Agnolo Niccolini and Tommaso Minerbetti received letters from Marsilio Ficino, and both men were diplomats during these years, Niccolini twice and Minerbetti once.[78] Antonio Pucci, diplomat once, had two learned sons, Antonio and Puccio, both of whom were friends of Bartolomeo Fonzio.[79] A vernacular letter from Bartolomeo Scala, despite the epistle's lack of learned references, may strengthen Antonio's connection to the humanist movement.[80] Piero Minerbetti was a diplomat four times and had his tomb constructed by Andrea del Verocchio. While the tomb is no longer extant, surviving fragments suggest classical elements.[81] Another individual with weak connections to the humanist movement was Andrea Cresci, who hired a private grammar tutor and provided a humanist grammar book for his son.[82] Cresci was a diplomat twice in these decades.[83] Giovanni Canacci, diplomat twice during these years, possessed stronger links to the humanist movement: He both was listed as a protector of Marsilio Ficino in 1489 and later compared Savanolora to figures from classical history, including Helen of Troy, after the preacher was condemned by Rome in March 1498.[84] Stronger yet were the connections of Guidantonio Vespucci, frequently a diplomat, who amended a manuscript containing notes taken on lectures by Angelo Poliziano on Aristotle's *Ethics*.[85] Vespucci also received vernacular letters from Bartolomeo Scala and employed Piero di Cosimo and Botticelli to decorate his house with classical images.[86] He was a diplomat eight times by 1484.[87]

Numerous other diplomats between 1456 and 1485 have left tantalizing hints that they may have possessed humanist interests, but the evidence is at present too weak to consider them among the social humanists. Bernardo Altoviti, diplomat once, married one of the children of Benedetto Accolti. The standard issues of money and familial prestige explain the match between the two families, and it is unclear whether Bernardo shared the humanist interests of his father-in-law.[88] Simone Grazzini worked in the Florentine chancery and was a diplomat twice without leaving further known evidence for his potential humanist interets.[89] Bartolomeo Pucci received a vernacular letter without literary references from Bartolomeo Scala, in addition to his two diplomatic missions, all of which occurred before his sons unsuccessfully tried to break him out of prison in 1496.[90] Beyond Bartolomeo Pucci, numerous Florentine diplomats during these years corresponded in the vernacular with Bartolomeo Scala without leaving any evidence for a shared learned connection; they include Antonio de' Medici, Pier Giovanni Ricasoli, Bongianni Gianfigliazzi, Piero Nasi, and Giovanni Lanfredini.[91] Even excluding these men, literary and social humanists occupied at least 228 positions of 369 total diplomatic and commissarial positions in 1456–1485, or 61.7 percent.[92] Just as in previous decades, the typical diplomatic mission featured at least one humanist.

The sheer ubiquity of basic humanist learning increased the demand on cities to send individuals with the ability to offer outstanding cultural gifts. Previously, a demonstration of humanist rhetoric offered an exceptional performance, but by midcentury the typical diplomat could only offer the typical humanist words. That was enough for some missions, particularly as the prominence of residential ambassadors curtailed the ritual formalities at the beginning of missions, even to major powers. Yet, missions to new princes, victorious princes, and especially new popes required more than the standard performance. Florentine obedience missions provide a revealing case study of the high-stakes gift exchanges of key ceremonial missions in the latter fifteenth century. Not only did obedience missions require the best diplomats in Florence; the historical record has preserved the speeches delivered on every obedience mission sent by Florence between 1447 and 1484. As discussed in the last chapter, in 1447 the Florentines turned to Giannozzo Manetti, a man who combined lineage with the deepest rhetorical skill and reputation, to head their mission to Nicholas V. After Manetti's exile, the Florentines turned to high-ranking churchmen who supplemented their office with eloquent tongues in the 1450s and 1460s. The rise of Donato Acciaiuoli in 1471 brought a new figure into Florentine diplomatic circles who combined his familial history with his rhetorical abilities and learned reputation. With Acciaiuoli's death

in 1478 and the election of a new pope, Innocent VIII, in 1484, the
Florentines were faced again with finding a man with extraordinary eloquence to offer a valuable cultural gift. Rather than a churchman or a
person from old Florentine stock, this time they chose the parvenu
Bartolomeo Scala.

Between 1456 and 1485, Florence sent obedience missions to Pius II
(1458), Paul II (1464), Sixtus IV (1471), and Innocent VIII (1484) with
each mission featuring eloquent men who delivered a humanist oration.
In 1458, Agnolo Acciaiuoli, Luigi Guicciardini, Pierfrancesco de' Medici,
Piero de' Pazzi, and Antonio Pierozzi each possessed traceable ties to
humanism. Their colleague, Guglielmo Rucellai, was the only member of
the mission who seems to have lacked such ties, although Rucellai did use
Leonardo da Vinci's father as a notary in the same year.[93] That the
Acciaiuoli, Guicciardini, Medici, Pazzi, and Rucellai families were
ancient in Florence needs no elaboration here, while Antonio Pierozzi's
position as archbishop of Florence was the key consideration in his
selection. On this mission, the archbishop of Florence combined the
prestige of his office, his holy reputation, and eloquent words to offer
an extraordinary gift to the new pope at the moment of Florence's
obedience speech.

As in 1455, Antonio Pierozzi delivered a surviving humanist oration
that used many of the same rhetorical and content moves of his oration
three years earlier.[94] The similarities between the two orations are particularly striking given the reputation of the new pope, Pius II, as a first-rate
humanist author and orator. As earlier, Pierozzi's commission instructed
him to express to the pope the Florentines' collective joy, so great that "the
like of which is not remembered for any news that has ever been
announced in this city."[95] Although this election made all Christians
rejoice, the great devotion and friendship that has always existed between
the pope and Florentines means that they were particularly happy. The
commission granted Pierozzi unprecedented leeway to demonstrate their
unprecedented goodwill toward the pope.

We would have elaborated the words in more places, demonstrating how much one
ought how to speak, if it were not you, *messer* Archbishop, who was speaking
about this material before the Holy Pope. For this material we give you – as a man
most outstanding in every aspect – free commission regarding the before stated
things to say them as well as it seems to your Reverence, elaborating as much as is
fitting for the honor of this Republic and of the Holy Father. At the end, you will say
that you have some things to say to his holiness, which we will defer to another
more convenient time.[96]

Perhaps because of the tremendous success of his oration three years previously, this time Pierozzi's commission explicitly gave him the leeway to flesh out his commission as he saw fit.

Antonio Pierozzi used the same combination of deep knowledge of religious subjects and humanist eloquence to deliver an exceptional oration on this occasion as he had done three years previously. The following quotation demonstrates this technique (left untranslated for stylistic analysis).

Et certe nullum horum nec animam unam ad portum valuit perducere salutis aeternae, sed post haec inquit Daniel ipse propheta: Suscitabit Deus coeli regnum aliud, quod in aeternum non dissipabitur, nec regnum ipsum alteri tradetur, & comminuet omnia regna haec, & ipsum manebit in aeternum.[97]

The passage containing Pierozzi's original language, from "*Et*" to "*propheta*," features alliteration ("*nullum ... nec*", "*animam ... ad*", and "*portum ... perducere*") and assonance ("*nullum horum ... animam unam*"). He followed this display of rhetorical prowess with a quotation from the Bible, thus demonstrating his biblical learning. In addition to Daniel, cited and uncited references to the Bible fill the oration, to Psalms, Romans, the Gospels, and others.[98]

However, he also tailored part of his content to fit the interests of the new pope. For example, Pierozzi offered Gregory of Nazianus as proof of the supreme power of priests, introducing this thinker as "an outstanding teacher among the Greek theologians."[99] He urged the pope to take on the Turk. In the process, he compared the pope to illustrious figures in the past, such as Moses and Emperor Theodosius. According to Pierozzi, these men had defeated enemies more with oratory than with arms. He urged the pope to listen to the counsel of others, just as Alexander Severus had done. The pope must undertake clerical reform and appoint pious and qualified men to church positions.[100] Pierozzi offered this advice not as "Minerva," but as a "most affectionate son to the highest father."[101] Such references to antiquity fit into the broader context of his continued displays of biblical learning. For example, the result of the clerical reforms will be that "the skies are joyful and the earth exults with utterly complete rejoicing," a quote from the Psalms.[102] In fact, Pierozzi worried that his minor concessions combined with his humanist style and biblical learning would not be enough to offer an extraordinary oratorical performance. He stated, "Also, spare me punishment, Blessed Father, if I spoke too long, or if I was pronouncing things incorrectly, without style and without skill."[103] He hoped that if he had missed something, his colleagues would supply it.[104]

Florence continued to use learned churchmen, often from old families, to offer an extraordinary diplomatic gesture on the obedience mission to Paul II in 1464. On this mission, the city sent Archbishop Filippo de' Medici, the legal expert and experienced diplomat Otto Niccolini, as well as the powerful Medici insiders Tommaso Soderini, Luigi Guicciardini, Buonaccorso Pitti, and Carlo Pandolfini. As previously, most of these men – Filippo de' Medici, Otto Niccolini, Tommaso Soderini, and Luigi Guicciardini – possessed notable ties to the humanist movement. Yet, links for Buonaccorso Pitti and Carlo Pandolfini have not yet been located, and, as shown later, this trend of including individuals without known connections to the humanist movement on obedience missions continued into the 1480s. These selections deviated from the clear trend of humanist interests among Florentine diplomats after the 1420s, and thus future research may establish links currently unknown. Yet, even if these two men lacked humanist interests, they serve as a key reminder of arguments made earlier in this study: Members of the Florentine patriciate were not the same men as the members of the humanist movement. Humanist interests can be tracked through learned connections and these learned connections interacted with other types of connections already familiar to historians. Many but not all Florentine patricians were humanists; most but not all humanists were patricians. Connections rather than class or original literary compositions reveal participation in the humanist movement.

On this mission, once again a high-ranking church official – this time from the Medici family itself – was chosen to offer an extraordinary gesture to the pope.[105] Filippo had already officially headed the Florentine congratulatory mission to France in late 1461 and had successfully delivered a long humanist oration to the new king, Louis XI.[106] Filippo's position as an archbishop enhanced his diplomatic status, just as it had in the case of Antonio Pierozzi. Yet, whereas Pierozzi had relied on his office and saintly reputation to supplement heavily his otherwise modest familial background, Filippo's family presented no such problems. In fact, Filippo's close relationship with Cosimo and then Piero de' Medici made him an extraordinary diplomat with or without his church office.[107] Pierozzi and Filippo also differed in their choices of oratorical content. Pierozzi had used a combination of humanist rhetoric with displays of deep biblical learning. By contrast, Filippo de' Medici returned to the types of classical displays favored by Giannozzo Manetti. More than any previous or future fifteenth-century Florentine diplomat, in fact, the social humanist Filippo showed off his classical learning with piles of classical quotes.

Filippo de' Medici integrated humanist rhetoric and content into his speech for the obedience mission to Paul II in 1464. In it, Filippo used an ostentatious display of learned citations surrounded by humanist rhetoric. In terms of style, one example is "*Nos enim et si parva diximus animi tamen tui sapientiam et magnitudinem liberalitatem et clementiam pietatemque non ignoramus, quibus omnia nobis fausta et felicita futura esse non dubitamus,*" which features alliteration (*fausta . . . felicita futura*), assonance (*sapientiam . . . magnitudinem liberalitatem . . . clementiam pietatemque*), and prolepsis ("*nos*" is outside the "*si*" clause into which it grammatically fits).[108] In terms of content, Filippo offered stories about Demosthenes, Scaevola, and Moses as his proof of the greatness of the Holy See and his fear speaking before it.[109] He also offered references to the church fathers: "since the words of the Blessed Gregory come to my mind."[110] Additionally, he wrote that, if the pope works for the good of God, "you will receive the reward of eternal happiness not only thirty or sixty, but also 100 times."[111] These numbers are a direct reference to a parable of Christ recorded in Matthew 13:3–8, where Jesus states that a farmer dropped seeds in various places, some of which "fell on good soil and brought forth grain, some a hundredfold, some sixty, some thirty."[112] Just before the oration's conclusion, Filippo told the story of Matthias and Barabas, which he drew from Acts 1:23–26.[113]

Filippo further enhanced his oration through creative content. He presented two standard metaphors of the pope as shepherd of the Christian flock and righter of the Christian ship; in these roles the pope will unify all Christians. The topic of Christian unity enabled Filippo to praise the pope's family. Namely, Filippo described the efforts of Pope Eugenius IV, an uncle of Pope Paul, to unify the Greek and Latin churches. Beyond praising the pope's ancestors, referring to this event implied the devotion of the Florentines to the papacy and the pope's family: Eugenius's church council had taken place in Florence while the pope was seeking asylum in the city. Moreover, this reference led up to the payoff of the entire oration. Pope Paul II will exceed his familial ancestor and perfectly fulfill the mission of the pope as Christian unifier. Whereas the Turks had only trembled at the name of Eugenius, they will flee in terror before the name of the new pope, before their final submission to his will. The pope will rule the world. A lengthy section of praise for the pope's virtues proves his worth to be a judge over the world.[114]

In 1471 the Florentines turned to Donato Acciaiuoli, who possessed the rare mixture of ancient familial lineage, political loyalty to the Medici, and a strong humanist reputation, to head their obedience mission to the new pope, Sixtus IV. Acciaiuoli overcame questionable political allegiances in his youth to become one of Lorenzo's trusted allies by the latter 1460s.[115] When Sixtus IV was elected pope, Acciaiuoli accompanied Lorenzo de' Medici himself, as well as Domenico Martelli, Bongianni Gianfigliazzi, Piero Minerbetti, and Angelo della Stufa, to offer the Florentine obedience. Acciaiuoli, Lorenzo de' Medici, and Domenico Martelli have left strong evidence for their humanist interests, while Bongianni Gianfigliazzi and Angelo della Stufa have yet to be linked.[116] The fact that Donato Acciaiuoli was a member of the mission and that he delivered a surviving oration in a classical style is not surprising, given the antiquity of his family and his learned reputation. Moreover, that the oration was copied and translated suggests the continued importance attached to the cultural gift in the latter Quattrocento.[117]

Donato Acciaiuoli's popular oration reveals the continued function of humanist oratory as a cultural gift in diplomacy.[118] The oration began by presenting the pope as a "present" and a "gift" that God had given to the world.[119] Acciaiuoli described the incredible joy of the Florentines toward this unprecedented gift. Then he moved on to the quality of the gift that God had given to the world. Acciaiuoli contended that "great thanks must be offered to immortal God, who has ornamented you with such talents, by you and no less by us. On our behalf He gave so distinguished a shepherd for men and brought him forth into the light."[120] Acciaiuoli feared that his oration would not be enough to reach the level of gift required for such a divine offering:

But since now it is the old custom of almost all orators, who in their first audience approach this most holy See, to give an oration full of congratulations and joy, I fear that you might think that I speak in this standard style on behalf of the Florentine people. I speak not in this standard style, not a sermon, not in the habit usually seized upon by all, but in devotion, observance, and affection for the apostolic See.[121]

Rather than the oratorical custom, Acciaiuoli hoped that the pope would recognize that his oration offered something new by surpassing the typical oratorical performance. He was offering, in short, a cultural gift.

The multitude of evidentiary threads woven in this chapter joined in the Florentine obedience mission to Pope Innocent VIII in 1484.[122] The mission, as usual, demanded the most extraordinary men Florence had to offer, so long as they also possessed deep ties to the Medici family. To meet these requirements, the mission featured several key Mediceans from ancient families, including Antonio Canigiani, Agnolo Niccolini, Francesco Soderini, Giovanni Tornabuoni, and Guidantonio Vespucci.[123] Yet, alongside these prestigious knights, lawyers, and members of ancient Florentine families, the Florentine government charged the humanist parvenu Bartolomeo Scala to deliver the opening oration. Scala's presence and his oratorical role are even more compelling because he was not the only person on the mission with humanist interests: While Giovanni Tornabuoni has yet to be linked to the humanist movement, Antonio Canigiani, Agnolo Niccolini, Francesco Soderini, and Guidantonio Vespucci were all social humanists discussed elsewhere in this study. In fact, Francesco Soderini not only carried the prestige of a church office, he had also delivered a successful oration to a pope on a previous diplomatic oration. In 1480, Soderini had led a large mission to convince Pope Sixtus IV to lift the interdict on Florence imposed after the Pazzi Conspiracy. On that occasion, Soderini delivered an oration that was both copied and praised.[124] Scala's inclusion marked the final step of the integration of humanism into diplomacy, for on this mission Florence looked past the social background of a humanist parvenu and sent him as head of its most ceremonial, most demanding diplomatic mission.

Scala described his background to Angelo Poliziano in 1494. He wrote, "I came to the republic naked, disadvantaged, of the lowest parentage, full of confidence but absolutely penniless, without reputation, patrons or kinsmen," a statement that Alison Brown's exhaustive biography affirms.[125] In the latter 1450s, Scala began working in the service of the Medici family, first under Pierfrancesco and then as the Medicis' hand-picked chancellor of Florence in 1465.[126] Soon Scala was enjoying prominent political positions outside the chancery. After a position on the Priors in 1473, Scala's career reached new heights by 1480. In that year, Scala was appointed to the Balìa. The highest office in Florence – the position of Standard Bearer of Justice – followed in 1486.[127] Across and outside his political roles, Scala wrote numerous humanist treatises, poems, orations, and the beginning of a *History of Florence*.[128] In domestic settings, Scala's success had precedent. Moreover, his position was helped by his legal training, an attribute that had helped other men with little familial history to rise to political prominence, such as Bernardo Buongirolamo.[129] Scala's relationship with the Medici combined with his rhetorical abilities and legal training to make up for the deficiencies of his familial background and enable Scala to hold domestic offices by the mid-1480s.

Yet, Scala's humanist abilities were worth more in the 1480s than at any previous time in Renaissance Florence. Although his legal training and relationship with the Medici helped Scala's status, his humanist abilities were the primary reason for his selection as a diplomat. In fact, the Florentine Signoria elected Scala exclusively to deliver the congratulatory oration. Scala arrived in Rome on December 7. One week later on December 15, he gave his speech. He was granted rewards for his oration on December 25 and 28. He had already planned his route back to Florence on December 31. He returned to the city on January 12.[130] Scala, in short, went to Rome, gave his oration, and returned home. The Florentine government had elected individuals for a similarly limited diplomatic role on obedience missions in previous decades. Both Antonio Pierozzi and Donato Acciaiuoli had also been elected for obedience missions, delivered their orations, and returned shortly thereafter.[131] Like Pierozzi and Acciaiuoli, Scala was elected to give an opening oration. Like his predecessors, Scala was expected to offer an extraordinary cultural gift through his oratorical performance. Unlike the churchman Pierozzi and the member of the ancient Acciaiuoli house, Scala carried a literary reputation but lacked a prominent church office or familial status. This key difference suggests a rise in prestige attached to humanist learning by the 1480s.

Given his learning, the classically styled oration that Bartolomeo Scala delivered on the occasion is not surprising. Scala returned to the ostentatious use of a classical oratorical framework preferred by Giannozzo Manetti. Like Manetti's, Scala's oration contained a clear partition followed by an obvious demarcation of each oratorical section.[132] Moreover, Scala devoted a great deal of attention to the stylistic organization of his material. For example, note the beginning consonants of the words in the following phrase: "*fidemque faciat venturae vitae qui non quae nobis*" (f, f, v, v, q, n, q, n).[133] Scala repeatedly used rhetorical questions to stress his praise of the papacy, a technique that he employed more than his predecessors had.[134] These types of stylistic and structural moves placed his oration well into the realm of an acceptable oratorical performance.

Scala also added creative content to his speech. In particular, he compared the virtues of the new pope with those of Christ himself. The pope has power over the salvation and damnation of souls. Scala stated, "Who has learned to open the gates of heaven for us, to close them, to damn and to give salvation for men? The highest Pope."[135] According to Scala, God takes direct action in the selection of the pope in order to prevent filling such a powerful position with wicked men. The qualities that God looks for in this position are the same as the virtues that Christ possessed.[136] As Christ said, "I gave my example to you, as I have done, you ought to do."[137] God picks popes who possess spiritual and intellectual talents in order to meet the pope's obligations as shepherd for the Christian flock. Scala subsequently listed a variety of virtues that the pope ought to share with Jesus Christ.[138] He then concluded his list with passages further connecting the power and virtues of Christ with the pope. In particular, Christ and the pope share the same task. Christ had stated that he was the "good shepherd."[139] He then told Peter, the founder of the papal seat, to take care of his flock. The new pope has selected the name Innocent, just like the "innocent lamb Christ is often called in holy writings."[140] In possession of Christ-like virtues and handpicked by God, the new pope must emulate the virtuous actions of his predecessors and work for peace.

Despite his background, the humanist parvenu's oration was a stunning success. On Christmas day, the pope dubbed Scala a knight and a senator of Rome as reciprocation for Scala's cultural gift. Three days later, Innocent VIII granted Scala patronage of a church in Scala's hometown of Val d' Elsa. One of Scala's assistants in the chancery, Filippo Redditi, copied the oration in the same book used to record instructions to diplomats.[141] This inclusion gave the oration an official quality. Just as members of the Florentine government could look back to books of ceremony and various examples of diplomatic dispatches for models to follow, future diplomats could look at Scala's 1484 oration as an extraordinarily successful example of a diplomatic speech. The title of the oration reads, "Oration of Bartolomeo Scala, Florentine Diplomat, to the Highest Pope Innocent VIII."[142] For the first time in Florentine diplomacy, "the social position of the speaker was a matter of perfect indifference; what was desired was simply the most cultivated humanistic talent."[143] The son of a miller had surpassed the status requirements of a diplomatic reception ritual through his literary reputation. He had subsequently used his stunning rhetorical abilities to offer the pope a cultural gift.

Scala's mission capped developments that had begun decades earlier in Florence. By the 1420s and 1430s large numbers of Florentines from different walks of life had begun to cultivate humanist letters. They did so through reading rather than writing texts and primarily to prepare and/ or participate in frequent social, political, and religious rituals that called for displays of humanist eloquence. The case study of diplomacy demonstrates that humanist learning was but one of many traits determining who spoke in which rituals and at what times. In diplomacy, an ancient familial history of political power in Florence was the primary characteristic in selections. At first, Florentines turned to individuals who supplemented their traditional marks of status with abilities in humanist rhetoric.

Consequently, by the latter 1420s and early 1430s the majority of Florentine diplomats can be linked both to ancient families and to the humanist movement. These men delivered humanist orations – cultural gifts – and initially their unusual performances sufficed among the ceremonial, symbolic gifts that dominated the beginning of diplomatic missions. Over time, basic humanist displays became so common that increasing value was placed upon the learning of the most exceptionally talented humanists, people who were able to exceed the norm through their rhetorical abilities. This increased value – combined with the changes in political culture in Florence under the Medici family – enabled Bartolomeo Scala to ascend to the pinnacle of political and social status in and outside Florence in the 1480s. Proficiency in humanist letters carried more prestige in the 1480s than it had earlier in the century, and this increased prestige enhanced the social status of parvenu literary humanists. This increased prestige also encouraged more and more people to pursue humanist studies, with the effect of the even further expansion of the humanist movement. The size and success of the humanist movement were the tangible effects of the learned interests of the social humanists.

Conclusion

On an unspecified date during the fifteenth century, a Florentine man stepped before the new Signoria. He probably had been thrilled the week before when he had learned that his name had been pulled as one of the four men to represent his quarter of Florence among the Sixteen Standard Bearers. This excitement probably had dissolved into nerves when he learned that he had been chosen to deliver the customary *Exhortation to Justice*. Why, he must have thought, was I chosen? He was not an orator, not a scholar, and yet there he stood, facing some of the city's most eminent men, all of whom awaited the beginning of his speech. He began, having decided beforehand that he would hide neither his lack of eloquence nor what he thought. An elaborate parsing of the meaning of "justice," he said, using learned philosophers and theologians, would be superfluous among such prominent men with such *virtù*. Therefore, he skipped the topic that was so customary in dozens of other surviving speeches delivered on similar occasions. Instead, he focused on the writing he knew best: the Bible, or perhaps just a saying from it he had heard in a sermon or other conversation. Citing Matthew 5:10, he claimed that sufferers for the sake of justice were blessed and possessors of the Kingdom of Heaven. Those who ruled without justice could expect "the worst misery" and "eternal damnation."[1] For these reasons he beseeched the governors to rule with "mercy" while always caring for those who could not care for themselves.[2]

Clearly not everyone in fifteenth-century Florence was a humanist, even if the broad definition of a person who has left evidence of an interest in the history, writings, and rhetoric of antiquity is applied. Not even all men eligible to hold a position among the *tre maggiori* possessed enough humanist learning to pull off even a single, eloquent, vernacular oration, despite the numerous, widely accessible set orations available for copying in Latin and the vernacular. The survival of this unlettered anonymous speech suggests its unusual lack of quality, just as the survival of the speeches of Giannozzo Manetti and other humanists suggest their quality at the other end of the spectrum. Most *protesti* were undoubtedly in between, their normalcy and routine nature neither worthy of comment nor of copying for future reference. In terms of orations, as in so much else, the historical record tends to leave large amounts of the exceptional from the past, with smatterings of the more mundane thrown in by chance.

The evidence in this book suggests that the humanist movement encompassed an enormous number of people whose humanist interests and abilities ranged from superficial dabbling to mastery of the history and rhetoric of the ancient world. A small fraction of these individuals wrote original texts in Latin, while most humanists were content to study the works of others and cultivate spoken eloquence. That most humanists did not write Latin treatises should not devalue the humanist texts surviving for historical study. Expanding the humanist movement to include all of the individuals interested in humanism does not cheapen it into meaningless boundaries. The movement grows exponentially, but scholarly conception of it *should* grow exponentially. Bartolomeo Bardi, Giuliano Davanzati, Matteo Strozzi, and Giannozzo Manetti were different in the extent of their intellectual interests, not their type. Certainly, humanist literature offers one of the few remaining areas where truly exciting, important, and new texts can be introduced to new audiences through locating a text, editing it, publishing it, and perhaps translating it as well. Even pivotal works of the literary humanists remain unedited, particularly historical works, speeches, and letters. It remains a lost literature and this is an exciting time to be a historian of humanism. Nevertheless, the excitement should not overshadow that these texts and their authors were not the whole of the humanist movement in fifteenth-century Florence. In fact, they constituted a tiny fraction of it.

Learned connections provide historians with the best evidentiary source for participation in the humanist movement, while these connections themselves open new avenues for historical inquiry. Scholars have long studied the economic, familial, marital, geographical, and political connections among people for any number of insights into Renaissance society. Learned connections too bound people together and drove them apart. In some cases, learned connections reinforced other types of social bonds:

They often followed patrilineal nuclear familial units even as a few extended families, such as the Strozzi, possessed humanists across the broader familial clan. Learned interests could shape marital matches by allowing men to marry up because their learning enhanced their social status. Like other forms of social connections, a person's learned connections both reinforced and removed political and geographical boundaries. Humanist dialogues and dedications were a very public and permanent way of tying people together, a risky business in a society that placed such a premium on artfully saying nothing.[3] The growth in community studies, analyses of historical networks, and the minor resurgence of traditional statistically based social history make these points about the historical significance of learned connections particularly pertinent today.[4] Learned connections should be part of the conversation just as they were part of the ties that bound and severed relationships in Renaissance Florence. This book has attempted to introduce these learned connections into the broader historiographical discussion.

Investigating the humanist movement in its entirety by means of learned connections reveals just how differentiated humanists were in terms of their individual interests in the ancient world and their backgrounds. Figures like Leonardo Bruni and Giannozzo Manetti were clearly central to the humanist movement, yet their interests were shared at a lesser level by Matteo Strozzi, Dietisalvi Neroni, Antonio Ridolfi, Tommaso Ceffi, Matteo Castellani, Niccolò Guasconi, and Bernardo Buongirolamo, people who themselves differed in the strength of their connections to the humanist movement. This book has offered two basic, fluid categories to differentiate people at the center of the movement from other humanists. The general categories of literary and social humanists enable scholars to continue to acknowledge the centrality of the literary humanists to the intellectual history and the history of ideas of the Renaissance. At the same time, the inclusion of the social humanists in the humanist movement enables scholars to give those men and women their historical due as well. Assigning people to the literary humanist or social humanist categories is not always obvious: The categories overlap and are intended to describe two key sections of the range of learned interests encompassed by participants in the humanist movement. Concerns over exact categorization should not distract from the point of the categories in the first place: to create a conception of the humanist movement that takes seriously the entire range of people – in terms of social, political, and economic background as well as strength of humanist interests – involved in it and the broad range of ways that these men and women expressed their humanist interests.

It is indisputable that the surviving evidence points to a preponderance of patricians in the humanist movement. Indeed, knowledge of humanism by the second half of the fifteenth century was part of the way status could be determined in Renaissance Florence. But these observations do not mean that humanist learning was limited to the social elites. On the one hand, it seems to have been relatively easy to cultivate enough rhetoric and content knowledge to join the ranks of the social humanists, if for no other reason than the surprisingly high literacy rates among Florentines and availabilty of vernacular translations of Latin or Greek texts. On the other hand, arguments that associate humanism with class overshadow the diversity and size of the Florentine patriciate, which encompassed a third of the entire population.[5] The fact that humanism can be traced among people even further down the social ladder is itself a testament to just how widespread humanist learning was in fifteenth-century Florence. Moreover, if the Florentine patriciate is considered an open group with room for upward or downward mobility – as recent sociological and economic studies have argued – then humanism was more a tool available to men looking to maintain or change their place in the world than a factor closing off avenues for social mobility.[6] The translation of both classical and original humanist texts into vernacular languages suggests just how far humanist interests spread. The sheer numbers of social humanists discussed in this study, many of whom had rudimentary knowledge of Latin, suggest that basic Latin literacy was far more pronounced in Florence than is traditionally assumed. In short, the humanist movement appears to have been open to people from at least the upper half of the Florentine population, rather than only to the neo-Latin writers traditionally associated with humanism.

The driving force behind the spread of the humanist movement was the search for social status. Humanist learning became valuable currency in the market of social status in Renaissance Florence, at times weighing more heavily than more traditional indicators of social position. As such, the spread of humanism can be largely explained by the hopes and expectations of people who had to offer a humanist performance, in Latin or the vernacular, in a public or private event. This book has offered a case study of diplomatic oratory and ritual, but other occasions with learned demands abounded. If the demands of formal, prestigious diplomatic ceremonies represented one end of the spectrum, appearing learned among acquaintances at a dinner party represented the other. The ability to appear learned and the prestige it carried allowed an individual to uphold his or her honor and increase his or her status.

That was the unifying theme of the humanist movement in fifteenth-century Florence.

Such humanist performances interacted with other aspects of Renaissance society to shape where and when people could put their learning into practice. In diplomacy, familial status, humanist learning, and other factors determined selection for diplomatic assignments by the latter 1420s. By the 1450s loyalty to the Medici family was another important criterion, while deep knowledge of humanist rhetoric had increased in value. In political and diplomatic situations, the lack of traditional markers of social status tended to push most literary humanists into secretarial positions, while the demands of the cultural gift prodded Florentine patricians to develop their rhetorical skills. Yet, diplomatic rituals and secretarial positions were both a fraction of the situations where humanist learning came into play. Requirements for speakers in confraternities differed from those for diplomats; speakers for the Guelf Party in Florence needed different tools than speakers in the *pratiche* or speakers at the home of Franco Sacchetti or other countless occasions lost in the historical shadows where people sought to impress or persuade others with their learning. These contexts largely shaped the people who participated in the humanist movement and the ways that they experienced it. These contexts also shaped the surviving literature that came out of the humanist movement: Frankly, much of the surviving humanist literature simply cannot be understood without deep analysis of the specific situations surrounding each text, especially not with any hope of understanding how Renaissance people themselves may have understood it.

These ritualized occasions brought about an expansion of the humanist movement that accompanied an increase in prestige attached to humanist learning. This study largely upholds the timeline of previous scholars for key developments in this process. As Ronald Witt has argued, this study contends that humanism was becoming fairly widespread in Florence by the 1420s; as Robert Black has asserted, it seems that many effects of this spread were most keenly felt by the 1470s, when educational reforms reflected the increased value attached to humanist letters. The learned connections of hundreds of Florentines have been brought forth to show just how widespread humanist learning became in Florence, both before 1470 and after. With so many men capable of humanist rhetoric, the abilities of the few most learned individuals became especially prized, a development that helps explain the diplomatic careers of Matteo Palmieri and Bartolomeo Scala.

The nature of the evidence on which this book is based, namely, correspondences between men and official diplomatic documents, has forced women out of this study. Recent studies suggest the potential for wide-spread humanist interests among women and even respect for their ora-torical abilities among men.[7] However, different types of evidentiary sources would have to be brought to bear to examine female social human-ists, their specific conglomerate of social attributes, and the learned demands of the specific occasions in which they could reasonably expect to find themselves. The finding that Florence does not seem to have sent a woman as an official diplomat in the fifteenth century (0/2,266 diplomatic positions in the database for this study was occupied by a woman) does not mean that other occasions did not provide women with opportunities to demonstrate their learning. After all, they too possessed extraordinarily high levels of at least vernacular literacy and they too lived in a city saturated with humanist forms and performances.

Although a systematic study has not been completed, the trends identi-fied in Florence in this book seem to have continued after Bartolomeo Scala's successful mission to Pope Innocent VIII in 1484. Individuals with learned reputations but without strong familial backgrounds continued to enter diplomatic ranks, with Niccolò Michelozzi and Alessandro Braccesi serving as two notable examples of prominent diplomats in the 1480s and 1490s.[8] A surviving speech that Angelo Poliziano wrote for other Florentine diplomats in 1496 points to the continuation of the cultural gift in diplomacy.[9] That Poliziano wrote this oration for other diplomats may even point to the renewal of the importance attached to more tradi-tional markers of status after the fall of the Medici and the restoration of a more republican system of government in Florence after 1494: Namely, without a pseudoprince to impact diplomatic selections, the Florentines closed the door to their diplomatic ranks and returned to a reliance on familial history as the sine qua non for political prominence. Such hypoth-eses, however, are speculative and await more in-depth study.

Beyond the specific context of Florence, the humanist movement con-tinued to spread across geographical and social boundaries throughout the early modern period. By the mid-sixteenth century republics and kingdoms across Europe possessed humanists, even as the most innovative intellec-tual trends shifted toward theology, metaphysics, and the natural sciences. Humanism remained an intellectual force, its influence still being felt in surprising places – such as figures traditionally associated with the Scientific Revolution – in the seventeenth century and beyond. Anthony Grafton has pointed to the humanist interests of Johannes Kepler even as Francis Bacon and Descartes held sharply contrary views on humanism.[10] Humanist schools came to dominate Europe in the centuries ahead, a point undisputed even as scholars have debated just how revolutionary their educational changes actually were.[11]

This book has argued that, at least in Florence, this spread and influence were possible because ritualized situations began demanding displays of humanist learning and, in turn, humanist learning became a marker of social status attainable by vast numbers of the population. Although arguments about the rest of Europe or even just the Italian peninsula based on Florence have rightly been criticized by historians over the past several decades, in this case, it seems probable that the large numbers of humanists and the reasons behind the appeal of humanist learning were the same elsewhere as in Florence.[12] Diplomacy suggests that this was the case. First, anecdotes cited in this book point to audiences of hundreds who attended humanist speeches in places outside Florence. Second, diplomacy hinged upon the successful exchanges of gifts: A gift of an eloquent humanist oration simply would not work if the ruler(s) addressed did not at some level appreciate the gesture. These rulers, in turn, had to send both letters and diplomats who could reciprocate the cultural gift. Once humanism infiltrated diplomacy – the comments of Giangaleazzo Visconti on the value of Salutati's letters in the late Trecento suggest they probably served more or less as a starting point – the demands of the gift exchange required humanist performances on both sides. The appeal of humanist letters to non-Florentines undoubtedly varied in its particulars across different localities, but the general argument about the relationship between social status and learning probably holds. In and outside Florence, large numbers of people pursued humanist letters largely through study rather than original literary production and did so hoping to apply their learning in practical situations in order to enhance their own status and that of their families.

The enormous number of social humanists also helps answer other sometimes asked but rarely answered questions among scholars of Renaissance Europe: For whom did the humanists write and translate, and at whom were the ubiquitous classical allusions in rituals, art, literature, orations, buildings, and so on, aimed? Or, phrased slightly differently, why speak for an hour in Latin if nobody understood what the speaker said? The arguments of this book suggest that many, many people in the audience *could* understand these orations: The social humanists, whose ranks were far larger than has been traditionally assumed and who varied in their humanist interests, all possessed the basic knowledge necessary to participate in the dialogue of classical allusions. Not all of them caught every reference, but many understood enough to make the classically inspired gestures worthwhile. Jacob Burckhardt was correct that humanism was a form of entertainment, and as with all forms of entertainment, different readers and viewers took different things from texts and performances. This book has sought to shed light on the people who acted as the engines behind the spread of the humanist movement and explain why humanism appealed to them. They populated a deeper Renaissance than has been usually assumed in the recent historiography. This Renaissance was the product of the social humanists.

Notes

Introduction: A Social Conception of the Humanist Movement

1. Ronald G. Witt, *In the Footsteps of the Ancients: The Origins of Humanism from Lovato to Bruni* (Leiden: Brill, 2000).
2. Paul Oskar Kristeller, *Renaissance Thought and Its Sources*, ed. Michael Mooney (New York: Columbia University Press, 1979). See also Benjamin G. Kohl, "The Changing Concept of the *studia humanitatis* in the Early Renaissance," *Renaissance Studies* 6, no. 2 (June 1992): 185–202.
3. Hans Baron, *The Crisis of the Early Italian Renaissance: Civic Humanism and Republican Liberty in an Age of Classicism and Tyranny*, rev. ed. (Princeton, NJ: Princeton University Press, 1966).
4. Eugenio Garin, *Italian Humanism: Philosophy and Civic Life in the Renaissance* (Westport, CT: Greenwood Press, 1975).
5. Christopher S. Celenza, *The Lost Italian Renaissance: Humanists, Historians, and Latin's Legacy* (Baltimore: Johns Hopkins University Press, 2004), 54.
6. Paul Oskar Kristeller, "Marsilio Ficino as a Man of Letters and the Glosses Attributed to Him in the Caetani Codex of Dante," *Renaissance Quarterly* 36, no. 1 (Spring 1983): 3–11.
7. On this historiography, see James Hankins, "The 'Baron Thesis' after Forty Years and Some Recent Studies of Leonardo Bruni," *Journal of the History of Ideas* 56, no. 2 (April 1995): 309–338; see also "Forum on the Baron Thesis," *American Historical Review* 100, no. 5 (1995): 107–144.
8. For a rare opposing view, see Robert Black, review of *Renaissance Civic Humanism: Reappraisals and Reflections*, ed. James Hankins, *The English Historical Review* 116, no. 467 (June 2001): 716. cf. Mark Jurdjevic, "Hedgehogs and Foxes: The Present and Future of Italian Renaissance Intellectual History," *Past and Present* 195 (May 2007): 258.
9. Arthur Field, *The Origins of the Platonic Academy in Florence* (Princeton, NJ: Princeton University Press, 1988); Margery Ganz, "The Humanist as Citizen: Donato di Neri Acciaiuoli, 1428–1478" (PhD diss., Syracuse University, 1979); Mark Jurdjevic, "Civic Humanism and the Rise of the Medici," *Renaissance Quarterly* 52, no. 4 (Winter 1999): 994–1020, with further bibliography on 998. On civic humanism in general, see James Hankins, ed. *Renaissance Civic Humanism: Reappraisals and Reflections* (Cambridge: Cambridge University Press, 2000).

10. On Garin, his ideas, and his method, see Celenza, *The Lost*, 28–40 and 54–57.
11. For the most recent study of Renaissance humanism, see Angelo Mazzocco, ed., *Interpretations of Renaissance Humanism* (Leiden: Brill, 2006).
12. James Hankins, "A Lost Continent of Literature," in *Humanism and Platonism in the Italian Renaissance* (Rome: Edizioni di Storia e Letteratura, 2003), 1:541–550; see also Celenza, *The Lost*.
13. Lauro Martines, *The Social World of the Florentine Humanists 1390–1460* (Princeton, NJ: Princeton University Press, 1963), 12–13.
14. Ibid., 12.
15. Ibid., 12–14.
16. On this point in general, see Field, *The Origins*.
17. Martines, *The Social*, 12.
18. Vanna Arrighi, "Griso Griselli," in *DBI*, available online at "Griso Griselli in Dizionario Biografico – Treccani," Treccani.it, http://www.treccani.it/enciclo-pedia/griso-griselli_(Dizionario-Biografico)/ (accessed June 21, 2011). For Manetti's letterbook from Venice, see Vat. Lat. 931. On Griselli, see also Nadia Lerz, "Il diario di Griso di Giovanni," *Archivio Storico Italiano* 117, no. 2 (1859): 247–278.
19. Arnaldo della Torre, *Storia dell' Accademia platonica di Firenze* (Florence: G. Carnesecchi e figli, 1902), 279, 337, 343–344. On the published version of this conversation, called the *Dialogus in symposio*, see David Marsh, "Boccaccio in the Quattrocento: Manetti's *Dialogus in symposio*," *Renaissance Quarterly* 33, no. 3 (Autumn 1980): 337–350; and Gabriella Albanese, "Manetti tra politica, novellistica e filosofia: il "Dialogus in Symposio," in *Dignitas et excellentia hominis: Atti del convegno internazionale di studi su Giannozzo Manetti*, ed. Stefano Ugo Baldassarri (Florence: Le Lettere, 2008), 15–83.
20. Arrighi, "Griselli."
21. Martines, *The Social*, 14–15.
22. Ibid., 14.
23. Ibid., 305.
24. Celenza, *The Lost*, 52.
25. On the prevalence of non-writers among Venetian humanists in the fifteenth century, see Margaret L. King, *Venetian Humanism in an Age of Patrician Dominance* (Princeton, NJ: Princeton University Press, 1986).
26. On this point, see also Mark Jurdjevic, *Guardians of Republicanism: The Valori Family in the Florentine Renaissance* (Oxford: Oxford University Press, 2008), 170–173.
27. James Hankins, "The Popularization of Humanism in the Fifteenth Century: The Writings of Leonardo Bruni in Latin and the Vernacular," in *Language and Cultural Change: Aspects of the Study and Use of Language in the Later Middle Ages and the Renaissance*, ed. Lodi Nauta (Leuven: Peeters, 2006), 133–136.
28. Angelo Mazzocco, *Linguistic Theories in Dante and the Humanists: Studies in Language and Intellectual History in Late Medieval and Early Renaissance Italy* (Leiden: Brill, 1993). For further leads, see Brian Jeffrey Maxson, "'This Sort of Men': the Vernacular and the Humanist Movement in Fifteenth-

Century Florence," in *I Tatti Studies*, ed. Andrea Rizzi and Eva del Soldato (forthcoming).

29. On chancery letters in fifteenth-century Florence, see Ronald G. Witt, *Coluccio Salutati and his Public Letters* (Geneva: Librairie Droz, 1976); Paolo Viti, *Leonardo Bruni e Firenze: Studi sulle lettere pubbliche e private* (Rome: Bulzoni, 1992), 3–274; Robert Black, *Benedetto Accolti and the Florentine Renaissance* (Cambridge: Cambridge University Press, 1985), 109–110 and 141–150; Alison Brown, *Bartolomeo Scala, 1430–1497, Chancellor of Florence: The Humanist as Bureaucrat* (Princeton, NJ: Princeton University Press, 1979), 138–145 and 168–186.

30. See the examples in Francesco Filarete and Angelo Manfidi, *The Libro Cerimoniale of the Florentine Republic*, ed. Richard C. Trexler (Geneva: Librairie Droz, 1978), 86, 91, 94, and 96. The *Libro Cerimoniale* does not record every oration that occurred during the ceremonies that it describes. For example, it records nothing about the orations that accompanied the entrance of Frederick III into Florence (Filarete and Manfidi, *The Libro*, 72). However, the *Priorista* records three during these ceremonies: when the emperor actually entered the city in January; when he returned in May; and when the Signoria and the Dieci di Balìa went to greet the emperor at Santa Maria Novella on the emperor's return trip. Pagolo di Matteo Petriboni and Matteo di Borgo Rinaldi, *Priorista (1407–1459)*, ed. Jacqueline A. Gutwirth with Gabriella Battista (Rome: Edizioni di Storia e Letteratura, 2001), 352, 354, and 362–363.

31. Michael Baxandall, *Giotto and the Orators: Humanist Observers of Painting in Italy and the Discovery of Pictorial Composition, 1350–1450* (Oxford: Clarendon Press, 1971); cf. Witt, *In the Footsteps*, 502.

32. On humanism and education, see Paul Grendler, *Schooling in Renaissance Italy* (Baltimore: Johns Hopkins University Press, 1989) and Robert Black, *Humanism and Education in Medieval and Renaissance Italy* (Cambridge: Cambridge University Press, 2001).

33. Robert Black, *Education and Society in Florentine Tuscany: Teachers, Pupils and Schools, c. 1250–1500* (Leiden: Brill, 2007), 1–42. Black may exaggerate this figure slightly, as the *catasto* underrepresents people who were probably illiterate. See Richard A. Goldthwaite, *The Economy of Renaissance Florence* (Baltimore: Johns Hopkins University Press, 2009), 563–565. For contrasting statistics, see Brian Richardson, *Printing, Writers and Readers in Renaissance Italy* (Cambridge: Cambridge University Press, 1999), 109–112.

34. On Chrysoloras and Argyropoulos, see James Hankins, "The Study of Greek in the Latin West," in *Humanism and Platonism in the Italian Renaissance* (Rome: Edizioni di Storia e Letteratura, 2003), 1:284–285; on the Florentine university, see Jonathan Davies, *Florence and its University during the Early Renaissance*. Leiden: Brill, 1998; on the wealth of Florentine humanists, see Martines, *The Social*, 85–144.

35. Kenneth Gouwens, "Perceiving the Past: Renaissance Humanism after the 'Cognitive Turn,'" *American Historical Review* 103, no. 1 (February 1998): 80.

36. Martines, *The Social*, 98–99.

37. Ibid., 267.
38. For an introduction to this literature, see R. C. Richardson, *The Debate on the English Revolution*, 3rd ed. (Manchester: Manchester University Press, 1998); for a group model based on social class, see Christopher Hill, *The Century of Revolution, 1603–1714* (London: Routledge Classics, 2002); for a sampling of revisionist literature, see Peter Gaunt, *The English Civil War: The Essential Readings* (Oxford: Blackwell, 2000).
39. See especially, Gene Brucker, *The Civic World of Early Renaissance Florence* (Princeton, NJ: Princeton University Press, 1977); F. W. Kent, *Household and Lineage in Renaissance Florence* (Princeton, NJ: Princeton University Press, 1977); Dale Kent, *The Rise of the Medici* (Oxford: Oxford University Press, 1978); F. W. Kent and Dale Kent, *Neighbours and Neighbourhoods in Renaissance Florence: The District of the Red Lion in the Fifteenth Century* (Locust Valley, NY: J. J. Augustin, 1982); Ronald F. E. Weissman, *Ritual Brotherhood in Renaissance Florence* (New York: Academic Press, 1982); Nicholas A. Eckstein, *The District of the Green Dragon* (Florence: Leo S. Olschki, 1995); Nicolai Rubinstein, *The Government of Florence under the Medici (1434–1494)*, 2nd ed. (Oxford: Clarendon Press, 1997); Sharon Strocchia, *Nuns and Nunneries in Renaissance Florence* (Baltimore: Johns Hopkins University Press, 2009), 39–71, with further bibliographic leads on the study of neighborhoods on 208–209.
40. Two good entry points into this literature are Jurdjevic, *Guardians*, 168–169, and Thomas Kuehn, *Heirs, Kin, and Creditors in Renaissance Florence* (Cambridge: Cambridge University Press, 2008), 107–111.
41. As a start, see Strocchia, *Nuns*, 39–40 and 208–209.
42. This appendix is found at Martines, *The Social*, 303–350.
43. Mario Cosenza, *Bibliographical Dictionary of the Italian Humanists and the World of Classical Scholarship, 1300–1800* (Boston: G. K. Hall, 1962–1967); Field, *The Origins;* Arthur Field, "Leonardo Bruni, Florentine Traitor? Bruni, the Medici, and an Aretine Conspiracy of 1437," *Renaissance Quarterly* 51, no. 4 (1998): 1109–1150; James Hankins, "The Myth of the Platonic Academy of Florence," *Renaissance Quarterly* 44, no. 3 (1991): 429–475, esp. 463–471; Davies, *Florence*, 106–124; della Torre, *Storia;* Emilio Santini, *Firenze e i suoi "oratori" nel Quattrocento* (Milan: Remo Sandron, 1922); Armando Verde, *Lo studio fiorentino, 1473–1503: Ricerche e Documenti* (Florence: Leo S. Olschki, 1973–2010); Antonio Manfredi, "Notizie su Antonio Ferrantini canonico di San Lorenzo e umanista," in *Il capitolo di San Lorenzo nel quattrocento*, ed. Paolo Viti (Florence: Leo S. Olschki, 2006), 65–80. Numerous conferences have been held in Italy that shed light on the lives and writings of literary humanists as well as more marginal figures; for a sampling of these see the notes to Chapter 2 of this study.
44. Anthony F. D'Elia, *The Renaissance of Marriage in Fifteenth-Century Italy* (Cambridge, MA: Harvard University Press, 2004); John M. McManamon, *Funeral Oratory and the Cultural Ideals of Italian Humanism* (Chapel Hill: University of North Carolina Press, 1989); Alison Brown, "Platonism in Fifteenth-Century Florence," in *The Medici in Florence* (Florence: Leo S. Olschki, 1992), 215–245; Hankins, "The Popularization;" cf. James Hankins, "Humanism in the Vernacular: The Case of Leonardo Bruni,"

in *Humanism and Creativity in the Renaissance: Essays in Honor of Ronald G. Witt*, ed. Christopher S. Celenza and Kenneth Gouwens (Leiden: Brill, 2006), 11–29.

45. Christian Bec, *Les Marchands Écrivains: Affaires et Humanisme à Florence, 1375–1434* (Paris: Mouton, 1967); Christian Bec, *Cultura e Società a Firenze nell' Età della Rinascenza* (Rome: Salerno Editrice, 1984); Christian Bec, *Les Livres des Florentins (1413–1608)* (Florence: Leo S. Olschki, 1984); John M. Najemy, *Corporatism and Consensus in Florentine Electoral Politics, 1280–1400* (Chapel Hill: University of North Carolina Press, 1982); and John M. Najemy, *A History of Florence, 1200–1575* (Malden, MA: Blackwell, 2006), 200–218; see also Dale Kent, *Cosimo de' Medici and the Florentine Renaissance* (New Haven, CT: Yale University Press, 2000), esp. 81–98; Paula C. Clarke, "Middle Class Culture in Florence on the Eve of the Renaissance," in *Firenze alla vigilia del rinascimento: Antonio Pucci e i suoi contemporanei*, ed. Maria Bendinelli Predelli (Fiesole: Edizioni Cadmo, 2006), 111–124.

46. Fubini's list of publications is too vast to list in its entirety here. For example, see Riccardo Fubini, *Italia quattrocentesca: Politica e diplomazia nell'età di Lorenzo il Magnifico* (Milan: Franco Angeli, 1994); Riccardo Fubini, *Quattrocento fiorentino: Politica, diplomazia, cultura* (Pisa: Pacini, 1996); and Riccardo Fubini, *Storiografia dell'umanesimo in Italia da Leonardo Bruni ad Annio da Viterbo* (Rome: Edizioni di Storia e Letteratura, 2003); see also Gary Ianziti, *Humanistic Historiography under the Sforzas: Politics and Propaganda in Fifteenth-Century Milan* (Oxford: Clarendon Press, 1988); Gary Ianziti, *Writing History in Renaissance Italy: Leonardo Bruni and the Uses of the Past* (Cambridge, MA: Harvard University Press, 2012); Sharon Strocchia, *Death and Ritual in Renaissance Florence* (Baltimore: Johns Hopkins University Press, 1992); Jurdjevic, *Guardians*; Stephen Milner, "Political Oratory and the Public Sphere in Early Quattrocento Florence," *New Readings* 1 (1995): 41–64; Stephen Milner, "Citing the Balcony: The Politics of Place and Public Address in Trecento Florence," *Italian Studies* 55 (2000): 53–82; Stephen Milner, "The Piazza della Signoria as Practiced Place," in *Renaissance Florence: A Social History*, ed. Roger J. Crum and John T. Paoletti (Cambridge: Cambridge University Press, 2006), 83–103; Ronald G. Witt, "Civic Humanism and the Rebirth of the Ciceronian Oration," *Modern Language Quarterly* 51, no. 2 (1990): 178–181; Witt, *In the Footsteps*, 451–454; see also James Hankins, "Cosimo de' Medici as a Patron of Humanistic Literature," in *Humanism and Platonism in the Italian Renaissance* (Rome: Edizioni di Storia e Letteratura, 2003), 1:427–455.

47. Witt, "Civic Humanism," 178–181.

48. Witt, *In the Footsteps*, 453.

49. Ibid. and Witt, "Civic Humanism," 180–181.

50. Witt, *In the Footsteps*, 451–454.

51. Black's numerous shorter publications on Tuscan and Florentine education culminated in the publication of Black, *Humanism*, and Black, *Education*.

52. Black, *Education*, xii.

53. Ibid., xv and xviii.

1. Learned Connections and the Humanist Movement

1. Phyllis Goodhart Gordan, ed. and trans., *Two Renaissance Book Hunters: The Letters of Poggius Bracciolini to Nicholas Niccolis* (New York: Columbia University Press, 1974), 91.
2. Ibid., 91.
3. On Bardi as bank manager in Rome, see ibid., 281. On Bardi more generally, see Kent, *The Rise*, 72, 73, and 83.
4. C. Monzani, "di Leonardo Bruni Aretino," *Archivio Storico Italiano*, new series, 5 (1857): 30 and ASF Dieci Miss. 2, 85v.
5. Poggio Bracciolini, *Lettere*, ed. Helene Harth (Florence: Leo S. Olschki, 1984), 2:33; after Bruni's mission had ended, Poggio again referred to contact between Bruni and Bardi in a letter dated from October of the same year; see Gordan, *Two Renaissance*, 110 and 296.
6. Poggio's whereabouts are known from his letters. A letter dated July 1426 was sent from Rome; see Bracciolini, *Lettere*, 2:55. Corroborating evidence is in a letter dated September 25, 1426, in which Poggio stated that he had left Rome only two months before, thus placing him in the city with Bruni and Bardi until mid-July; see Bracciolini, *Lettere*, 2:64.
7. Field, "Leonardo Bruni," 111I.
8. Francesco Paolo Luiso, *Studi su l'epistolario di Leonardo Bruni* (Rome: Istituto Storico Italiano per il Medio Evo, 1980), 103–104; cf. Leonardo Bruni, *Epistolarum libri VIII recensente Laurentio Mehus (1741)*, ed. James Hankins (Rome: Edizioni di Storia e Letteratura, 2007), 1:141–142. I have been unable to find any letters to or from Cosimo de' Medici in ASF MAP from this period.
9. Kenneth Setton, *The Papacy and the Levant*, 4 vols. (Philadelphia: American Philosophical Society, 1976–1984), 2:46.
10. For documents related to Barbaro and Mauroceno's negotiations in Rome, see ASV Sen. Sec. 9, 98r, 106v, 117v, 120v, 121r, 129v, 131r, 132v, 133v, 136v, 138v, 142v, 147r, 149v, 158v, and 163; for the order for Bruni and Tornabuoni to work closely with them, see Monzani, "di Leonardo," 26–27, 30, and 32.
11. Francesca Trivellato, "La missione diplomatica a Venezia del fiorentino Giannozzo Manetti a meta quattrocento," *Studi Veneziani* 28 (1994): 231–235. For Manetti's learned discussions while abroad, see Albanese, "Manetti," 22–26.
12. Gordan, *Two Renaissance*, 99.
13. Ibid., 99, 126, 127, 132, and 287. For Bardi's date of death, see ibid., 313.
14. Bec, *Les Livres*, 174.
15. Viti, *Leonardo Bruni e Firenze*, 379.
16. ASF Sig. Leg. 10, 109v.
17. On the *Otto di Custodia (Otto di Guardia)*, see Rubinstein, *The Government*, 56 and passim.
18. ASF Sig. Dieci OttoLeg. Miss. Resp. 2, 77r.
19. The letter is published in Viti, *Leonardo Bruni e Firenze*, 381–382.
20. Witt, *In the Footsteps*, 446.

21. Cesare Guasti, *Commissioni di Rinaldo degli Albizzi per il Comune di Firenze dal MCCCXCLIX al MCCCCXXXIII* (Florence: M. Cellini E.C.), 1:276.

22. Black, *Education*, 169 and 428.

23. Giuseppe M. Cagni, *Vespasiano da Bisticci e il suo epistolario* (Rome: Edizioni di Storia e Letteratura, 1969), 205.

24. These *filze* are found at Sig. Dieci Otto Leg. Miss. Resp. 2, 5, 60, 61, 62, and 75; see also Marcello del Piazzo, ed., *Signori, Dieci di Balìa, Otto di Pratica Legazioni e Commissarie, Missive e Responsive* (Rome: n.p, 1960), 9–10, 12–13, 39–41, and 55.

25. For a survey of this literature, see Brian Jeffrey Maxson, "Kings and Tyrants: Leonardo Bruni's *Hiero* in Early Renaisance Florence," *Renaissance Studies* 24, no. 2 (April 2010): 190–191.

26. For the *Dialogues*, see Gordon Griffiths, James Hankins, and David Thompson, eds., *The Humanism of Leonardo Bruni* (Binghamton, NY: Medieval & Renaissance Texts and Studies, 1987), 63–84. See also the Latin version at Leonardo Bruni, *Histoire, Eloquence et Poésie à Florence au Début du Quattrocento*, ed. and trans. Laurence Bernard-Pradelle (Paris: Honoré Champion Editeur, 2008), 316–391; on Sermini as the chancellor of Florence, see Carol Quillen, "The Uses of the Past in Quattrocento Florence: A Reading of Leonardo Bruni's *Dialogues*," *Journal of the History of Ideas* 71, no. 3 (July 2010): 363–364; for Sermini's role in the Guelf Party, see Field, "Leonardo Bruni," 1117.

27. Albanese, "Manetti," 25–26.

28. Ibid., 29–30.

29. Ibid. See also Marsh, "Boccaccio," 342.

30. Albanese, "Manetti," 18 and 24–25.

31. della Torre, *Storia*, 185, 191, and passim.

32. Ibid., 401–402; cf. Vespasiano da Bisticci, *Le Vite*, ed. Aulo Greco (Florence: Istituto Nazionale di Studi sul Rinascimento, 1976), 2:215–217.

33. On the identity of teachers and students in fifteenth-century Florence, see Black, *Education*.

34. On gifts, see Chapter 4.

35. Michael Baxandall, *Painting and Experience in Fifteenth-Century Italy* (Oxford: Oxford University Press, 1988); F. W. Kent and Patricia Simons with J. C. Eade, eds., *Patronage, Art, and Society in Renaissance Italy* (Oxford: Clarendon Press, 1987); Melissa Meriam Bullard, *Lorenzo il Magnifico: Image, Anxiety, Politics and Finance* (Florence: Leo S. Olschki, 1994), 111–117.

36. Margery A. Ganz, "A Florentine Friendship: Donato Acciaiuoli and Vespasiano da Bisticci," *Renaissance Quarterly* 43, no. 2 (Summer 1990): 380–381; see also Albinia de la Mare, "Vespasiano da Bisticci e i copisti fiorentini di Federico," in *Federico di Montefeltro*, ed. Giorgio Cerboni Baiardi, Giorgio Chittolini, and Piero Floriani (Rome: Bulzoni Editore, 1986), 3:87.

37. Frances Amelia Yates, *Giordano Bruno and the Hermetic Tradition* (London: Routledge and Kegan Paul, 1964), 12–14.

38. Christopher S. Celenza, "Parallel Lives: Plutarch's Lives, Lapo da Castiglionchio the Younger (1405–1438) and the Art of Italian Renaissance Translation," *Illinois Classical Studies* 22 (1997): 130–132.

39. Ibid., 132–134.

40. Ibid., 134–138; on his death, see ibid., 121.

41. Brian Jeffrey Maxson, "Establishing Independence: Leonardo Bruni's *History of the Florentine People* and Ritual in Fifteenth-Century Florence," in *Foundation, Dedication and Consecration Rituals in Early Modern Culture*, ed. Maarten Delbeke, Jan de Jong, and Minou Schraven (Leiden: Brill, 2012), 79–96.

42. Daniela Gatti, *La Vita Caroli di Donato Acciaiuoli: La legenda di Carlo Magno in funzione di una historia di gesta* (Bologna: Patron, 1981), 116 and more generally 115–118; "Illud autem loco summae gloriae Florentiae urbi tribuendam puto" cf. Leonardo Bruni, *History of the Florentine People*, ed. and trans. James Hankins (Cambridge, MA: Harvard University Press, 2001–2007), 1:86–89. Illud autem loco summae gloriae Florentiae urbi tribuendam puto.

43. C. Milanesi, "Il viaggio degli ambasciatori fiorentini al Re di Francia nel MCCCCLXI descritto da Giovanni di Francesco di Neri Cecchi loro Cancelliere," *Archivio Storico Italiano* ser. 3, vol. 1 (1865): part one, 25.

44. Francesco Guicciardini, *Diario del viaggio in Spagna; memorie di famiglia*, ed. Roberto Palmarocchi with preface by Bruno Maier and notes by Mario Spinella (Pordenone: Edizioni Studio Tesi, 1993), 41.

45. Many of these letters appear in Car. Strozzi III, 112. For examples, see 1r, 2r, 3r, 4r, and passim.

46. Luiso, *Studi*, 108–109; and Bruni, *Epistolarum*, 2:31–33.

47. Brucker, *The Civic World*, 292; and Black, *Benedetto Accolti*, 137.

48. ASF Sig. Dieci Otto Leg. Miss. Resp, 75. On 10r there is a vernacular letter in Piero's hand. The Latin letter from 10r–10v, however, is in a different hand. On 10v there is another vernacular letter and Piero's hand returns. The same change occurs in the Latin letters on 11v–12r, 12v, and 18r, all of which are signed in Piero's name. On 18r is the vernacular letter, clearly in Piero's hand, that ends with the statement that the letter was sent to the Dieci di Balìa and written in Piero's own hand. The Latin letter on the same page simply states that it was sent to the Dieci, omitting any comment on who wrote it.

49. Matteo Palmieri, *Vita civile*, ed. Gino Belloni (Florence: Sansoni, 1982), 7–8.

50. ASF Car. Strozzi. III 112, 80r.

51. Richard C. Trexler, *The Libro Cerimoniale of the Florentine Republic* (Geneva: Librairie Droz S.A., 1978), 85–88. The quote, "fecie inoppinato degna risposta," is from p. 86; on Marsuppini, see Chapter 4.

52. For his copy of Bruni's book, see BML Plut. 3, 378, and Paul Oskar Kristeller, *Iter Italicum* (Leiden: Brill, 1963–1992), 6:177; for his manuscript with rhetorical works by Cicero, see BL Harl. 3925, with ownership marks on 94r and 188v.

53. Guicciardini, *Diario*, 93, "sanza lettere."

54. della Torre, *Storia*, 610; Kristeller, "Marsilio Ficino," 28.

55. ASF Car. Strozzi. I 137, 41r.

56. On Jacopo's diplomatic career, see Chapter 7; Bartolomeo Scala, *Humanistic and Political Writings*, ed. Alison Brown (Tempe: Arizona Center for Medieval and Renaissance Texts and Studies, 1997), 145–148.

57. della Torre, *Storia*, 727.

58. Ibid. See also Marsilio Ficino, *Three Books on Life*, ed. and trans. Carol V. Kaske and John R. Clark (Binghamton, NY: Medieval & Renaissance Texts & Studies, 1989), 394–401; Jill Kraye, "Ficino in the Firing Line: A Renaissance Neoplatonist and His Critics," in *Marsilio Ficino: His Theology, His Philosophy, His Legacy*, ed. Michael J. B. Allen and Valery Rees with Martin Davies (Leiden: Brill, 2002), 377–378; for the letter from Ficino to Piero Guicciardini, see Marsilio Ficino, *Opera omnia*, ed. Paul Oskar Kristeller (Turin: Bottega d'Erasmo, 1962), 1:754.

59. Ficino, *Three*, 196–197.

60. Ibid., 196–199.

61. Ibid., 198–199.

62. Ibid., 396; Kraye, "Ficino," 377–378.

63. Ficino, *Three*, 396–397.

64. Ibid., 398–399.

65. BNC Magl. VIII 1437, 9v–12r. See also Hankins, "The Myth," 466; on Piero's election, see *Florentine Renaissance Resources, Online Tratte of Office Holders, 1282–1532*, machine-readable data file, ed. David Herlihy, R. Burr Litchfield, Anthony Molho, and Roberto Barducci (Providence, RI: Florentine Renaissance Resources/STG: Brown University, 2002), search for Guicciardin under surnam1. There will be only one Piero di Iacopo listed.

66. Niccolò Machiavelli, *Florentine Histories*, trans. Laura F. Banfield and Harvey C. Mansfield, Jr. (Princeton, NJ: Princeton University Press, 1988), 181.

67. BNC Magl. VIII 54, 33r has the date September 29, 1467; 99v has an ownership mark of Giovanni Guicciardini.

68. David Herlihy, *Women, Family and Society in Medieval Europe: Historical Essays, 1978–1991* (Providence, RI: Berghahn Books, 1995), 204–205, has leads on the guild matriculation of members of this branch of the Guicciardini family, but nothing on potential intellectual interests.

69. John R. Spencer, *Andrea del Castagno and his Patrons* (Durham, NC: Duke University Press, 1991), 15–31; on his diplomatic career, see Chapter 6.

70. On the location of Bernadetto's house, see Dale Kent, *Friendship, Love and Trust in Renaissance Florence* (Cambridge, MA: Harvard University Press, 2009), 101.

71. Brian Jeffrey Maxson, "The Many Shades of Praise: Politics and Panegyrics in Fifteenth-Century Florence," in *Rhetorik in Mittelalter und Renaissance: Konzepte – Praxis – Diversität*, ed. Georg Strack and Julia Knödler (Munich: Utz, 2011), 404; on Davanzati in general, see Martines, *The Social*, 328–329.

72. On the Davanzati as neighbors of the Strozzi, see Kent, *The Rise*, 182 and 184. The Palazzo Davanzati in Florence was not owned by the Davanzati family until well outside the temporal limits of this book, but it also suggests the proximity of the family to the Strozzi. The house features a coat of arms and record of Giuliano Davanzati's knighthood at the hands of Pope Eugenius IV, evidently moved from an older dwelling of the Davanzati. See Walter Bombe,

"A Florentine House in the Middle Ages: The Davizzi-Davanzati Palace," *Architectural Record* 31 (1912): 580.

73. ASF Car. Strozzi. III, 112, 78r and 79r.
74. Cagni, *Vespasiano*, plate 10, which appears between pp. 144 and 145.
75. Ibid., 47.
76. The rough dating of these decorations is from an oral discussion, in situ, with an expert of Renaissance architecture in Florence. My thanks Dr. Brenda Preyer for her time and generosity with this information.
77. Alessandro Guidotti, "Nuovi documenti su Vespasiano da Bisticci la sua bottega e la sua famiglia," in *Federico di Montefeltro*, ed. Giorgio Cerboni Baiardi, Giorgio Chittolini, and Piero Floriani (Rome: Bulzoni Editore, 1986), 3:103–104. Cf. Albinia de la Mare, "New Research on Humanistic Scribes in Florence," in *Miniatura fiorentina del Rinascimento 1440–1525*, ed. Annarosa Garzelli (Florence: Giunta Regionale Toscana, 1985), 1:400, which records that the shop of Vespasiano's master and later partner, Michele di Giovanni Guarducci, was on "the corner of the Via del Proconsolo facing the Palazzo del Podestà."
78. On Agnolo in general, see da Bisticci, *Le Vite*, 2:261–284.
79. Vespasiano da Bisticci, *Renaissance Princes, Popes, and Prelates*, trans. William George and Emily Waters (New York: Harper & Row: 1963), 247–250.
80. Ibid., 246–247.
81. Ricc. 3903, 3r.
82. Leon Battista Alberti, *The Family in Renaissance Florence*, trans. Renée Neu Watkins (Columbia: University of South Carolina Press, 1969), 3.
83. da Bisticci, *Le Vite*, 2:262.
84. Luiso, *Studi*, 132–133; cf. Bruni, *Epistolarum*, 2:194–195.
85. On the friendship between Filippo and Bruni, see Field, "Leonardo," 1124; on the actual genealogy of Filippo, see da Bisticci, *Renaissance*, 319, who claims that Filippo descended from "a very poor man of Vertine di Chianti." On Filippo and the Badia, see Anne Leader, *The Badia of Florence: Art and Observance in a Renaissance Monastery* (Bloomington: Indiana University Press, 2011), 90–91. My thanks to Anne Leader for sharing chapter 3 of her monograph before it appeared in print.
86. Maxson, "*This Sort.*"
87. Kent, *The Rise*, 157; see Leonardo Bruni, *Opere letterarie e politiche*, ed. Paolo Viti (Turin: Unione Tipografico, 1996), 200–201 and more generally, 200–241.
88. On the diplomatic career of these two men, see Chapter 6.
89. Cagni, *Vespasiano*, 136–137.
90. On the attribution, see Shelley E. Zuraw, "The Public Commemorative Monument: Mino da Fiesole's Tombs in the Florentine Badia," *Art Bulletin* 80, no. 3 (September 1998): 473. For an image of the tomb, see Anne Markham Schulz, *The Sculpture of Bernardo Rossellino and His Workshop* (Princeton, NJ: Princeton University Press, 1977), plate 215, referred to on p. 71; see also Leader, *The Badia*, 56 and 58.

91. These letters are all unpublished. The letter to Pandolfo from Donato Acciaiuoli survives in several manuscripts, all listed in the *Iter Italicum*. For example, see BNC Magl. XXXII 39 and BNC Magl. XXXIX 86. The letters from Giannozzo Manettti, Piero Acciaiuoli, and Alamanno Rinuccini are in Ricc. 3903, but are not listed in the *Iter*. Ricc. 3903 also contains the only known copy of the funerary oration written by Giannozzo Manetti on the death of Giannozzo Pandolfini, which has never been published.

92. della Torre, *Storia*, 385.

93. BNC Magl. XXV, 348, 14r–22r.

94. Ficino, *Opera omnia*, 1:918; on Pierfilippo's library, see Annaclara Cataldi Palau, "La biblioteca Pandolfini." *Italia medioevale e umanistica* 31 (1988): 259–399; Annaclara Cataldi Palau, "La biblioteca di Pierfilippo Pandolfini," in *Protrepticon*, ed. Sesto Prete (Milan: Istituto Francesco Petrarca, 1989), 17–28; Concetta Bianca, "Un nuovo codice Pandolfini" *Rinascimento* 34 (1994): 153–155.

95. These letters are found at BNC Magl. VI, 166, 104r–114v.

96. Alamanno Rinuccini, *Lettere ed orazioni*, ed. Vito R. Giustiniani (Florence: Leo S. Olschki, 1953), 175.

97. Verde, *Lo Studio*, 4:385.

98. Gene Brucker, *Living on the Edge in Leonardo's Florence, Selected Essays* (Berkeley: University of California Press, 2005), 146 and 191.

99. Melissa Meriam Bullard, *Filippo Strozzi and the Medici: Favor and Finance in Sixteenth-Century Florence and Rome* (Cambridge: Cambridge University Press, 1980), 125.

100. della Torre, *Storia*, 388; Rinuccini, *Lettere*, 126–130.

101. Cagni, *Vespasiano*, 191–195, 200–205, 215–220; cf. della Torre, *Storia*, 388.

102. Angelo Poliziano, *I detti piacevoli*, ed. Mariano Festa (Montepulciano: Editori del Grifo, 1985), 28.

103. Marita Horster, *Andrea del Castagno: Complete Edition with a Critical Catalogue* (Ithaca, NY: Cornell University Press, 1980), 179.

104. Spencer, *Andrea*, 37–42.

105. Christian L. Joost-Gaugier, "Castagno's Humanistic Program at Legnaia and Its Possible Inventor," *Zeitschrift für Kunstgeschichte* 45, no. 3 (1982): 279–282.

106. Philine Helas, "Der 'fliegende Kartograph.' Zu dem Federico da Montefeltro und Lorenzo de' Medici gewidmeten Werk." Le septe giornate della geographia" von Francesco Berlinghieri und dem Bild der Erde im Florenz des Quattrocento," *Mitteilungen des Kunsthistorischen Institutes in Florenz* 46 (2002): 311.

107. Cagni, *Vespasiano*, 150–153.

108. Cosenza, *Bibliographical*, 3:2572; cf. della Torre, *Storia* 388, which mistakenly states "Piero." In a note on the same page, in fact, he refers to "Priore."

109. The information regarding the location of Agnolo Pandolfini's home, beside the fifteenth-century Pazzi Palace, was generously shared with me by Brenda Preyer.

110. della Torre, *Storia*, 389–391.

111. Rinuccini, *Lettere*, 173–175.
112. Several sermons and orations by Pierfilippo (not seen) are listed throughout the volumes of Kristeller, *Iter*.
113. *Online Catasto of 1427*, version 1.3, ed. David Herlihy, Christian Klapisch-Zuper, R. Burr Litchfield, and Anthony Molho (machine-readable data file based on D. Herlihy and C. Klapisch-Zuber, [*Census and Property Survey of Florentine Domains in the Province of Tuscany, 1427–1480*] Florentine Renaissance Resources/STG: Brown University, Providence, RI, 2002. Search for Rinuccini under family name.
114. The Palazzo Acciaiuoli, Palazzo Strozzi, and Palazzo Strozzino still exist to document the strength of these families in the Santa Maria Novella quarter of the city, as does the Brancacci Chapel in Santa Maria del Carmine to document the presence of that family in the *oltrarno*. On Donato Acciaiuoli's relatives, see Eugenio Garin, *Portraits from the Quattrocento*, trans. Victor A. Velen and Elizabeth Velen (New York: Harper & Row, 1972), 57.
115. On the Manetti family and their neighborhood, see Eckstein, *The District*, 23–24.
116. Griffiths, *The Humanism*, 65.
117. Marco Parenti, *Lettere*, ed. Maria Marrese (Florence: Leo s. Olschki, 1996), 169; for a partial genealogy of the Pazzi family, see Lauro Martines, *April Blood: Florence and the Plot against the Medici* (Oxford: Oxford University Press, 2003), xvi.
118. BNC Magl. VI, 166, 109v.
119. Martines, *April*, 65.
120. Brucker, *Living*, 143–144.
121. da Bisticci, *Renaissance*, 268–269; see also the letter from Ferrante to Florence announcing Pandolfo's death at ASF Cop. Resp. 1, 134r-134v.
122. Martines, *April*, 208.
123. F. W. Kent, *Bartolommeo Cederini and His Friends: Letters to an Obscure Florentine* (Florence: Leo. S. Olschki, 1991), 30.
124. Ibid., 1115–1118.
125. Field, "Leonardo Bruni," 1119–1122.
126. Kent, *The Rise*, 355–357.
127. Kent, *The Rise*, 345.
128. On Agnolo Acciaiuoli, see the discussion and leads in Chapter 2; on Manetti, see Martines, *The Social*, 178–191.
129. Martines, *April*, 57.
130. Anthony Molho, *Florentine Public Finances in the Early Renaissance, 1400–1433* (Cambridge, MA: Harvard University Press, 1971), 181, 216, and 218.
131. William J. Connell, "The Humanist Citizen as Provincial Governor," in *Florentine Tuscany: Structures and Practices of Power*, ed. William J. Connell and Andrea Zorzi (Cambridge: Cambridge University Press, 2000), 158–161; on Manetti's self-imposed exile, see Luca Boschetto, "L'esilio volontario di Manetti," in *Dignitas et Excellentia Hominis: Convegno di studi su Giannozzo Manetti*, ed. Stefano U. Baldassarri (Florence: Le Lettere, 2008), 117–145.
132. Boschetto, "L'esilio," 123–124.

133. Martines, *April*, 259.

134. Martines, *The Social*, 201–210.

135. Ibid., 117–121.

136. Luiso, *Studi*, 98.

137. Bec, *Les Livres*, 166 and 179; and Kent, *The Rise*, 158.

138. Martines, *The Social*, 204.

139. Ibid., 365–366

140. For the location of Bruni's home, see James Hankins, "The Dates of Leonardo Bruni's Later Works (1437–1443)," *Studi medievali e umanistici* 5–6 (2007–2008), 37; on the location of the Peruzzi and Castellani families, see Kent, *The Rise*, 157; for the intermarriage between the Castellani and Peruzzi, see Kent, *The Rise*, 158.

141. On the role of the Castellani in the Guelf Party in Florence, see Kent, *The Rise*, 158; on Bruni's involvement with the Guelfs, see Bruni, *Opere*, 793–802 and Maxson, "Kings," 200–202 and 204.

142. Martines, *April*, 32–33.

143. For Bruni's election, see ASF Sig. Dieci Otto Leg. Miss. Resp. 8, 20v; for Bruni's neighbor, see Hankins, "The Dates," 37; see also Luca da Panzano, "*Brighe, affanni, volgimenti di stato*": *Le ricordanze quattrocentesche di Luca di Matteo di messer Luca dei Findolfi da Panzano* (Florence: SISMEL, 2010), 73 and 123.

144. ASF Sig. Dieci Otto Leg. Miss. Resp. 8, 20v, "impedimenti."

145. Ibid. On Jacopo Niccoli as a lawyer and as Niccolò Niccoli's brother, see Martines, *The Social*, 161.

146. Martines, *The Social*, 161.

147. On the political status of the Niccoli, see ibid. 160–161.

148. For these connections, see Chapter 7.

149. *Florentine Renaissance Resources*, search for Medici under surname and Niccolo under name.

150. ASF Cons. Prat. 46, 149v, "nostri honoris inminutione."

151. Ibid.

152. Stefano Ugo Baldassarri and Bruno Figliuolo, *Manettiana. La biografia anonima in terzine e altri documenti inediti su Giannozzo Manetti* (Rome: Roma nel Rinascimento, 2010), 11–12.

153. Ibid., 12; and Martines, *The Social*, 185.

154. The speech is published at F. Sandeo, *De regibus siciliae et apuliae* (Hanover: 1611), 169–175.

155. da Bisticci, *Le Vite*, 2:542–543.

156. Sandeo, *De regibus*, 177.

157. Da Bisticci, *Le Vite*, 2:543, "altro che l'abaco" and "vegano quanto onore è a una città et a una casa un simile cittadino."

158. da Bisticci, *Renaissance*, 375–376.

159. Ibid., 71–72.

2. Literary and Social Humanists

1. On Marsili, see Martines, *The Social*, 306–308; della Torre, *Storia*, 185–190; Graziano Micheli, *La figura di Luigi Marsili, precursore della civiltà umanistica a Firenze* (Florence: Editore de Bono, 1992).
2. On Salutati, see Berthold L. Ullman, *The Humanism of Coluccio Salutati* (Padua: Editrice Antenore, 1963); Witt, *Coluccio Salutati*; Ronald G. Witt, *Hercules at the Crossroads: The Life, Works, and Thought of Coluccio Salutati* (Durham, NC: Duke University Press, 1983); Associazione Culturale Buggiano Castello, *Atti del convegno Coluccio Salutati cancelliere e letterato* (Signa: Nova Arti Grafiche, 2007); Concetta Bianca, ed., "Novità su Coluccio Salutati: Seminario a 600 anni dalla morte," in *Medioevo e Rinascimento: Annuario del Dipartimento di Studi sul Medioevo e il Rinascimento dell'Università di Firenze* new ser. 19 (2008).
3. On Bruni, see Griffiths, *The Humanism*; Paolo Viti, ed., *Leonardo Bruni Cancelliere della Repubblica di Firenze* (Florence: Leo S. Olschki, 1990); Viti, *Leonardo Bruni e Firenze*; Field, "Leonardo Bruni"; James Hankins, *Humanism and Platonism in the Italian Renaissance* (Rome: Edizioni di Storia e Letteratura, 2003); Gary Ianziti, "Leonardo Bruni, the Medici, and the Florentine Histories," *Journal of the History of Ideas* 69, no. 1 (2008): 1–22; Maxson, "Kings"; Maxson "Establishing"; Ianziti, *Writing History*.
4. On Poggio, see Ernst Walser, *Poggius Florentinus, Leben und Werke* (Leipzig: Teubner, 1914); *Poggio Bracciolini, 1380–1980, nel VI centenario della nascita* (Florence: Sansoni, 1982); Gordan, *Two Renaissance*; Bracciolini, *Lettere*; Frederick Krantz, "Between Bruni and Machiavelli: History, Law and Historicism in Poggio Bracciolini," in *Politics and Culture in Early Modern Europe*, ed. Phyllis Mack and Margaret C. Jacob (Cambridge: Cambridge University Press, 1987), 119–151, with further bibliography on p. 119.
5. Charles L. Stinger, *Humanism and the Church Fathers: Ambrogio Traversari (1386–1439) and Christian Antiquity in the Italian Renaissance* (Albany: State University of New York Press, 1977), 6 and 30. On Traversari in general, see also Gian Carlo Garfagnini, ed., *Ambrogio Traversari nel VI centenario della nascita* (Florence: Leo S. Olschki, 1988); William Hyland, "The Climacteric of Late Medieval Camaldolese Spirituality: Ambrogio Traversari, John-Jerome of Prague, and the *Linea salutis heremitarum*," in *Florence and Beyond: Culture, Society, and Politics in Renaissance Italy*, ed. David S. Peterson with Daniel Bornstein (Toronto: Centre for Reformation and Renaissance Studies, 2008), 107–120; Martines, *The Social*, 311–312.
6. On Filelfo, see *Francesco Filelfo nel quinto centenario della morte* (Padua: Editrice Antenore, 1986); Diana Robin, *Filelfo in Milan: Writings 1451–1477* (Princeton, NJ: Princeton University Press, 1991), with further bibliography; Paolo Viti, "Francesco Filelfo," in *DBI*, available online at "Francesco Filelfo in Dizionario Biografico – Treccani," Treccani.it, http://www.treccani.it/enciclopedia/francesco-filelfo_%28Dizionario-Biografico%29/ (accessed April 13, 2012); W. Scott Blanchard, "Patrician Sages and the Humanist Cynic: Francesco Filelfo

and the Ethics of World Citizenship," *Renaissance Quarterly* 60, no. 4 (Winter 2007): 1107–1169.

7. On Manetti, see Heinz Willi Wittschier, *Giannozzo Manetti, das Corpus der Orationes* (Cologne: Böhlau, 1968); Paul Botley, "Giannozzo Manetti, Alfonso of Aragon and Pompey the Great: A Crusading Document of 1455," *Journal of the Warburg and Courtauld Institutes* 67 (2004): 129–156; Paul Botley, *Latin Translation in the Renaissance: The Theory and Practice of Leonardo Bruni, Giannozzo Manetti, and Erasmus* (Cambridge: Cambridge University Press, 2004), 63–114; Christine Smith and Joseph F. O'Connor, *Building the Kingdom: Giannozzo Manetti on the Material and Spiritual Edifice* (Tempe: Arizona Center for Medieval and Renaissance Texts and Studies, 2006); Stefano Ugo Baldassarri, ed. *Dignitas et excellentia hominis* (Florence: Le Lettere, 2008), with further bibliographic leads; Baldassarri and Figliuolo *Manettiana*.

8. On Acciaiuoli, see Garin, *Portraits*, 55–117; Ganz, "The Humanist"; Gatti, *La Vita*; Margery Ganz, "Donato Acciaiuoli and the Medici: A Strategy for Survival in '400 Florence,'" *Rinascimento* 22 (1982): 33–73; Ganz, "A Florentine."

9. On Ficino, see Paul Oskar Kristeller, *Supplementum Ficinianum* (Florence: Leo S. Oschki, 1937); Gian Carlo Garfagnini, ed., *Marsilio Ficino e il ritorno di Platone* (Florence: Leo S. Olschki, 1986); Paul Oskar Kristeller, *Marsilio Ficino and His Work after Five Hundred Years* (Florence: Leo S. Olschki, 1987); Michael J. B. Allen and Valery Rees with Martin Davies, eds., *Marsilio Ficino: His Theology, His Philosophy, His Legacy* (Leiden: Brill, 2002); Sebastiano Gentile and Stéphane Toussaint, eds., *Marsilio Ficino, Fonti, Testi, Fortuna* (Rome: Edizioni di Storia e Letteratura, 2006).

10. On Scala, see Brown, *Bartolomeo Scala*; Anna Bellinazzi, *La casa del cancelliere: Documenti e studi sul Palazzo di Bartolomeo Scala a Firenze* (Florence: Edifir, 1998).

11. On Niccoli, see Giuseppe Zippel, *Niccolò Niccoli* (Florence: Bocca, 1890); Berthold L. Ullman and Philip A. Stadter, *The Public Library of Renaissance Florence: Niccolò Niccoli, Cosimo de' Medici and the Library of San Marco* (Padua: Editrice Antenore, 1972); Albinia de la Mare, *The Handwriting of Italian Humanists* (Oxford: Oxford University Press, 1973), 1:44–61; M. C. Davies, "An Emperor without Clothes? Niccolò Niccoli under Attack," in *Maistor: Classical, Byzantine and Renaissance Studies for Robert Browning*, ed. Ann Moffatt (Canberra: Australian Association for Byzantine Studies, 1984), 296–308.

12. On Palla di Nofri Strozzi, see Martines, *The Social*, 316–318; Giuseppe Fiocco, "La biblioteca di Palla Strozzi," in *Studi di bibliografia e di storia in onore di Tammaro de Marinis* (Verona: Valdonega, 1964), 2:289–310; Kent and Kent, *Neighbours;* Heather Gregory "Palla Strozzi's Patronage and Pre-Medicean Florence," in *Patronage, Art and Society in Renaissance Italy*, ed. F. W. Kent and Patricia Simons with J. C. Eade (Oxford: Clarendon Press, 1987), 201–220; Lorenzo Fabbri, "The Memory of Exiled Families: The Case of the Strozzi," in *Art, Memory, and Family in Renaissance Florence*, ed. Giovanni Ciappelli and Patricia Lee Rubin (Cambridge: Cambridge University Press, 2000), 253–261; Sergio Tognetti, "Gli affari di Messer

Palla Strozzi (e di suo padre Nofri). Imprenditoria e mecenatismo nella Firenze del primo Rinascimento," *Annali di Storia di Firenze* 4 (2009): 7–88; a summary of publications related to Palla di Nofri's artistic commissions is found in Patricia Lee Rubin, *Images and Identity in Fifteenth-Century Florence* (New Haven, CT: Yale University Press, 2007), 318–319.

13. Carlo Marsuppini has received little attention from scholars. For him in general, see Giuseppe Zippel, *Carlo Marsuppini d'Arezzo: Notizie, biografiche, raccolte* (Trento: Giovanni Zippel, 1897); Martines, *The Social,* passim; Roberto Cardini and Paolo Viti, *I cancellieri aretini della Repubblica di Firenze* (Florence: Polistampa, 2003), 73–97; Remigio Sabbadini, "Briciole umanistiche," *Giornale storico della letteratura italiana* 17 (1891): 212–218; and Alessandra Rocco, ed., *Carlo Marsuppini traduttore d'Omero: La prima traduzione umanistica in versi dell'Iliade (primo e nono libro)* (Padua: Il poligrafo, 2000); my thanks to Arthur Field and Timothy Kircher for the references to Sabbadini and Rocco, respectively.

14. F. W. Kent, *Lorenzo de' Medici and the Art of Magnificence* (Baltimore: Johns Hopkins University Press, 2004), 1–9.

15. da Bisticci, *Le Vite,* 1:115, 175, and passim.

16. See Chapter 4.

17. Letters between Manetti and Vespasiano exist from 1449 and continue until 1457. See Cagni, *Vespasiano,* 121–129 and 131–139.

18. della Torre, *Storia,* 345; on Vespasiano and the Acciaiuoli, see Ganz, "A Florentine."

19. della Torre, *Storia,* 404–405; cf. Cagni, *Vespasiano,* 149–150.

20. della Torre, *Storia,* 383. cf. Cagni, *Vespasiano,* 125.

21. della Torre, *Storia,* 404 and 411; BNC Magl. VIII, 1390, 23r; for Scala's letters, see Scala, *Humanistic,* 183.

22. ASF Car. Strozzi. I, 137, 41r.

23. ASF Car. Strozzi. III, 247, 280r, "priegovi quando vi trovai con cari amici e parenti viricordai."

24. ASF Car. Strozzi. III, 247, 298r; further letters between the two men are found at Car. Strozzi. III, 145, 84r; 178, 23r, and passim.

25. Ganz, "A Florentine," 372–374.

26. de la Mare, "New Research," 1:401–404 and 406–408.

27. della Torre, *Storia,* 287–291; Field, "Leonardo Bruni," 1113.

28. Margaret Haines, "Oligarchy and Opera: Institution and Individuals in the Administration of the Florentine Cathedral," in *Florence and Beyond: Culture, Society, and Politics in Renaissance Italy,* ed. David S. Peterson with Daniel E. Bornstein (Toronto: Centre for Reformation and Renaissance Studies, 2008), 161–162.

29. ASF Car. Strozzi. III, 112, 69r, 71r, 74r, 75r; 114, 1r, 3r, 5r.

30. Witt, *In the Footsteps,* 446.

31. The potential political undertones of the antagonism between Guasconi and Niccoli were kindly pointed out to me by Arthur Field; on Biagio Guasconi, see also Bec, *Les Marchands,* 405; Raffaella Maria Zaccharia, "Biagio Guasconi," in *DBI,* available online at "Biagio Guasconi in Dizionario Biografico – Treccani,"

Treccani.it, http://www.treccani.it/enciclopedia/biagio-guasconi_%28Dizionario-Biografico%29/ (accessed April 16, 2012).

32. ASF Car. Strozzi. III, 114, 25r.

33. ASF Car. Strozzi. III, 112, 50r; cf. Field, "Leonardo Bruni," 1113.

34. da Bisticci, *Le Vite*, 2:424–425.

35. della Torre, *Storia*, 289. Letters from Domenico to Matteo are found at Car. Strozzi. III, 112, 139r, 141r, and 147r. See also Bec, *Les Marchands*, 404–405.

36. Nicolai Rubinstein, "Florentine Constitutionalism and Medici Ascendancy in the Fifteenth Century," in *Florentine Studies: Politics and Society in Renaissance Florence*, ed. Nicolai Rubinstein (London: Faber and Faber, 1968), 460.

37. Kent, *Friendship*, 175.

38. Machiavelli, *Florentine*, 293.

39. della Torre, *Storia*, 288; cf. Field, "Leonardo Bruni," 1113.

40. Charles Trinkaus, *In Our Image and Likeness* (Constable: Garden City Press, 1970), 238; Remigio Sabbadini, *La scuola e gli studi di Guarino Guarini Veronese* (Catania: Francesco Galati, 1896), 39.

41. de la Mare, "New Research," 1:427; Martines, *The Social*, 318–319; on Corbinelli in general, see Rudolfo Blum, *La biblioteca della Badia fiorentina e i codici di Antonio Corbinelli* (Vatican City: Biblioteca Apostolica Vaticana, 1951), 39–110 and 173–179; Antonio Rollo, "Sulle tracce di Antonio Corbinelli," *Studi medievali e umanistici* 2 (2004): 25–95.

42. de la Mare, "New Research," 1:427.

43. For the letter, see Car. Strozzi. III, 112, 21r; see also Bisticci, *Le Vite*, 2:376; Francesco Filelfo, *Satyrae*, ed. Silvia Fiaschi (Rome: Edizioni di Storia e Letteratura, 2005), 1:35–42.

44. da Bisticci, *Le Vite*, 2:377–378.

45. de la Mare, "New Research," 1:427.

46. Ibid., 1:400.

47. Botley, *Latin Translation*, 75.

48. Alessandra Strozzi, *Selected Letters*, ed. Heather Gregory (Los Angeles: University of California Press, 1997), 84–85.

49. On this dialogue, see Giannozzo Manetti, *Dialogus Consolatorius*, ed. Alfonso de Petris (Rome: Edizioni di Storia e Letteratura, 1983); Francesco Bausi, "Le due redazioni del *Dialogus Consolatorius* di Giannozzo Manetti," in *Dignitas et Excellentia Hominis*, ed. Stefano U. Baldassarri (Florence: Le Lettere, 2008), 77–104.

50. Botley, *Latin Translation*, 75.

51. For the biography of Agnolo Acciaiuoli, see Serena Ferente, "The Ways of Practice: Angelo Acciaiuoli, 1450–1470," in *From Florence to the Mediterranean and Beyond*, ed. Diogo Ramada Curto, Eric R. Dursteler, Julius Kirshner, and Francesca Trivellato (Florence: Leo S. Olschki, 2009), 1:103–116; and Martines, *The Social*, 335–336; for Agnolo's interactions with the emperor of Constantinople, see Setton, *Papacy*, 4:64.

52. Botley, *Latin*, 71; see also Smith and O'Connor, *Kingdom*, 31–49 and 305–359. On the familial relationship between Manetti and Acciaiuoli, see Martines, *The Social*, 335; see also Ferente, "The Ways," 1:107.

53. della Torre, *Storia*, 234–237.
54. Cagni, *Vespasiano*, 129.
55. See Ambrogio Traversari, *Latinae epistolae*, ed. Lorenzo Mehus (Florence: Caesareo, 1759), 2:259; on Filelfo, see della Torre, *Storia*, 330–331 (with additional epistolary leads not seen); on Barbaro, see Francesco Barbaro, *Epistolario*, ed. Claudio Griggio (Florence: Leo S. Olschki, 1999), 2:86–87, 116, 517–518, 589–590; cf. Kent, *The Rise*, 134.
56. Kent, *Friendship*, 28.
57. Field, "Leonardo Bruni," 1126; cf. Cosenza, *Dictionary*, 1:23.
58. Francesco Filelfo, *Cent-dix letters grecques de François Filelfe*, ed. Émile Legrand (Paris: Ernest Leroux, 1892), 54–55; cf. della Torre, *Storia*, 369.
59. Cosenza, *Dictionary* 1:23.
60. M. D. Reeve, "Statius' Silvae in the Fifteenth Century," *Classical Quarterly* n.s. 27, no. 1 (1977), 202.
61. Sir John Edwin Sandys, *A Short History of Classical Scholarship* (Cambridge: Cambridge University Press, 1915), 167–170.
62. Reeve, "Statius' Silvae," 220.
63. Ibid., 223.
64. Reeve does not specify the name of Antonio's father, but I have found this information through the Online Tratte. See *Florentine Renaissance Resources*. Search for "Barbadori" under surname. I have yet to establish the connection between Bartolomeo da Montepulciano and Giovanni Barbadori.
65. Reeve, "Statius' Silvae," 223.
66. ASF Car. Strozzi. III, 112, 107r; on Filelfo's translation of Aristotle's *Rhetoric*, see Viti, "Francesco." The finding guide in the Florentine State Archive lists the sender as "*incerto*" and Christian Bec published the letter in its entirety without speculating on the sender's identity. See Bec, *Les Marchands*, 401.
67. Dale Kent, "Michele del Giogante's House of Memory," in *Society and Individual in Renaissance Florence*, ed. William J. Connell (Berkeley: University of California Press, 2002), 113.
68. da Bisticci, Le Vite, 2:397, "dotto," "buona notitia de le lettere latine," and "religiosissimo."
69. Griffiths, Hankins, and Thompson, *The Humanism*, 331.
70. Botley, *Latin*, 75; da Bisticci, *Le Vite*, 2:397–404; Traversari, *Latinae*, 2:261.
71. ASF Car. Strozzi. III, 112, 110r, 115r, and passim. The letters are published in Francesco Flamini, "Leonardo di Piero Dati, poeta latino del secolo XV," *Giornale storico della letteratura italiana* 16, no. 1 (1890): 82–94.
72. Field, "Leonardo Bruni," 1114; see also Cesare Guasti, "Raimondo Mannelli alla battaglia di Rapallo," *Archivio Veneto* 10 (1875): 54–70.
73. della Torre, *Storia*, 304; see also letters from Niccolò to Matteo at ASF Car. Strozzi. III, 112, 17r, 25r, 29r, 80r; Ricc. 1166, 53v.
74. Letters by Niccolò are found at Ricc. 1166 and BNC Magl. XXI 170; on the familial relationship between Matteo Strozzi and Niccolò della Luna, see della Torre, *Storia*, 306. Alessandra Strozzi, Niccolò's mother, was the sister of Simone Strozzi, who was Matteo's father.
75. Martines, *The Social*, 341–342.

76. della Torre, *Storia*, 293–294; Howard Saalman, *Filippo Brunelleschi: The Buildings* (University Park: Pennsylvania State University Press, 1993), 36–37 and 49–52.
77. Philip Gavitt, *Charity and Children in Renaissance Florence: The Ospedale degli Innocenti, 1410–1536* (Ann Arbor: University of Michigan Press 1990), 145–146.
78. Ibid., 149.
79. Ibid.
80. Ibid.
81. da Bisticci, *Renaissance*, 322–323.
82. Gavitt, *Charity*, 149; and Alison Brown, "Insiders and Outsiders: The Changing Boundaries of Exile," in *Society and Individual in Renaissance Florence*, ed. William J. Connell (Berkeley: University of California Press, 2002), 379; cf. Ullman and Stadter, *The Public*, 26; Black, *Education*, 168–169, who states it was a "virtual exile"; da Bisticci, *Renaissance*, 323.
83. Brown, "Inside," 374.
84. della Torre, *Storia*, 307.
85. della Torre, *Storia*, 307; and Martines, *The Social*, 342.
86. Kent, *Friendship*, 17; and della Torre, *Storia*, 311–312.
87. della Torre, *Storia*, 315–316; on the learning of Andrea Alamanni, see BNC Magl. XXI 170, 52r-54v; Alessandro Perosa, "Andrea Alamanni," in *DBI*, available at "Andrea Alamanni in Dizionario Biografico – Treccani," Treccani. it, http://www.treccani.it/enciclopedia/andrea-alamanni_%28Dizionario_Biografico%29/ (accessed April 16, 2012); della Torre, *Storia*, 368–371; Field "Leonardo Bruni," 1121; Martines, *The Social*, 345–346.
88. della Torre, *Storia*, 316–320.
89. Leonardo Dati, *Epistolae* (Florence, 1743), XIX-XXV, 1–2; and Ricc. 1166, 29r, 29v, 30r, 54r, 54v, 55r, 56r, 56v. cf. della Torre, *Storia*, 295–296, 312–313.
90. della Torre, *Storia*, 295–296.
91. Ibid., 295; The source is Juvenal, *Satires*, 2.121; the original Latin is "o procures, censore opus est an haruspice nobis?" The translation is from Susanna Morton Braund, ed. and trans., *Juvenal and Persius* (Cambridge, MA: Harvard University Press, 2004).
92. della Torre, *Storia*, 295–296, although della Torre was uncertain as to the identity of this Benedetto.
93. Raffaele Maria Zaccaria, "Nicola de' Medici," in *DBI*, available at "Nicola de' Medici in Dizionario Biografico – Treccani," Treccani.it, http://www. treccani.it/enciclopedia/nicola-de-medici_(Dizionario-Biografico)/ (accessed June 21, 2011).
94. Ibid.
95. della Torre, *Storia*, 293 and 296; da Bisticci, *Renaissance*, 237.
96. della Torre, *Storia*, 292–293 and 295–296; cf. Ricc. 1166, 33r and 54v; for the identification of Palla and Lorenzo in Gentile da Fabirano's painting, see Keith Christiansen, *Gentile da Fabriano* (Ithaca, NY: Cornell University Press, 1982), 98 with a detail on plates 32 and 33.
97. Field, "Leonardo," 1119.

98. Martines, *The Social*, 338.
99. Da Bisticci, *Renaissance* 455–456. Brown, "Insiders," 381 claims a date of 1434 but does not provide a source. On p. 363, Brown refers to Kent, *The Rise*, 357 for the exiles in 1434; however, Kent, *The Rise*, 357 does not list Lorenzo.
100. da Bisticci, *Renaissance*, 457.
101. Ibid., 458. That the youth was a Florentine is from ibid., 244.
102. Ricc. 1166, 33r.
103. Field, "Leonardo," 1113.
104. Brown, "Insiders," 381.
105. della Torre, *Storia*, 300.
106. Oren Margolis, "The Politics of Culture in the World of René of Anjou" (PhD diss., University of Oxford, 2011), 173–175. My thanks to Oren Margolis for permission to cite his unpublished dissertation.
107. della Torre, *Storia*, 309–310.
108. See Ricc. 1166, 13r, where Niccolò referred to Bruni as "our Leonardo (huic nostro admodum Leonardo)."
109. Ricc. 1166, 13v–14r; cf. della Torre, *Storia*, 309.
110. On these participants, see Field, "Leonardo," 1127–1128 and Giacomo Ferraù, "Le <<Commentationes florentinae de exilio>>," in *Francesco Filelfo nel quinto centenario della morte* (Padua: Editrice Antenore, 1986), 375 and 381.
111. Field, "Leonardo," 1127.
112. A. Astorri, "Benedetto Fortini," in *DBI*, available at "Benedetto Fortini in Dizionario Biografico – Treccani," Treccani.it, http://www.treccani.it/enci-clopedia/benedetto-fortini_%28Dizionario-Biografico%29/ (accessed July 19, 2011).
113. della Torre, *Storia*, 299–300; Martines, *The Social*, 341.
114. Field, "Leonardo," 1118.
115. Brown, "Insiders," 371.
116. della Torre, *Storia*, 297–299; cf. Rinuccini, *Lettere*, 220–221.
117. The letter is in Ricc. 1166, 55v–56r; for Quaratesi's book, see Black, *Education*, 156; on the Quaratesi in general, see Martines, *The Social*, 341.
118. The general dates of these ownership records match the Giuliano mentioned in Niccolò's letter, but without an adequate family tree of the Quaratesi family it is impossible to discern whether both books were owned by the same Giuliano and whether this Giuliano, in turn, was the brother mentioned in the letter. For the ownership records, see Salomone Morpugo, *I mano-scritti della Biblioteca Riccardiana di Firenze* (Rome: Tipografia Giachetti, 1900), 1:377; and Concetto Marchesi, "Il compendio volgare dell'*Etica* aristotelica e le fonti del VI libro del <Tresor>," *Giornale storico della letteratura italiana* 42 (1903): 71.
119. Hugh Chapman, *Michelangelo, Drawings: Closer to the Master* (New Haven, CT: Yale University Press, 2005), 209–211, with image on 210.
120. Janet Ross, *Florentine Palaces and Their Stories* (London: J. M. Dent, 1905), 174.
121. On Matteo Palmieri, see George M. Carpetto, *The Humanism of Matteo Palmieri* (Rome: Bulzoni, 1984); Claudio Finzi, *Matteo Palmieri dalla 'Vita*

Civile' alla *'Città di Vita'* (Rome: Giuffrè Editore, 1984); Alessandra Mita Ferraro, *Matteo Palmieri: Una biografia intellettuale* (Genoa: Name, 2005).

122. della Torre, *Storia*, 297.
123. Cristoforo Landino, *Poems*, trans. Mary P. Chatfield (Cambridge, MA: Harvard University Press, 2008), 231 and 370.
124. Anthony Grafton, *Leon Battista Alberti: Master Builder of the Italian Renaissance* (Cambridge, MA: Harvard University Press, 2002), 174.
125. On Ridolfi, see Benedetto Luschino, *Vulnera diligentis*, ed. Stefano dall' Aglio (Florence: Tavarnuzze, 2002), 319–320; Ida Giovanna Rao, Paolo Viti, and Raffaella Maria Zaccaria, eds., *I processi di Girolamo Savonarola (1498)* (Florence: SISMEL edizioni del Galluzzo, 2001), 75–76. My thanks to Stefano dall'Aglio for kindly supplying me with these references. Riccardo Fubini, "Discorrendo di cose fiorentine: La provvisione effimera del gonfaloniere Giovan Battista Ridolfi (7 settembre 1512)," in *From Florence to the Mediterranean and Beyond: Essays in Honour of Anthony Molho*, ed. Diogo Ramada Curto, Eric R. Dursteller, Julius Kirshner, and Francesca Trivellato, (Florence: Leo S. Olschki, 2009), 1:3–12.
126. Lisa Jardine, *Worldly Goods: A New History of the Renaissance* (New York: W. W. Norton, 1996), 143–145.
127. ASF Car. Strozzi. I, 137, 89r-104r; cf. Cesare Guasti, *Le carte strozziane del R. Archivio di Stato in Firenze* (Florence: Galileiana, 1884), 1:594.
128. Humphrey Butters, "Machiavelli and the Medici," in *The Cambridge Companion to Machiavelli*, ed. John M. Najemy (Cambridge: Cambridge University Press, 2010), 65.
129. Ibid.
130. Robert Black, "Machiavelli, Servant of the Florentine Republic," in *Machiavelli and Republicanism*, ed. Gisela Bock, Quentin Skinner, and Maurizio Viroli (Cambridge: Cambridge University Press, 1990), 90; further leads on Jacopo Salviati's learning are found in Paul Oskar Kristeller, "An Unpublished Description of Naples by Francesco Bandini," in *Studies in Renaissance Thought and Letters* (Rome: Edizioni di Storia e Letteratura, 1969), 1:401, 414, 428–435.
131. Georg Luck, "A Late Greek Manuscript in the Walters Art Gallery," *Journal of the Walters Art Gallery* 41 (1983): 67.
132. della Torre, *Storia*, 689
133. Ibid., 719–721.
134. Ibid., 832–833; and Baldesar Castiglione, *The Book of the Courtier*, ed. Daniel Javitch (New York: W. W. Norton, 2002), 45; on Diacceto in general, see Paul Oskar Kristeller, "Francesco da Diacceto and Florentine Platonism in the Sixteenth Century," in *Studies in Renaissance Thought and Letters* (Rome: Edizioni di Storia e Letteratura, 1969), 1:295–327.
135. Rinuccini, *Lettere*, 34–36, 139–141; page 241 has a useful index with letter summaries and further leads on references to Capponi in Rinuccini's letters.
136. della Torre, *Storia*, 826.

137. Niccolò del Benino does not appear in della Torre or Cosenza; however, a *protesto* survives by him at BNC Magl. XXV, 348, 22v-29r (dated March 16, 1477). Two letters from Ficino survive to him from 1494 in Ficino, *Opera*, 1:959.

138. della Torre, *Storia*, 187 and 198–199; on Rossi in general, see Aldo Manetti, "Roberto de Rossi," *Rinascimento* 2 (1951): 33–55; Martines, *The Social*, 108–110, 155–159, 256–257, and 415; Roberto Weiss, *Medieval and Humanist Greek* (Padua: Antenor, 1977), 7, 232, 246–247, 258, and 262.

139. Marianne Pade, *The Reception of Plutarch's Lives in Fifteenth-Century Italy* (Copenhagen: Museum Tusculanum Press, 2007), 1:170.

140. See Chapter 1 as well as della Torre, *Storia*, 194.

141. Pade, *The Reception*, 1:170–171.

142. della Torre, *Storia*, 198.

143. Ibid., 198.

144. Davies, *Florence*, 115 and 146.

145. della Torre, *Storia*, 198.

146. G. Pampaloni, "Alessandro Alessandri," in DBI, available online at "Alessandro Alessandri in Dizionario Biografico – Treccani.it, http://www.treccani.it/enciclopedia/alessandro-alessandri_%28Dizionario-Biografico%29/ (accessed May 8, 2012); the altarpiece can be viewed online at the Metropolitan Museum of Art, "Saint Lawrence Enthroned with Saints and Donors," http://www.metmuseum.org/Collections/search-the-collections/110001341 (accessed October 17, 2011).

147. Martines, *The Social*, 329–330. For the location of Agnolo Pandolfini's house, see earlier. For Matteo Palmieri, see Strocchia, *Nuns*, 60 and 95; the survival of the Palazzo degli Alessandri on the modern Borgo degli Albizzi attests to the proximity of the Alessandri family to these two men.

148. Raffaella Maria Zaccaria, "Nicola di Vieri dei Medici," in *Alberti e la cultura del quattrocento*, ed. Roberto Cardini and Mariangela Regoliosi (Florence: Edizioni Polistampa, 2007), 1:418–423; on Nicola in general, see also Martines, *The Social*, 323–324.

149. Zaccaria, "Nicola," 1:417–418 and 1:423–425.

150. Biondo Flavio, *Italia Illustrata*, ed. and trans. Catherine J. Castner (Binghamton, NY: Global Academic, 2005), 1:49.

151. Hankins, "The Popularization," 142.

152. della Torre, *Storia*, 310.

153. Biondo Flavio, *Italy Illustrated*, ed. and trans. Jeffrey A. White (Cambridge, MA: Harvard University Press, 2005), 1:305.

154. See especially ASF Car. Strozzi. III 111, 119, 125, and 191.

155. Darrell D. Davisson, "New Documents on Gentile da Fabriano's Residence in Florence, 1420-1422," *Burlington Magazine* 122, no. 932 (November 1980): 759–760.

156. ASF Car. Strozzi. III, 111, 1r.

157. ASF Car. Strozzi. III, 125, 118r-160r; 191, 40r; see also Field, "Leonardo Bruni," 1112; Maxson, "The Many Shades."

158. Luiso, *Studi*, 69–70.

159. Jane Schuyler, *Florentine Busts: Sculpted Portraiture in the Fifteenth Century* (New York: Garland, 1976), 122, with image of the bust on 270, fig. 3.
160. Luigi Chiapelli, "Inventario dei manoscritti raccolti dal lanaiolo fiorentino Dietisalvi di Nerone (a. 1433)," *La Bibliofilia* 25, no. 8–9 (1923): 247–252.
161. ASF Cons. Prat. 52, 124v.
162. ASF Cons. Prat. 52, 122v; on his exile, Rubinstein, *The Government*, 115–117, 123–124, and 137; Brown, "Insiders," 374.
163. Chiapelli, "Inventario," 249–251; on Zenobi Guasconi, see Lauro Martines, *Lawyers and Statecraft in Renaissance Florence* (Princeton, NJ: Princeton University Press, 1968), 484–485; Raffaella Maria Zaccaria, "Zenobi Guasconi," in *DBI*, available at "Zenobi Guasconi in Dizionario Biografico – Treccani," Treccani.it, http://www.treccani.it/enciclopedia/zenobi-guasconi_res-5d8c3d23-87ee-11dc-8e9d-0016357eee51_%28Dizionario-Biografico%29/ (accessed October 10, 2011).
164. Zaccaria, "Zenobi."
165. Cagni, *Vespasiano da Bisticci*, 127–128.
166. Ibid., 128–129.
167. Ibid., 106 and 171; BL Add. 28272, 11v and 12r contains letters from Pandolfo Pandolfini to his brother Pierfilippo at the bank of Francesco Neroni.
168. BL. Add. 28272, 10v.
169. ASF Car. Strozzi. I, 137, 37v, and 38v. Li altri nostri carissimi amici.
170. da Bisticci, *Le Vite*, 2:310 and 315; cf. della Torre, *Storia*, 392; Martines, *The Social*, 342–343.
171. On these discussions, see della Torre, *Storia*, 223–226.
172. The Pazzi Palace coincides with the general location of Piero's home and that of his brothers. See Howard Saalman, "The Authorship of the Pazzi Palace," *Art Bulletin* 46, no. 3 (September 1964): 389.
173. Black, *Education*, 428.
174. Kristeller, *Supplementum*, 2:84–85.
175. da Bisticci, *Le Vite*, 2:309.
176. della Torre, *Storia*, 382 and 391–392.
177. Ibid., 392. Another letter between Piero and Acciaiuoli is at ibid., 409–410.
178. della Torre, *Storia* 402. della Torre wrote "confessiamo poi al lettore di non essere riusciti a trovare nessuna notizia su quel *Carlo d' Antonio di Silvestro* ivi nominato." The Online Tratte reveals that there were eighteen individuals among Florentine officeholders in the database named "Carlo Antonio." Only one of them features a third name of "Salvestro," which is Carlo Antonio Salvestro Serristori, who was born in 1425 and started being drawn for offices in 1439, although he was still a minor. His extensive officeholding career began in 1454. *Florentine Renaissance Resources*. Search Carlo under Name1 and Antonio under Name2. Include births in the search.
179. On Serristori, see F. W. Kent, "'Be Rather Loved than Feared': Class Relations in Quattrocento Florence," in *Society and Individual in Renaissance Florence*, ed. William J. Connell (Berkeley: University of California Press, 2002), 43; see also Sergio Tognetti, *Da Figline a Firenze:*

Ascesa economica e politica della famiglia Serristori (secoli XIV-XVI) (Florence: Opus Libri, 2003).

180. Mark Phillips, *The Memoir of Marco Parenti: A Life in Medici Florence* (Princeton, NJ: Princeton University Press, 1987), 62.
181. Ibid., 55–57.
182. Also found at Ibid., 55–62.
183. Ibid., 54.
184. della Torre, *Storia*, 393 and 401.
185. Rinuccini, *Lettere*, 143 (dated January 21, 1475).
186. Eckstein, *The District*, 20; and Nicholas Eckstein, "Neighborhood as Microcosm," in *Renaissance Florence: A Social History*, ed. Roger J. Crum and John T. Paoletti (Cambridge: Cambridge University Press, 2006), 228.
187. The will is published at Niccolò Machiavelli, *Opere complete* (Milan: Ernesto Oliva, 1850), 1:lviii–lxi. On Filippo and Machiavelli's friendship, see also John M. Najemy, "The Controversy Surrounding Machiavelli's Service to the Republic," in *Machiavelli and Republicanism*, ed. Gisela Bock, Quentin Skinner, and Maurizio Viroli (Cambridge: Cambridge University Press, 1990), 109–117.
188. Najemy, "The Controversy," 109–111; on Filippo Casavecchia, see also Paolo Malanima, "Filippo Casavecchia" in *DBI*, available at "Filippo Casavecchia in Dizionario Biografico – Treccani," Treccani.it, http://www.treccani.it/enciclopedia/filippo-casavecchia_(Dizionario-Biografico)/ (accessed October 17, 2011).
189. Black, *Education*, 424.
190. Bruni, *Epistolarum*,1:124–125; cf. Luiso, *Studi*, 88–89 (the letter dates to the second half of 1417).
191. Luiso, *Studi*, 89.
192. On Lorenzo de' Medici's learning, see Martines, *The Social*, 332–333; Barbaro, *Epistolario*, 2:65–66, 84–85, and passim; John Paoletti, "Fraternal Piety and Family Power: The Artistic Patronage of Cosimo and Lorenzo de' Medici," in *Cosimo 'il Vecchio' de' Medici, 1389–1464*, ed. Francis Ames-Lewis (Oxford: Clarendon Press, 1992), 198.
193. On this treatise, see C. C. Bayley, *War and Society in Renaissance Florence: The De Militia of Leonardo Bruni* (Toronto: University of Toronto Press, 1961); and Bruni, *Opere*, 651–701.
194. Witt, *In the Footsteps*, 446.
195. Guasti, *Commissioni*, 1:270–271 and 3:672.
196. For these letters, see especially ASF Car. Strozzi. III, 114, 131, 133, 144, 178, 180, and 247.
197. Parenti, *Lettere;* see also Phillips, *The Memoir.*
198. ASF Car. Strozzi. III, 247, 52r.
199. See ASF Car. Strozzi. III, 145, 84r; 178, 23r, 44r, and passim.
200. ASF Car. Strozzi. III, 247, 252r.
201. ASF Car. Strozzi. III, 250r.
202. Strozzi, *Selected Letters*, 84–85.
203. J. Russell Sale, *Filippino Lippi's Strozzi Chapel in Santa Maria Novella* (New York: Larland, 1979), 34.

204. Ibid., 38–43.
205. Ibid., 33.
206. Ibid., 43.
207. Ann Crabb, *The Strozzi of Florence: Widowhood and Family Solidarity in the Renaissance* (Ann Arbor: University of Michigan Press, 2000), 219; on this chapel more generally, see Sale, *Filippino.*
208. On this sculpture, see Schuyler, *Florentine,* 114–134; Schuyler's account should be read with the critiques of Mary D. Garrard, Review of *Florentine Busts: Sculpted Portraiture in the Fifteenth Century,* by Jane Schuyler; *The Colossal Sculpture of the Cinquecento,* by Virginia Bush; and *The Early Sculpture of Bartolommeo Ammanati,* by Peter Kinney, *Art Bulletin* 61, no. 3 (September 1979): 485–490.
209. Field, "Leonardo Bruni," 1114; cf. Luiso, *Studi,* 102; on Niccolò more generally, see Amelia Dainelli, "Niccolò da Uzzano nella vita politica dei suoi tempi," *Archivio Storico Italiano* ser. 6, vol. 17 (1932): 35–86 and 185–216.
210. Brown, *Bartolomeo Scala,* 24–25.
211. Martines, *The Social,* 331–332.
212. Michael Winterbottom, "Fifteenth-Century Manuscripts of Quintilian," *Classical Quarterly* n.s. 17, no. 2 (November 1967): 346; Rubinstein, *The Government,* 112.
213. Ginevra Niccolini di Camugliano, *The Chronicles of a Florentine Family 1200–1470* (London: Jonathan Cape, 1933), 204–307.
214. della Torre, *Storia,* 397. cf. di Camugliano, *The Chronicles,* 197; on Scala, see Scala, *Humanistic,* 18–19; on Accolti and Ficino, see Robert Black, "Ancients and Moderns in the Renaissance: Rhetoric and History in Accolti's Dialogue on the Preeminence of Men of His Own Time," *Journal of the History of Ideas* 43, no. 1 (January–March 1982): 20.
215. di Camugliano, *The Chronicles,* 181.
216. Bec, *Les Marchands,* 368.
217. For Pitti's friendship with Roberto Rossi, see Gene Brucker, ed., *Two Memoirs of Renaissance Florence: The Diaries of Buonaccorso Pitti and Gregorio Dati,* trans. Julia Martines (Prospect Heights, IL: Waveland Press, 1991), 95; for Salutati and Pitti, see Bec, *Les Marchands,* 371, "frater meus."
218. P. Bigazzi, "Vita di Bartolommeo Valori (il Vecchio)," *Archivio Storico Italiano* 4 (1843): 274; on this oration in general, see also Jurdjevic, *Guardians,* 96–123.

3. The Social Origins of the Florentine Humanists

1. Kent, *Friendship,* 95–111.
2. Kent, "Michele," 120–121; and Kent, *Cosimo,* 91–93.
3. Kent, *Cosimo,* 48.
4. On the Lotteringhi family see Anthony Molho, *Marriage Alliance in Late Medieval Florence* (Cambridge, MA: Harvard University Press, 1994), 371 and 394; on his classical texts see Kent, *Friendship,* 106–107.

5. Kent, *Cosimo*, 83, 85, 87, and 89. Kent attributes the secular content to Valerian, but the source is probably Valerius Maximus; see later discussion.

6. Goldwaite, *Economy*, 546–547, and Molho, *Marriage*, 211.

7. Anthony Molho, "Domenico di Leonardo Buoninsegni's Istoria Fiorentina," *Renaissance Quarterly* 23, no. 3 (Autumn 1970): 261.

8. Ibid., 264; on Buoninsegni in general, see Anthony Molho, "Domenico Buoninsegni," in *DBI*, available at "Domenico Buoninsegni in Dizionario Biografico – Treccani," Treccani.it, http://www.treccani.it/enciclopedia/ domenico-buoninsegni_res-278f3a94-187e9-11dc-8e9d-0016357eee51_%28 Dizionario_Biografico%29/ (accessed April 23, 2012).

9. Saundra Weddle, "Saints in the City and Poets at the Gates: The Codex Rustici as a Devotional and Civic Chronicle," in *Florence and Beyond: Culture, Society and Politics in Renaissance Italy*, ed. David S. Peterson with Daniel Bornstein (Toronto: Centre for Reformation and Renaissance Studies, 2008), 180.

10. Ibid., 188–189.

11. Ibid., 187–191.

12. On this translation, see Maxson, "'This Sort.'"

13. Ibid.

14. Martines, *April*, 168; for Acciaiuoli's publication of a translation of Bruni's history, see Maxson, "Establishing," 94.

15. On Jacopo Bracciolini see C. Vasoli, "Iacopo Bracciolini," in *DBI*, available at "Iacopo Bracciolini in Dizionario Biografico – Treccani," Treccani.it, http:// www.treccani.it/enciclopedia/iacopo-bracciolini_%28Dizionario-Biografico%29/ (accessed April 23, 2012); see also F. Polidori, "Due vite di Filippo Scolari," *Archivio Storico Italiano* 4 (1843): 119–184, esp. 163–184; de la Mare, "New Research," 448; Martines, *April*, 168; on Pippo Spano, see also Goldthwaite, *The Economy*, 240; Katalin Prajda, "The Florentine Scolari Family at the Court of Sigismund of Luxemburg in Buda," *Journal of Early Modern History* 14, no. 6 (2010): 513–533.

16. Martines, *April*, 125.

17. Ibid., 168.

18. Piero di Marco Parenti, *Storia fiorentina*, ed. Andrea Matucci (Florence: Leo S. Olschki, 1994), 1:IX–X.

19. de la Mare, "New Research," 411; cf. Strocchia, *Nuns*, 77–78. See also Richardson, *Printing*, 113–118, esp. 113–114.

20. de la Mare, "New Research," 406.

21. Ibid., 412. On printing in early modern Europe in general, see Andrew Pettegree, *The Book in the Renaissance* (New Haven, CT: Yale University Press, 2010). Short sections on fifteenth-century Florence are found at 19–20 and 51–53. See also Richardson, *Printing*.

22. Bec, *Les Livres*, 11–13. On the process of inheritance in Florence in general, see Kuehn, *Heirs*.

23. Molho, *Marriage*, 365–375; cf. Kuehn, *Heirs*, 144.

24. Raffaella Maria Zaccaria, "Niccolò Guasconi," in *DBI*, available at "Niccolò Guasconi in Dizionario Biografico – Treccani," Treccani.it, http://www.treccani.it/enciclopedia/niccolo-guasconi_(Dizionario-Biografico)/ (accessed October 24, 2011).

25. Bec, *Les Livres*, 149–150.
26. For the status of the Tanagli family, see Molho, *Marriage*, 374 and 404.
27. Bec, *Les Livres*, 156, 162, and 171.
28. Martines, *April*, 33; cf. Phillips, *The Memoir*, 155; Martines, *The Social*, 60.
29. Martines, *April*, 31–33.
30. Molho, *Marriage*, 373.
31. Martines, *The Social*, 78–79.
32. Rubinstein, *The Government*, 246.
33. Ricc. 2621. The letters of Michele Verino are published in Verde, *Lo Studio*, 3:671–720.
34. Paolo Giovio, *Elogi degli uomini illustri*, ed. Franco Minonzio, trans. Andrea Guasparri and Franco Minonzio (Turin: Giulio Einaudi, 2006), 161.
35. Anthony M. Cummings, *The Maecenas and the Madrigals: Patrons, Patronage, and the Origins of the Italian Madrigal* (Philadelphia: American Philosophical Society, 2004), 21–25.
36. Giovio, *Elogi*, 161. "Addolorato per l'insolenza di quell'oltraggio morí in pochi giorni."
37. Bec, *Les Livres*, 164.
38. Molho, *Marriage*, 373.
39. For the status of the Bonciani family, see Molho, *Marriage*, 367; for the wealth of the Riccardi in 1427, 1457/8, and 1480 see Molho, *Marriage*, 381; for the marriage, see Paolo Malanima, *I Riccardi di Firenze: Una famiglia e un patrimonio nella Toscana dei Medici* (Florence: Leo S. Olschki, 1977), 6.
40. Malanima, *I Riccardi*, 7–8.
41. Ibid., 8–12.
42. Bec, *Les Livres*, 160–161. For the status of the Nobili family, see Molho, *Marriage*, 372.
43. Michael Rocke, *Forbidden Friendships: Homosexuality and Male Culture in Renaissance Florence* (Oxford: Oxford University Press, 1996), 74 and 181.
44. Molho, *Marriage*, 371.
45. Anthony Molho, "Créditeurs de Florence en 1347. Un aperçu statistique du quartier de Santo Spirito," in *Firenze nel Quattrocento* (Rome: Edizioni di storia e letteratura, 2006), 1: 100–101.
46. Giovanni Boccaccio, *The Decameron*, 2nd ed., trans. G. H. McWilliam (London: Penguin Books, 1995), 486; on Alberti's Chapel, see Ludwig H. Heydenreich, *Architecture in Italy, 1400–1500*, revised by Paul Davies (New Haven, CT: Yale University Press, 1996), 40.
47. Boccaccio, *The Decameron*, 485–490.
48. *Florentine Renaissance Resources*. Search for "Lotteringhi" under surname.
49. *Online Catasto of 1427*. Search for "Lotteringhi" under family name.
50. Lotteringo's age can be found at ibid.
51. Molho, *Marriage*, 394.
52. Kent, *Cosimo*, 89–90 and 431. Kent provides Sandro's quotation on p. 431: "Dice e narra Valerio libro quarto chapitolo primo d'uno che piangneva la morte del nimicho suo perochè avea chonosciuta la vita sua esser hutile alla repubblica cioè al ben chomune." Kent attributes the quote to "Valerian" but it may be from book 4, chapter 1 of Valerius Maximus's *Memorable Doings*

and Sayings. There V. Maximus describes how Macedonicus and Scipio Africanus despised one another, but upon learning of Scipio's death Macedonicus summoned the citizens to lament the great man's death and the loss it meant to Rome. See Valerius Maximus *Memorable Deeds and Sayings* 4.1.

53. Kent, *Cosimo*, 431.
54. Kent, *Friendship*, 107.
55. Alison Brown, "The Language of Empire," in *Florentine Tuscany*, ed. William J. Connell and Andrea Zorzi (Cambridge: Cambridge University Press, 2000), 39; Rinuccini, *Lettere*, 55–56; on the epitaph, see L. Miglio, "Donato Cocchi Donati," in *DBI*, available at "Donato Cocchi Donati in Dizionario Biografico – Treccani," Treccani.it, http://www.treccani.it/enciclopedia/donato-cocchi-donati_(Dizionario-Biografico)/ (accessed October 28, 2011).
56. Miglio, "Donato."
57. L. Miglio, "Antonio Cocchi Donati," in *DBI*, available at "Antonio Cocchi Donati in Dizionario Biografico – Treccani," Treccani.it, http://www.treccani.it/enciclopedia/antonio-cocchi-donati_%28Dizionario-Biografico%29/ (accessed April 23, 2012).
58. Ibid.
59. Kent, *Cosimo*, 71, and 420; Morpurgo, *I manoscritti*, 162–165; I have not seen this manuscript. For Jacopo's position as Prior, see *Florentine Renaissance Resources*; search for Donati under surnam1.
60. BNC Magl. VIII 1439. This manuscript in its modern form is a compilation of several previously distinct manuscripts. For example, Jacopo Cocchi-Donati's hand begins at folio 37r, but the page begins in the middle of a letter and also carries the older number 94. The transcription of Donato Acciaiuoli's oration with Jacopo's claim to have been present occupies folii 57v-59v.
61. The book is now in the Pierpont Morgan Library in New York. See Kristeller, *Iter*, 5:347 (not seen).
62. Bec, *Les Livres*, 154–155.
63. John Pope-Hennessy, *Luca della Robbia* (Ithaca, NY: Cornell University Press, 1980), 84. According to Luca della Robbia's tax return in 1446, he possessed "Una chasa da llavoratore, possta nel popolo di Santa Maria al Tartagl<i>ese di Valdarnno di sopra, nel borgho del Tartagl<i>ese" and "Una chasetta possta dirieto a detta chasa, fàssene istalla da best<i>e, in detto popolo, a I via, [a] II Filippo di firenze del Pancia, [a] II e a IIII rede di Piero Teci."
64. Bec, *Les Livres*, 159.
65. Martines, *The Social*, 373.
66. Ibid., 377.
67. Bec, *Les Livres*, 158.
68. Ibid., 184–185.
69. Ibid., 185.
70. *Online Catasto of 1427*; search for Vinaccesi under family name.
71. Martines, *The Social*, 358 and 371. Martines lists Bartolomeo's wealth at 3,310 florins.
72. Ibid., 356–359 and 369–372.
73. *Online Florentine Resources*; search for Vinaccesi under sunam1.

74. Black, *Benedetto*, 168. The record is at ASF Cons. Prat. 53, 240v.
75. The Nuti were not listed among Molho's lists of patrician families. See Molho, *Marriage*, 372 and 397; on Bernardo Nuti as a schoolteacher, see Black, *Education*, xiii and 417.
76. Landino, *Poems*, xiv–xv and 329.
77. Black, *Benedetto*, 171. On Gaddi, see Black, "Machiavelli," 75–76 and later discussion.
78. Landino, *Poems*, 22–23, 62–65, and passim.
79. James Hankins, *Repertorium Brunianum: A Critical Guide to the Writings of Leonardo Bruni* (Rome: Istituto Storico Italiano per il Medio Evo, 1997), passim. See also Maxson, "'*This Sort.*'"
80. On Renaissance secretaries in general, see Marcello Simonetta, *Rinascimento segreto: Il mondo del segretario da Petrarca a Machiavelli* (Milan: FrancoAngeli, 2004).
81. de la Mare, "New Research," 1:396–397.
82. Gordan, *Two Renaissance*, 93.
83. de la Mare, "New Research," 1:396–398.
84. Ibid., 1:418.
85. Ibid., 1:397.
86. James Hankins, "Notes on the Composition and Textual Tradition of Leonardo Bruni's *Historiarum florentini populi libri XII*," in *Classica et Beneventana*, ed. F. T. Coulson and A. A. Grotans (Turnhout, Belgium: Brepols, 2008), 96; cf. de la Mare, "New Research," 1:397.
87. de la Mare, "New Research," 482–484.
88. Albinia de la Mare, "Messer Piero Strozzi, a Florentine Priest and Scribe," in *Calligraphy and Paleography: Essays Presented to Alfred Fairbank*, ed. A. S. Osley (New York: October House, 1965), 56.
89. Ibid., 56–57.
90. Ibid., 58.
91. Ibid., 63 and the plate facing page 58.
92. Ibid., 62–68.
93. de la Mare, "New Resarch," 1:420.
94. A partial lineage can be found at Amanda Lillie, *Florentine Villas in the Fifteenth Century: An Architectural and Social History* (Cambridge: Cambridge University Press, 2005), 262, and another note to the brother can be found at 278. Benedetto's dates were 1387–1458; Messer Piero was born in 1416; Pagholo was born in 1424/25; and Francesco was born in 1427/8.
95. A partial lineage can be found at ibid., 263. Lillie's table has been supplemented with Crabb, *The Strozzi*, 71 and Strozzi, *Selected*, 226.
96. Lillie, *Florentine*, 291–292; Heather Gregory, "A Florentine Family in Crisis: The Strozzi in the Fifteenth Century" (PhD diss., University of London, 1981), 160; Crabb, *The Strozzi*, 149.
97. Heather Gregory, "The Return of the Native: Filippo Strozzi and Medicean Politics," *Renaissance Quarterly* 38, no. 1 (Spring 1985): 7; Strozzi, *Selected*, 60–61.
98. Crabb, *The Strozzi*, 66.
99. ASF Car. Strozzi. V, 15, 80r. My thanks to Judith Bryce for this reference.

100. Gregory, "Return," 7, and more generally 6–7, "chè non è oggi in Italia più singhulare uomo di lui."
101. Strozzi, *Selected*, 74–79.
102. Ibid., 154–157.
103. For Francesco, the Opera, and Paolo Uccello's famous equestrian painting, see Franco and Stefano Borsi, *Paolo Uccello*, trans. Elfreda Powell (New York: Thames and Hudson, 1994), 303, which also contains leads to archival documents; cf. John Temple-Leader and Giuseppe Marcotti, *Sir John Hawkwood (L'Acuto)*, trans. Leader Scott (London: T. Fisher Unwin, 1889), 295; documents related to Francesco's tenure on the Operai can be found at Margaret Haines, ed., "The Years of the Cupola, 1417–1436," Opera di Santa Maria del Fiore, http://www.operaduomo.firenze.it/cupola/home_eng.HTML (accessed November 14, 2011); click on "Indices" at the top, then "Surnames Etc." on the left, then "Surnames (which appears below "Surnames Etc."), then "S." Francesco di Benedetto di Caroccio Strozzi appears numerous times in 1424/25 and 1433.
104. Carl Brandon Strehlke, "Zanobi di Benedetto di Caroccio degli Strozzi, known as Zanobi Strozzi," in *Painting and Illumination in Early Renaissance Florence*, ed. Laurence B. Kanter, Barbara Drake Boehm, Carl Brandon Strehlke, Gaudenz Freuler, Christa C. Mayer Thurman, and Pia Palladino (New York: Harry N. Abrams, 1994), 349–350, with images of his work on 350–361; see also Dillian Gordon, "Zanobi Strozzi's 'Annunciation' in the National Gallery," *Burlington Magazine* 140, no. 1145 (August 1998), 517–524; Maria S. Tacconi, *Cathedral and Civic Ritual in Late Medieval and Renaissance Florence* (Cambridge: Cambridge University Press, 2005), passim.
105. B. Santi, "Bernardo Cennini," in *DBI*, available at "Bernardo Cennini in Dizionario Biografico – Treccani," Treccani.it, http://www.treccani.it/enciclopedia/bernardo-cennini_%28Dizionario-Biografico%29/ (accessed November 15, 2011); cf. Brian Richardson, *Print Culture in Renaissance Italy: The Editor and the Vernacular Text, 1470–1600* (Cambridge: Cambridge University Press, 1994), 43.
106. Richardson, *Print*, 43.
107. Bartolomeo Fonzio, *Letters to Friends*, ed. Alessandro Daneloni and trans. Martin Davies (Cambridge, MA: Harvard University Press, 2011), 200; cf. Girolamo Mancini, "Il bel s. Giovanni e le feste patronali di Firenze descritte nel 1475 da Piero Cennini," *Rivista d'Arte* 6 (1909): 209–210.
108. Fonzio, Letters, 10–13, 14–17, 18–21, and 44–53; cf. Bartolomeo Fonzio, *Epistolarum libri*, ed. Alessandro Daneloni (Messina: Centro Interdipartimentale di Studi Umanistici, 2008), 1:8–9, 12–17, 36–43; on Michelozzi and Braccesi, see later discussion.
109. M. Palma, "Piero Cennini," in *DBI*, available at "Piero Cennini in Dizionario Biografico – Treccani," Treccani.it, http://www.treccani.it/enciclopedia/piero-cennini_%28Dizionario-Biografico%29/ (accessed November 15, 2011); cf. Kristeller, "An Unknown," 342.
110. ASF Car. Strozzi. I, 137, 244r; and Fonzio, *Letters*, 94–97. Scala also wrote a vernacular letter to Tommaso Ridolfi; see Scala, *Humanistic*, 94 and 104.

111. Mancini, "Il bel," 212–213; cf. Palma, "Piero."
112. Mancini, "Il bel," 220–227.
113. de la Mare, "New Research," 1:445 and 1:526–529; Berthold L. Ullman, "More Humanistic Manuscripts," in *Calligraphy and Palaeography*, ed. A. S. Osley (New York: October House, 1965), 52–53; see also Mancini, "Il bel," 210–215.
114. de la Mare, "New Research," 526–527; cf. Ullman, *Origin and Development*, 125, "invidiosus," "nil puto cordis habes," and "falleris invidia, inscitia."
115. On these points, compare the similar findings of Andrew Pettegree on the types of books published in the late fifteenth century: Pettegree, *The Book*, 58–60. See also Richardson, *Printing*, 135–151, esp. 135–140.
116. Bec, *Les Livres*, 33.
117. Ibid., 49.
118. Chiappelli, "Inventario," 250–252.
119. Giuseppe M. Cagni, "I codici Vaticani Palatino-Latini appartenuti alla biblioteca di Giannozzo Manetti," *La Bibliofilia* 62, no. 1 (1960): 19–42. On the libraries of other humanists, see Walser, *Poggius*, 418–423; Blum, *La biblioteca*, 73–96; Ullman, *Humanism of Coluccio*, 129–280; Fiocco, "La biblioteca," 306–310; Ullman and Stadter, *The Public Library*; de la Mare, *The Handwriting*, 41–43 and 112–138; and the references to the library of Pierfilippo Pandolfini earlier.
120. On fifteenth-century copies of classical works, see Albinia de la Mare, "Florentine Manuscripts of Livy in the Fifteenth Century," in *Livy*, ed. T. A. Dorey (London: Routledge & Kegan Paul, 1971), 177–199; Winterbottom, "Fifteenth-Century Manuscripts," 339–369; Reeve, "Statius' Silvae," 202–225; Pade, *The Reception;* the multivolume *Catalogus translationum et commentariorum*, also contains leads on the readers of classical works in the fourteenth, fifteenth, and sixteenth centuries.
121. Pearl Kibre, "The Intellectual Interests Reflected in Libraries of the Fourteenth and Fifteenth Centuries," *Journal of the History of Ideas* 7, no. 3 (June 1946): 257–297.
122. Hankins, *Repertorium*, 256–257. Compare the following analysis with a similar one done for Bruni's *On the Italian War against the Goths* and *On the Origin of Mantua* in Maxson, "'This Sort.'"
123. Hankins, *Repertorium*, 68.
124. Ibid., 42.
125. Ibid., 110.
126. On Rinuccini, see Martines, *The Social*, 347–348; Watkins, *Humanism*, 186–224; Vito R. Giustiniani, *Alamanno Rinuccini, 1426–1499: Materialien und Forschungen zur Geschichte des Florentinischen Humanismus* (Graz: Böhlau Verlag, 1965); Martines, *April*, 214–220.
127. On Antonio Canigiani, see Maxson, "'This Sort.'"
128. Hankins, *Repertorium*, 55.
129. Arnaldo Ganda, *Filippo Cavagni da Lavagna: Editore, tipografo, commerciante a Milano nel Quattrocento* (Florence: Leo S. Olschki, 2006), 88–89,

which contains a photocopy of Vespucci's record of ownership of Eusebius. See also della Torre, *Storia*, 772–774; de la Mare, *Handwriting*, 1:106–138; on Vespucci's status at San Marco, see Clements R. Markham, ed. and trans., *The Letters of Amerigo Vespucci and Other Documents Illustrative of His Career* (London: Hakluyt Society, 1894), iii.

130. Markham, *The Letters*, iii.

131. Ibid., 2.

132. On Ficino, see Ficino, *Opera omnia*, 1:753–754, 806, and 842; on the book exchange, see della Torre, *Storia*, 347–348 and 772–774; in general, see also Black, *Education*, 136–138.

133. Hankins, *Repertorium*, 50–51.

134. Tacconi, *Cathedral*, 154; three additional owners may have been fifteenth-century Florentines but have not yet been identified: Bartolomeo di Ghoro di Donato Vinati (Hankins, *Repertorium*, 50), Niccolò d' Antonio Bizzeri and Forese Bizzeri (Hankins, *Repertorium*, 55), and Francesco di Messer Giovanni di Francesco di Ruberto di Iacopo di Francesco Venturi (Hankins, *Repertorium*, 72).

135. Hankins, *Repertorium*, 51. The Online Tratte (*Florentine*) reveals two and possibly more individuals named Andrea da Verrazzano in the fifteenth and sixteenth centuries. Search "Andrea" under name1 and "daverrazzan" under surnam1 and include births in the search. The results provide two listings with the first name "Andrea" and the surname "daverrazzan." However, the listing under "Andrea Amerigo daVerrazzan" seems to contain three different individuals. An Andrea Amerigo was born in 1389 and first held office in 1425 (he was a minor in 1422). An Andrea Amerigo was a minor in 1466, making him unlikely to be the same individual. Another Andrea Amerigo, this time with the added third name of Niccolo da Verrazzano, was a minor in 1491. Andrea Amerigo Niccolo da Verrazzano was dead in 1493. The results also list an Andrea Lorenzo da Verrazzano, who was born in 1511.

136. de la Mare, "New Research," 480.

137. Paul Saenger, *A Catalogue of Pre-1500 Western Manuscript Books at the Newberry Library* (Chicago: University of Chicago Press, 1989), 187; cf. Hankins, *Repertorium*, 27. Hankins contains the scribal information, but not the location where the work was copied.

138. Hankins, *Repertorium*, 86; on Carlo's possible role in the book's translation, see earlier discussion.

139. Ibid., 42 and 121; on Giovanni da Stia, see de la Mare, "New Research," 420 and 499–500; Hankins, "Notes," 98.

140. Hankins, *Repertorium*, 89 and 217; Kent, *Cosimo*, 71.

141. Hankins, *Repertorium*, 62.

142. Ibid., 51, 58, 65, and 123; Kent, *Cosimo*, 83.

143. Molho, *Marriage*, 365 and 376. Molho lists the Adimari as a high-status family.

144. Stefano Ugo Baldassarri and Arielle Saiber, *Images of Quattrocento Florence: Selected Writings in Literature, History and Art* (New Haven, CT: Yale University Press, 2000), 129.

145. Molho, *Marriage*, 365–375.

146. W. Leonard Grant, "The Life of Naldo Naldi," *Studies in Philology* 60, no. 4 (October 1963): 606–610.
147. Paul Oskar Kristeller, "An Unknown Correspondence of Alessandro Braccesi with Niccolò Michelozzi, Naldo Naldi, Bartolomeo Scala, and Other Humanists (1470–1472) in ms. Bodl. Auct. F. 2. 17," in *Studies in Renaissance Thought and Letters* (Rome: Edizioni di Storia e Letteratura, 1985), 349.
148. Grant, "The Life," 610–617.
149. Rinuccini's problems with Lorenzo de' Medici stemmed in part from letters written while he was a diplomat to Rome in 1475–1476. Renée Neu Watkins, ed., *Humanism and Liberty: Writings on Freedom from Fifteenth-Century Florence* (Columbia, SC: University of South Carolina Press, 1978), 187; see also Fubini, *Quattrocento fiorentino*, 108–122; Rinuccini, *Lettere*, 214–218.
150. da Bisticci, *Commentario*, 1.
151. Grant, "The Life," 609. Grant also includes Albiera degli Albizzi as the recipient of a poem, but the poem probably honored Albiera after her death.
152. Ristori, "Amerigo Corsini."
153. Ibid.; see also Fonzio, *Letters*, 2–3.
154. Alfonso Lazzari, *Ugolino e Michele Verino: Studii biografici e critici* (Turin: Libreria Carlo Clausen, 1897). Many of Verino's works have been published.
155. For a table of much of this correspondence, see Kristeller, "An Unknown," 368–372; on Braccesi more generally, see Bice Agnoletti, *Alessandro Braccesi: Contributo alla Storia dell'Umanesimo e della Poesia Volgare* (Florence: G. Passeri, 1901); Alessandro Perosa, "Alessandro Braccesi," in *DBI* available at "Alessandro Braccesi in Dizionario Biografico – Treccani," Treccani.it, http://www.treccani.it/enciclopedia/alessandro-braccesi_%28 Dizionario-Biografico%29/ (accessed December 14, 2011); Paolo Viti, "Il carteggio della seconda missione romana di Alessandro Braccesi," in *Forme letterarie umanistiche: Studi e ricerche* (Lecce: Conte Editore, 1999), 361–388.
156. Richard Hunter, *Plato's Symposium* (Oxford: Oxford University Press, 2004), 133–134.
157. della Torre, *Storia*, 566–568 and 647–654; see also Hankins, "Myth," 444; Arthur Field, "The Platonic Academy of Florence," in *Marsilio Ficino: His Theology, His Philosophy, His Legacy*, ed. Michael J. B. Allen and Valery Rees with Martin Davies (Leiden: Brill, 2002), 369–370.
158. Vanna Arrighi, "Piero del Nero," in *DBI*, available at "Piero del Nero in Dizionario Biografico – Treccani," Treccani.it, "http://www.treccani. it/enciclopedia/piero-del-nero_%28Dizionario-Biografico%29/ (accessed December 14, 2011).
159. Nicolai Rubinstein, "Michelozzo and Niccolò Michelozzi in Chios 1466–1467," in *Cultural Aspects of the Italian Reniassance: Essays in Honour of Paul Oskar Kristeller*, ed. Cecil H. Clough (Manchester: Manchester University Press, 1976), 216. Leads on Niccolò Michelozzi can also be found at Alison Brown, "Women, Children and Politics in the Letters of a Florentine Notary, Ser Pace di Bambello," in *Florence and Beyond: Culture, Society and Politics in Renaissance Italy*, ed. David S. Peterson with Daniel

E. Bornstein (Toronto: Centre for Reformation and Renaissance Studies, 2008), esp. 233.

160. For an index of this correspondence, see Nancy Isenberg, "Censimento delle lettere di Niccolò Michelozzi," *Giornale italiano di filologia* n.s. 13 (1982): 280–291. Isenberg's article should be used with the comments in Paolo Viti, "Note su Niccolò Michelozzi," in *Forme letterarie umanistiche: Studi e ricerche* (Lecce: Conte Editore, 1999), 267–273. Ficino himself wrote to Michelozzi; see Kristeller, *Supplementum*, 2:90–91.

161. della Torre, *Storia*, 717; della Torre discusses Michelozzi more generally on pp. 716–719.

162. Viti, "Note," 278–279.

163. Paolo Viti identified the group attending the speech on December 5 as the *Proconsul* of the guild, ser Alberto di ser Alberto dei ser Ruchi, and the *consiglieri* of the guild, Domenico Martelli, Pietro da Iesi, Antonio Bartolomei, Bartolomeo Berti, Gabriele Leoni, Paolo Benivieni, Pietro Cecchi, Niccolò da Romena, Angelo Bandini, Girolamo da Colle, and Paolo Grassi. See Viti, "Note," 273.

164. Ibid.

165. On this poem, see also della Torre, *Storia*, 669.

166. Molho, *Marriage*, 367–375.

167. Ibid., 384 and 396.

168. Ibid., 387 and *Florentine Renaissance Resources*; search for "delcaccia" under surnam1.

169. Niccolò Michelozzi: ASF Sig. Dieci Otto Leg. Miss. Resp. 11, 1; Otto Leg. 4, 18r; 7, 89r; 9, 4v; Sig. Leg. 21 84r; Dieci Leg. 11, 18r; Lorenzo de' Medici: ASF Sig. Leg. 16, 160r; 17, 111r; 21, 43r; Alamanno Rinuccini: ASF Sig. Leg. 18, 156r; Piero del Nero: ASF Sig. Leg. 21, 89v; Giovanni Cavalcanti: ASF Sig. Leg. 21, 133r. li altri nostri carissimi amici.

170. See appendices in Rubinstein, *The Government*, 321–362.

171. *Florentine Renaissance Resources*; search for "cavalcanti" under surnam1. The relevant result is Giovanni di Niccolo Cavalcanti.

172. Ibid.; search for "corsini" under surnam1 and make sure that "guild" is checked. See also R. Ristori, "Amerigo Corsini," in *DBI*, available at "Americo Corsini in Dizionario Biografico – Treccani," Treccani.it, http:// www.treccani.it/enciclopedia/amerigo-corsini_%28Dizionario-Biografico% 29/ (accessed November 23, 2011).

173. *Florentine Renaissance Resources*; search for "delcaccia" under surnam1.

174. Ibid.; search for "delnero" under surnam1. Piero del Nero also held a small number of positions outside Florence, but nothing to suggest a more prom-inent political role than has been suggested here. See Arrighi, "Piero del Nero."

175. *Florentine Renaissance Resources*; search for "rinuccini" under surnam1.

176. Perosa, "Alessandro Braccesi."

177. *Florentine Renaissance Resources*; search for "pazzi" under surnam1.

178. Ibid.; search for "michelozzi" under surnam1.

179. Lazzari, *Ugolino*; for examples of offices, see 64, 77, 78, 81, and 90.

4. The Humanist Demands of Ritual

1. Trexler, *The Libro*, 71–72.
2. Ibid., 72.
3. Petriboni and Rinaldi, *Priorista*, 353–354.
4. Vespasiano da Bisticci, *Commentario della vita di messer Giannozzo Manetti*, ed. Piero Fanfani (Turin: Unione Tipografico, 1862), 64–65.
5. Ibid., 65.
6. Ibid., 65–66.
7. da Bisticci, *Renaissance*, 321.
8. Ibid.
9. Ibid.
10. Ibid., 319.
11. See Bruni, *Opere*, 815–823; da Bisticci, *Commentario*, 203–228; F. Sansovino, *Historia di casa Orsina e degli huomini illustri della famiglia* (Venice: 1565), 3:39–46; Scala, *Humanistic*, 215–223; two upublished examples by Marcello Virgilio are in Ricc. 767 and Ricc. 811.
12. Scala, *Humanistic*, 205–211.
13. See the discussion of two such orations delivered by Palla di Nofri Strozzi later. See also ASF Sig. Risp. Verb.; Black, *Benedetto Accolti*, 164–165; and Scala, *Humanistic*, 191–198, 211–215, and 232–238.
14. On visitors to the Signoria, see Nicolai Rubinstein, *The Palazzo Vecchio 1298–1532: Government, Architecture, and Imagery in the Civic Palace of the Florentine People* (Oxford: Clarendon Press, 1995), 37 and 38, which shows the location of the chancery in Palazzo Vecchio in the fifteenth century. See also Black, "Machiavelli," 73.
15. On the *ringhiera*, see Milner, "Citing," 53–82, with a list of events involving the *ringhiera* on 61–62; Trexler, *Public*, 49–50 and 315–318; images of the *ringhiera* can be found at Ulrich Meier, "Die Sichet-und Hörbarketi der Macht: Der Florentiner Palazzo Vecchio im Spätmittelalter," in *Zwischen Gotteshaus und Taverne. Öffentliche Räumein Spätmittelalter und Früher Neuzeit*, ed. Susanne Rau and Gerd Schwerhoff (Cologne: Böhlau, 2004), 238 and 239.
16. Bruni, *History*, 2:268–269. On page 559, Hankins provides that Donato Acciaiuoli translated Bruni's term *"pro rostris"* as "in su la ringhiera." See also Milner, "Citing," 71–77; on the *rostrum* or *rostra* in Roman antiquity, see Robert Morstein-Marx, *Mass Oratory and Political Power in the Late Roman Republic* (Cambridge: Cambridge University Press, 1989), 42–57.
17. Maxson, "Establishing Independence," 91.
18. Brucker, *The Civic*, 293; Alison Williams Lewin, *Negotiating Survival: Florence and the Great Schism, 1378–1417* (Madison, NJ: Fairleigh Dickinson University Press, 2003), 12; Black, *Benedetto*, 157–164.
19. Rubinstein, *The Palazzo*, 20.
20. Emilio Santini, "La protestatio de iustitia nella Firenze medicea del Sec XV" *Rinascimento* 10, no. 1 (June 1959): 34–35. See also Milner, "Political Oratory," 51–55; Uwe Neumahr, *Die Protestatio de Iustitia in der Florentiner Hochkultur* (Münster: Lit Verlage, 2002).

21. McManamon, *Funeral Oratory*; d'Elia, *The Renaissance*.
22. Witt, *In the Footsteps*, 360–361; cf. Paul Oskar Kristeller, "The Scholar and His Public in the Late Middle Ages and the Renaissance," in *Medieval Aspects of Renaissance Learning*, ed. Edward P. Mahoney (Durham, NC: Duke University Press, 1974), 10–11.
23. Brucia Witthoft, "Marriage Rituals and Marriage Chests in Quattrocento Florence," *Artibus et Historiae* 3, no. 5 (1982): 53–54.
24. On the *Certame Coronario*, see Kent, *Friendship*, 17; Lucia Bertolini, ed., *De vera amicitia: i testi del primo Certame Coronario* (Modena: F. C. Panini, 1993); Lucia Bertolini, "ΑΓΩΝ ΣΤΕΦΑΝΙΤΗΣ il progetto del Certame Coronario (e la sua ricezione)" in *Il volgare come lingua di cultura dal trecento al cinquecento*, ed. Arturo Calzona, Francesco Paolo Fiore, Alberto Tenenti, and Cesare Vasoli (Florenze: Leo S. Olschki, 2003), 51–70; Mazzocco, *Linguistic*, 91–94; della Torre, *Storia*, 311–312.
25. Rab Hatfield, "The Compagnia de' Magi," *Journal of the Warburg and Courtauld Institutes* 33 (1970): 128–135, 153–161; cf. Christopher F. Black, *Italian Confraternities in the Sixteenth Century* (Cambridge: Cambridge University Press, 1989), 90–91.
26. Kent, *Friendship*, 95–111; and Kent, *Cosimo*, 43–54.
27. Nirit Ben-Aryeh Debby, *Renaissance Florence in the Rhetoric of Two Popular Preachers* (Turnhout, Belgium: Brepols, 2001), 37–39, 66–68, and 97–111.
28. Debby, *Renaissance*, 199; and da Bisticci, *Renaisssance*, 166–167; Bernardino and Dominici's relations with literary humanists were not all favorable, with Poggio Bracciolini the leading critical voice against both men. See Debby, *Renaissance*, 201–205.
29. Debby, *Renaissance*, 200.
30. Jacob Burckhardt, *The Civilization of the Renaissance in Italy*, trans. S. G. C. Middlemore (London: Penguin Books, 1990), 154.
31. Garrett Mattingly, *Renaissance Diplomacy* (Boston: Houghton Mifflin, 1971), 52–54.
32. Donald E. Queller, *The Office of the Ambassador in the Middle Ages* (Princeton, NJ: Princeton University Press, 1967), 155.
33. F. Pintor, "Le due ambascerie di Bernardo Bembo a Firenze e le sue relazioni coi Medici," in *Studi letterari e linguistici dedicati a Pio Ranjna nel quarantesimo anno del suo insegnamento* (Florence: Enrico Ariani, 1911), 785–815; Donald Weinstein, *Ambassador from Venice: Pietro Pasqualigo in Lisbon, 1501* (Minneapolis: University of Minnesota Press, 1960); Patricia H. Labalme, *Bernardo Giustiniani: A Venetian of the Quattrocento* (Rome: Edizioni di Storia e Letteratura, 1969); Fubini, *Quattrocento Fiorentino*, 99–122; Giovanna Petti Balbi, "Un uomo delle istituzioni: Gottardo Stella di Sarzana, cancelliere e diplomatico genovese del '400," *Archivio Storico Italiano* 167, no. 2 (2004): 259–289.
34. Daniela Frigo, *Politics and Diplomacy in Early Modern Italy: The Structure of Diplomatic Practice, 1450–1800*, trans. Adrian Belton (Cambridge: Cambridge University Press, 2000); Vincent Ilardi, *Studies in Italian Renaissance Diplomatic History* (London: Variorum, 1986); Paul Dover, "The Economic Predicament of Italian Renaissance Ambassadors," *Journal*

of Early Modern History 12 (2008): 137–167, with a discussion of the role of humanism in framing protestations of poverty on 140–142. My thanks to Paul Dover for sharing copies of his work with me. A recent German study on Florentine diplomacy and diplomats was called to my attention too late to fully incorporate its findings into this study; see Heinrich Lang, *Cosimo de' Medici, die Gesandten und die* Condottieri: *Diplomatie und Kriege der Republik Florenz im 15. Jahrhundert* (Paderborn: Ferdinand Schöningh, 2009), with Italian summary provided on pp. 488–489. My thanks to Oren Margolis for this reference.

35. Robert Black, "Florence," in *The Renaissance in National Context,* ed. Roy Porter and Mikulás Teich (Cambridge: Cambridge University Press, 1992), 31; Dale Kent, "The Florentine Reggimento in the Fifteenth Century," *Renaissance Quarterly* 28, no. 4 (Winter 1975): 575–638.

36. Brian Jeffrey Maxson, "Gifts and Status in Diplomacy: A Case-Study of Florence, Pius II, and Jacopo Piccinino in 1458," in *Languages of Power in Italy, 1300–1600,* ed. Daniel Bornstein and Laura Gaffuri (Turnhout, Belgium: Brepols, forthcoming).

37. R. J. Walsh, *Charles the Bold and Italy (1467–1477): Politics and Personnel* (Liverpool: Liverpool University Press, 2005), 268.

38. Pius II, *Commentaries,* ed. and trans. Margaret Meserve and Marcello Simonetta (Cambridge, MA: Harvard University Press, 2007), 2:32–35.

39. Richard C. Trexler, *Public Life in Renaissance Florence* (Ithaca, NY: Cornell University Press, 1991), 315–318; Edward Muir, *Ritual in Early Modern Europe,* 2nd ed. (Cambridge: Cambridge University Press, 2005), 262–264.

40. Milanesi, "Il Viaggio," 7–8, 10–11, and 23–24. Abel Desjardins and Giuseppe Canestrini, *Négociations Diplomatiques de la France avec la Toscane: Documents Recueillis par Giuseppe Canestrini* (Paris: Impériale, 1859), 1:124.

41. Trexler, *Public,* 324.

42. Ibid., 323–326.

43. Ibid., 323; Bullard, *Lorenzo il Magnifico,* 28–34 and 51–53.

44. Marcel Mauss, *The Gift: Forms and Functions of Exchange in Archaic Societies,* trans. Ian Cunninson (London: Cohen & West, 1970), 1–2.

45. David Swartz, *Culture and Power: The Sociology of Pierre Bourdieu* (Chicago: University of Chicago Press, 1997), 90.

46. On this mission and its diplomatic correspondence, see Baldassarri and Figliuolo, *Manettiana,* 21–26.

47. Setton, *Papacy,* 2:53–54 and 2:62.

48. da Bisticci, *Renaissance,* 31–42.

49. Baldassarri and Figliuolo, *Manettiana,* 21.

50. For the following anecdote, see da Bisticci, *Le Vite,* 2:550–555. Vespasiano claimed to be an eyewitness on p. 555.

51. da Bisticci, *Le Vite,* 2:551, "onore fuori dell'ordinario."

52. Ibid., "Io voglio fare grandissimo onore a' Fiorentini, perché io darò loro udienza in concestoro publico dove si dà a' Re et agli Imperadori, per dare loro questo principio."

53. Ibid., "Rispose che io non mi maravigliassi, che, essendo lui in corte di Roma, dove si trovavano tutti i singulari uomini che avevano i Cristiani, più in questo tempo che già è lungo tempo non v'erano istati."

54. Ibid., "et che la mattina seguente poteva poco guadagnare e perdere assai, perché molti hanno decto bene come lui o meglio."

55. Ibid., 2:551–552, "et se per mia disgratia mi venisse errato, io perdo la fatica d'anni quaranta ch'io ho studiato, et dove? nel primo luogo de' Cristiani, dove si può perdere assai e guadagnare poco, sì ché non ti maravigliare se io mi sono alterato."

56. Ibid., 2:552. "Aveva detto il cardinale Niceno et altri cardinali che v'era venuti uomini degni discosto da Roma più di cento cinquanta miglia, solo per vederlo e per udire isporgli l'ambasciata, tutte queste cose lo facevano temere."

57. Ibid., 2:553–554.

58. Ibid., 2:554, "Questo acto di parlare in concestoro publico fu de' primi che facesseno mai i Fiorentini, perché questo luogo era de' Re, et degli Imperadori, el Papa lo dette a' Fiorentini per fare loro questo onore."

59. Ibid., "Messer Giannozo gli dette principio, donde hanno preso dipoi tutti gli altri che v'hanno parlato l'ordine della sua oratione, essendo nuova consuetudine come era e l'oratione oggi molto degna."

60. Ibid., "E' Cardinali mandorono a Vinegia la copia della sua oratione, et veddesi poi in quella de' Vinitiani avervi messo alle volte parecchi versi di quella di messer Giannozo."

61. Ibid., "Nel partirsi dipoi dal Papa, Neri di Gino si volse a messer Giannozo et sì gli disse: Io non ho mai considerato il pericolo che la città nostra ha portato."

62. Ibid., "se tu non c'eri, dove si trovava l'onore della nostra città et l'onore nostro?"

63. Ibid., "La nostra patria, et noi in ispezialtà, te ne restiamo obligati."

64. Ibid., 2:554–555, "Consideri ogniuno quanto onore et gloria abbia avuto la città di Firenze questa mattina, et a questo si conosce quanto vaglia uno singulare uomo a una republica. Questa andata gli fu maggiore onore che l'essere raffermo capitano di Pistoia."

65. See the discussion on this mission and Manetti's oration in Maxson, "The Many," 388–390.

66. da Bisticci, Le Vite, 2:570–571, "Giunto l'uno dì, l'altro dì gli dette la maestà del Re udienza publica, dove recitò una degnissima oratione latina de pace observanda. Ebbe la mattina grandissimo onore, perché v'era, oltra alla maestà del Re, tutti i signori et ambasciadori di tutte le potentie di Italia e fuori di Italia." The title of the speech translates to "On Observing the Peace."

67. ASF Sig. Leg. 13, 11r, "il giorno seguente quello clarissimo ambasciadore et poeta in conspecto di questa Signoria et del vinitiano ambasciadore et d tucto il nostro collegio agiunto il numero d molti nostri principali citadini ebbe oratione elegantissima gravissima et ornata."

68. ASF Sig. Leg. 13, 11v, "Tu come prudente in nome d questa Signoria renderai innumerabili gratie alla maesta del re in avere mandati si clarissimi ambasciadori et con si humanissima legatione."

69. ASF Sig. Leg. 13, 13r, "vera Gloria."

70. ASF Sig. Leg. 13, 13r, "cie stata confermata e stabilita dalli suoi ambasciadori i quali exposono con tanta humanita et affectione d cotesto serenissimo re verso questa re publica che sanza dubbio si suo dire la sua maesta havere gia tucti glianimi d questo nostro popolo. Tu se prudentissimo et con ogni studio et diligentia tingegnerai conservare tale benivolentia." The letter uses the plural when referring to the king's ambassador because he arrived in Florence with a Venetian diplomat who reiterated his basic points. ASF Sig. Leg. 13, 11r.

71. The commission is published in Naddo da Montecatini and Iacopo Salviati, *Croniche fiorentine*, ed. Ildefonso di San Luigi (Florence: Gae. Cambiagi, 1784), 1:362–371.

72. Ibid., 1:291–292.

73. Ibid., 1:362, "veri figliuoli."

74. Ibid., "chome veri figliuoli e servidori che sempre siamo istati de suoi serenissimi progenitori e della sua maesta."

75. Ibid., 1:363, "possibile e honesta."

76. The oration is published in ibid., 1:371–381.

77. Both Cicero and Pseudo-Cicero recommended praising external things, physical attributes, and internal qualities. See Cicero *De inventione* 2.177 and Pseudo-Cicero *Rhetorica ad Herennium* 3:10.

78. On this oration, see the detailed analysis in Chapter 6.

79. da Montecatini and Salviati, *Croniche*, 1:363., "Dopo questa espositione ho inchontinente ho in quel tempo che vi parra piu utile."

80. Ibid., 1:380 and 381.

81. Ibid., 1:292–293, "L'altra mattina tutti insieme l'andammo a visitare, et a sporre la nostra Ambasciata; et prima parlammo noi, et per noi parlò Mess. Filippo Magalotti, e fu nel Palagio del Papa a S. Piero, et haveva esso Re gran quantità di notabili Baroni, e Cavalieri per magnificenza di se, e fu tenuto per ogni huomo, che detto Mess. Filippo parlasse tanto altamente, e notabilmente quanto fusse udito già fa gran tempo. Et è vero, che questo parlare non fu di cose sustantiali, ma fu circa alle raccomandigie, et offerte, che s'usano ne' principii, et oltra ciò mostrare quanta stretta, et lunga amicitia era stata sempre intra i suoi antenati, et il nostro popolo; et poi conchiudendo, che altre parti più secrete gli si sporrebbero a sua volontà."

82. For the political situation involving Florence, Venice, Milan, and Naples in 1477, see the commission for this mission found at ASF Sig. Leg. 19, 132v–137r (new numbering). See also Giustiniani, *Alamanno*, 239–243; Fubini, *Italia*, 220–252; Vincent Ilardi, "The Assassination of Galeazzo Maria Sforza and the Reaction of Italian Diplomacy," in *Violence and Civil Disorder in Italian Cities, 1200–1500*, ed. Lauro Martines (Berkeley: University of California Press, 1972), 72–103.

83. ASF Sig. Leg. 19, 133v (new numbering), "Et cosi dipoi seguirete in honorare lafesta accomodandovi altempo et alla qualita della cosa."

84. ASF Sig. Leg. 19, 133v., "Aluogho et a tempo farete ilpresente nostro ornandolo con quelle parole che viparra convenienti."

85. ASF Sig. Leg. 19, 133v., "volonta."

86. ASF Sig. Leg. 19, 133v., "Nella vostra prima audientia non direte altro che in genere la cagione prima della vostra andata pelle noze."

87. Rinuccini, *Lettere*, 72, "Nonnulla sunt praeterea, serenissime rex, quae tuae maiestati seorsum referre mandarint praesides nostri, quae, cum illius commodo nobis licebit, enarrabimus."

88. Ibid., "Ut autem florentini populi benivolentiam devotionemque erga regiam maiestatem in hac nuptiali pompa non solum praesentia nostra et oratione testemur, attulimus novae reginae munuscula quaedam, ut putamus, non aspernanda."

89. ASF Sig. Leg. 19, 137v (new numbering), "la maesta del re dello honore factovi nella vostra entrata come scrivete a 30 et della grata audientia et delle dimostrationi damore facte come scrivete a 31."

90. Giustiniani, *Alamanno*, 240, "Vidimus et excepimus libentissime legatos quos ad nostras honestandas nuptias misistis. Eorum enim adventus et in ipsis peragendis nuptiis iucundissima fuit, et munus quo nos vestro nomine donarunt longe gratissimum; accepimus illud ut a vobis quos nostri amantissimos scimus perfectum equissimo animo. Agimus igitur vobis maximas gratias et pro ipsis oratoribus missis et pro ipso munere et tante vostri in nos amoris et benivolencie significationes et, memores futuros et cum usus postulaverit gratiam prolixe relaturos pollicemur."

91. See the discussion of Florentine diplomatic personnel in Chapter 5 of this study.

92. Maxson, "The Many," 373.

93. ASF Sig. Leg. 15, 11v.

94. ASF Sig. Leg. 15, 10v.

95. Maxson, "The Many," 373–374.

96. ASF Sig. Miss. I 15, 18r, "affectuosamente quanto piu si potra e per lo modo consueto."

97. ASF Sig. Leg. 1, 114r, "affectuosamente."

98. ASF Sig. Leg. 1, 117v, "affectuosamente."

99. ASF Sig. Leg. 2, 13r.

100. ASF Sig. Leg. 2, 45v.

101. See, for example, the long instructions to Filippo Magalotti and the other Florentine diplomats charged with congratulating King Ladislaus of Naples on his conquest of Rome in 1408. da Montecatini and Salviati, *Croniche*, 1:362–363.

102. ASF Sig. Leg. 6, 61r, "saluterete e conforterete con largheza di parole et commodo a loro grato."

103. ASF Sig. Leg. 6, 92v, "salutatalo e confortatolo affectuosamente come singulare fratello e amico nostro."

104. ASF Sig. Leg. 6, 100r, "Quando sarai a ferrara o ove sara lo illustre signore marchese predetto salutatolo o confortatolo per parte della signoria nostra come singularissimo e buono fratello e amico et offertogli generalmente con quelle parole e modi si richiede fra buoni amici e fratelli."

105. ASF Sig. Leg. 6, 125v, "tipresentarai alloro conspecto et per parte della nostra Signoria come intimi et singularissimi nostri amici affectuosissimamente saluterai et conforterai et ledebite et consuete offerte farai."

106. ASF Sig. Leg. 7, 35v., "quelle effectuose et calde parole che conosci disiderarsi et convenirsi al caso." These findings fit with those of the Italian historian

Emilio Santini, who argued that diplomatic commissions changed in the early
fifteenth century in terms of both form and content as a result of the increasing influence of humanism. See Santini, *Firenze*, esp. 123–124.

107. Giovanni Cavalcanti, *Istorie fiorentine*, ed. Filippo Luigi Polidori (Florence:
Tipografia all' Insegna di Dante, 1839), 2:374. "In prima espongano l'usate
salute e conforti, come a nostri buoni, veri e cordialissimi magiori frategli, con
quelle dolci e larghe parole, che alla loro prudenzia parrà convenirsi."

108. Ibid., 2:395, "In prima conferitosi a Perugia, saluti et conforti et profferisca a
quelli Signori Priori come veri et buoni fratelli et perfectissimi amici della
nostra Communità, sì come è usanza, et la sua prudentia saprà ben fare."

109. ASF Sig. Leg. 12, 4r, "quando sara tempo presentata prima laletter della
credentia con leriverentie debite et convenienti per parte diquesta saluterai et
conforterai con parole amichevoli honorifice et piene daffectione facendogli
larghe et generali offerte monstrandogli che nelalingua nelingegno ne lituoi
gesti sarebbono sufficienti apotere exprimere et narrare quanto e lamore et la
dilectione di questa signoria et di questa signoria di tucto questo popolo
inverso la sua."

110. ASF Sig. Leg. 12, 63v, "quando sara il tempo presentata prima la lettera della
credentia con le debite et consuete reverentie per parte di questa signoria
conforterai et saluterai la sua excellentia con parole affectuose honorifice et
piene disingulari affectioni facendogli larghe offerte in generale con quelle
parole che paranno alla tua prudentia essere accommodate al tempo alla
materia et alla persona la quale rapresenti et similemente a quella apresso alla
quale hai adire."

111. ASF Sig. Leg. 11, 185v–186r, (^ ^ indicates an inserted word) "quando visara
dato il tempo va presenterete al conspecto del Sanctissimo padre et facte le
debite reverentie et cerimonie presentata la lettera della credentia baciando
prima decta lettera come e diconsuetudine vicongratulerete et rallegherrete
con la sua Sanctita con parole ample et grandi et honorifice et piene di
devotione et difiliale affecto della felice assumptione della sua Beatudine
dimonstrando lo immenso gaudio et exultatione che questa Signoria et
tucto questo popolo et principali desso hanno avuto della sua electione di
^sì^ sancto et optimo pastore et che non e alcuno che siricordi mai essere
venuto alla cita nostra novella si felice per la quale universalmente da tucta la
cita et da qualunque persona dessa si prendesse tanto immenso gaudio et
incredibile letitia et questo non dovea essere admiratione adalcuno perche
ogni fedele christiano considerato laltissimo dio avere perveduto di tale
successore di piero et di tale governatore nel quale erano excellentissime
virtu admirabilissima doctrina una somma et paternale carita et dilectione
verso tucto il popolo fedele meritamente si dovea rallegrare et giubilare adio
di tale assumptione et se adalcuno questo era conveniente era necessario et
debito officio alla cita nostra la quale ama observa et in sommo honore
riverentia et devotione la sua Beatidine et da essa et per lo passato et per lo
presente sente et intende essere et dilecta et amata Ma non era vostro propo-
sito velersi extendere in narrare ne la letitia et il ga^u^dio nella singulare
devotione et reverentia di questo popolo verso la ^sua^ Sanctita perche ne
lingegno vostro ne la eloquentia ne alcuna copia o fiume dornate parole

sarebbono sufficienti apotere explicare queste parti et questo primo congresso vuole essere exposto con parole grandi et sonanti et apte adimonstrare tanto gaudio et tanta lititia quanto per tucti se preso di tale asumptione Et per la prima volta distesovi in questa congratulatione quanto giudichera essere utile le vostre prudentie et facte le debite recommendationi di tucti e nostri citadini mercatati et prelati et etiandio lofferte farete fine subgiugnendo che altra volta quando pratera alla sua Beatitudine sarete apiedi dessa per dire alcune altre cose a voi commesse."

112. Pierozzi's commission from 1458 appears in ASF Sig. Leg. 15, 2v-7r and is published in Cesare Guasti, *Due legazioni al Sommo Pontefice per il Comune di Firenze presedute da Sant' Antonino Arcivescovo* (Florence: Bianchi E. C. Barbera, 1857), 45–52. Filippo de' Medici's commission from 1464 appears in ASF Sig. Leg. 15, 125v-128r.

113. Guasti, *Due legazioni*, 46 and ASF Sig. Leg. 15, 125v.

114. ASF Sig. Dieci Otto Leg. Miss. Resp. 75, 91r, "Et dirai essere mandato da noi parendoci necessario fare questa dimonstratione al presente di nuovo imbasciadore nostro alla excellente signore non per altro bisogno."

115. For orations by Florentine diplomats from the 1490s and later, see Desjardins and Canestrini, *Négociations*, 1:335–337; Florence Gragg, ed., *Latin Writings of the Italian Humanists* (New York: Charles Scribner's Sons, 1927), 199–201; Manlio Fancelli, ed., *Orazioni politiche del cinquecento* (Bologna: Nicola Zanichelli, 1941); ASF Acquisti 140, insert 9, 166r-167v contains an anonymous oration by Florentine diplomats to the pope. The oration is undoubtedly for an obedience mission (see the congratulations offered by the diplomats at the bottom of folio 166r through the top of 166v). The reference to "Dux Soderinus" on 166v points to the election of Julius II in 1503 as the most likely event for the speech.

116. Muir, *Ritual*, 264.

117. Ibid., 264–65.

118. Stephen J. Milner, "Communication, Consensus and Conflict: Rhetorical Precepts, the *Ars concionandi*, and Social Ordering in Late Medieval Italy," in *The Rhetoric of Cicero in Its Medieval and Early Renaissance Commentary Tradition*, ed. Virginia Cox and John O. Ward (Leiden: Brill, 2006), 365–408. On oratorical models in general, see Witt, *In the Footsteps*, 351–494. For an example of a handbook, see BNC Naz. II II 72.

119. Black, *Benedetto*, 157–164.

120. Trexler, *Libro*, 86–88.

121. ASF Sig. Risp. Verb. 2, 41v and 43v.

122. Scala, *Humanistic*, 224.

5. Civic Failure of the Literary Humanists or Literary Failure of the Civic Humanists?

1. See, for example, the discussion of class and gender equality at Burckhardt, *The Civilization*, 230–235 and 250–253.

2. Ibid., passim; cf. Celenza, *The Lost*, 11–15.

3. Burckhardt, *The Civilization*, 153.

4. McManamon, *Funeral Oratory*, 25; D'Elia, *The Renaissance*, 47.

5. Martines, *The Social*, 145–198.

6. Martines, *The World*, 178–193.

7. Ibid., 147–148, 165–166, and 168; Witt, *Hercules*, 111–177; Viti, *Leonardo Bruni Cancelliere*; Black, *Benedetto*, 85–183; Brown, *Bartolomeo Scala*, 42–60 and 135–192; Demetrio Marzi, *La cancelleria della Repubblica fiorentina* (Rocca San Casciano: Licinio Cappelli, 1910), 1: 106–259.

8. Maxson, "The Many," 379–388, esp. 386–388.

9. Black, *Benedetto Accolti*, 224–285.

10. Ibid., 259–270.

11. Martines, *The Social*, 147–154.

12. Ibid., 158, and more generally at 154–158.

13. Ibid., 160–165.

14. On the following points, cf. Robert Black, "Florentine Political Traditions and Machiavelli's Election to the Chancery" *Italian Studies* 40 (1985): 1–5; Black, "Machiavelli," 71–81.

15. Martines, *The Social*, 103.

16. *Florentine Renaissance Resources*; search for "rinuccini" under surnam1.

17. Martines, *The Social*, 264.

18. *Florentine Renaissance Resources*; search for "bracciolini" under surnam1; cf. Black, *Benedetto*, 90.

19. Martines, *The Social*, 260.

20. *Florentine Renaissance Resources*; search for "marsuppini" under surnam1.

21. Grafton, *Leon*, 6–9.

22. Martines, *The Social*, 168–175; cf. Hankins, "The Dates," 21–22.

23. Martines, *The Social*, 176–191; Raffaella Maria Zaccaria, "Documenti su Giannozzo Manetti," in *Dignitas et excellentia hominis*, ed. Stefano U. Baldassarri (Florence: Le Lettere, 2008), 333–345.

24. On these origins see the discussion in Chapter 7.

25. Martines, *The Social*, 192; on Manetti, see Boschetto, "L'esilio," 117–118.

26. Martines, *The Social*, 192–193.

27. Jurdjevic, *Guardians*, 53–54; on humanists in the chancery, see the citations in Black, "Florentine," and Black, "Machiavelli."

28. Black, "Machiavelli," 78–81.

29. On Florentine diplomatic documents in general, see Vincent Ilardi, "Fifteenth-Century Diplomatic Documents in Western European Archives and Libraries (1450–1494)," *Studies in the Renaissance* 9 (1962): 79–83; see also Irene Fabii, "Sulla trasmissione dei carteggi diplomatici della Repubblica Fiorentina: Le antiche segnature," *Medioevo e Rinascimento* XVII (2003): 135–139.

30. ASF Cons. Mar. 3, 2v; ASF Car. Cor. 51, 56v-56r, 121r, 122v; ASF Sig. Dieci Otto Leg. Miss. Resp. 8, 185r.

31. ASF Sig. Leg. 13, 31r, 32v and Dieci Leg. 4, 22r.

32. ASF Dieci Leg. 4, 59r and ASF Sig. Leg. 13, 44v.

33. Giuseppe Pampaloni, "Gli organi della Repubblica fiorentina per le relazioni con l'estero," *Rivista di studi politici internazionali* 20 (1953): 285.

34. ASF Dieci Miss. 2 76v-77r, 85r-86r, 93v-95r, 98r-98v, 103v-104r, 109r, and 113r-113v; cf. the correspondence with the Signoria at Monzani, "di Leonardo," 25–34.

35. On this episode, see Laura de Angelis, "I canonici di San Lorenzo e loro disputa con i canonici della cattedrale," in *Il Capitolo di San Lorenzo nel Quattrocento*, ed. Paolo Viti (Florence: Leo S. Olschki, 2006), 21–34.

36. Guasti, *Commissioni*, 1:33.

37. ASF Sig. Dieci Otto Leg. Miss. Resp. 8 and ASF Car. Cor. 51. Excerpts from a third election book covering 1428–1435, now lost, are found at ASF Car. Strozzi. III 191, 128r-129v.

38. For example, see ASF Sig. Leg. 16, 206r, 208r; Sig. Leg. 17, 112r; Sig. Leg. 19, 132r; cf. Fubini, *Quattrocento*, 86–87.

39. While building this database I viewed the relevant files for both the Signoria and the Dieci di Balìa in situ. For the Otto di Pratica, I have relied on the descriptions for these files found in *Carteggi delle magistrature dell'età repubblicana: Otto di Pratica* (Florence: Leo S. Olschki, 1987). All archival references to Otto di Pratica derive from this inventory and have not been seen.

40. On the various series of surviving Florentine diplomatic documents, see Marzi, *La cancelleria*, 527–532; del Piazzo, *Signori*; Fabii, *Sulla trasmissione*, 3–5; at least two more registers are found outside the Archivio di Stato in Florence. A register of letters written by Leonardo Bruni is at BNC Panc. 148 (letters to rulers from February 12, 1435 to February 16, 1444). A register of letters written by Carlo Marsuppini that covers February 25, 1451, to October 16, 1452, is in BMore. Bigazzi, 193.

41. ASF Dieci Deb. & Cred. 2, 128v-129r, 279v, 316v-317r, 407v; 3, 34v.

42. Domenico Giugni, for example, performed ambassadorial duties in Hungary on an unofficial basis. See Scala, *Humanistic*, 128; Giannozzo Manetti continued to perform diplomatic activities for the Florentines in the 1450s after his voluntary exile. See Connell, "The Humanist Citizen," 161.

43. Fubini, *Quattrocento*, 89–98; cf. Bullard, *Lorenzo*, 54–56.

44. For these individuals, see notes 51 and 52.

45. Their diplomatic missions are as follows: Donato Acciaiuoli: ASF Sig. Leg. 15, 148r; 17, 20r, 84r, 111r, 144r, 159r, 161v, 167r; 18, 90r, 97r; 19, 75r, 155r; 20, 20r; Sig. Dieci Otto Leg. Miss. Resp. 75, 34. Giannozzo Manetti: ASF Car. Cor. 51, 22v; ASF Sig. Leg. 11, 56r, 185v; 12, 56v, 119r; 13, 3v, 32v, 41r; Dieci Leg. 4, 61v; Martines, *The Social*, 185–186; Matteo Palmieri: ASF Dieci Leg. 4, 23r; Sig. Leg. 13, 131v; 15, 7v; 16, 26r, 35r, 153v; 17, 168r; Carpetto, *The Humanism*, 22; Palla di Nofri Strozzi: ASF Sig. Leg. 4, 126r, 127v, 129v; 5, 97v, 102r; 6, 57r, 97v; 7, 39r; 9, 32r, 40v, 50v, 76v, 109v; Guasti, *Commissioni*, 3:357, 3:360; Cavalcani, *Istorie*, 2:313; Matteo Palmieri, *Annales*, ed. Giosue Carducci, Vittorio Fiorini, and L. A. Muratori, *Raccolta degli storici italiani dal cinquecento al millecinquecento* 26, no. 1 (Città di Castello: S. Lapi, 1906), 137.

46. For Bruni's first election as diplomat, see ASF Sig. Dieci Otto Leg. Miss. Resp 8, 20v; on Bruni's diplomatic missions in 1426, see earlier discussion. On Bruni's domestic officeholding, see Martines, *The Social*, 165–176.

47. Martines, *The Social*, 160–165.

48. This mission is found at ASF Sig. Leg. 18, 156r. On Rinuccini's fall from favor with Lorenzo de' Medici, see earlier discussion.

49. On Scala's missions, see in general Brown, *Bartolomeo Scala*, 87–90 and 106–108; Scala, *Humanistic*, 24; for Scala's hometown, see Brown, *Bartolomeo Scala*, 3.

50. Kent, *The Rise*, 56–57; and Molho, *Marriage*, 252–253.

51. The 17 individuals who served on more then 20 missions were (with the year that their family entered the *tre maggiori* in parentheses) Agnolo Acciaiuoli (1291), Luca degli Albizzi (1284), Maso degli Albizzi (1284), Rinaldo degli Albizzi (1284), Neri di Gino Capponi (1304), Filippo Corsini (1326), Rinaldo Gianfigliazzi (1382), Vieri Guadagni (1289), Luigi Guicciardini (1302), Filippo Magalotti (1287), Bernadetto de' Medici (1291), Pierfilippo Pandolfini (1304), Bartolomeo Popoleschi (1390), Antonio Ridolfi (1287), Lorenzo Ridolfi (1287), Cristofano Spini (1286), and Niccolò da Uzzano (1363). For these dates, see *Florentine Renaissance Resources*. I have included the earliest dates listed for each relevant surname.

52. The individuals serving between 10 and 19 times as a diplomat were Donato Acciaiuoli (1291), Filippo Adimari (1387), Alessandro Alessandri (1378), Palmieri Altoviti (1282), Matteo Arrighi (1287), Biliotto Biliotti (1297), Bernardo Buongirolamo (1467), Felice Brancacci (1317), Gino Capponi (1287), Matteo Castellani (1317), Paolo Diaccetto (1294), Giuliano Davanzati (1358), Dietisalvi di Dietisalvi Neroni (1292), Jacopo Gianfigliazzi (1382), Bernardo Giugni (1291), Niccolò Giugni (1291), Bernardo Guadagni (1289), Jacopo Guicciardini (1302), Piero Guicciardini (1302), Lorenzo Machiavelli (1283), Bardo Mancini (1291), Giannozzo Manetti (1306), Nello Martini (none found); Piero Nasi (1376), Otto Niccolini (1341), Agnolo Pandolfini (1304), Carlo Pandolfini (1304), Benedetto Peruzzi (1286), Ridolfo Peruzzi (1286), Buonaccorso Pitti (1283), Giovannozzo Pitti (1283), Francesco Rucellai (1302), Tommaso Sacchetti (1333), Jacopo Salviati (1302), Tommaso Soderini (1282), Marcello Strozzi (1284), Palla di Nofri Strozzi (1284), Angelo della Stufa (1323), Francesco Tornabuoni (1428), Marsilio Vecchietti (1371), and Andrea Vettori (1320). See ibid.

53. On the Adimari, see Molho, *Marriage*, 253; on the Alessandri (from the Albizzi), see Molho, *Marriage*, 205; on the Vecchietti, see Kent, *The Rise*, 146.

54. For the identification of lawyers, I have relied on the appendices in Martines, *Lawyers*, 481–508. The lawyers were Bernardo Buongirolamo, Filippo Corsini, Giuliano Davanzati, Nello Martini, Otto Niccolini, Bartolomeo Popoleschi, Lorenzo Ridolfi, and Marcello Strozzi.

55. For the identification of knightly status, I have relied on the titles used to address diplomats in diplomatic commissions and correspondences. The breakdown is as follows: *Started diplomatic career as a knight*: Maso degli Albizzi, Rinaldo Gianfigliazzi, Filippo Magalotti, Cristofano Spini, Filippo Adimari, Palmieri Altoviti, Jacopo Gianfigliazzi, Francesco Rucellai, Tommaso Sacchetti; *attained knighthood during diplomatic career*: Agnolo Acciaiuoli, Rinaldo degli Albizzi, Luigi Guicciardini, Antonio Ridolfi, Alessandro Alessandri, Matteo Castellani, Dietisalvi di Dietisalvi Neroni,

Bernardo Giugni, Giannozzo Manetti, Carlo Pandolfini, Buonaccorso Pitti, Giovannozzo Pitti, Jacopo Salviati, Tommaso Soderini, Palla di Nofri Strozzi, Angelo della Stufa.; cf. Gaetano Salvemini, *La Dignità Cavalleresca nel Comune di Firenze* (Florence: M. Ricci, 1896), 130–137 and 144–148.

56. Martines, *The Social*, 117, 123, and 127. See also Cardini and Viti, *I cancellieri*.

57. Martines, *The Social*, 311.

58. Ibid., 148–149.

59. *Florentine Renaissance Resources.* Search Niccoli under surname. The Niccoli family had one person serve in the *tre maggiori* on only one occasion in the fourteenth century.

60. Martines, *The Social*, 155 and 265.

61. Alessandro Perosa, "Lo zibaldone di Giovanni Rucellai," in *Studi di filologia umanistica*, ed. Paolo Viti (Rome: Edizioni di Storia e Letteratura, 2000), 2: 112–113.

62. ASF Cons. Prat. 52, 44v.

63. For these references to Bernadetto's diplomatic missions, see ASF Sig. Leg. 11, 93v, 150v; 12, 45r, and 54r.

64. ASF Sig. Miss. I 37, 112r.

65. Palmieri, *Annales*, 157.

66. ASF Sig. Leg. 26, 40v–72r. A statute limiting embassies and passed in 1494 – thus outside the temporal reaches of this study – has received some scholarly attention. See Michael Mallett, "Ambassadors and Their Audiences in Renaissance Italy," *Renaissance Studies* 8, no. 3 (1994): 234; Riccardo Fubini, "La figura politica dell'ambasciatore negli siluppi dei regimi oligarchici quattrocenteschi abbozzo di una ricerca (a guisa di lettera aperta)," in *Forme e tecniche del potere nella città (secoli XIV-XVII)* (Perugia: Tipografia Guerra, 1979–1980), 46 and 55.

67. da Bisticci, *Le Vite*, 1:480–481 and 2:527–528. A similar example occurs at 2:550, where Donato di Leonardo Bruni nominates Manetti to go to the new pope Nicholas V in 1447.

68. ASF Car. Cor. 51, 15v and ASF Sig. Leg. 10, 109v.

69. ASF Car. Cor. 51, 24r and ASF Sig. Dieci Otto Leg. Miss. Resp. 2 and 5.

70. ASF Car. Cor. 51, 55r.

71. Giuseppe Vedovato, *Note sul diritto diplomatico della Repubblica Fiorentina* (Florence: G. C. Sansoni, 1946), 60–61.

72. Ibid., 49–52.

73. Desjardins and Canestrini, *Négociations*, 1:127, "ci fu in pubblico data audienza."

74. For example, see Dante Catellaci, "Diario di Felice Brancacci ambasciatore con Carlo Federighi al Cairo per il Comune di Firenze," *Archivio Storico Italiano* ser. 4, vol. 8 (1881): 157–188; Lerz, "Il Diario," 247–278; Milanesi, "Il Viaggio"; and P. J. Jones, "Travel Notes of an Apprentice Florentine Statesman, Giovanni di Tommaso Ridolfi," in *Florence and Italy*, ed.

Peter Denley and Caroline Elam (London: Westfield College, Committee for Medieval Studies, 1988), 263–280.

75. Ermolao Barbaro, *De coelibatu, De officio legati*, ed. Vittore Branca (Florence: Leo S. Olschki, 1969), 163.

76. For the surviving examples of diplomatic oratory by fifteenth-century Florentines, see Maxson, "The Many Shades," 375–376.

77. Witt, *In the Footsteps*, 451.

78. di Camugliano, *The Chronicles*, 216.

79. K. J. P. Lowe, *Church and Politics in Renaissance Italy: The Life and Career of Cardinal Francesco Soderini (1453–1524)* (Cambridge: Cambridge University Press, 1993), 20 and 276.

80. Hankins, "Cosimo," 431. Hankins suggests that a copy of this oration may survive in a fifteenth-century manuscript compiled between the 1420s and 1450s by the papal secretary and humanist Rinuccio Aretino, but internal evidence in the speech suggests that it may have been delivered years earlier than the date of the monk's letter to Cosimo. See Chapter 6.

81. Monzani, "di Leonardo," 32.

82. On this mission, see earlier discussion.

83. Bruni, *Opere*, 806–809.

84. Ibid., 808–811.

85. On classical panegyrics and external praise, see Pseudo-Cicero *Rhetorica ad Herennium* 3:10 and Cicero *De inventione* II 177.

86. Bruni, *Opere*, 808. "Per que enim loca nunquam nisi extremo vite periculo et summa formidine vadebatur."

87. Ibid., "latrociniis."

88. Ibid. "Itaque valles ipse et nemora, que prius metum exanimem viatoribus afferebant."

89. Ibid. Trees are exhorted to praise the Lord in Isa. 44:23: "Sing for joy, O heavens, for the LORD has done this; shout aloud, O earth beneath. Burst into song, you mountains, you forests and all your trees, for the LORD has redeemed Jacob, he displays his glory in Israel" (New International Version).

90. Bruni, *Opere*, 808–810.

91. Ibid., 810.

92. ASF Sig. Rap. 2, 97v. The Italian is "giunto in castello e vicitato i Priori premesse ledebite salutioni conforti e offerte."

93. ASF Sig. Rap. 1, 22v. The report, in its entirety, provides the dates of the diplomats' departure from and return to Florence, the signatures of the two diplomats with the standard formulaic pronouncements that the report is true and signed in their own respective hands, and one additional, descriptive statement: "La praticha tralloro e noi fu lungha e niente conchudemo cholloro."

94. Martines, *The Social*, 85–144.

95. Robert Black, "The Revival of Latin and Humanist Education," in *Italy in the Age of the Renaissance: 1300–1550*, ed. John M. Najemy (Oxford: Oxford University Press, 2004), 30.

96. Bruni, *Opere*, 861. "Questa è la risposta che vi si fa per parte de' miei magnifici Signori con diliberatione et consenso non solamente di questa numerosa

multitudine de' spettabili cittadini, i quali vedete essere presente et audienti; ma ancora con consenso et diliberatione di tutta la città acciò che intendiate tutto il popolo nostro essere d'uno volere et d'uno consenso et d'un pezzo."

97. Louis Haas, "Il mio buono compare: Choosing Godparents and the Uses of Baptismal Kinship in Renaissance Florence," *Journal of Social History* 29, no. 2 (1995): 346. See also Trexler, *Public Life*, 285; Queller, *The Office*, 48–49. The Venetians tried to limit this role for Venetian diplomats, see legislation passed on July 18, 1409 in Donald E. Queller and Francis R. Swietek, *Two Studies on Venetian Government* (Geneva: Librairie Droz, 1977), 39.

98. "Diario di Palla di Noferi Strozzi." *Archivio Storico Italiano* ser. 4, vol. 11 (1883): 35–37.

99. Ibid., 37–38.

100. Ibid. 37. "And first, with the owed reverence, they undertook with a most gracious mind the greetings of so great a majesty. As if by a father, protector, and benefactor of this state, they recommend humbly themselves and all their state."

101. Ibid.

102. For example, see Desjardins and Canestrini, *Négociations*, 64 and 78.

103. Bruni, *History*, 1:95–97. See also Maxson, "Establishing," 84–86.

104. Bruni, *Opere*, 853–855.

105. Ibid., 855–856.

106. Ibid., 856.

107. Ibid., 857–858.

108. Ibid., 858–859.

109. Ibid., 859–860.

110. Ibid., 860.

111. Ibid., 860–861.

112. James Hankins attributed this oration to the Florentine mission to either the coronation of Albrecht III in 1438 or that of Frederick III in 1440. See James Hankins, "Unknown and Little-Known Texts of Leonardo Bruni," in *Humanism and Platonism in the Italian Renaissance* (Rome: Edizioni di Storia e Letteratura, 2003), 1:61. No record of a diplomatic mission to Frederick III in 1440 exists. The diplomatic records in the Florentine archives for 1440 are admittedly fragmentary; however, the election book of diplomats sent by the Signoria for that year does survive and does not possess any record for a congratulatory mission to the new emperor in 1440 or his coronation in 1442. See ASF Car. Cor. 51. The file is chronological with the years 1438–1442 appearing at 26r–41r. The fact that Bruni undoubtedly wrote an oration for Giuliano Davanzati on a mission in 1442 may also suggest that he wrote a speech for the same man in 1438. See Maxson, "The Many," 380–381.

113. Bruni, *Opere*, 836, "Vidimus stellam eius in Oriente et venimus adorare eum."

114. ASF Car. Cor. 51, 155v. The diplomats were Giuliano Davanzati, Carlo Federighi, and Bernardo Giugni.

115. Bruni, *Opere*, 836. "Serenissime atque gloriosissime princeps, non sine probabili ratione similtudo facta est ab antiquis inter fastigium imperiale et astra in celo fulgentia."

116. Ibid., "Que quidem omnia, ne nunc noviter a me reperta putes, audi quid dicat Vergilius poetarum doctissimus: <<Ecce Dionei processit Cesaris astrum, / astrum quo segetes gauderent frugibus et quo / duceret apricis in collibus uva colorem>>."

117. Ibid., "tranquilitatem et pacem."

118. Ibid., 838, "fides," "moderatio," "fortitudo," "clementia," "incorrupta iustitia," "admirabilis sapientia," "altitudo consilii," "civitatibus et populis."

119. "sapientia," "consilium," "fortitudo," "iustitia," "fides." Latin from B. Fischer, I. Gribomont, H. F. D. Sparks, W. Thiele, Robert Weber, H. I. Frede, and Roger Gryson, eds., *Biblia sacra vulgata* (Stuttgart: Hendrickson, 1994).

120. Bruni, *Opere*, 838, "Quod, licet per litteras iam pridem significarit, tamen vivis etiam affatibus per nos oratores suos demonstrari plenius voluit, ac presentes tuo culmini sublimissimo gratulari pro hac felici adsumptione tua."

121. Ibid., "Ceterum, serenissime princeps, nonnulla seorsum exponere habemus, que cum dabitur locus et tempus tue maiestati seriosius exprimemus."

122. ASF Sig. Risp. Verb. 1 and 2.

123. For example, see the exchange between the Florentines and the Sienese ambassador at ASF Sig. Risp. Verb. 2, 4r-5r. In this particular example, the response of the Florentines to the Sienese political oration is not provided; instead the entry cuts off on 5r with a statement that the Standard Bearer of Justice conferred with the citizens of Florence and that they reached a consensus on what to do.

124. For my arguments that Bruni wrote the speech for Biagio Guasconi in 1432, see Maxson, "The Many," 375 and 383. For opposing opinions, see Hans Baron, *Humanistic and Political Literature in Florence and Venice at the Beginning of the Quatrocento* (Cambridge, MA: Harvard University Press, 1955), 176–177; Bruni, *Opere*, 826; and Concetta Bianca, "Le orazioni di Leonardo Bruni," in *Leonardo Bruni cancelliere della Repubblica di Firenze*, ed. Paolo Viti (Florence: Leo S. Olschki, 1990), 229–230.

125. On this oration, see Maxson "The Many," 379–383.

126. Scala, *Humanistic*, 242.

127. The social prominence of the Guicciardini is well known. The Pandolfini enjoyed a particularly close bond with the kings of Naples. Giannozzo Pandolfini, Pandolfo's father, was knighted by King Alfonso. See Kent, *Bartolommeo*, 84. King Ferrante served as godfather to Pandolfo's son, named Ferrante. See da Bisticci, *Le Vite*, 2:350.

128. Rinuccini, *Lettere*, 68.

129. On the Rinuccini family's history in Florence, see *Florentine Renaissance Resources* and search for Rinuccini under surnam1. On Rinuccini's diplomatic career, see earlier discussion.

6. The Rise of the Social Humanists, 1400–1455

1. William Shepherd, *The Life of Poggio Bracciolini* (Liverpool: J. M'Creery, 1802), 439–440.
2. Poggio Bracciolini, *The Facetiae or Jocose Tales of Poggio* (Paris: Isidore Liseux, 1879), 2:7.
3. Ibid.
4. Ibid., 2:7–8.
5. For this story, see ibid., 2:6–8.
6. Witt, *In the Footsteps*, 367.
7. Ibid., 363–370.
8. Ibid., 363–366. For Lapo's orations, see Robert Davidsohn, "Tre orazioni di Lapo da Castiglionchio ambasciatore fiorentino a Papa Urbano V e alla curia in Avignone," *Archivio Storico Italiano* 20 (1897): 234–246.
9. Davidsohn, "Tre," 234–246.
10. Brucker, *The Civic*, 293.
11. Ibid.; cf. Brucker, *Renaissance Florence*, 296.
12. Brucker, *The Civic*, 293.
13. This and subsequent lists of diplomatic missions in this study refer to the first page of commissions whenever possible. For missions for which a commission has not been found, an archival reference that places that person as a diplomat on the mission has been provided. Gianfigliazzi's missions are found at ASF Sig. Leg. 1, 14v, 79v; 2, 51v; 6, 14r; 28, 7r; ASF Dieci Relazioni 1, 1v; ASF Dieci Leg. 2, 1v, 9v, 68v; 3, 65v, 90r, 93r; ASF Sig. Dieci Otto Leg. Miss. Resp. 8, 12r; Luiso, *Studi*, 30. Gianfigliazzi was also a frequent diplomat before 1394. See in general ASF Dieci Leg. 1.
14. ASF Sig. Leg. 1, 2r; 2, 7v, 21r, 25r, 35v, 42v; 3, 59v; 4, 14v, 26v, 91v; 6, 31v; 28, 7r; ASF Dieci Leg. 2, 46v; 3, 65v; ASF Dieci Relazioni 1, 1v, 5v. Corsini was also a frequent diplomat before 1394. See in general ASF Dieci Leg. 1.
15. ASF Dieci Relazioni 1, 7v; ASF Dieci Leg. 2, 23r, 45r; 3, 9v; ASF Dieci Miss. 2, 1r; ASF Sig. Leg. 2, 13r, 60r; 4, 42v, 45r, 50v, 55r, 108r, 143r; 5, 127v; 6, 16r, 57r, 90r, 108v, 111v; 9, 32r; 28, 29r, 124r; ASF Sig. Miss. I 31, 22r; ASF Sig. Dieci Otto Leg. Miss. Resp. 8, 12r; ASF Sig. Rap. 1, 43r, 44r; ASF Car. Cor. 51, 6r.
16. His speech is found at BNC Magl. VI 134, 12r-13v and dates from 1392. The first part of the oration may be modeled on the beginning of Cicero's *Pro Roscio*. It also cites a letter of Cicero at the end of 12v. BNC Panc. 147 contains Ridolfi's manuscript with letters to Salutati and others as well as further evidence for his interest in humanist studies. See also, Lawrin Armstrong, *Usury and Public Debt in Early Renaissance Florence: Lorenzo Ridolfi and the Monte Comune* (Toronto: Pontifical Institute of Mediaeval Studies, 2003), 107–108.
17. ASF Dieci Leg. 2, 52r; 3, 20v, 59r, 94v, 85r; ASF Dieci Relazioni 1, 42v; ASF Sig. Leg. 1, 74v, 86r, 93r, 100v, 101r; 2, 2v, 13r, 30v, 51v; 3, 51v; 4, 42v, 55r; 28, 13r, 23r; ASF Sig. Rap. 1, 19v.
18. On this mission, see earlier discussion.

19. For further political analyses of orations that ostensibly lacked a political component, see Maxson, "Many Shades," passim.

20. Magalotti cited Boccaccio (da Montecatini and Salviati, *Croniche*, 1:371–372), Vergil (1:372), Cicero (1:372, 373), Seneca (1:372), Petrarch (1:373), Dante (1:374), Aristotle (1:376), Didymus of Alexandria (381), books of the Bible (1:372, 373, 374, 375, 379, 381).

21. Ibid., 1:371–373.

22. Ibid., 1:381. I have been unable to identify Magalotti's source for this quotation, but Magalotti may be trying to appear to cite Didymus the Blind, a late fourth-century teacher at Alexandria. On him, see Richard A. Layton, *Didymus the Blind and His Circle in Late-Antique Alexandria* (Urbana: University of Illinois Press, 2004).

23. da Montecatini and Salviati, *Croniche*, 1:371. "El chuore spaventa e triema conosciendosi di pocho ingengnio e meno arte e minimo esercitio siche glispiriti che nutrischano reghano exercitano i membri richorrono al suo sochorso chome alla loro fonte abbandonando la lingua per actitudine del parlare pensando alla gloriosa progenia della vostra serenita."

24. Ibid., 1:371–372.

25. Ibid., 1:372–373, "ispaventato" and "tanti notabili baroni principi e singnori."

26. Ibid., 1:373.

27. Ibid., "divino aiuto," "da mihi sermonem rectum," and "inperfetione del mio dire."

28. Ibid., 1:381, "dengnita."

29. Ibid.

30. Ibid., 1:371, "considering."

31. Ibid., 1:372–373. "Having to speak in the presence of your glorious excellence and of your serenity's amazing profundity of intellect, as well as in the so magnificent presence of so many notable barons, princes, and rulers, in a place where a decorated speech is offered every time because of the importance of the many things determined and also the deep level of skill [of those present], I, of little reputation, scared and speechless, am so stunned that I do not trust myself to speak."

32. Najmey, *A History*, 195–196.

33. Eric Cochrane, *Historians and Historiography in the Italian Renaissance* (Chicago: University of Chicago Press, 1981), 14.

34. Published in Guasti, *Commissioni*.

35. Cochrane, *Historians*, 14.

36. Kent, *The Rise*, 211–215. See also G. Canestrini "Versi fatti da Niccolò da Uzzano, predicendo la mutazione dello stato," *Archivio Storico Italiano* 4 (1843): 297–300.

37. da Bisticci, *Renaissance*, 318; cf. da Bisticci, *Le Vite*, 2:136.

38. See the notes to the edition of this text in Armstrong, *Usury*, 131–260. Whereas Ridolfi made countless references to scholastic writers throughout the text, he referred to only a handful of classical sources. For example, pages 163 and 217 have quotations from Valerius Maximus, Cicero appears on 216, and Livy on 217.

39. On the match between the Castellani and Bruni, see Martines, *The Social*, 121–123 and 199–210; on the connection between Pitti and Salutati, see earlier discussion.
40. Kent, *The Rise*, 211 and 220.
41. Martines, *The Social*, 240–241.
42. *Florentine Renaissance Resources*, search for "gianfigliaz" under surname.
43. Kent, *The Rise*, 219. See also Field, "Leonardo Bruni," 1115.
44. Brucker, *The Civic*, 266.
45. G. Canestrini, "Testamento del Cardinale Baldassarre Coscia, già Papa col nome di Giovanni XXIII," *Archivio Storico Italiano* 4 (1843): 295.
46. da Montecatini and Salviati, *Croniche*, 1:368 and 369.
47. Martines, *Lawyers*, 369 and 483.
48. For Capponi at Pisa, see ASF Dieci Leg. 3, 117v, 120v, and 121r; ASF Sig. Leg. 28, 30v; for Capponi's history, see Cochrane, *Historians*, 23; for Palmieri's version, see Carpetto, *The Humanism*, 100–111.
49. Brucker, *The Civic*, 263–264.
50. ASF Dieci Leg. 3, 41r, 51v, 78v, 86v, 87v, and 129r.
51. Guasti, *Commissioni*, 1:307.
52. Bigazzi, "Vita," 274.
53. Guasti, *Commissioni*, 1:305.
54. Machiavelli, *Florentine*, 181.
55. On these business dealings, see Martines, *The Social*, 128–29 and 232; for Filelfo's dialogue, see Field, "Leonardo Bruni," 1127.
56. Marcello Strozzi was often the contact between Florence and Rome between 1409 and the 1440s. Martines, *Lawyers*, 483. Moreover, he was a diplomat to various popes at least seven times: ASF Dieci Leg. 3, 3r; ASF Sig. Leg. 6, 90r; 7, 28v; 9, 28v; 28, 19v; ASF Sig. Miss. I 28, 52v; ASF Car. Cor. 51, 6r.
57. Guasti, *Commissioni*, 1:306–307.
58. Ibid., 1:305.
59. Paolo Viti, "Leonardo Dati," in *DBI*, available online at "Leonardo Dati in Dizionario Biografico – Treccani.it," http://www.treccani.it/enciclopedia/leo-nardo-dati_res-de29ae09–87eb-11dc-8e9d-0016357eee51_%28Dizionario-Biografico%29/ (accessed May 8, 2012); Stefano Orlandi, *Necrologio di S. Maria Novella 1235–1504: Testo e commenti biografici cardinali, vescovi, teologi, letterati, missionari, artisti fiorentini* (Florence: Leo S. Olschki, 1955), 2:134–166; for references to Gregorio's brother Leonardo in Gregorio's diary, see, for example, Brucker, *Two*, 132 and 140.
60. Guasti, *Commissioni*, 1:292–293, which publishes Rieti's commission and report. See also ASF Sig. Dieci Otto Leg. Miss. Resp. 8, 77r (election record), ASF Sig. Leg. 6, 78r (commission), and ASF Sig. Rap. 2, 47v (report).
61. ASF Sig. Leg. 6, 43r and Guasti, *Commissioni*, 1:292.
62. Guasti, *Commissioni*, 1:296, "ambasciadore."
63. Viti, "Leonardo Dati."
64. Viti, "Leonardo Dati," "grande sapienza retorica."
65. Orlandi, *Necrologio*, 2:142–143 and 163–164; Viti, "Leonardo Dati."
66. Viti, "Leonardo Dati," which contains a good discussion of the issues involved in attributing this work to Leonardo Dati.

67. Aiazzi, *Ricordi*, lvi. "Trovammo il detto papa Martino a Milan, e quivi si fe'la prima vicitazione, e feccla il generale, e durò circa a un'ora, che mai s'udì simile orazione, che v'era forse cento calamai a scriverla mentre che diceva, e fece grandissimo onore a se e al commune."

68. Ibid. Rinuccini was a youth under Bartolomeo Valori along with Niccolò di Domenico Giugni.

69. See, for example, a sermon delivered on September 15, 1415, in Johannes Hollnsteiner von Heinrich Finke, *Acta concilii constanciensis* (Münster: I. W. Regensberg, 1923), 417–419.

70. Ibid., 488.

71. Ibid., 418, "canones antiqui."

72. Ibid., 488–492.

73. For the *Manipulus Florum*, see Chris L. Nighman, "What Is the *Manipulus florum?*" Description of the *Manipulus florum*, http://info.wlu.ca/~wwwhist/faculty/cnighman/page2.html (accessed April 25, 2010). This Web page is part of the broader Electronic *Manipulus florum* Project, edited by Chris L. Nighman of Wilfrid Laurier University in Ontario, Canada, which aims to make accessible and searchable this influential collection of quotations. Dati's quotations were found by searching within this project. The stable URL is http://info.wlu.ca/~wwwhist/faculty/cnighman/MFedition/index.html (accessed April 25, 2010). This URL provides a list of section headings. Socrates is under *rapina l*; Anacharsis is under *lex*; Seneca is listed under *curiositas AN*; the second Seneca quotation is under *curiositas am*. Compare, for example, the references to Socrates. Dati stated, "cum semel a Socrate quesitum fuisset, cur rideret, respondit: video magnos latrones ducentes ad suspendium parvos latrones: sacrilegia, inquit, minuta puniuntur, sed magna in triumphis feruntur." The *Manipulus florum* has "Quesitum erat a Socrate cur rideret. Respondens ait: Video magnos latrones ducentes paruum latronem ad suspendium qui digniores sunt suspendio. Sacrilega, inquit, minuta puniuntur sed magna in triumphis feruntur."

74. See, for example, Finke, *Acta*, 481.

75. Ibid., 507–513, esp. 508 and 510.

76. For a contrasting argument, see Hankins, "Cosimo," 431.

77. For the text of this oration, see James Hankins, "A Zibaldone of Rinuccio Aretino," in *Humanism and Platonism in the Italian Renaissance* (Rome: Edizioni di Storia e Letteratura, 2003), 120–121. The quotation translates to "After we heard that you, most holy Father, were elected to the Apostolic See (literally, "into the pontificate of the Holy See") by the influence of God, we were moved by such joy that we disdain never to be able to set it out in words." The quotation from Cicero is, Cicero *Epistularum ad familiares* XV, 7, and translates to "I was moved by the greatest joy when I heard that you were made consul."

78. Hankins, "A Zibaldone," 121, "The kind of pastor that the church was especially desiring and pushing for, it has, and a Colonna has been verified (that is, agreed upon as the true pope), in whom no one better to erect, establish, and fortify it could be desired or hoped for."

79. Their missions from 1425 and earlier are found at: Cosimo: ASF Sig. Leg. 6, 108v; 7, 28r, 36v; Palla di Nofri Strozzi: ASF Sig. Leg. 4, 126r, 127v, 129v; 6, 57r, 6, 97v; 7, 39r.

80. Crabb, *The Strozzi*, 27.

81. ASF Sig. Leg. 6, 22r; 7, 15r.

82. Paul M. Kendall and Vincent Ilardi, eds., *Dispatches with Related Documents of Milanese Ambassadors in France and Burgundy* (Athens: Ohio University Press, 1970–1981), xli.

83. ASF Sig. Leg. 6, 50v, 68v; Sig. Miss. I, 29, 109v; Sig. Dieci Otto Leg. Miss. Resp. 3, 23.

84. ASF Sig. Leg. 6, 29r, 43r, 90r, 131r; 7, 17v.

85. ASF Sig. Leg. 6, 63r, 96r, 138r; Sig. Dieci Otto Leg. Miss. Resp. 5.

86. ASF Sig. Leg. 6, 123v; 7, 15r, 32v; ASF Sig. Minutari 6, 4r; ASF Sig. Miss. I 31, 27r.

87. ASF Sig. Leg. 6, 81r, 115v; 7, 5r; Sig. Dieci Otto Leg.Miss.Resp. 8, 22v.

88. ASF Sig. Leg. 6, 107r; 7, 25r; Car. Strozzi. III 119, 19r; 37r; 125, 1r.

89. Agnolo's missions prior to and including 1425 are found at ASF Dieci Leg. 3, 1v, 78r; ASF Sig. Dieci Otto Leg. Miss. Resp. 8, 4r; ASF Sig. Leg. 6, 6v, 36r, 68v, 79r, 98r, 139r; 7, 46r.

90. ASF Sig. Rap. 1, 40r; Dieci Leg. 3, 58r, 78r; ASF Sig. Leg. 4, 1r; 6, 63r, 97v, 136v.

91. On the fascinating figure of Felice Brancacci, see Garin, *Portraits*, 57 and 103; Anthony Molho, "The Brancacci Chapel: Studies in Its Iconography and History," *Journal of the Warburg and Courtauld Institutes* 40 (1977): 50–98 and 322; Leonida Pandimiglio, *Felice di Michele vir clarissimus e un consoteria* (Olivetta: Tipografica Varese, 1989), which contains an edition of the letter from Lorenzo di Palla Strozzi to Brancacci in Rome that discusses Biondo Flavio on page 120; Nicholas Eckstein, ed., *The Brancacci Chapel: Form, Function and Setting* (Cambridge, MA: Harvard University Press, 2007).

92. ASF Sig. Leg. 4, 146v; 6, 86r, 89r, 115v; 7, 1r.

93. Molho, *Florentine*, 153.

94. Mallet, *The Florentine*, 38–39.

95. For Strozzi's reputation, see Brucker, *The Civic*, 286; for his diplomatic career, see ASF Sig. Leg. 2, 76r, 76v; 6, 9r, 46r; 7, 2v.

96. Brucker, *Renaissance Florence*, 238.

97. Enzo Carli, *All the Paintings of Paolo Uccello*, trans. Marion Fizallan (London: Oldbourne, 1963), 62. The relevant document is available at *The Years of the Cupola. Digital Archive of the Sources of the Opera di Santa Maria del Fiore, 1417–1436*, Margaret Haines, ed. (Florence, Opera di Santa Maria del Fiore, 2009), http://duomo.mpiwg-berlin.mpg.de/eng/IN/INlist21552So.HTM (accessed February 9, 2012).

98. ASF Sig. Leg. 4, 113r; 6, 87v.

99. ASF Car. Strozzi. III 132, 291r and 292r.

100. della Torre, *Storia*, 309.

101. ASF Sig. Leg. 6, 95v.

102. ASF Sig. Leg. 7, 13r and for the dedication and work, see Bruni, *Histoire*, 696–807. An English translation of the text is available at Griffiths, *The Humanism*, 267–282.
103. Martines, *The Social*, 324–325; and Davies, "An Emperor," 275–277.
104. Benvenuti was a diplomat to Bologna and Ferrara in 1419 (ASF Sig. Leg. 6, 100r); Genoa in 1420 (ASF Sig. Leg. 6, 111v); and Città di Castello (ASF Sig. Leg. 6, 140v).
105. Witt, *In the Footsteps*, 489–490.
106. Witt discusses the weak domestic culture of humanism in early fifteenth-century Milan at ibid., 477.
107. On the humanism of Pandolfini and Strozzi, see earlier discussion. Pandolfini's missions between these years are found at ASF Sig. Leg. 5, 39r, 51r, 76v, 119v. Strozzi's missions between these years are found at ASF Sig. Leg. 5, 97v, 102r; 9, 32r, 40v, 50v, 76v, 109v; Cavalcanti, *Istorie*, 2:313ff; Palmieri, *Annales*, 137.
108. Alessandro Alessandri: ASF Sig. Leg. 8, 85r; 9, 28v, 85v; Luca degli Albizzi: ASF 7, 76v; 9, 91r, 135v; Sig. Dieci Otto Leg. Miss. Resp. 5, 304; Rinaldo degli Albizzi: ASF Sig. Leg. 5, 97v, 102r; 7, 52v, 59v; 9, 40r, 55v; Felice Brancacci: ASF Dieci Miss. 2, 42r; Sig. Leg. 7, 70r; 9, 28v; 8, 1r, 9r, 20r; 9, 88v, 97r, 117r; Piero Guicciardini: ASF Sig. Leg. 5, 133r; 7, 76v; 9, 1r, 51r, 135v; 10, 2v; Ridolfo Peruzzi: ASF Dieci Miss. 2, 60r; Sig. Leg. 5, 12v; 9, 32r, 53r, 12v, 119v, 122v; Francesco Soderini: ASF Sig. Leg. 5, 127v; 7, 71v; 8, 46r; 9, 85r, 99v; Marcello Strozzi: ASF Sig. Leg. 5, 10v; 7, 59v; 9, 38v; 10, 15r; Guasti, *Commissioni*, 3:360.
109. Cochrane, *Historians*, 23; and Santini, *Firenze*, 183–185. For Capponi's missions between 1426 and 1435 see (one position was given two commissions) ASF Sig. Leg. 5, 95r, 96r, 9, 28v, 130v.
110. Cochrane, *Historians*, 26.
111. Schulz, *The Sculpture*, 69–74, esp. 71, with images shown from plate 114 to 119.
112. On Guadagni, see Raffaella Maria Zaccaria, "Bernardo Guadagni," in *DBI* available online at "Bernardo Guadagni in Dizionario Biografico – Treccani. it," http://www.treccani.it/enciclopedia/bernardo-guadagni_%28Dizionario-Biografico%29/ (accessed May 8, 2012); for Astore's diplomatic missions, see Guasti, *Commissioni*, 3:360; ASF Sig. Leg. 5, 34v; 8, 76r; 9, 64r. For Astore's role in the Florentine war with Lucca, see Machiavelli, *Florentine*, 166–168.
113. Leonardo Bruni: ASF Sig. Leg. 7, 50r; Dieci Miss. 2, 133v; Cosimo de' Medici: ASF Sig. Miss. I 31, 33r; Sig. Leg. 9, 40v, 65v; Lorenzo de Medici: ASF Sig. Leg. 5, 105v; 9, 32r; Matteo Strozzi: Crabb, *The Strozzi*, 27.
114. Piero Beccanugi: ASF Sig. Leg. 5, 71r; 7, 70r; Matteo Castellani: ASF Sig. Leg. 5, 43v, Giuliano Davanzati: ASF Sig. Leg. 5, 10r; 9, 32r; Biagio Guasconi: ASF Sig. Leg. 8, 79r; 9, 44r, 82v; Zenobi Guasconi: ASF Sig. Leg. 9, 32r, 55v; Raimondo Mannelli: ASF Sig. Leg. 9, 78r; Lorenzo Ridolfi: ASF Sig. Leg. 5, 127v; 9, 32r; Lorenzo di Palla Strozzi: ASF Sig. Leg. 9, 85r; Palla di Palla Strozzi: ASF Car. Strozzi. III 119, 37r; 125, 1r.

115. della Torre, *Storia*, 229; on the performances at San Martini, see Kent, *Friendship*, 95–111; Alberti's missions between 1426 and 1435 are found at ASF Sig. Leg. 9, 98r.

116. Marzi, *La cancelleria*, 160–161 and 182–186. On Paolo Fortini more generally, see Giovanni Ciappelli, "Paolo Fortini," in *DBI*, available at "Paolo Fortini in Dizionario Biografico – Treccani.it," http://www.treccani.it/enciclopedia/paolo-fortini_%28Dizionario-Biografico%29/ (accessed January 16, 2012); on his sons, see earlier discussion. On his diplomatic mission, see ASF Sig. Leg. 5, 47v.

117. On Martini and his speech, see Maxson, "The Many," 398–401; on Martini more generally, see Martines, *Lawyers*, 499 and passim. Nello Martini is sometimes referred to as Nello da San Gimignano or Nello Cetti.

118. Diplomats not yet connected to humanism but who filled three or more positions between 1426 and 1435 were the following: *three missions*: Mariotto Baldovinetti, Nerone Dietisalvi, Guido Magalotti, Bindaccio Ricasoli, and Francesco Tornabuoni; *four missions*: Astore Gianni and Bernardo Guadagni.

119. ASF Sig. Leg. 9, 32r.

120. Diplomatic missions, especially to major powers, often featured more than one diplomat. For the purposes of the analysis in this paragraph, each mission, regardless of the number of diplomats it involved, has been counted only a single time. This method provides a sense of the frequency of diplomatic exchanges between Florence and other parties.

121. For a political and cultural approach to the history of the state system in Italy during the mid Quattrocento, see Serena Ferente, *La sfortuna di Jacopo Piccinino: Storia del Bracceschi in Italia, 1423–1465* (Florence: Leo S. Olschki, 2005).

122. ASF Car. Cor. 51, 22v; Sig. Leg. 11, 56r, 185v; 12, 16v, 119r; 13, 3v, 32v, 41r; Dieci Leg. 4, 61v; Martines *The Social*, 185–186; cf. Baldassarri and Figliuolo, *Manettiana*, 11–66, which discusses and publishes much of the relevant documentation.

123. ASF Sig. Leg. 10, 37r; 11, 4r, 158v, 185v; 12, 91v, 120v; 13, 36r; Dieci Leg. 4, 37v, 59r; Car. Cor. 51, 6r, 11v, 21r, 28v, 35v, 40v, 44r, 47v; Sig. Dieci Otto Leg. Miss. Resp. 61, 143; Kendall and Ilardi, eds., *Dispatches*, 1:xli; di Camugliano, *The Chronicles*, 211 and 224.

124. ASF Car. Cor. 51, 30v; Dieci Leg. 4, 4r, 13v, 29v, 44v, 57r, 69v; Sig. Leg. 11, 167r; 12, 69v, 137v; 13, 44v, 85v; 28, 40r; Sig. Dieci Otto Leg. Miss. Resp. 7, 1.

125. ASF Dieci Leg. 4, 65r; ASF Sig. Leg. 10, 109v, 164v; 11, 38v; 12, 97r; ASF Sig. Dieci Otto Leg. Miss. Resp. 2, 95; 5, 351, 399, 415; 60, 73; 62, 74; Car. Cor. 51, 30r, 34v; Palmieri, *Annales*, 165.

126. ASF Sig. Leg. 10, 43r; 11, 41v, 92r; 12, 52v; 13, 101r; ASF Sig. Dieci Otto Leg. Miss. Resp. 9, 1; 62, 37; ASF Dieci Leg. 4, 51r, 65r, 68v.

127. ASF Sig. Leg. 10, 67r; 11, 27v, 89r, 143r, 185v; 12, 24r, 132v, 137v, 154v; Car. Cor. 51, 21v, 35v; 36r, 41v, 48v; Sig. Dieci Otto Leg. Miss. Resp. 7, 1; 61, 143; Palmieri, *Annales*, 157.

128. ASF Car. Cor. 51, 6r, 40r; Sig. Leg. 10, 155v, 161r; 11, 1r, 143r; 12, 24r, 69v; 13, 31r, 32v, 42r; 28, 40r.
129. On this tomb, see Zuraw, "The Public," 452–477.
130. da Bisticci, *Le Vite*, 2:321.
131. Ficino, *Opera*, 1:611–612.
132. His diplomatic missions for these years are found at ASF Sig. Leg. 10, 163r; 11, 185v; 12, 45r, 60r, 96r, 97r; 13, 24v, 42r; Car. Cor. 51, 26v, 37v, 38r, 102r.
133. Davies, *Florence*, 116–117.
134. His diplomatic missions are at ASF Sig. Leg. 10, 56r, 59v, 70v; 11, 12r, 93v, 150v; 12, 45r, 54r; 13, 85v, 173r; Car. Cor. 51, 32r, 34r, 35r, 35v, 41v, 102v; Dieci Leg. 4, 40r, 42r, 53r, 61v; Palmieri, *Annales*, 157 and 165.
135. Spencer, *Andrea*, 15–31.
136. These men and their missions were Alessandro Alessandri: ASF Sig. Leg. 10, 44v; 11, 185v; 12, 60r, 63v; Car. Cor. 51, 25v, 35r, 122r, 143v; Dieci Leg. 4, 70r; Piero Beccanugi: ASF Sig. Leg. 10, 41v; Car. Cor. 51, 23v, 32v; Donato Cocchi-Donati's diplomatic missions are at ASF Car. Cor. 51, 43r; Sig. Leg. 11, 50v, 145v, 174r; 12, 159r, 13, 21r; Dieci Leg. 4, 31r; Giuliano Davanzati: ASF Sig. Leg. 10, 32r, 34v, 60v, 155v; ASF Car. Cor. 51, 26r, 35r, 40r, 47v; Piero Guicciardini: ASF Car. Cor. 51, 6r, 24v, 29r, 31r; Sig. Leg. 10, 37r, 162v; Sig. Dieci Otto Leg. Miss. Resp. 1, 11; Domenico Martelli: ASF Sig. Leg. 11, 113r; 12, 99r, 103v; Dieci Leg. 4, 63r; Car. Cor. 51, 39r; Cosimo de' Medici: ASF MAP 11, 365; 124, 652; Lorenzo de' Medici: ASF Car. Cor. 51, 6r, 29r, 31v; Sig. Leg. 10, 64v, 81v, 158v; Piero de' Medici: ASF Sig. Leg. 11, 185v; 12, 137v, 154v; 13, 48r; Otto Niccolini: ASF Dieci Leg. 4, 15v, 21r, 67v; Sig. Leg. 13, 31r, 41r, 44v, 136v; Palmieri, *Annales*, 171; Matteo Palmieri: ASF Dieci Leg. 4, 23r; Sig. Leg. 13, 131v; Giannozzo Pandolfini: ASF Sig. Leg. 11, 5r; 12, 129r, 175r; 13, 48r, 136v; Car. Cor. 51, 122r, 143v; Palmieri, *Annales* 165; Piero de' Pazzi: ASF Dieci Leg. 4, 67r; Antonio Ridolfi: ASF Sig. Leg. 12, 36r, 187v; 13, 94r, 136v; Dieci Leg. 4, 26v; Lorenzo Ridolfi: ASF Car. Cor. 51, 6r; Alamanno Salviati: ASF Car. Cor. 51, 6r, 10r, 39v, 41r; Sig. Leg. 10, 75v; 12, 28v; 13, 6v; Marcello Strozzi: ASF Car. Cor. 51, 6r, 14r; Sig. Leg. 10, 148r; Guglielmo Tanagli: ASF Sig. Leg. 11, 144r; 13, 69r; Dieci Leg. 4, 22r; Sig. Dieci Otto Leg. Miss. Resp. 4, 7r; Car. Cor. 51, 43v; Palmieri, *Annales*, 161.
137. The relevant letter is at Rinuccini, *Lettere*, 33. Ridolfi's diplomatic missions are at ASF Sig. Leg. 12, 32v, 102v, 115v, 157v, 168r; 13, 153v.
138. On these orations, see later discussion and Chapter 7. His mission in 1455 is at ASF Sig. Leg. 13, 136v.
139. On Giovanni de' Medici's learning, see Vittorio Rossi, "L' indole e gli studi di Giovanni di Cosimo de' Medici," in *Rendiconti della reale accademia dei Lincei*, series 5, vol. 2 (Rome: Tipografia della Accademia, 1893), 38–60, 129–150; see also della Torre, *Storia*, 527–528; Cagni, *Vespasiano*, 55–57; Kristeller, *Supplementum*, 2:79–80; his missions are at ASF Sig. Leg. 13, 136v, 158r; Car. Cor. 51, 143v.
140. Hatfield, "The Compagnia," 156–157. Bernardo's diplomatic missions are found at ASF Car. Cor. 51, 36r and 47r.

141. da Bisticci, *Le Vite*, 2:213; Sacchetti's diplomatic missions are at ASF Sig. Leg. 11, 59v; 12, 129r, 165v.
142. Saalman, *Brunelleschi*, 228–233 and Black, *Humanism*, 245.
143. ASF Car. Cor. 51, 39r.
144. Black, *Education*, 398–399, 434.
145. Ibid., 126 and 164; Buongirolamo's connections to humanism beyond this employment were quite weak. See Martines, *Lawyers*, 63–64 and 504; Paolo Mari, "Bernardo Buongirolami," in *DBI*, available online at "Bernardo Buongirolami in Dizionario Biografico – Treccani.it," http://www.treccani.it/enciclopedia/bernardo-buongirolami_%28Dizionario-Biografico%29/ (accessed May 8, 2012). Alison Brown related that Bartolomeo Scala corresponded with Bernardo Buongirolamo in a "semi-official capacity;" see Brown, *Bartolomeo Scala*, 200. However, Brown wrote nothing about Buongirolamo sharing Scala's intellectual interests. Scala did write a surviving vernacular letter to Bernardo Buongirolamo without literary references. See Scala, *Humanistic*, 154. His diplomatic missions are at ASF Sig. Leg. 15, 11r, 42r, 51r, 87r; 16, 35r, 154r, 189r; 17, 15r, 96r, 132r; 18, 113r; Sig. Dieci Otto Leg. Miss. Resp. 12; Dieci Leg. 5, 262r; Dieci Miss. 19, 111v.
146. His mission is at ASF Sig. Leg. 10, 50r; for his activities as a scribe, see de la Mare, "New Research," 425, 516–518.
147. On Antonio and Leonardo Salutati, see Martines, *The Social*, 149; for their missions, see ASF Sig. Leg. 10, 107v and Car. Cor. 51, 24r.
148. Spencer, *Andrea*, 42–56, esp. 55–56; Schulz, *The Sculpture*, (64–68, esp. 66) with images at plates 106–113.
149. Roger J. Crum, "Roberto Martelli, the Council of Florence, and the Medici Palace Chapel," *Zeitschrift für Kunstgeschichte* 59, no. 3 (1996): 404–406.
150. On the relationship between Donatello and Roberto Martelli, see Patricia Lee Rubin, *Giorgio Vasari: Art and History* (New Haven, CT: Yale University Press, 1995), 348–355, esp. 352, where the relationship between Donatello and Roberto Martelli is explicitly discussed; see also Rubin, *Images*, 109; cf. Giorgio Vasari, *Lives of the Artists*, vol. 1, trans. George Bull (London: Penguin, 1987), 174 and 181; for the fraternal relationship between Domenico and Roberto, see *Florentine Renaissance;* search for Martelli under surnam1. Both men share the same name2, which suggests the same father.
151. da Bisticci, *Renaissance*, 206–207.
152. Viti, *Leonardo Bruni*, 16; the mission is at ASF Sig. Leg. 11, 10r.
153. Crabb, *The Strozzi*, 198–204.
154. ASF Car. Cor. 51, 37r.
155. Black, *Benedetto Accolti*, 179–180; his mission is at ASF Sig. Leg. 13, 164r.
156. Rhiannon Daniels, *Boccaccio and the Book: Production and Reading in Italy 1340–1520* (London: Modern Humanities Research Association, 2009), 174; his mission is at ASF Sig. Leg. 10, 39v.
157. Rossella Bessi, *Umanesimo volgare: Studi di letteratura fra Tre e Quattrocento* (Florence: Leo S. Olschki, 2005), 67. Della Stufa was also a

member of the Signoria that Donato Acciaiuoli described as full of merchants rather than learned men. See della Torre, *Storia* 365. On his missions, see ASF Car. Cor. 51, 46v; Sig. Miss. I 37, 26r; Sig. Leg. 12, 109v; Dieci Leg. 4, 11v, 13r, 20r, 27v, 41v, 64v.

158. Haines, "Oligarchy," passim, esp. 157 and 164; see also Haines, "The Years," http://www.operaduomo.firenze.it/cupola/ENG/IN/INlist15447So. HTM (accessed February 13, 2012), which lists many of the documents related to Niccolò Alessandri among other Alessandri family members.

159. Dale Kent, "A Window on Cosimo de' Medici, *Paterfamilias* and Politician, from within His Own Household: The Letters of his Personal Assistant, Ser Alesso Pelli," in *Florence and Beyond: Culture, Society and Politics in Renaissance Italy, Essays in Honour of John M. Najemy*, ed. David S. Peterson with Daniel E. Bornstein (Toronto: Centre for Reformation and Renaissance Studies, 2008), 355–367. Pelli's missions are at ASF Dieci Leg. 4, 41r and Car. Cor. 51, 16v.

160. da Bisticci, *Renaissance*, 352.

161. ASF Sig. Dieci Otto Leg. Miss. Resp. 7, 15. This document is a letter to Antonio while he was near Renè of Anjou. Antonio's commission seems to be lost.

162. Fonzio, *Letters*, 4–10 and 200, where the editor of the *Letters*, Alessandro Daneloni, lists the recipient of this letter as born in 1451; a different Puccio Pucci was a diplomat in 1446 and 1447; see ASF Sig. Leg. 11, 157r; 12, 49v.

163. Beyond the individuals in this paragraph, those not yet connected to humanism who were diplomats three or more times between 1436 and 1455 are the following: *three missions*: Antonio Albizzi, Mariotto Bencini, Giovanni Cafferecci, Mariotto Lippi, Filippo Tornabuoni; *four missions*: Nerone Dietisalvi, Piero Rucellai, Domenico Sapiti, Francesco Ventura; *five missions*: Paolo Diaccetto, Giovanni Vespucci; *six missions*: Nofri Parenti; *seven missions*: Niccolò Giugni; *nine missions*: Carlo Pandolfini; *twenty-four missions*: Bernadetto de' Medici.

164. ASF Sig. Leg. 11, 185v; cf. Baldassarri and Figliuolo, *Manettiana*, 21–26, which publishes the commission and a subsequent letter to Acciaiuoli and Manetti.

165. For Manetti's oration in general, see BML Plut. 52 15, 1r-9r. See also Wittschier, *Giannozzo Manetti*, 79–84.

166. BML Plut. 52 15, 1v, "partium divisione."

167. BML Plut. 52, 15, 2v, "quem si antiques hystorias veteres annales et cronicos libros parumper ante occulos posueris."

168. On Nello Martini's examples, see Maxson, "Many Shades," 399.

169. BML Plut. 52 15, 3r. "ut greci elegantius & expressius dicunt atheus qui in religiosos & sine deo Manfredus."

170. BML Plut. 52, 15, 6r.

171. For Numa, Augustus, and the name Nicholas, see BML Plut. 52, 15, 7r-7v.

172. ASF Sig. Leg. 11, 185v.

173. ASF Sig. Leg. 11 186r; "fine subguignendo che altra volta quando pratera alla sua Beatitudine. sarete apiedi dessa per dire alcune altre cose a voi commesse." For the peace more generally, ASF Sig. Leg. 11, 186r-187v.

174. For this statement, see BML Plut. 52 15, 9r, "Caeterum quadam alia restant quae cum sanctitati tuae placuerit opportunioribus locis atque temporibus referemus (Certain other things remain which, when it pleases your holiness, we will speak about at a more fitting place and time.)"

175. ASF Sig. Leg. 13, 136v.

176. Guasti, *Due Legazioni*, 3–4. "et che nella città nostra non è memoria anticha, che si ricordi venire mai nuova reputata felice quanto questa, et per la quale universalmente da tucta la città, grandi piccoli et mezzani, et d'ogni grado et d'ogni sexo, se ne prendesse si smisurato guadio et letitia."

177. See each page of the oration found at Antonino, *Chronicorum* (1586), 3:585– 589. The sixteenth-century editor has noted when the language echoes a biblical passage.

178. Ibid., 3:586–587, 587, and 588. The quotations to the *Etymologies* and the *Donation of Constantine* are explicitly stated; however, Antonino quotes the *De consideratione* silently. The passages are "tu igitur sacerdos ... unctione Christus" (book II, ch. 8 of *De consideratione)* and "formam fore iustitae ... Pharaonis" (book IV, ch. 7). I have accessed an online version of Bernard's *De consideratione* at http://www.binetti.ru/bernardus/10.shtml (accessed May 11, 2010) and verified the accuracy of its transcription of the relevant passages in Bernard of Clairvaux, *De Consideratione ad Eugenium Papam Tertium*, ed. Gerardus Vossius (Rome: Guielmi Facciotti, 1594). In this edition, the first passage "tu ... Christus" appears in book II, ch. 9, pp. 57– 58. The second passage, "formam ... Pharaonis," appears in book IV, ch. 11, p. 143.

179. Antonino, *Chronicorum*, 3:585–587, "Laetatus sum in iis, quae dicta sunt mihi."

180. Ibid.

181. Ibid., 3:587–588.

182. Ibid., 3:588, "angelum sathanae."

183. Ibid.

184. On Antonino's appearance, see da Bisticci, *Le Vite*, 1:234.

185. Antonino, *Chronicorum*, 3:585; "Blessed father and lord, because it happens that whoever speaks before your sanctity is shaken up and trembles, partly because of the celestial nature of your throne, which among people nothing is higher; partly because of your intelligence, which, by a heavenly gift is golden and abundant in your familiarity with both law and holy wisdom; no less because of the presence of the most reverend lord cardinals, most venerable bishops, and learned doctors with their vast knowledge; is it any wonder if I, who am sufficient in neither knowledge nor words, pale and almost lose my voice when approaching those who are owed such majesty?"

186. Bernard of Clairvaux, *De Consideratione*, book IV, ch. 7, http://www.binetti. ru/bernardus/10.shtml (accessed June 15, 2010); the passage is a description of things that the pope should be: "Form of justice, mirror of holiness, example of piety, asserter of truth, defender of the faith, teacher of nations, leader of the Christians, friend of the groom, paranymph of the bride, appointer of the clergy, pastor of the plebs, teacher of the foolish, refuge of the oppressed, advocate of the poor, hope of the wretched, guardian of

orphans, judge of widows, eye of the blind, tongue of the mute, crutch of the
aged, avenger of wickedness, dread of the wicked, glory of the good, rod of
the mighty, hammer of tyrants, father of kings, administrator of laws,
dispensator of canons, salt of the earth, light of the world, priest of the
Almighty, vicar of Christ, Christ of the Lord, and finally god of the
Pharaoh."

187. Antonino, *Chronicorum*, 3:587.

7. Humanism as a Means to Social Status, 1456–1485

1. Scala, *Humanistic*, 224.
2. Angelo M. Bandini, *Collectio veterum aliquot monimentorum* (Arezzo: Michele Bellotti, 1752), 86–100; cf. Brown, *Bartolomeo*, 205.
3. Scala, *Humanistic*, 224.
4. On these events, see Najemy, *History*, 250–306 and 341–374, as well as the classic account in Rubinstein, *Government*.
5. Rubinstein, *Government*, 145–146.
6. On these ritualized developments, see Trexler, *Public*, 419–462.
7. Franca Leverotti, *Diplomazia e governo dello stato: I <<famigli cavalcanti>> di Francesco Sforza (1450–1466)* (Pisa: ETS Editrice, 1992), 11.
8. Luiso, *Studi*, 51.
9. On this development during the fifteenth century, see Fubini, *Quattrocento*, 11–98.
10. On these points, see the lists supplied in Chapter 5.
11. Brucker, *The Civic*, 278–279.
12. On these points, see Chapter 5.
13. Martines, *Lawyers*, 63–64.
14. On the familial origins of Nello Martini, see Ibid., 73 and 499.
15. Ibid., 73–75.
16. Ibid., 206 and 504.
17. Nello's missions are found at ASF Sig. Miss. I 28, 125v; Sig. Leg. 4, 100v; 5, 92v; 6, 46r, 74r, 84r; 7, 10r, 29v, 46r, 52v.
18. Maxson, "Gifts."
19. Ibid.
20. *Florentine Renaissance Resources*. Search for "palmieri" under surname.
21. da Bisticci, *Le Vite*, 1:563. "naque di parenti di mediocre conditione, dette principio alla casa sua, et nobilitolla per le sua singulari virtù."
22. Rinuccini, *Lettere*, 80. "Mattheus igitur Palmerius honestis parentibus natus, quippe qui in germanos quosdam principes originis suae primordia referat."
23. Ferraro, *Matteo*, 23, and more generally 17–24.
24. Rubinstein, *The Government*, 161 and 325.
25. On this mission, see Ferraro, *Matteo*, 92–95.
26. Ibid., 99–103.
27. Ibid., 108–113.
28. Guasti, *Commissioni*, 1: 292–293.

29. Ibid., 292, "con modo cauto e secreto" and "alcuno altro non abbia a sentire."
30. Ibid., 292–293.
31. On this mission, see earlier discussion.
32. Ferraro, *Matteo*, 132–134.
33. Ibid., 137–138; cf. Carpetto, *The Humanism*, 22.
34. Ferraro, *Matteo*, 139–146.
35. Ibid., 146–148 and 155–163. For a list of Palmieri's diplomatic missions more generally, see earlier discussion; cf. Martines, *The Social*, 192; Carpetto, *The Humanism*, 12 and 22. Ferraro describes a mission not found in the database for this project, namely, Palmieri's role as one of the twenty ambassadors sent to greet Frederick III in 1452. These escort missions rarely have left significant traces in the historical record and thus have been excluded from this study unless otherwise noted. The identity of these twenty men, for example, would be lost to history, if not for the writings of Palmieri himself. See Ferraro, *Matteo*, 90. Escort diplomats were not usually recorded in the election books for diplomats or given explicit, recorded commissions – or if they were, such documents no longer survive in the standard archival sources.
36. Palmieri, *Annales*, 184. cf. ASF Sig. Leg. 16, 35r; Ferraro, *Matteo*, 136–137.
37. Bayley, *War and Society*, 82–85; cf. Brucker, *The Civic*, 447ff.
38. On this mission, see the documents published in Guasti, *Commissioni*, 2:320–533.
39. da Bisticci, *Renaissance*, 250–251 and 316–318; Armstrong, *Usury*, 25–26.
40. Bayley, *War and Society*, 89.
41. Ibid., 85–90; Peter Partner, *The Papal State under Martin V: The Administration and Government of the Temporal Power in the Early Fifteenth Century* (London: British School at Rome, 1958), 86–90.
42. For the negotiations with Savoy, see ASV Sen. Sec. 9, 142v, 147r and ASF Dieci Miss. 2, 95v–96r, 98v and 103v. For Palla di Palla Strozzi's commission to Savoy, see ASF Car. Strozzi III, 119, 37r. For a copy of the capitals of the agreement with Savoy, see ASF Car. Strozzi III, 125, 7r.
43. G. Canestrini, "Discorso sopra alcune relazioni della Repubblica fiorentina col Re d'Ungheria e con Filippo Scolari," *Archivio Storico italiano* 4 (1843): 204–206.
44. Monzani, "di Leonardo," 47 and part 2, 26.
45. On this mission, see ASF Dieci Miss. 2, 133v; Hankins, *Plato*, 2:385–386; and Viti, *Leonardo*, 128; and the unpublished payment records cited in Chapter 5.
46. ASF Dieci Miss. 2, 133v.
47. Bayley, *War and Society*, 76; Martines, *The Social*, 205; Roberto Bizzocchi, *Chiesa e potere nella Toscana del Quattrocento* (Bologna: Società editrice il Mulino, 1987), 21–22 and 47; Field, "Leonard Bruni," 1132.
48. Field, "Leonardo Bruni," 1132.
49. Leonardo Bruni, "Memoirs," in *History of the Florentine People*, vol. 3, ed. and trans. James Hankins with D. J. W. Bradley (Cambridge, MA: Harvard University Press, 2007), 356–363.

50. Germano Gualdo, "Leonardo Bruni segretario papale," in *Leonardo Bruni Cancelliere della Repubblica di Firenze*, ed. Paolo Viti (Florence: Leo S. Olschki, 1990), 80.

51. The pope had left Florence and entered Rome by September of 1420; see Monzani, "di Leonardo," 46. Bruni was elected a diplomat only in November.

52. Gualdo, "Leonardo," 81 and 92. Gualdo, however, is unsure of the level to which Bruni was used. Bruni argued against his fellow Florentines in favor of letting Pope Eugenius leave the city after the conclusion of the Council of Florence. See da Bisticci, *Renaissance*, 362–364. Giovanni Dominici had advised Rinaldo degli Albizzi as early as 1406 to work with Leonardo Bruni at the curia. See Guasti, *Commissioni*, 1:104.

53. Leonardo Bruni, *Humanistisch-Philosophische Schriften mit einer Chronologie seiner Werke und Briefe*, ed. Hans Baron (Leipzig: B. G. Teubner, 1928), 75–76.

54. Luiso, *Studi*, 104–105.

55. Trexler, *Public*, 287.

56. Ibid., 288.

57. "Consueverunt, Beatissime Pater, qui legationis officio fungentes sedem apostolicam et sanctissimam adeunt, quantum ipsi verbis oreque adniti possunt, exquisitissimis eam laudibus conari extollere. Quos tamen cum sepe presens diligenter accurateque audiverim, atque una ex parte verba illorum, alia vero ex parte amplitudinem maiestatemque sedis huius pensitarem, usque adeo deficere verba animadverti, ut laudatores ipsi eorum conatus omnes ridiculi viderentur. Neque sane id immerito evenire constat. Quis enim mentis compos humanis verbis digne huius laudes referre se posse credat, cuius auctoritas atque potestas non contenta terris neque maris ambitu celos insuper penetrat et transcendit angustisque sententiis amplitudinem huius sedis equare se posse existimet? Mea quidem sententia qui se hoc factuarum sperat, imbecillitatem suam non cognoscit. Qui vero attentare ausus est, temerarius reperitur. Ut recte a philosophis dictum sit, bonorum alia esse laudis, alia venerationis; laudis ea esse que in commendationem cadunt humanam; venerationis autem, illa que diviniora maioraque exsistunt, quam ad ea laudationes nostre queant accedere." Viti, *Opere*, 806–808.

58. Ibid., 808.

59. Their missions between these years are found at Donato Acciaiuoli: ASF Sig. Leg. 15, 148r; 17, 20r, 84r, 111r, 144r, 159r, 161v, 167r; 18, 90r, 97r; 19, 75r, 155r; 20, 20r; Sig. Dieci Otto Leg. Miss. Resp. 75, 34. Bernardo Buongirolamo: ASF Sig. Leg. 15, 11r, 42r, 51r, 87r; 16, 35r, 154r, 189r; 17, 15r, 96r, 132r; 18, 113r; Sig. Dieci Otto Leg. Miss. Resp. 12; Dieci Leg. 5, 262r; Dieci Miss. 19, 111v. Jacopo Guicciardini: ASF Dieci Leg. 5, 298v; 6, 1r; Otto Leg. 3, 3v; Sig. Leg. 16, 7r, 42r, 160r, 180r, 208r; 17, 22r, 57r; 19, 3r; 20, 2r 21, 26r; 28, 42r; Sig.Dieci Otto Leg. Miss. Resp 14, 1; 60, 1; filze 12 and 78 both contain letters regarding a mission to Milan in 1483; Luigi Guicciardini: ASF Otto Leg 1, 1rv; Sig. Leg. 15, 2v, 8r, 86r, 123v, 125r, 145r; 16, 20r, 113r, 164v, 172r, 193v, 219r; 17, 166r; 18, 90r; 19, 34r, 67r; 20, 76r; 21, 24v, 37r; Sig. Dieci Otto Leg. Miss. Resp. 60, 1; Otto Niccolini: ASF Sig. Leg. 15, 31v, 92r, 120v; 123r, 125r; 16, 158r, 191r, 208r; 17, 25r; 28, 42r; Palmieri,

Annales, 188; Pierfilippo Pandolfini: ASF Dieci Miss. 22, 91v; Otto Leg. 1, 1v; 3, 84rv; Sig. Leg. 17, 188r; 19, 132r; 20, 6r, 56r, 72r; 21, 28r, 43r, 60v; Antonio Ridolfi: ASF Car. Cor. 51, 157v, 160r; Otto Leg. 1, 10rv; Sig. Leg. 13, 181r; 15, 26v, 61r, 66v, 75r, 134r; 16, 37v, 164v, 185r; 213r; 17, 75r, 119r; 19, 92r; 20, 2r, 83r.

60. On Soderini's learning in general, see Paula C. Clarke, *The Soderini and the Medici* (Oxford: Clarendon Press, 1991), 134; his diplomatic missions are at ASF Sig. Leg. 15, 103r, 125r; 16, 35r, 173r; 17, 74r, 102r, 145r, 174r; 18, 84r, 19, 65r; 20, 48r; Sig. Dieci Otto Leg. Miss. Resp. 4, 33r.

61. Ferraro, *Matteo,* 39–40 and 87; cf. Clarke, *The Soderini,* 147.

62. Matteo Palmieri: ASF Sig. Leg. 15, 7v; 16, 26r, 35r, 153v; 17, 168r; Piero de' Pazzi; ASF Sig. Leg. 14, 42r; 15, 2v, 31v, 54v, 123r; Bernardo Rucellai: ASF Sig. Leg. 17, 155r; 20, 86r; 21, 35r, 59r; Otto Leg. 3, 105r; Dietisalvi Neroni: ASF Sig. Leg. 15, 63v, 90r, 127v; 16, 3v; Antonio Canigiani: ASF Sig. Leg. 21, 48v, 51v; Otto Leg. 4, 1r; Filippo de' Medici: ASF Sig. Leg. 15, 54v, 125r; 16, 192r; Lorenzo de' Medici: ASF Sig. Leg. 16, 160r; 17, 111r; 21, 43r; Pierfrancesco de' Medici: ASF Sig. Leg. 15, 2v, 86r; 17, 56r; Giuliano Ridolfi: ASF Sig. Leg. 14, 28v; 15, 1r, 37v; Tommaso Ridolfi: ASF Sig. Leg. 21, 17r, 40v; Sig. Dieci Otto Leg. Miss. Resp. 4, 11; Agnolo Acciaiuoli: ASF Sig. Leg. 15, 2v, 8r; Bernardo Giugni: ASF Sig. Leg. 16, 10r, 19r; Domenico Martelli: ASF Sig. Leg. 14, 40v; 17, 111r; Niccolò Michelozzi: ASF Sig. Dieci Otto Leg. Miss. Resp. 11, 1; Otto Leg. 4, 18r; Pandolfo Pandolfini: ASF Sig. Leg. 15, 58r, 145r; Franco Sacchetti: ASF Sig. Leg. 15, 26v, 44v; Bartolomeo Scala: ASF Sig. Leg. 21, 51v; Scala, *Humanistic,* 56; Piero Acciaiuoli: ASF Sig. Leg. 15, 80r; Maso degli Albizzi: ASF Sig. Leg. 21, 22r; Alessandro Alessandri: ASF Sig. Leg. 15, 31v; Piero de' Medici: ASF Dieci Miss. 5, 63v; Domenico Pandolfini: ASF Sig. Leg. 18, 150r; Antonio Pierozzi: ASF Sig. Leg. 15, 2v; Alamanno Rinuccini: ASF Sig. Leg. 18, 156r.

63. His diplomatic missions are found at ASF Dieci Miss. 5, 151v; Sig. Leg. 21, 40v, 43r. For his participation in the so-called Platonic Academy, see della Torre, *Storia,* 30.

64. Cecil Grayson, "Gentile Becchi," in *DBI,* available online at "Gentile Becchi in Dizionario Biografico – Treccani.it," http://www.treccani.it/enciclopedia/gentile-becchi_%28Dizionario-Biografico%29/ (accessed May 8, 2012); Desjardins and Canestrini, *Négociations,* 317–318 and his oration at pp. 335–337; Black, *Education,* 159 and 428; his diplomatic missions are at ASF Sig. Leg. 21, 48v; Otto Leg. 4, 1r.

65. For the dedication, see della Torre, *Storia,* 555–558; on his learning in general, see Eugenio Ragni, "Tommaso Benci," in *DBI,* available online at "Tommaso Benci in Dizionario Biografico – Treccani.it," http://www.treccani.it/enciclopedia/tommaso-benci_%28Dizionario-Biografico%29/ (accessed May 8, 2012); his diplomatic mission is at ASF Sig. Leg. 15, 71r.

66. Brown, "Platonism," 228; his diplomatic missions are at ASF Sig. Leg. 16, 70r, 140r; 17, 67r, 95r; 19, 1r; 21, 18v, 24v.

67. da Bisticci, *Le Vite,* 2:409; his diplomatic missions are at ASF Sig. Leg. 16, 135r, 189r.

68. For his friendship with Scala and Poliziano, see della Torre, *Storia*, 730. For further learned connections, see Ficino, *Opera*, 1:892; Bartolomeo Fonzio, *Epistolarum libri*, ed. Alessandro Daneloni, (Messina: Centro Interdipartimentale di Studi Umanistici, 2008), 1:10–11, 14–15; cf. Fonzio, *Letters*, 14–15 and 16–19; and Lionello Sozzi, "Lettere inedite di Philippe de Commynes a Francesco Gaddi," in *Studi di bibliografia e di storia in onore di Tammaro de Marinis* (Verona: Valdonega, 1964), 4:209–212; Black, "Machiavelli," 75–76; his diplomatic missions are found at ASF Sig. Leg. 21, 19v, 41v; Otto Leg. 3, 171r.

69. Christopher S. Celenza, *Renaissance Humanism and the Papal Cura: Lapo da Castiglionchio the Younger's De curiae commodis* (Ann Arbor: University of Michigan Press, 1999), 48; his diplomatic mission is found at ASF Sig. Leg. 19, 29r.

70. della Torre, *Storia*, 30; his diplomatic mission is found at ASF Dieci Miss. 21, 162v.

71. Ristori, "Amergo."

72. della Torre, *Storia*, 542; his diplomatic missions are found at ASF Sig. Leg. 21, 48v; Otto Leg. 4, 1r.

73. della Torre, *Storia*, 602; the missions are at ASF Sig. Leg. 21, 38r; Dieci Miss. 21, 64v.

74. The letter is found at ASF Car. Strozzi. III 112, 18r. The missions are at ASF Sig. Leg. 15, 25v, 68v, 135v; Car. Cor. 51, 153v.

75. On this oration, see Chapter 5; the mission is at ASF Sig. Leg. 21, 51v.

76. della Torre, *Storia*, 726, "carissimo;" for his mission, see ASF Sig. Dieci Otto Leg. Miss. Resp. 22, 1r. He was also a diplomat after 1485; see esp. ASF Sig. Leg. 21.

77. Francesco Guicciardini, *Dialogue on the Government of Florence*, ed. Alison Brown (Cambridge: Cambridge University Press, 1994), 179; Jurdjevic, *Guardians*, passim, has information on Capponi's political role in Florence in the 1490s before his death in 1496; see also Michael Mallett, "Piero Capponi," in *DBI*, available online at "Piero Capponi in Dizionario Biografico – Treccani.it," http://www.treccani.it/enciclopedia/piero-capponi_%28Dizionario-Biografico%29/ (accessed March 7, 2012). For Capponi's missions up to 1484, see ASF Sig. Leg. 20, 47r; 21, 37r; Dieci Miss. 21, 201v.

78. The letters to Niccolini are at Ficino, *Opera*, 1:642–643, 919, 954–955, his missions are at ASF Sig. Leg. 21, 26v and 51v; letters to Minerbetti are at Ficino, *Opera*, 1:635, his mission is at ASF Sig. Leg. 17, 160r.

79. On Antonio's sons, see Fonzio, *Letters*, 4–9, 156–169, and 200; for Antonio's mission, see ASF Dieci Miss. 21, 59v.

80. Scala, *Humanistic*, 109.

81. For his missions, see ASF Sig. Leg. 17, 112r, 168r; 19, 34r; 21, 36v; on his tomb, see Andrew Butterfield, *The Sculptures of Andrea del Verrocchio* (New Haven, CT: Yale University Press, 1997), 49 and 246; Vasari, *Lives*, 238.

82. Black, *Education*, 140 and 433. The grammar was by Niccolò Perotti; see esp. 161–162.

83. ASF Sig. Leg. 18, 153r; 19, 150r.

84. Peter Godman, *From Poliziano to Machiavelli: Florentine Humanism in the High Renaissance* (Princeton, NJ: Princeton University Press, 1998), 168; Jurdjevic, *Guardians*, 49; della Torre, *Storia*, 732; for his missions, see ASF Sig. Leg. 17, 165r; 18, 130r.

85. James Hankins, "The Ethics Controversy," in *Humanism and Platonism in the Italian Renaissance* (Rome: Edizioni di Storia e Letteratura, 2003), 218.

86. Scala, *Humanistic*, 94, 115, 117, and 150–151; for his artistic patronage, see Langton Douglas, "The *Fall of Man* by Piero di Cosimo," *Burlington Magazine for Connoisseurs* 86, no. 507 (June 1945): 134, 136, and 137.

87. ASF Sig. Leg. 17, 132r; 20, 26r, 41r; 21, 20r, 33r, 46r, 51v; Otto Leg. 2, 11rv.

88. Black, *Benedetto Accolti*, 333–334; his mission is at ASF Dieci Miss. 5, 3v.

89. Black, *Benedetto Accolti*, 131–132; his missions are at ASF Sig. Leg. 19, 122r and Otto Leg. 4, 20r.

90. Scala, *Humanistic*, 131; on the prison break, see Luca Landucci, *A Florentine Diary from 1450 to 1516*, trans. Alice de Rosen Jervis, (New York: Arno Press, 1969), 108; his missions are at ASF Sig. Leg. 19, 140r and 21, 41r.

91. For Scala's letters to these men, see Scala, *Humanistic*, passim; their missions are at Pier Giovanni Ricasoli: ASF Dieci Miss. 6, 12v; Sig. Leg. 20, 85r; 21, 40v; Piero Nasi: ASF Sig. Leg. 17, 11r, 35r, 169r; 18, 21r, 74r; 20, 62r, 83r; 21, 47v; Antonio de' Medici: ASF Sig. Leg. 20, 66r; 21, 24v; Giovanni Lanfredini: ASF Sig. Leg. 21, 59v; Bongianni Gianfigliazzi: ASF Sig. Leg. 17, 112r; 19, 132r; 21, 30v; Dieci Miss. 21, 54v, 66r; Sig. Dieci Otto Leg. Miss. Resp. 60, 1; Otto Leg. 4, 8v.

92. Individuals who are not yet associated with humanism but who served as diplomats three or more times were the following: *three missions*: Girolamo Albizzi, Giovanni Lorini, Paolo Machiavelli, Piero Vettori; *four missions*: Jacopo Lanfredini; *five missions*: Bartolomeo Popoleschi, Angelo della Stufa; *eight missions*: Bernardo Corbinelli.

93. ASF Sig. Leg. 15, 2v. For the Rucellai and Leonardo da Vinci's father, see Mirella Ferrari, *Medieval and Renaissance Manuscripts at the University of California, Los Angeles*, ed. R. H. Rouse (Berkeley: University of California Press, 1991), 66–67 (Belt Library 66, not seen).

94. On this oration, see Chapter 6.

95. Guasti, *Due Legazioni*, 45. "che simile mai per alcuna nuova qui adnuntiata in questa città essere stato non si ricorda."

96. Ibid., 46, "Saremoci in più lunghe parole distesi, dimostrando quanto dire si dovesse; se non che voi, messer l'Arcivescovo, intorno a questa materia dinanzi al Padre sancto a dire harete, al quale come huomo in ogni cosa prestantissimo diamo libera conmissione intorno alle predette cose dire egregiamente come alla Reverenza vostra parrà, distendendovi tanto quanto allo honore di questa Republica si conviene et del sancto Padre. Et nella fine direte, voi avere alcuna cosa alla Sanctità sua a dire, le quali in altro tempo più congruo si differiranno."

97. Antonino, *Chronicorum*, 3:594, "Certainly, none of these (empires) strove to lead a single soul to the door of eternal salvation, but after these empires, the prophet Daniel said 'God will awaken a certain kingdom of heaven, which will never be dispersed, nor will that kingdom be exchanged for another, and it will crush all these other kingdoms and it will last forever.'"

98. Ibid., 3:593–598; again, the sixteenth-century editor has marked Antonino's references to biblical and patristic sources.
99. Ibid., 3:594, "inter Graecos theologos doctor praecipuus."
100. Ibid., 3:596–597.
101. Ibid., 3:597, "Minervam" and "filius affectuosissimus patri optimo."
102. Ibid., 3:598, "laetentur coeli & exultet terra gratulatione pernimia"; this phrase appears repeatedly throughout the speech (3:593 (twice), 3:595, 3:596, and 3:598) and ultimately is from Psalms 95:11. However, it was also the opening lines to the bull joining the Greek and Latin churches at the Council of Florence in 1439.
103. Ibid., "Mihi quoque, pater beatissime supplico parcas, si prolixus fui, vel si non recte, non apte, non idonee pronunciaverim iniuncta."
104. Ibid.
105. For a discussion of these instructions, see Chapter 4. Although the surviving oration is anonymous, the instructions for the mission are directed to the archbishop.
106. For this oration, see Desjardins and Canestrini, *Négociations*, 117–124.
107. For Filippo's relationship with Cosimo and Piero, see D. S. Chambers, "Cardinal Francesco Gonzaga in Florence." In *Florence and Italy: Renaissance Studies in Honour of Nicolai Rubinstein*, ed. Peter Denley and Caroline Elam (London: Committee for Medieval Studies, 1988), 260; Martines, *April*, 48; on Filippo more generally, see Giovanni Ciccaglioni, "Filippo de' Medici," in *DBI*, available online at "Filippo de' Medici in Dizionario Biografico – Treccani.it," http://www.treccani.it/enciclopedia/filippo-de-medici_%28Dizionario-Biografico%29/author? (accessed May 8, 2012); Michele Luzzatini, "Filippo de' Medici, Arcivescovo di Pisa e le Visite pastorale del 1462–1463, *Bollettino storico pisano* 33–35 (1964–1966): 361–401.
108. BUP M.S. 537, 30r. "Indeed, even if we say few things about your mind, nevertheless we are not unaware of your wisdom, great generosity, clemency, and piety, because of which we have no doubt that all future things will be auspicious and happy."
109. Ibid., 28r–28v.
110. Ibid., 29r, "cum michi beati Gregorii verba veniunt in mentem."
111. Ibid., 29v, "non solum trigesimam aut sexagesimam, sed etiam centesimam eterne felicitatis eris recepturus mercedem."
112. The translation is the New Revised Version.
113. BUP, M.S. 537, 31v.
114. Ibid., 29v–31v.
115. On Acciaiuoli, see earlier discussion.
116. On Gianfigliazzi, see also Vanna Arrighi and Francesca Klein, "Da mercante avventuriero a confidente dello stato: Profilo di Bongianni Gianfigliazzi attraverso la sue *ricordanze*," *Archivio Storico Italiano* 161 (2003): 53–79; on della Stufa, see Chapter 6.
117. Ganz, "The Humanist," 214 and 339–342.
118. On this oration and mission in general, see Margery Ganz, "Donato Acciaiuoli and the Medici: A Strategy for Survival in '400 Florence," *Rinascimento* 22 (1982): 58–59.

119. BNC Magl. XXXII 39, 77v, "donum" and "munus."
120. Ibid., 78v, "cum immortali deo qui te tantis virtutibus ornavit maximae sunt a te gratiae habendae non minores a nobis agendae sunt quibus hominem tam ornatum pastorem dedit in lucem pertulit."
121. Ibid., 79r, the entire passage reads, "sed cum iam inveteratae consuetudinis sit omnium ferme oratum qui primum ad hanc sanctissimam sedem veniunt ut orationem habeant gratulationis & laetitie plenam vereor ne de populo florentino hac communi consuetudine me loqui putes. Non est haec communi consuetudo non sermo non mos ab omnibus usurpari solitus sed est devotio observantia caritas in apostolicam sedem natura nobis primum innata deinde multis nostrae reipublicae in eacclisia meritis multis suis in nos officiis confirmata quem facit ut omni eacclisae prosperitate laetemur ut nostra calamitate doleamus." Cf. Santini, *Firenze*, 213.
122. For the commission, see ASF Sig. Leg. 21, 51v.
123. For the connections of these families with the Medici, see Rubinstein, *The Government*, 123, 219, 221, and 354.
124. Lowe, *Church*, 20 and 276; on Soderini's diplomatic career more generally, see Lowe, *Church*, 27–35.
125. Brown, *Bartolomeo Scala*, 217.
126. Ibid., 22–46.
127. Ibid., 67 and 97–100.
128. Ibid., 83–101 and 257–326.
129. On Bernardo Buongirolamo as a new man, see ibid., 202; for Buongirolamo's diplomatic missions, see earlier discussion.
130. Ibid., 107–108.
131. See Guasti, *Due legazioni*, 53 and 58; Ganz, "Donato," 58–59.
132. Scala, *Humanistic*, 225. "De qua quidem nos ... orationi modum."
133. Ibid., 227; the entire sentence is "Quo enim pacto aliis futuram gloriam proponet fidemque faciet venturae vitae qui non quae nobis salvator noster est pollicitus cuncta tanquam ea, quae certissima habentur, sibi persuaserit?" "By this agreement he (the pope) puts forward future glory for others and builds faith for the afterlife. Who has not been convinced of these promises, just like all those, which are considered most certain, that our savior has promised to us?"
134. Ibid., 224.
135. Ibid., 225, "Quis aperire caeli nobis portas, quis claudere edidicit damnareque et dare salutem hominibus? Summus pontifex."
136. Ibid., 226–227.
137. Ibid., 227, "Exemplum meum dedi vobis ut quemadmodum ego feci, et vos faciatis."
138. Ibid., 227–228.
139. Ibid., 228, "pastor bonus."
140. Ibid., 229, "agnus innocens Christus in sacris saepe litteris appellatur."
141. Scala, *Humanistic*, 224; on Redditi, see Brown, *Bartolomeo Scala*, 205.
142. Scala, *Humanistic*, 224, "Oratio Bartholomei Scalae Florentini Oratoris ad Summum Pontificem Innocentium octavum."
143. Burckhardt, *The Civilization*, 153.

Conclusion

1. BNC Magl. XXV 348 11r-11v, "grandissima miseria" and "damnatione eterna."
2. Ibid., "miserichordia."
3. Ronald F. E. Weissman, "The Importance of Being Ambiguous: Social Relations, Individualism, and Identity in Renaissance Florence," in *Urban Life in the Renaissance*, ed. Susan Zimmerman and Ronald Weissman (Newark: University of Delaware Press, 1989), 269–280; cf. Edward Muir, "In *Some* Neighbors We Trust: On the Exclusion of Women from the Public in Renaissance Italy," in *Florence and Beyond: Culture, Society and Politics in Renaissance Italy*, ed. David S. Peterson with Daniel E. Bornstein (Toronto: Centre for Reformation and Renaissance Studies, 2008), 274–275; my thinking here has also been informed through conversations with Nic Baker about a conference paper he delivered at the American Historical Association in 2010, a project currently being revised for publication.
4. See especially Paul McLean, *The Art of the Network: Strategic Interaction and Patronage in Renaissance Florence* (Durham, NC: Duke University Press, 2007); and John F. Padgett, "An Open Elite? Social Mobility, Marriage, and Family in Florence, 1282–1494," *Renaissance Quarterly* 63, no. 2 (Summer 2010): 357–404.
5. Goldthwaite, *Economy*, 546–547; and Molho, *Marriage*, 211.
6. Padgett, "An Open," passim, with summary of major points on pp. 401–405; Goldthwaite, *Economy*, 546–560, esp. 550–554, although on 557–558 Goldthwaite implies that humanism and the artistic culture it encouraged were factors closing off social mobility.
7. Virginia Cox, "Gender and Eloquence in Ercole de' Roberti's *Portia* and *Brutus*," *Renaissance Quarterly* 62, no. 1 (Spring 2009): 81–95.
8. Michelozzi's missions between 1485 and 1494 are found at ASF Otto Leg. 7, 89rv; 9, 4v; Sig. Leg. 21, 84r; Dieci Leg. 11, 18r; Braccesi's are found at ASF Otto Leg. 9, 1v and Sig. Dieci Otto Leg. Miss. Resp. 27, 59.
9. The speech is found at Gragg, *Latin*, 199–201.
10. Anthony Grafton, *Defenders of the Text: The Traditions of Scholarship in an Age of Science, 1450–1800* (Cambridge, MA: Harvard University Press, 1994), 1–5. Kepler in particular receives extensive treatment in Grafton's book; see 178–203.
11. On these debates, Black, *Humanism*; Grendler, *Schooling*; Anthony Grafton and Lisa Jardine, *From Humanism to the Humanities* (Cambridge, MA: Harvard University Press, 1986).
12. On the historiography as moving beyond Florence, see Gene Brucker "Florence Redux," in *Beyond Florence: The Contours of Medieval and Early Modern Italy*, ed. Paula Findlen, Michelle Fontaine, and Duane J. Osheim (Stanford: Stanford University Press, 2003), 5–12, and the further bibliographic leads therein.

Bibliography

Abbreviations

ASF: Archivio di Stato, Florence
  Acquisti: Acquisti e Doni
  Car. Cor.: Carte di Corredo
  Car. Strozzi.: Carte Strozziane
  Cons. Mar.: Consoli del Mare
  Cons. Prat.: Consulte e Pratiche
  Cop. Resp.: Copiari di Responsive
  Dieci Deb. & Cred.: Dieci di Balìa, Debitori e Creditori
  Dieci Leg.: Dieci di Balìa, Legazioni e Commissarie
  Dieci Miss.: Dieci di Balìa, Missive
  Dieci Relazioni: Dieci di Balìa, Relazioni di oratori fiorentini
  MAP: Medici avanti il Principato
  N.A.: Notarile anticosimiano
  Otto Leg.: Otto di Pratica, Legazioni e Commissarie
  Sig. Dieci Otto Leg. Miss. Resp.: Signori, Dieci di Balìa, Otto di Pratica.
    Legazioni e Commissarie, Missive, Responsive
  Sig. Leg.: Signori, Legazioni e Commissarie
  Sig. Minutari: Signori, Minutari
  Sig. Miss. I: Signori, Missive I Cancelleria
  Sig. Rap.: Signori, Rapporti e relazioni di oratori fiorentini
  Sig. Risp. Verb.: Signori, Risposte verbali di oratori forestieri
ASV: Archivio di Stato, Venice
  Sen. Sec.: Senato Secrete
BL: British Library
  Add.: Additional
  Harl.: Harley
BML: Biblioteca Medicea Laurenziana, Florence
  Plut.: Plutei
BMore.: Biblioteca Moreniana, Florence
BNC: Biblioteca Nazionale Centrale, Florence
  Magl.: Magliabechiana

Naz.: Fondo Nazionale
Panc.: Manoscritti Panciatichiani
BUP: Biblioteca Universitaria, Padua
DBI: Dizionario Biografico degli Italiani
Ricc.: Biblioteca Riccardiana, Florence
Vat. Lat.: Latina, Biblioteca Apostolica Vaticana, Vatican City

Primary and Secondary Works Cited

Agnoletti, Bice. *Alessandro Braccesi: Contributo alla storia dell' umanesimo e della poesia volgare.* Florence: G. Passeri, 1901.

Aiazzi, Giuseppe, ed. *Ricordi storici di Filippo di Cino Rinuccini dal 1282 al 1460 colla continuazione di Alamanno e Neri, suoi figli, fino al 1560.* Florence: Stamperia Piatti, 1840.

Albanese, Gabriella. "Manetti tra politica, novellistica e filosofia: Il "Dialogus in Symposio." In *Dignitas et excellentia hominis: Atti del convegno internazionale di studi su Giannozzo Manetti*, edited by Stefano Ugo Baldassarri, 15–83. Florence: Le Lettere, 2008.

Alberti, Leon Battista. *The Family in Renaissance Florence.* Translated by Renée Neu Watkins. Columbia: University of South Carolina Press, 1969.

Allen, Michael J. B. and Valery Rees with Martin Davies, eds. *Marsilio Ficino: His Theology, His Philosophy, His Legacy.* Leiden: Brill, 2002.

de Angelis, Laura. "I canonici di San Lorenzo e loro disputa con i canonici della cattedrale." In *Il Capitolo di San Lorenzo nel Quattrocento*, edited by Paolo Viti, 21–34. Florence: Leo S. Olschki, 2006.

Armstrong, Lawrin. *Usury and Public Debt in Early Renaissance Florence: Lorenzo Ridolfi and the Monte Comune.* Toronto: Pontifical Institute of Mediaeval Studies, 2003.

Arrighi, Vanna. "Griso Griselli." In *DBI*, http://www.treccani.it/enciclopedia/griso-griselli_(Dizionario-Biografico)/ (accessed June 21, 2011).

Arrighi, Vanna. "Piero del Nero." In *DBI*, http://www.treccani.it/enciclopedia/piero-del-nero%28Dizionario-Biografico%29/ (accessed December 14, 2011).

Arrighi, Vanna and Francesca Klein. "Da mercante avventuriero a confidente dello stato: Profilo di Bongianni Gianfigliazzi attraverso la sue ricordanze." *Archivio Storico Italiano* 161 (2003): 53–79.

Associazione Culturale Buggiano Castello. *Atti del convegno Coluccio Salutati cancelliere e letterato.* Signa: Nova Arti Grafiche, 2007.

Astorri, A. "Benedetto Fortini." In *DBI*, http://www.treccani.it/enciclopedia/benedetto-fortini_%28Dizionario-Biografico%29/ (accessed July 19, 2011).

Balbi, Giovanna Petti. "Un uomo delle istituzioni: Gottardo Stella di Sarzana, cancelliere diplomatico genovese del '400." *Archivio Storico Italiano* 167, no. 2 (2004): 259–289.

Baldassarri, Stefano Ugo, ed. *Dignitas et excellentia hominis.* Florence: Le Lettere, 2008.

Baldassarri, Stefano Ugo and Arielle Saiber. *Images of Quattrocento Florence: Selected Writings in Literature, History and Art.* New Haven, CT: Yale University Press, 2000.

Baldassarri, Stefano Ugo and Bruno Figliuolo, eds. *Manettiana. La biografia anonima in terzine e altri documenti inediti su Giannozzo Manetti*. Rome: Roma nel Rinascimento, 2010.

Bandini, Angelo M. *Collectio veterum aliquot monimentorum*. Arezzo: Michele Bellotti, 1752.

Barbaro, Ermolao. *De coelibatu, De officio legati*. Edited by Vittore Branca. Florence: Leo S. Olschki, 1969.

Barbaro, Francesco. *Epistolario*. Edited by Claudio Griggio. Florence: Leo S. Olschki, 1999.

Baron, Hans. *The Crisis of the Early Italian Renaissance: Civic Humanism and Liberty in an Age of Classicism and Tyranny*. Rev. ed. Princeton, NJ: Princeton University Press, 1966.

Baron, Hans. *Humanistic and Political Literature in Florence and Venice at the Beginning of the Quattrocento*. Cambridge, MA: Harvard University Press, 1955.

Bausi, Francesco. "Le due redazioni del Dialogus Consolatorius di Giannozzo Manetti." In *Dignitas et Excellentia Hominis*, edited by Stefano U. Baldassarri, 77–104. Florence: Le Lettere, 2008.

Baxandall, Michael. *Giotto and the Orators: Humanist Observers of Painting in Italy and the Discovery of Pictorial Composition, 1350–1450*. Oxford: Clarendon Press, 1971.

Baxandall, Michael. *Painting and Experience in Fifteenth-Century Italy*. Oxford: Oxford University Press, 1988.

Bayley, C. C. *War and Society in Renaissance Florence: The De Militia of Leonardo Bruni*. Toronto: University of Toronto Press, 1961.

Bec, Christian. *Cultura e società a Firenze nell' età della Rinascenza*. Rome: Salerno Editrice, 1984.

Bec, Christian. *Les Livres des Florentins (1413–1608)*. Florence: Leo S. Olschki, 1984.

Bec, Christian. *Les Marchands Écrivains: Affaires et Humanisme à Florence, 1375–1434*. Paris: Mouton, 1967.

Bellinazzi, Anna. *La casa del cancelliere: Documenti e studi sul Palazzo di Bartolomeo Scala a Firenze*. Florence: Edifir, 1998.

Bertolini, Lucia, ed. *De vera amicitia: I testi del primo Certame Coronario*. Modena: F. C. Panini, 1993.

Bertolini, Lucia. "ΑΓΩΝ ΣΤΕΦΑΝΙΤΗΣ il progetto del Certame Coronario (e la sua ricezione)." In *Il volgare come lingua di cultura dal trecento al cinquecento*, edited by Arturo Calzona, Francesco Paolo Fiore, Alberto Tenenti, and Cesare Vasoli, 51–70. Florence: Leo S. Olschki, 2003.

Bessi, Rossella. *Umanesimo volgare: Studi di letteratura fra Tre e Quattrocento*. Florence: Leo S. Olschki, 2005.

Bianca, Concetta. "Un nuovo codice Pandolfini." *Rinascimento* 34 (1994): 153–155.

Bianca, Concetta, ed. "Novità su Coluccio Salutati: Seminario a 600 anni dalla morte." In *Medioevo e Rinascimento: Annuario del Dipartimento di Studi sul Medioevo e il Rinascimento dell' Università di Firenze* new ser. 19 (2008).

Bianca, Concetta. "Le orazioni di Leonardo Bruni." In *Leonardo Bruni Cancelliere della Repubblica di Firenze*, edited Paolo Viti, 227–245. Florence: Leo. S. Olschki, 1990.

Bigazzi, P. "Vita di Bartolommeo Valori (il Vecchio)." *Archivio Storico Italiano* 4 (1843): 235–383.

da Bisticci, Vespasiano. *Commentario della vita di messer Giannozzo Manetti*. Edited by Piero Fanfani. Turin: Unione Tipografico, 1862.

da Bisticci, Vespasiano. *Le Vite*. Edited by Aulo Greco. Florence: Istituto Nazionale di Studi sul Rinascimento, 1976.

da Bisticci, Vespasiano. *Renaissance Princes, Popes, and Prelates*. Translated by William George and Emily Waters. New York: Harper & Row, 1963.

Bizzocchi, Roberto. *Chiesa e potere nella Toscana del Quattrocento*. Bologna: Società editrice il Mulino, 1987.

Black, Christopher F. *Italian Confraternities in the Sixteenth Century*. Cambridge: Cambridge Univesity Press, 1989.

Black, Robert. "Ancients and Moderns in the Renaissance: Rhetoric and History in Accolti's Dialogue on the Preeminence of Men of His Own Time." *Journal of the History of Ideas* 43, no. 1 (January–March 1982): 3–32.

Black, Robert. *Benedetto Accolti and the Florentine Renaissance*. Cambridge: Cambridge University Press, 1985.

Black, Robert. *Education and Society in Florentine Tuscany: Teachers, Pupils and Schools, c. 1250–1500*. Leiden: Brill, 2007.

Black, Robert. "Florence." In *The Renaissance in National Context*, edited by Roy Porter and Mikulás Teich, 21–41. Cambridge: Cambridge University Press, 1992.

Black, Robert. "Florentine Political Traditions and Machiavelli's Election to the Chancery." *Italian Studies* 40 (1985): 1–16.

Black, Robert. *Humanism and Education in Medieval and Renaissance Italy*. Cambridge: Cambridge University Press, 2001.

Black, Robert. "Machiavelli, Servant of the Florentine Republic." In *Machiavelli and Republicanism*, edited by Gisela Bock, Quentin Skinner, and Maurizio Viroli, 71–99. Cambridge: Cambridge University Press, 1990.

Black, Robert. "Review of Renaissance Civic Humanism: Reappraisals and Reflections," edited by James Hankins. *English Historical Review* 116, no. 467 (June 2001): 715–716.

Black, Robert. "The Revival of Latin and Humanist Education." In *Italy in the Age of the Renaissance: 1300–1550*, edited by John M. Najemy, 29–36. Oxford: Oxford University Press, 2004.

Blanchard, W. Scott. "Patrician Sages and the Humanist Cynic: Francesco Filelfo and the Ethics of World Citizenship." *Renaissance Quarterly* 60, no. 4 (Winter 2007): 1107–1169.

Blum, Rudolfo. *La biblioteca della Badia fiorentina e i codici di Antonio Corbinelli*. Vatican City: Biblioteca Apostolica Vaticana, 1951.

Boccaccio, Giovanni. *The Decameron*, 2nd ed. Translated by G. H. McWilliam. London: Penguin Books, 1995.

Bombe, Walter. "A Florentine House in the Middle Ages: The Davizzi-Davanzati Palace." *Architectural Record* 31 (1912): 580–590.

Borsi, Franco and Stefano Borsi. *Paolo Uccello.* Translated by Elfred Powell. New York: Thames and Hudson, 1994.

Boschetto, Luca. "L'esilio volontario di Manetti." In *Dignitas et Excellentia Hominis: Convegno di studi su Giannozzo Manetti,* edited by Stefano U. Baldassarri, 117–145. Florence: Le Lettere, 2008.

Botley, Paul. "Giannozzo Manetti, Alfonso of Aragon and Pompey the Great: A Crusading Document of 1455." *Journal of the Warburg and Courtauld Institutes* 67 (2004): 129–156.

Botley, Paul. *Latin Translation in the Renaissance: The Theory and Practice of Leonardo Bruni, Giannozzo Manetti, and Erasmus.* Cambridge: Cambridge University Press, 2004.

Bracciolini, Poggio. *The Facetiae or Jocose Tales of Poggio.* Paris: Isidore Liseux, 1879.

Bracciolini, Poggio. *Lettere.* Edited by Helene Harth. Florence: Leo S. Olschki, 1984.

Braund, Susanna Morton, ed. and trans. *Juvenal and Persius.* Cambridge, MA: Harvard University Press, 2004.

Brown, Alison. *Bartolomeo Scala, 1430–1497, Chancellor of Florence: The Humanist as Bureaucrat.* Princeton, NJ: Princeton University Press, 1979.

Brown, Alison. "Insiders and Outsiders: The Changing Boundaries of Exile." In *Society and Individual in Renaissance Florence,* edited by William J. Connell, 337–383. Berkeley: University of California Press, 2002.

Brown, Alison. "The Language of Empire." In *Florentine Tuscany,* edited by William J. Connell and Andrea Zorzi, 32–47. Cambridge: Cambridge University Press, 2000.

Brown, Alison. "Platonism in Fifteenth-Century Florence." In *The Medici in Florence,* 215–245. Florence: Leo S. Olschki, 1992.

Brown, Alison. "Women, Children and Politics in the Letters of a Florentine Notary, Ser Pace di Bambello." In *Florence and Beyond: Culture, Society and Politics in Renaissance Italy,* edited by David S. Peterson with Daniel E. Bornstein, 229–255. Toronto: Centre for Reformation and Renaissance Studies, 2008.

Brucker, Gene. *The Civic World of Early Renaissance Florence.* Princeton, NJ: Princeton University Press, 1977.

Brucker, Gene. "Florence Redux." In *Beyond Florence: The Contours of Medieval and Early Modern Italy,* edited by Paula Findlen, Michelle Fontaine, and Duane J. Osheim, 5–12. Stanford, CA: Stanford University Press, 2003.

Brucker, Gene. *Living on the Edge in Leonardo's Florence, Selected Essays.* Berkeley: University of California Press, 2005.

Brucker, Gene. *Renaissance Florence.* Berkeley: University of California Press, 1969.

Brucker, Gene, ed. *Two Memoirs of Renaissance Florence: The Diaries of Buonaccorso Pitti and Gregorio Dati.* Translated by Julia Martines. Prospect Heights, IL: Waveland Press, 1991.

Bruni, Leonardo. *Epistolarum libri VIII recensente Laurentio Mehus (1741).* Edited by James Hankins. Rome: Edizioni di Storia e Letteratura, 2007.

Bruni, Leonardo. *Histoire, Eloquence et Poésie à Florence au Début du Quattrocento*. Edited and translated by Laurence Bernard-Pradelle. Paris: Honoré Champion Editeur, 2008.

Bruni, Leonardo. *History of the Florentine People*. Edited and translated by James Hankins. Cambridge, MA: Harvard University Press, 2001–2007.

Bruni, Leonardo. *Humanistisch-Philosophische Schriften mit einer Chronologie seiner Werke und Briefe*. Edited by Hans Baron. Leipzig: B. G. Teubner, 1928.

Bruni, Leonardo. *Opere letterarie e politiche*. Edited by Paolo Viti. Turin: Unione Tipografico, 1996.

Bullard, Melissa Meriam. *Filippo Strozzi and the Medici: Favor and Finance in Sixteenth-Century Florence and Rome*. Cambridge: Cambridge University Press, 1980.

Bullard, Melissa Meriam. *Lorenzo il Magnifico: Image, Anxiety, Politics and Finance*. Florence: Leo S. Olschki, 1994.

Burckhardt, Jacob. *The Civilization of the Renaissance in Italy*. Translated by S. G. C. Middlemore. London: Penguin Books, 1990.

Butterfield, Andrew. *The Sculptures of Andrea del Verrocchio*. New Haven, CT: Yale University Press, 1997.

Butters, Humfrey. "Machiavelli and the Medici." In *The Cambridge Companion to Machiavelli*, edited by John M. Najemy, 64–79. Cambridge: Cambridge University Press, 2010.

Cagni, Giuseppe M. "I codici Vaticani Palatino-Latini appartenuti alla biblioteca di Giannozzo Manetti." *La Bibliofilia* 62, no. 1 (1960): 1–42.

Cagni, Giuseppe M. *Vespasiano da Bisticci e il suo epistolario*. Rome: Edizioni di Storia e Letteratura, 1969.

di Camugliano, Ginevra Niccolini. *The Chronicles of a Florentine Family 1200–1470*. London: Jonathan Cape, 1933.

Canestrini, G. "Discorso sopra alcune relazioni della Repubblica fiorentina col Re d'Ungheria e con Filippo Scolari. *Archivio Storico Italiano* 4 (1843): 185–232.

Canestrini, G. "Testamento del Cardinal Baldassarre Coscia, già Papa col nome di Giovanni XXIII." *Archivio Storico Italiano* 4 (1843): 292–296.

Canestrini, G. "Versi fatti da Niccolò da Uzzano, predicendo la mutazione dello stato." *Archivio Storico Italiano* 4 (1843): 297–300.

Cardini, Roberto and Paolo Viti. *I cancellieri aretini della Repubblica di Firenze*. Florence: Polistampa, 2003.

Carli, Enzo. *All the Paintings of Paolo Uccello*. Translated by Marion Fizallan. London: Oldbourne, 1963.

Carpetto, George M. *The Humanism of Matteo Palmieri*. Rome: Bulzoni Editore, 1984.

Carteggi delle magistrature dell'età repubblicana: Otto di Pratica. Florence: Leo S. Olschki, 1987.

Castiglione, Baldesar. *The Book of the Courtier*. Edited by Daniel Javitch. New York: W. W. Norton, 2002.

Catellacci, Dante. "Diario di Felice Brancacci ambasciatore con Carlo Federighi al Cairo per il Comune di Firenze." *Archivio Storico Italiano* ser. 4, vol. 8 (1881): 157–188.

Cavalcanti, Giovanni. *Istorie fiorentine*. Edited by Filippo Luigi Polidori. Florence: Tipografia all' Insegna di Dante, 1838–1839.

Celenza, Christopher S. *The Lost Italian Renaissance: Humanists, Historians, and Latin's Legacy*. Baltimore: Johns Hopkins University Press, 2004.

Celenza, Christopher S. "Parallel Lives: Plutarch's Lives, Lapo da Castiglionchio the Younger (1405–1438) and the Art of Italian Renaissance Translation." *Illinois Classical Studies* 22 (1997): 121–155.

Celenza, Christopher S. *Renaissance Humanism and the Papal Cura: Lapo da Castiglionchio the Younger's De curiae commodis*. Ann Arbor: University of Michigan Press, 1999.

Chambers, D. S. "Cardinal Francesco Gonzaga in Florence." In *Florence and Italy: Renaissance Studies in Honour of Nicolai Rubinstein*, edited by Peter Denley and Caroline Elam, 241–261. London: Committee for Medieval Studies, 1988.

Chapman, Hugh. *Michelangelo Drawings: Closer to the Master*. New Haven, CT: Yale University Press, 2005.

Chiappelli, Luigi. "Inventario dei manoscritti raccolti dal lanaiolo fiorentino Dietisalvi di Nerone (a. 1433)." *La Bibliofilia* 25, no. 8–9 (1923): 247–52.

Christiansen, Keith. *Gentile da Fabriano*. Ithaca, NY: Cornell University Press, 1982.

Ciappelli, Giovanni. "Paolo Fortini." In *DBI*, http://www.treccani.it/enciclopedia/paolo-fortini_%28Dizionario-Biografico%29/ (accessed January 16, 2012).

Ciccaglioni, Giovanni. "Filippo de' Medici," in *DBI*, http://www.treccani.it/enciclopedia/filippo- de-medici_%28Dizionario-Biografico%29/ (accessed May 8, 2012).

Clairvaux, Bernard of. *De consideratione ad Eugenium Papam Tertium*. Edited by Gerardus Vossius. Rome: Gulielmi Facciotti, 1594.

Clarke, Paula C. *The Soderini and the Medici*. Oxford: Clarendon Press, 1991.

Clarke, Paula C. "Middle Class Culture in Florence on the Eve of the Renaissance." In *Firenze alla vigilia del rinascimento: Antonio Pucci e i suoi contemporanei*, edited by Maria Bendinelli Predelli, 111–124. Fiesole: Edizioni Cadmo, 2006.

Cochrane, Eric. *Historians and Historiography in the Italian Renaissance*. Chicago: University of Chicago Press, 1981.

Connell, William J. "The Humanist Citizen as Provincial Governor." In *Florentine Tuscany: Structures and Practices of Power*, edited by William J. Connell and Andrea Zorzi, 144–164. Cambridge: Cambridge University Press, 2000.

Cosenza, Mario. *Bibliographical Dictionary of the Italian Humanists and the World of Classical Scholarship, 1300–1800*. Boston: G. K. Hall, 1962–1967.

Cox, Virginia. "Gender and Eloquence in Ercole de' Roberti's Portia and Brutus." *Renaissance Quarterly* 62, no. 1 (Spring 2009): 61–101.

Crabb, Ann. *The Strozzi of Florence: Widowhood and Family Solidarity in the Renaissance*. Ann Arbor: University of Michigan Press, 2000.

Crum, Roger J. "Roberto Martelli, the Council of Florence, and the Medici Palace Chapel." *Zeitschrift für Kuntsgeschichte* 59, no. 3 (1996): 403–417.

Cummings, Anthony M. *The Maecenas and the Madrigalist. Patrons, Patronage, and the Origins of the Italian Madrigal*. Philadelphia: American Philosophical Society, 2004.

Dainelli, Amelia. "Niccolò da Uzzano nella vita politica dei suoi tempi." *Archivio Storico Italiano* ser. 6, vol. 17 (1932): 35–86 and 185–216.

Daniels, Rhiannon. *Boccaccio and the Book: Production and Reading in Italy 1340–1520.* London: Modern Humanities Research Association, 2009.

Dati, Leonardo. *Epistolae.* Florence, 1743.

Davidsohn, Robert. "Tre orazioni di Lapo da Castiglionchio ambasciatore fiorentino a Papa Urbano V e alla curia in Avignone." *Archivio Storico Italiano* 20 (1897): 225–246.

Davies, Jonathan. *Florence and Its University during the Early Renaissance.* Leiden: Brill, 1998.

Davies, M. C. "An Emperor without Clothes? Niccolò Niccoli under Attack." In *Maistor: Classical, Byzantine and Renaissance Studies for Robert Browning,* edited by Ann Moffatt, 269–308. Canberra: Australian Association for Byzantine Studies, 1984.

Davisson, Darrell D. "New Documents on Gentile da Fabriano's Residence in Florence, 1420–1422." *Burlington Magazine* 122, no. 932 (November 1980): 759–760, 763.

Debby, Nirit Ben-Aryeh. *Renaissance Florence in the Rhetoric of Two Popular Preachers.* Turnhout, Belgium: Brepols, 2001.

Desjardins, Abel and Giuseppe Canestrini. *Négociations Diplomatiques de la France avec la Toscane: Documents Recueillis par Giuseppe Canestrini.* Paris: Impériale, 1859.

"Diario di Palla di Noferi Strozzi." *Archivio Storico Italiano* ser. 4, vol. 11 (1883): 20–48, 145–156, 293–309; ser. 4, vol. 12 (1883): 3–22; ser. 4, vol. 13 (1884): 153–170; ser. 4, vol. 14 (1884): 3–18.

Douglas, Langton. "The Fall of Man by Piero di Cosimo." *Burlington Magazine for Connoisseurs* 86, no. 507 (June 1945): 134–139.

Dover, Paul. "The Economic Predicament of Italian Renaissance Ambassadors." *Journal of Early Modern History* 12 (2008): 137–167.

Eckstein, Nicholas, ed. *The Brancacci Chapel: Form, Function and Setting.* Cambridge, MA: Harvard University Press, 2007.

Eckstein, Nicholas. *The District of the Green Dragon.* Florence: Leo S. Olschki, 1995.

Eckstein, Nicholas. "Neighborhood as Microcosm." In *Renaissance Florence: A Social History,* edited by Roger J. Crum and John T. Paoletti, 219–239. Cambridge: Cambridge University Press, 2006.

d'Elia, Anthony F. *The Renaissance of Marriage in Fifteenth-Century Italy.* Cambridge, MA: Harvard University Press, 2004.

Fabbri, Lorenzo. "The Memory of Exiled Families: The Case of the Strozzi." In *Art, Memory, and Family in Renaissance Florence,* edited by Giovanni Ciappelli and Patricia Lee Rubin, 253–261. Cambridge: Cambridge University Press, 2000.

Fabii, Irene. "Sulla trasmissione dei carteggi diplomatici della Repubblica Fiorentina: Le antiche segnature." *Medioevo e Rinascimento* XVII (2003): 135–171.

Fancelli, Manlio, ed. *Orazioni politiche del cinquecento.* Bologna: Nicola Zanichelli, 1941.

Ferente, Serena. *La sfortuna di Jacopo Piccinino: Storia del Bracceschi in Italia, 1423–1465*. Florence: Leo S. Olschki, 2005.

Ferente, Serena. "The Ways of Practice: Angelo Acciaiuoli, 1450–1470." In *From Florence to the Mediterranean and Beyond*, edited by Diogo Ramada Curto, Eric R. Dursteler, Julius Kirshner, and Francesca Trivellato, 103–116. Florence: Leo S. Olschki, 2009.

Ferrari, Mirella. *Medieval and Renaissance Manuscripts at the Unviversity of California, Los Angeles*. Edited by R. H. Rouse. Berkeley: University of California Press, 1991.

Ferraro, Alessandra Mita. *Matteo Palmieri: Una biografia intellettuale*. Genoa: Name, 2005.

Ferraù, Giacomo. "Le <<Commentationes florentinae de exilio.>>." In *Francesco Filelfo nel quinto centenario della morte*, 369–388. Padua: Editrice Antenore, 1986.

Ficino, Marsilio. *Opera omnia*. Edited by Paul Oskar Kristeller. Turni: Bottega d'Erasmo, 1962.

Ficino, Marsilio. *Three Books on Life*. Edited and translated by Carol V. Kaske and John R. Clark. Binghamton, NY: Medieval & Renaissance Texts & Studies, 1989.

Field, Arthur. "Leonardo Bruni, Florentine Traitor? Bruni, the Medici, and an Aretine Conspiracy of 1437." *Renaissance Quarterly* 51, no. 4 (1998): 1109–1150.

Field, Arthur. *The Origins of the Platonic Academy in Florence*. Princeton, NJ: Princeton University Press, 1988.

Field, Arthur. "The Platonic Academy of Florence." In *Marsilio Ficino: His Theology, His Philosophy, His Legacy*, edited by Michael J. B. Allen and Valery Rees with Martin Davies, 359–376. Leiden: Brill, 2002.

Filarete, Francesco and Angelo Manfidi. *The Libro Cerimoniale of the Florentine Republic*. Edited by Richard C. Trexler. Geneva: Librairie Droz, 1978.

Filelfo, Francesco. *Cent-dix letters grecques de François Filelfe*. Edited by Émile Legrand. Paris: Ernest Leroux, 1892.

Filelfo, Francesco. *Satyrae*. Edited by Silvia Fiaschi. Rome: Edizioni di Storia e Letteratura, 2005.

Finke, Heinrich and Johannes Hollnsteiner. *Acta concilii constanciensis*. Münster: I. W. Regensberg, 1923.

Finzi, Claudio. *Matteo Palmieri dalla "Vita Civile" alla "Città di Vita."* Rome: Giuffrè Editore, 1984.

Fiocco, Giuseppe. "La biblioteca di Palla Strozzi." In *Studi di bibliografia e di storia in onore di Tammaro de Marinis*, vol. 2, 289–310. Verona: Valdonega, 1964.

Fischer, B., I. Gribomont, H. F. D. Sparks, W. Thiele, Robert Weber, H. I. Frede, and Roger Gryson, eds. *Biblia sacra vulgate*. Stuttgart: Hendrickson, 1994.

Flamini, Francesco. "Leonardo di Piero Dati, poeta latino del secolo XV." *Giornale storico della letteratura italiana* 16, no. 1 (1890): 1–107.

Flavio, Biondo. *Italia Illustrata*. Edited and translated by Catherine J. Castner. Binghamton, NY: Global Academic, 2005–2011.

Flavio, Biondo. *Italy Illustrated*. Edited and translated by Jeffrey A. White. Cambridge, MA: Harvard University Press, 2005.

Florentine Renaissance Resources, Online Tratte of Office Holders, 1282–1532. Machine readable data file. Edited by David Herlihi, R. Burr Litchfield, Anthony Molho, and Roberto Barducci. Providence, RI: Florentine Renaissance Resources/STG, Brown University, 2002.

Fonzio, Bartolomeo. *Epistolarum libri.* Edited by Alessandro Daneloni. Messina: Centro Interdipartimentale di Studi Umanistici, 2008.

Fonzio, Bartolomeo. *Letters to Friends.* Edited by Alessandro Daneloni and translated by Martin Davies. Cambridge, MA: Harvard University Press, 2011.

"Forum on the Baron Thesis." *American Historical Review* 100, no. 5 (1995): 107–144.

Francesco Filelfo nel quinto centenario della morte. Padua: Editrice Antenore, 1986.

Frigo, Daniela. *Politics and Diplomacy in Early Modern Italy: The Structure of Diplomatic Practice, 1450–1800.* Translated by Adrian Belton. Cambridge: Cambridge University Press, 2000.

Fubini, Riccardo. "Discorrendo di cose fiorentine: La provvisioni effimera del gonfaloniere Giovan Battista Ridolfi (7 settembre 1512). In *From Florence to the Mediterranean and Beyond: Essays in Honor of Anthony Molho,* edited by Diogo Ramada Curto, Eric R. Dursteller, Julius Kirshner, and Francesca Trivellato, vol. 1, 3–12. Florence: Leo S. Olschki, 2009.

Fubini, Riccardo. "La figura politica dell'ambasciatore negli siluppi dei regimi oligarchici quattrocenteschi abbozzo di una ricerca (a guisa di lettera aperta)." In *Forme e tecniche del potere nella città (secoli XIV–XVII),* 35–59. Perugia: Tipografia Guerra, 1979–1980.

Fubini, Riccardo. *Italia quattrocentesca: Politica e diplomazia nell'età di Lorenzo il Magnifico.* Milan: Franco Angeli, 1994.

Fubini, Riccardo. *Quattrocento fiorentino: Politica, diplomazia, cultura.* Pisa: Pacini, 1996.

Fubini, Riccardo. *Storiografia dell'umanesimo in Italia da Leonardo Bruni ad Annio da Viterbo.* Rome: Edizioni di Storia e Letteratura, 2003.

Ganda, Arnaldo. *Filippo Cavagni da Lavagna: Editore, tipografo, commerciante a Milano nel Quattrocento.* Florence: Leo S. Olschki, 2006.

Ganz, Margery A. "Donato Acciaiuoli and the Medici: A Strategy for Survival in '400 Florence." *Rinascimento* 22 (1982): 33–73.

Ganz, Margery A. "A Florentine Friendship: Donato Acciaiuoli and Vespasiano da Bisticci." *Renaissance Quarterly* 43, no. 2 (Summer 1990): 372–383.

Ganz, Margery A. "The Humanist as Citizen: Donato di Neri Acciaiuoli, 1428–1478." PhD diss., Syracuse University, 1979.

Garfagnini, Gian Carlo, ed. *Ambrogio Traversari nel VI centenario della nascita.* Florence: Leo S. Olschki, 1988.

Garfagnini, Gian Carlo, ed. *Marsilio Ficino e il ritorno di Platone.* Florence: Leo S. Olschki, 1986.

Garin, Eugenio. *Italian Humanism: Philosophy and Civic Life in the Renaissance.* Westport, CT: Greenwood Press, 1975.

Garin, Eugenio. *Portraits from the Quattrocento.* Translated by Victor A. Velen and Elizabeth Velen. New York: Harper & Row, 1972.

Garrard, Mary D. Review of *Florentine Busts: Sculpted Portraiture in the Fifteenth Century*, by Jane Schuyler, *The Colossal Sculpture of the Cinquecento*, by Virginia Bush, and *The Early Sculpture of Bartolommeo Ammanati*, by Peter Kinney. *Art Bulletin* 61, no. 3 (September 1979): 485–490.

Gatti, Daniela. *La Vita Caroli di Donato Acciaiuoli: La legenda di Carolo Magno in funzione di una historia di gesta*. Bologna: Patron, 1981.

Gaunt, Peter. *The English Civil War: The Essential Readings*. Oxford: Blackwell, 2000.

Gavitt, Philip. *Charity and Children in Renaissance Florence: The Ospedale degli Innocenti, 1410–1536*. Ann Arbor: University of Michigan Press, 1990.

Gentile, Sebastiano and Stéphane Toussaint, eds. *Marsilio Ficino, fonti, testi, fortuna*. Rome: Edizioni di Storia e Letteratura, 2006.

Giovio, Paolo. *Elogi degli uomini illustri*. Edited by Franco Minonzio and translated by Andrea Guaspani and Franco Minonzio. Turin: Giulio Einaudi, 2006.

Giustiniani, Vito R. *Alamanno Rinuccini, 1426–1499: Materialien und Forschungen zur Geschichte des Florentinischen Humanismus*. Graz: Böhlau Verlag, 1965.

Godman, Peter. *From Poliziano to Machiavelli: Florentine Humanism in the High Renaissance*. Princeton, NJ: Princeton University Press, 1998.

Goldthwaite, Richard A. *The Economy of Renaissance Florence*. Baltimore: Johns Hopkins University Press, 2009.

Gordan, Dillian. "Zanobi Strozzi's 'Annunciation' in the National Gallery." *Burlington Magazine* 140, no. 1145 (August 1998), 517–524.

Gordan, Phyllis Goodhard, ed. and trans. *Two Renaissance Book Hunters: The Letters of Poggius Bracciolini to Nicholas Niccolis*. New York: Columbia University Press, 1974.

Gouwens, Kenneth. "Perceiving the Past: Renaissance Humanism after the Cognitive Turn." *American Historical Review* 103, no. 1 (February 1998): 55–82.

Grafton, Anthony. *Defenders of the Text: The Traditions of Scholarship in an Age of Science, 1450–1800*. Cambridge, MA: Harvard University Press, 1994.

Grafton, Anthony. *Leon Battista Alberti: Master Builder of the Italian Renaissance*. Cambridge, MA: Harvard University Press, 2002.

Grafton, Anthony and Lisa Jardini. *From Humanism to the Humanities*. Cambridge, MA: Harvard University Press, 1986.

Gragg, Florence, ed. *Latin Writings of the Italian Humanists*. New York: Charles Scribner's Sons, 1927.

Grant, W. Leonard. "The Life of Naldo Naldi." *Studies in Philology* 60, no. 4 (October 1963): 606–617.

Grayson, Cecil. "Gentile Becchi." In *DBI*, http://www.treccani.it/enciclopedia/gentile-becchi_%28Dizionario-Biografico%29/ (accessed May 8, 2012).

Gregory, Heather. "A Florentine Family in Crisis: The Strozzi in the Ffiteenth Century." PhD {diss.}, University of London, 1981.

Gregory, Heather. "Palla Strozzi's Patronage and Pre-Medicean Florence." In *Patronage, Art and Society in Renaissance Florence*, edited by F. W. Kent and Patricia Simons with J. C. Eade, 201–220. Oxford: Clarendon Press, 1987.

Gregory, Heather. "The Return of the Native: Filippo Strozzi and Medicean Politics." *Renaissance Quarterly* 38, 1 (Spring 1985): 1–21.

Grendler, Paul. *Schooling in Renaissance Italy*. Baltimore: Johns Hopkins University Press, 1989.

Griffiths, Gordon, James Hankins, and David Thompson, eds. *The Humanism of Leonardo Bruni*. Binghamton, NY: Medieval & Renaissance Texts & Studies, 1987.

Gualdo, Germano. "Leonardo Bruni segretario papale." In *Leonardo Bruni Cancelliere della Repubblica di Firenze*, edited by Paolo Viti, 73–95. Florence: Leo S. Olschki, 1990.

Guasti, Cesare. *Le carte strozziane del R. Archivio di Stato in Firenze*. Florence: Galileina, 1884.

Guasti, Cesare. *Commissioni di Rinaldo degli Albizzi per il Comune di Firenze dal MCCCXCIX al MCCCCXXXIII*. Florence: M. Cellini E.C., 1867–1873.

Guasti, Cesare. *Due legazioni al Sommo Pontefice per il Comune di Firenze presedute da Sant'Antonino Arcivescovo*. Florence: Bianchi E. C. Barbera, 1857.

Guasti, Cesare. "Raimondo Mannelli alla battaglia di Rapallo." *Archivio Veneto* 10 (1875): 54–70.

Guicciardini, Francesco. *Dialogue on the Government of Florence*. Edited by Alison Brown. Cambridge: Cambridge University Press, 1994.

Guicciardini, Francesco. *Diario del viaggio in Spagna; memorie di famiglia*. Edited by Roberto Palmarocchi, with preface by Bruno Maier and notes by Mario Spinella. Pordenone: Edizioni Studio Tesi, 1993.

Guidotti, Alessandro. "Nuovi documenti su Vespasiano da Bisticci la sua bottega e la sua famiglia." In *Federico di Montefeltro*, edited by Giorgio Cerboni Baiardi, Giorgio Chittolini, and Piero Floriani, vol. 3, 97–111. Rome: Bulzoni Editore, 1986.

Haas, Louis. "*Il mio buono compare*: Choosing Godparents and the Uses of Baptismal Kinship in Renaissance Florence." *Journal of Social History* 29, no. 2 (1995): 341–356.

Haines, Margaret. "Oligarchy and Opera: Institution and Individuals in the Administration of the Florentine Cathedral." In *Florence and Beyond: Culture, Society, and Politics in Renaissance Italy*, edited by David S. Peterson with Daniel E. Bornstein, 153–177. Toronto: Centre for Reformation and Renaissance Studies, 2008.

Haines, Margaret. "The Years of the Cupola, 1417–1436." Opera di Santa Maria del Fiore, http://www.operaduomo.firenze.it/cupola/home_eng.HTML (accessed November 14, 2011).

Hankins, James. "The 'Baron Thesis' after Forty Years and Some Recent Studies of Leonardo Bruni." *Journal of the History of Ideas* 56, no. 2 (April 1995): 309–338.

Hankins, James. "Cosimo de' Medici as a Patron of Humanistic Literature." In *Humanism and Platonism in the Italian Renaissance*, vol. 1, 427–455. Rome: Edizioni di Storia e Letteratura, 2003.

Hankins, James. "The Dates of Leonardo Bruni's Later Works (1437–1443)." *Studi medievali e umanistici* 5–6 (2007–2008): 11–50.

Hankins, James. "The Ethics Controversy." In *Humanism and Platonism in the Italian Renaissance*, vol. 1, 193–239. Rome: Edizioni di Storia e Letteratura, 2003.

Hankins, James. *Humanism and Platonism in the Italian Renaissance*. Rome: Edizioni di Storia e Letteratura, 2003.

Hankins, James. "Humanism in the Vernacular: The Case of Leonardo Bruni." In *Humanism and Creativity in the Renaissance: Essays in Honor of Ronald G. Witt*, edited by Christopher S. Celenza and Kenneth Gouwens, 11–29. Leiden: Brill, 2006.

Hankins, James. "A Lost Continent of Literature." In *Humanism and Platonism in the Italian Renaissance*, vol. 1, 541–550. Rome: Edizioni di Storia e Letteratura, 2003.

Hankins, James. "The Myth of the Platonic Academy of Florence." *Renaissance Quarterly* 44, no. 3 (1991): 429–475.

Hankins, James. "Notes on the Composition and Textual Tradition of Leonardo Bruni's Historiarum florentini populi libri XII." In *Classica et Beneventana*, edited by F. T. Coulson and A. A. Grotans, 87–109. Turnhout: Brepols, 2008.

Hankins, James. "The Popularization of Humanism in the Fifteenth Century: The Writings of Leonardo Bruni in Latin and the Vernacular." In *Language and Cultural Change: Aspects of the Study and Use of Language in the Later Middle Ages and the Renaissance*, edited by Lodi Nauta, 133–147. Leuven: Peeters, 2006.

Hankins, James, ed. *Renaissance Civic Humanism: Reappraisals and Reflections*. Cambridge: Cambridge University Press, 2000.

Hankins, James. *Repertorium Brunianum: A Critical Guide to the Writings of Leonardo Bruni*. Rome: Istituto Storico Italiano per il Medio Evo, 1997.

Hankins, James. "The Study of Greek in the Latin West." In *Humanism and Platonism in the Italian Renaissance*, vol. 1, 273–291. Rome: Edizioni di Storia e Letteratura, 2003.

Hankins, James. "Unknown and Little-Known Texts of Leonardo Bruni." In *Humanism and Platonism in the Italian Renaissance*, vol. 1, 19–62. Rome: Edizioni di Storia e Letteratura, 2003.

Hankins, James. "A Zibaldone of Rinuccio Aretino." In *Humanism and Platonism in the Italian Renaissance*, vol. 1, 99–121. Rome: Edizioni di Storia e Letteratura, 2003.

Hatfield, Rob. "The Compagnia de' Magi." *Journal of the Warburg and Courtauld Institutes* 33 (1970): 107–161.

Helas, Philine. "Der 'fliegende Karthograph:' Zu dem Federico da Montefeltro und Lorenzo de' Medici gewidmeten Werk 'Le septe giornate della geographia' von Francesco Berlinghieri und dem Bild der Erde im Florenz des Quattrocento." *Mitteilungen des Kunsthistorischen Institutes in Florenz* 46 (2002): 270–320

Herlihy, David. *Women, Family and Society in Medieval Europe: Historical Essays, 1978–1991*. Providence, RI: Berghahn Books, 1995.

Heydenreich, Ludwig H. *Architecture in Italy, 1400–1500*. Revised by Paul Davies. New Haven, CT: Yale University Press, 1996.

Hill, Christopher. *The Century of Revolution, 1603–1714*. London: Routledge Classics, 2002.

Horster, Marita. *Andrea del Castagno: Complete Edition with a Critical Catalogue*. Ithaca, NY: Cornell University Press, 1980.

Hunter, Richard. *Plato's Symposium*. Oxford: Oxford University Press, 2004.

Hyland, William. "The Climacteric of Late Medieval Camaldolese Spirituality: Ambrogio Traversari, John-Jerome of Prague, and the Linea salutis heremitarum," in *Florence and Beyond: Culture, Society, and Politics in Renaissance Italy*, edited by David S. Peterson with Daniel Bornstein, 107–120. Toronto: Centre for Reformation and Renaissance Studies, 2008.

Ianziti, Gary. *Humanistic Historiography under the Sforzas: Politics and Propaganda in Fifteenth-Century Milan*. Oxford: Clarendon Press, 1988.

Ianziti, Gary. "Leonardo Bruni, the Medici, and the Florentine Histories." *Journal of the History of Ideas* 69, no. 1 (2008): 1–22.

Ianziti, Gary. *Writing History in Renaissance Italy: Leonardo Bruni and the Uses of the Past*. Cambridge, MA: Harvard University Press, 2012.

Ilardi, Vincent. "The Assassination of Galeazzo Maria Sforza and the Reaction of Italian Diplomacy." In *Violence and Civil Disorder in Italian Cities, 1200–1500*, edited by Lauro Martines, 72–103. Berkeley: University of California Press, 1972.

Ilardi, Vincent. "Fifteenth-Century Diplomatic Documents in Western European Archives and Libraries (1450–1494)." *Studies in the Renaissance* 9 (1962): 64–112.

Ilardi, Vincent. *Studies in Italian Renaissance Diplomatic History*. London: Variorum, 1986.

Isenberg, Nancy. "Censimento delle lettere di Niccolò Michelozzi." *Giornale italiano di filologia* n.s. 13 (1982): 271–291.

Jardine, Lisa. *Worldly Goods: A New History of the Renaissance*. New York: W. W. Norton, 1996.

Jones, P. J. "Travel Notes of an Apprentice Florentine Statesman, Giovanni di Tommaso Ridolfi." In *Florence and Italy*, edited by Peter Denley and Caroline Elam, 263–280. London: Committee for Medieval Studies, 1988.

Joost-Gaugier, Christian L. "Castagno's Humanistic Program at Legnaia and Its Possible Inventor." *Zeitschrift für Kuntsgeschichte* 45, no. 3 (1982): 274–282.

Jurdjevic, Mark. "Civic Humanism and the Rise of the Medici." *Renaissance Quarterly* 52, no. 4 (Winter 1999): 994–1020.

Jurdjevic, Mark. *Guardians of Republicanism: The Valori Family in the Florentine Renaissance*. Oxford: Oxford University Press, 2008.

Jurdjevic, Mark. "Hedgehogs and Foxes: The Present and Future of Italian Renaissance Intellectual History." *Past and Present* 195 (May 2007): 241–268.

Kendall, Paul M. and Vincent Ilardi, eds. *Dispatches with Related Documents of Milanese Ambassadors in France and Burgundy*. Athens: Ohio University Press, 1970–1981.

Kent, Dale. *Cosimo de' Medici and the Florentine Renaissance*. New Haven, CT: Yale University Press, 2000.

Kent, Dale. "The Florentine Reggimento in the Fifteenth Century." *Renaissance Quarterly* 28, no. 4 (Winter 1975): 575–638.

Kent, Dale. *Friendship, Love, and Trust in Renaissance Florence*. Cambridge, MA: Harvard University Press, 2009.

Kent, Dale. "Michele del Giogante's House of Memory." In *Society and Individual in Renaissance Florence*, edited by William J. Connell, 110–136. Berkeley: University of California Press, 2002.

Kent, Dale. *The Rise of the Medici*. Oxford: Oxford University Press, 1978.

Kent, Dale. "A Window on Cosimo de' Medici, Paterfamilias and Politician, from within His Own Household: The Letters of His Personal Assistant, Ser Alesso Pelli." In *Florence and Beyond: Culture, Society and Politics in Renaissance Italy*, edited by David S. Peterson with Daniel E. Bornstein, 355–367. Toronto: Centre for Reformation and Renaissance Studies, 2008.

Kent, F. W. *Bartolommeo Cederini and His Friends: Letters to an Obscure Florentine*. Florence: Leo S. Olschki, 1991.

Kent, F. W. "'Be Rather Loved Than Feared': Class Relations in Quattrocento Florence." In *Society and Individual in Renaissance Florence*, edited by William J. Connell, 13–50. Berkeley: University of California Press, 2002.

Kent, F. W. *Household and Lineage in Renaissance Florence*. Princeton, NJ: Princeton University Press, 1977.

Kent, F. W. *Lorenzo de' Medici and the Art of Magnificence*. Baltimore: Johns Hopkins University Press, 2004.

Kent, F. W. and Dale Kent. *Neighbours and Neighbourhoods in Renaissance Florence: The District of the Red Lion in the Fifteenth Century*. Locust Valley, NY: J. J. Augustin, 1982.

Kent, F. W. and Patricia Simons with J. C. Eade, eds. *Patronage, Art, and Society in Renaissance Italy*. Oxford: Clarendon Press, 1987.

Kibre, Pearl. "The Intellectual Interests Reflected in Libraries of the Fourteenth and Fifteenth Centuries." *Journal of the History of Ideas* 7, no. 3 (June 1946): 257–297.

King, Margaret L. *Venetian Humanism in an Age of Patrician Dominance*. Princeton, NJ: Princeton University Press, 1986.

Kohl, Benjamin G. "The Changing Concept of the *studia humanitatis* in the Early Renaissance." *Renaissance Studies* 6, no. 2 (June 1992): 185–202.

Krantz, Frederick. "Between Bruni and Machiavelli: History, Law and Historicism in Poggio Bracciolini." In *Politics and Culture in Early Modern Europe*, edited by Phyllis Mack and Margaret C. Jacob, 119–151. Cambridge: Cambridge University Press, 1987.

Kraye, Jill. "Ficino in the Firing Line: A Renaissance Neoplatonist and His Critics." In *Marsilio Ficino: His Theology, His Philosophy, His Legacy*, edited by Michael J. B. Allen and Valery Rees with Martin Davies, 377–397. Leiden: Brill, 2002.

Kristeller, Paul Oskar. "Francesco da Diacceto and Florentine Platonism in the Sixteenth Century." In *Studies in Renaissance Thought and Letters*, vol. 1, 287–336. Rome: Edizioni di Storia e Letteratura, 1969.

Kristeller, Paul Oskar. *Iter Italicum*. Leiden: Brill, 1963–1992.

Kristeller, Paul Oskar. *Marsilio Ficino and His Work after Five Hundred Years*. Florence: Leo S. Olschki, 1987.

Kristeller, Paul Oskar. "Marsilio Ficino as a Man of Letters and the Glosses Attributed to Him in the Caetani Codex of Dante." *Renaissance Quartery* 36, no. 1 (Spring 1983): 1–47.

Kristeller, Paul Oskar. *Renaissance Thought and Its Sources.* Edited by Michael Mooney. New York: Columbia University Press, 1979.

Kristeller, Paul Oskar. "The Scholar and His Public in the Late Middle Ages and the Renaissance." In *Medieval Aspects of Renaissance Learning*, edited by Edward P. Mahoney, 3–25. Durham, NC: Duke University Press, 1974.

Kristeller, Paul Oskar. *Supplementum Ficinianum.* Florence: Leo S. Olschki, 1937.

Kristeller, Paul Oskar. "An Unknown Correspondence of Alessandro Braccesi with Niccolò Michelozzi, Naldo Naldi, Bartolomeo Scala, and Other Humanists (1470–1472) in ms. Bodl. Auct. F. 2 17." In *Studies in Renaissance Thought and Letters*, vol. 2, 341–383. Rome: Edizioni di Storia e Letteratura, 1985.

Kristeller, Paul Oskar. "An Unpublished Description of Naples by Francesco Bandini." In *Studies in Renaissance Thought and Letters*, vol. 1, 395–435. Rome: Edizioni di Storia e Letteratura, 1969.

Kuehn, Thomas. *Heirs, Kin, and Creditors in Renaissance Florence.* Cambridge: Cambridge University Press, 2008.

Labalme, Patricia H. *Bernardo Giustiniani: A Venetian of the Quattrocento.* Rome: Edizioni di Storia e Letteratura, 1969.

Landino, Cristoforo. *Poems.* Translated by Mary P. Chatfield. Cambridge, MA: Harvard University Press, 2008.

Landucci, Luca. *A Florentine Diary from 1450–1516.* Translated by Alice de Rosen Jervis. New York: Arno Press, 1969.

Lang, Heinrich. *Cosimo de' Medici, die Gesandten und die Condottieri: Diplomatie und Kriege der Republik Florenz im 15. Jahrhundert.* Paderborn: Ferdinand Schöningh, 2009.

Layton, Richard A. *Didymus the Blind and His Circle in Late-Antique Alexandria.* Urbana: University of Illinois Press, 2004.

Lazzari, Alfonso. *Ugolino e Michele Verino: Studii biografici e critici.* Turin: Libreria Carlo Clausen, 1897.

Leader, Anne. *The Badia of Florence: Art and Observance in a Renaissance Monastery.* Bloomington: Indiana University Press, 2011.

Lerz, Nadia. "Il diario di Griso di Giovanni." *Archivio Storico Italiano* 117, no. 2 (1959): 247–278.

Leverotti, Franca. *Diplomazia e governo dello stato: I <<famigli cavalcanti>> di Francesco Sforza (1450–1466).* Pisa: ETS Editrice, 1992.

Lewin, Alison Williams. *Negotiating Survival: Florence and the Great Schism, 1378–1417.* Madison, NJ: Fairleigh Dickinson University Press, 2003.

Lillie, Amanda. *Florentine Villas in the Fifteenth Century: An Architectural and Social History.* Cambridge: Cambridge University Press, 2005.

Lowe, K. J. P. *Church and Politics in Renaissance Italy: The Life and Career of Cardinal Francesco Soderini (1453–1524).* Cambridge: Cambridge University Press, 1993.

Luck, Georg. "A Late Greek Manuscript in the Walters Art Gallery." *Journal of the Walters Art Gallery* 41 (1983): 67–70.

Luiso, Francesco Paolo. *Studi su l'epistolario di Leonardo Bruni.* Rome: Istituto Storico Italiano per il Medio Evo, 1980.

Luschino, Benedetto. *Vulnera diligentis.* Edited by Stefano dall' Aglio. Florence: Tavarnuzze, 2002.

Luzzati, Michele. "Filippo de' Medici, Arcivescovo di Pisa e le visite pastorale del 1462–1463." *Bollettino storico pisano* 33–35 (1964–1966): 361–408.

Machiavelli, Niccolò. *Florentine Histories.* Translated by Laura F. Banfield and Harvey C. Mansfield Jr. Princeton, NJ: Princeton University Press, 1988.

Machiavelli, Niccolò. *Opere complete.* Milan: Ernesto Oliva, 1850.

Malanima, Paolo. "Filippo Casavecchia." In *DBI*, http://www.treccani.it/enciclopedia/filippo-casavecchia_(Dizionario-Biografico)/ (accessed October 17, 2011).

Malanima, Paolo. *I Riccardi di Firenze: una famiglia e un patrimonio nella Toscana dei Medici.* Florence: Leo S. Oschki, 1977.

Mallett, Michael. "Ambassadors and Their Audiences in Renaissance Italy." *Renaissance Studies* 8, no. 3 (1994): 229–243.

Mallett, Michael. "Piero Capponi." In *DBI*, http://www.treccani.it/enciclopedia/piero-capponi_%28Dizionario-Biografico%29/ (accessed March 7, 2012).

Mancini, Girolamo. "Il bel s. Giovanni e le feste patronali di Firenze descritte nel 1475 da Piero Cennini," *Rivista d'Arte* 6 (1909): 185–227.

Manetti, Aldo. "Roberto de Rossi." *Rinascimento* 2 (1951): 33–55.

Manetti, Giannozzo. *Dialogus Consolatorius.* Edited by Alfonso de Petris. Rome: Edizioni di Storia e Letteratura, 1983.

Manfredi, Antonio. "Notizie su Antonio Ferrantini canonico di San Lorenzo e umanista." In *Il capitolo di San Lorenzo nel quattrocento*, edited by Paolo Viti, 65–80. Florence: Leo S. Olschki, 2006.

Marchesi, Concetto. "Il compendio volgare dell'Etica aristotelica e le fonti del VI libro del <Tresor>." *Giornale storico della letteratura italiana* 42 (1903): 1–74.

de la Mare, Albinia. "Florentine Manuscripts of Livy in the Fifteenth Century." In *Livy*, edited by T. A. Dorey, 177–199. London: Routledge & Kegan Paul, 1971.

de la Mare, Albinia. *The Handwriting of Italian Humanists.* Oxford: Oxford University Press, 1973.

de la Mare, Albinia. "Messer Piero Strozzi, a Florentine Priest and Scribe." In *Calligraphy and Paleography: Essays Presented to Alfred Fairbank*, edited by A. S. Osley, 55–68. New York: October House, 1965.

de la Mare, Albinia. "New Research on Humanistic Scribes in Florence." In *Miniatura fiorentina del Rinascimento 1440–1525*, edited by Annarosa Garzelli, vol. 1, 393–600. Florence: Giunta Regionale Toscana, 1985.

de la Mare, Albinia. "Vespasiano da Bisticci e i copisti fiorentini di Federico." In *Federico di Montefeltro*, edited by Giorgio Cerboni Baiardi, Giorgio Chittolini, and Piero Floriani, vol. 3, 81–96. Rome: Bulzoni Editore, 1986.

Margolis, Oren. "The Politics of Culture in the World of René of Anjou." PhD diss., University of Oxford, 2011.

Mari, Paolo. "Bernardo Buongirolami." In *DBI*, http://www.treccani.it/enciclopedia/bernardo-buongirolami_%28Dizionario-Biografico%29/ (accessed May 8, 2012).

Markham, Clements R. *The Letters of Amerigo Vespucci and Other Documents Illustrative of His Career.* London: Hakluyt Society, 1894.

Marsh, David. "Boccaccio in the Quattrocento: Manetti's Dialogus in symposio." *Renaissance Quarterly* 33, no. 3 (Autumn 1980): 337–350.

Martines, Lauro. *April Blood: Florence and the Plot against the Medici.* Oxford: Oxford University Press, 2003.

Martines, Lauro. *Lawyers and Statecraft in Renaissance Florence.* Princeton, NJ: Princeton University Press, 1968.

Martines, Lauro. *The Social World of the Florentine Humanists 1390–1460.* Princeton, NJ: Princeton University Press, 1963.

Marzi, Demetrio. *La cancelleria della Repubblica fiorentina.* Rocca San Casciano: Licianio Cappelli, 1910.

Mattingly, Garrett. *Renaissance Diplomacy.* Boston: Houghton Mifflin, 1971.

Mauss, Marcel. *The Gift: Forms and Functions of Exchange in Archaic Societies.* Translated by Ian Cunninson. London: Cohen & West, 1970.

Maxson, Brian Jeffrey. "Establishing Independence: Leonardo Bruni's History of the Florentine People and Ritual in Fifteenth-Century Florence." In *Foundation, Dedication and Consecration Rituals in Early-Modern Culture,* edited by Maarten Delbeke, Jan de Jong, and Minou Schraven, 79–98. Leiden: Brill, 2012.

Maxson, Brian Jeffrey. "Gifts and Status in Diplomacy: A Case-Study of Florence, Pius II, and Jacopo Piccinino in 1458." In *Languages of Power in Italy, 1300–1600,* edited by Daniel Bornstein and Laura Gaffuri. Turnhout: Brepols, forthcoming.

Maxson, Brian Jeffrey. "Kings and Tyrants: Leonardo Bruni's Hiero in Early Renaissance Florence." *Renaissance Studies* 24, no. 2 (April 2010): 188–206.

Maxson, Brian Jeffrey. "The Many Shades of Praise: Politics and Panegyrics in Fifteenth-Century Florence." In *Rhetorik in Mittelalter und Renaissance: Konzepte – Praxis – Diversität,* edited by Georg Strack and Julia Knödler, 393–412. Munich: Utz, 2011.

Maxson, Brian Jeffrey. "'This Sort of Men': The Vernacular and the Humanist Movement in Fifteenth-Century Florence." In *I Tatti Studies,* edited by Andrea Rizzi and Eva del Soldato (forthcoming).

Mazzocco, Angelo, ed. *Interpretations of Renaissance Humanism.* Leiden: Brill, 2006.

Mazzocco, Angelo. *Linguistic Theories in Dante and the Humanists: Studies in Language and Intellectual History in Late Medieval and Early Renaissance Italy.* Leiden: Brill, 1993.

McLean, Paul. *The Art of the Network: Strategic Interaction and Patronage in Renaissance Florence.* Durham, NC: Duke University Press, 2007.

McManamon, John M. *Funeral Oratory and the Cultural Ideals of Italian Humanism.* Chapel Hill: University of North Carolina Press, 1989.

Meier, Ulrich. "Die Sicht- und Hörbarkeit der Macht: Der Florentiner Palazzo Vecchio im Spätmittelalter." In *Zwischen Gotteshaus und Taverne. Öffentliche Räume in Spätmittelalter und Früher Neuzeit,* edited by Susanne Rau and Gerd Schwerhoff, 229–271. Cologne: Böhlau, 2004.

Micheli, Graziano. *La figura di Luigi Marsili, precursore della civilià umanistica a Firenze.* Florence: Editore de Bono, 1992.

Miglio, L. "Antonio Cocchi Donati." In *DBI,* http://www.treccani.it/enciclopedia/antonio-cocchi-donati_%28Dizionario-Biografico%29/ (accessed April 23, 2012).

Miglio, L. "Donato Cocchi Donati." In *DBI,* http://www.treccani.it/enciclopedia/donato-cocchi-donati_%28Dizionario-Biografico%29/ (accessed October 28, 2011).

Milanesi, C. "Il viaggio degli ambasciatori fiorentini al Re di Francia nel MCCCCLXI descritto da Giovanni di Francesco di Neri Cecchi loro Cancelliere." *Archivio Storico Italiano* ser. 3, vol. 1 (1865): part 1, 3–62.

Milner, Stephen. "Citing the Balcony: The Politics of Place and Public Address in Trecento Florence." *Italian Studies* 55 (2000): 53–82.

Milner, Stephen. "Communication, Consensus and Conflict: Rhetorical Precepts, the Ars concionandi, and Social Ordering in Late Medieval Italy." In *The Rhetoric of Cicero in Its Medieval and Early Renaissance Commentary Tradition*, edited by Virginia Cox and John O. Ward, 365–408. Leiden: Brill, 2006.

Milner, Stephen. "The Piazza della Signoria as Practiced Place." In *Renaissance Florence: A Social History*, edited by Roger J. Crum and John T. Paoletti, 83–103. Cambridge: Cambridge University Press, 2006.

Milner, Stephen. "Political Oratory and the Public Sphere in Early Quattrocento Florence." *New Readings* 1 (1995): 41–64.

Molho, Anthony. "The Brancacci Chapel: Studies in Its Iconography and History." *Journal of the Warburg and Courtauld Institutes* 40 (1977): 50–98.

Molho, Anthony. "Créditeurs de Florence en 1347: Un apercu statistique du quartier de Santo Spirito." In *Firenze nel Quattrocento*, vol. 1, 97–111. Rome: Edizioni di Storia e Letteratura, 2006.

Molho, Anthony. "Domenico Buoninsegni." In *DBI*, http://www.treccani.it/enciclopedia/domenico-buoninsegni_res-278f3a94–87e9-11dc-8e9d-0016357eee51_%28Dizionario_Biografico%29/ (accessed April 23, 2012).

Molho, Anthony. "Domenico di Leonardo Buoninsegni's Istoria Fiorentina." *Renaissance Quarterly* 23, no. 3 (Autumn 1970): 256–266.

Molho, Anthony. *Florentine Public Finances in the Early Renaissance, 1400–1433.* Cambridge, MA: Harvard University Press, 1971.

Molho, Anthony. *Marriage Alliance in Late Medieval Florence.* Cambridge, MA: Harvard University Press, 1994.

da Montecatini, Naddo and Iacopo Salviati. *Croniche fiorentine.* Edited by Ildefonso di San Luigi. Florence: Gae. Cambiagi, 1784.

Monzani, C. "di Leonardo Bruni Aretino." *Archivio Storico Italiano* new series, vol. 5 (1857): part 1, 29–54 and part 2, 3–34.

Morpugo, Salomone. *I manoscritti della Biblioteca Riccardiana di Firenze.* Rome: Tipografia Giachetti, 1900.

Morstein-Marx, Robert. *Mass Oratory and Political Power in the Late Roman Republic.* Cambridge: Cambridge University Press, 1989.

Muir, Edward. "In Some Neighbors We Trust: On the Exclusion of Women from the Public in Renaissance Italy." In *Florence and Beyond: Culture, Society and Politics in Renaissance Italy*, edited by David S. Peterson with Daniel E. Bornstein, 271–290. Toronto: Centre for Reformation and Renaissance Studies, 2008.

Muir, Edward. *Ritual in Early Modern Europe.* 2nd ed. Cambridge: Cambridge University Press, 2005.

Najemy, John M. "The Controversy Surrounding Machiavelli's Service to the Republic." In *Machiavelli and Republicanism*, edited by Gisela Bock,

Quentin Skinner, and Maurizio Viroli, 101–117. Cambridge: Cambridge University Press, 1990.

Najemy, John M. *Corporatism and Consensus in Florentine Electoral Politics, 1280–1400.* Chapel Hill: University of North Carolina Press, 1982.

Najemy, John M. *A History of Florence, 1200–1575.* Malden, MA: Blackwell, 2006.

Neumahr, Uwe. Die *Protestatio de Iustitia in der Florentiner Hochkultur.* Münster: Lit Verlag, 2002.

Nighman, Chris L. "What Is the *Manipulus florum?*" Description of the *Manipulus florum*, http://info.wlu.ca/~wwwhist/faculty/cnighman/page2.html (accessed April 25, 2010).

Online Catasto of 1427. Version 1.3. Edited by David Herlihy, Christiane Klapisch-Zuber, R. Burr Litchfield, and Anthony Molho. [Machine readable data file based on D. Herlihy and C. Klapisch-Zuber, *Census and Property Survey of Florentine Domains in the Province of Tuscany, 1427–1480.*] Providence, RI: Florentine Renaissance Resources/STG, Brown University, 2002.

Orlandi, Stefano. *Necrologio di S. Maria Novella 1235–1504: Testo e commenti biografici cardinali, vescovi, teologi, letterati, missionari, artisti fiorentini.* Florence: Leo S. Olschki, 1955.

Pade, Marianne. *The Reception of Plutarch's Lives in Fifteenth-Century Italy.* Copenhagen: Museum Tusculanum Press, 2007.

Padgett, John F. "An Open Elite? Social Mobility, Marriage, and Family in Florence, 1282–1494." *Renaissance Quarterly* 63, no. 2 (Summer 2010): 357–411.

Palau, Annaclara Cataldi. "La biblioteca Pandolfini." *Italia medioevale e umanistica* 31 (1988): 259–399.

Palau, Annaclara Cataldi. "La biblioteca di Pierfilippo Pandolfini." In *Protrepticon*, edited by Sesto Prete, 17–28. Milan: Istituto Francesco Petrarca, 1989.

Palma, M. "Piero Cennini." In *DBI*, http://www.treccani.it/enciclopedia/piero-cennini_%28Dizionario-Biografico%29/ (accessed November 15, 2011).

Palmieri, Matteo. *Annales.* Edited by Giosue Carducci, Vittorio Fiorini, and L. A. Muratori. *Raccolta degli storici italiani dal cinquecento al millecinquecento* 26, no. 1. Città di Castello: S. Lapi, 1906.

Palmieri, Matteo. *Vita civile.* Edited by Gino Beloni. Florence: Sansoni, 1982.

Pampaloni, Giuseppe. "Alessandro Alessandri." In *DBI*, http://www.treccani.it/enciclopedia/alessandro-alessandri_%28Dizionario-Biografico%29/ (accessed May 8, 2012).

Pampaloni, Giuseppe. "Gli organi della Repubblica fiorentina per le relazioni con l'estero." *Rivista di studi politici internazionali* 20 (1953): 261–296.

Pandimiglio, Leonida. *Felice di Michele vir clarissimus e un consoteria.* Olivetta: Tipografica Varese, 1989.

da Panzano, Luca. *"Brighe, affanni, volgimenti di stato": Le ricordanze quattrocentesche di Luca di Matteo di messer Luca dei Firidolfi da Panzano.* Edited by Anthony Molho and Franek Sznura. Florence: SISMEL, 2010.

Paoletti, John. "Fraternal Piety and Family Power: The Artistic Patronage of Cosimo and Lorenzo de' Medici." In *Cosimo 'il Vecchio' de' Medici, 1389–1464*, edited by Francis Ames-Lewis, 195–219. Oxford: Clarendon Press, 1992.

Parenti, Marco. *Lettere.* Edited by Maria Marrese. Florence: Leo S. Olschki, 1996.

Parenti, Piero di Marco. *Storia fiorentina.* Edited by Andrea Matucci. Florence: Leo S. Olschki, 1994.

Partner, Peter. *The Papal State under Martin V. The Administration and Government of the Temporal Power in the Early Fifteenth Century.* London: British School at Rome, 1958.

Perosa, Alessandro. "Alessandro Braccesi." In *DBI*, http://www.treccani.it/enciclopedia/alessandro-braccesi_%28Dizionario-Biografico%29/ (accessed December 14, 2011).

Perosa, Alessandro. "Andrea Alamanni." In *DBI*, http://www.treccani.it/enciclopedia/andrea-alamanni_%28Dizionario_Biografico%29/ (accessed April 16, 2012).

Perosa, Alessandro. "Lo zibaldone di Giovanni Rucellai." In *Studi di filologia umanistica*, edited by Paolo Viti, vol. 2, 59–147. Rome: Edizioni di Storia e Letteratura, 2000.

Petriboni, Pagolo di Matteo and Matteo di Borgo Rinaldi. *Priorista (1407–1459).* Edited by Jacqueline A. Gutwirth with Gabriella Battista. Rome: Edizioni di Storia e Letteratura, 2001.

Pettegree, Andrew. *The Book in the Renaissance.* New Haven, CT: Yale University Press, 2010.

Phillips, Mark. *The Memoir of Marco Parenti: A Life in Medici Florence.* Princeton, NJ: Princeton University Press, 1987.

del Piazzo, Marcello, ed. *Signori, Dieci di Balìa, Otto di Pratica Legazioni e Commissarie, Missive e Responsive.* Rome: n.p., 1960.

Pierozzi, Antonino. *Chronicorum.* 1586.

Pintor, F. "Le due ambascerie di Bernardo Bembo a Firenze e le sue relazioni coi Medici." In *Studi letterari e linguistici dedicati a Pio Ranjna nel quarantesimo anno del suo insegnamento*, 785–815. Florence: Enrico Ariani, 1911.

Pius II. *Commentaries.* Edited and translated by Margaret Meserve and Marcello Simonetta. Cambridge, MA: Harvard University Press, 2004–2007.

Plebani, Eleonora. *I Tornabuoni: Una famiglia fiorentina alla fine del medioevo.* Milan: Franco Angeli, 2002.

Plutarch. *Lives.* Edited by Bernadotte Perrin. Cambridge, MA: Harvard University Press, 1996.

Poggio Bracciolini, 1380–1980, nel VI centenario della nascita. Florence: Sansoni, 1982.

Polidori, F. "Due vite di Filippo Scolari." *Archivio Storico Italiano* 4 (1843): 119–184.

Poliziano, Angelo. *I detti piacevoli.* Edited by Mariano Festa. Montepulciano: Editori del Grifo, 1985.

Pope-Hennessy, John. *Luca della Robbia.* Ithaca, NY: Cornell University Press, 1980.

Prajda, Katalin. "The Florentine Scolari Family at the Court of Sigismund of Luxemburg in Buda." *Journal of Early Modern History* 14, no. 6 (2012): 513–533.

Queller, Donald E. *The Office of Ambassador in the Middle Ages.* Princeton, NJ: Princeton University Press, 1967.

Queller, Donald E. and Francis R. Swietek. *Two Studies on Venetian Government.* Geneva: Librairie Droz, 1977.

Quillen, Carol. "The Uses of the Past in Quattrocento Florence: A Reading of Leonardo Bruni's Dialogues." *Journal of the History of Ideas* 71, no. 3 (July 2010): 363–385.

Quintillian. *The Institutes Oratoria.* Edited by H. E. Butler. London: William Heinemann, 1920.

Ragni, Eugenio "Tommaso Benci." In *DBI*, http://www.treccani.it/enciclopedia/tommaso-benci_%28Dizionario-Biografico%29/ (accessed May 8, 2012).

Rao, Ida Giovanna, Paolo Viti, and Raffaella Maria Zaccaria, eds. *I Processi di Girolamo Savonarola (1498).* Florence: SISMEL edizioni del Galluzzo, 2001.

Reeve, M. D. "Statius' Silvae in the Fifteenth Century." *Classical Quarterly* n.s. 27, no. 1 (1977): 202–225.

Richardson, Brian. *Print Culture in Renaissance Italy: The Editor and the Vernacular Text, 1470–1600.* Cambridge: Cambridge University Press, 1994.

Richardson, Brian. *Printing, Writers and Readers in Renaissance Italy.* Cambridge: Cambridge University Press, 1999.

Richardson, R. C. *The Debate on the English Revolution.* 3rd ed. Manchester: Manchester University Press, 1998.

Rinuccini, Alamanno. *Lettere ed orazioni.* Edited by Vito R. Giustiniani. Florence: Leo S. Olschki, 1953.

Ristori, R. "Amerigo Corsini." In *DBI*, http://www.treccani.it/enciclopedia/amerigo-corsini_%28Dizionario-Biografico%29/ (accessed November 23, 2011).

Robin, Diana. *Filelfo in Milan: Writings 1451–1477.* Princeton, NJ: Princeton University Press, 1991.

Rocco, Alessandra, ed. *Carlo Marsuppini traduttore d'Omero: La prima traduzione umanistica in versi dell'Iliade (primo e nono libro).* Padua: Il poligrafo, 2000.

Rocke, Michael. *Forbidden Friendships: Homosexuality and Male Culture in Renaissance Florence.* Oxford: Oxford University Press, 1996.

Rollo, Antonio. "Sulle trace di Antonio Corbinelli." *Studi medievali e umanistici* 2 (2004): 25–95.

Ross, Janet. *Florentine Palaces and Their Stories.* London: J. M. Dent, 1905.

Rossi, Vittorio. "L'indole e gli studi di Giovanni di Cosimo de' Medici." In *Rendiconti della reale accademia dei Lincei,* ser. 5, vol. 2. Rome: Tipografia della Accademia, 1893.

Rubin, Patricia Lee. *Giorgio Vasari: Art and History.* New Haven, CT: Yale University Press, 1995.

Rubin, Patricia Lee. *Images and Identity in Fifteenth-Century Florence.* New Haven, CT: Yale University Press, 2007.

Rubinstein, Nicolai. "Florentine Constitutionalism and Medici Ascendancy in the Fifteenth Century." In *Florentine Studies: Politics and Society in Renaissance Florence*, edited by Nicolai Rubinstein, 442–462. London: Faber and Faber, 1968.

Rubinstein, Nicolai. *The Government of Florence under the Medici (1434–1494)*. 2nd ed. Oxford: Oxford University Press, 1997.

Rubinstein, Nicolai. "Michelozzo and Niccolò Michelozzi in Chios 1466–1467." In *Cultural Aspects of the Italian Renaissance: Essays in Honour of Paul Oskar Kristeller*, edited by Cecil H. Clough, 216–228. Manchester: Manchester University Press, 1976.

Rubinstein, Nicolai. *The Palazzo Vecchio 1298–1532: Government, Architecture, and Imagery in the Civic Palace of the Florentine People*. Oxford: Clarendon Press, 1995.

Saalman, Howard. "The Authorship of the Pazzi Palace." *Art Bulletin* 46, no. 3 (September 1964): 388–394.

Saalman, Howard. *Filippo Brunelleschi: The Buildings*. University Park: Pennsylvania State University Press, 1993.

Sabbadini, Remigio. "Briciole umanistiche." *Giornale Storico della Letteratura Italiana* 17 (1891): 212–218.

Sabbadini, Remigio. *La scuola e gli studi di Guarino Guarini Veronese*. Catania: Francesco Galati, 1896.

Saenger, Paul. *A Catalogue of the Pre-1500 Western Manuscript Books at the Newberry Library*. Chicago: University of Chicago Press, 1989.

Sale, J. Russell. *Filippino Lippi's Strozzi Chapel in Santa Maria Novella*. New York: Garland, 1979.

Salvemini, Gaetano. *La dignità cavalleresca nel Comune di Firenze*. Florence: M. Ricci, 1896.

Sandeo, F. *De regibus siciliae et apuliae*. Hanover: 1611.

Sandys, Sir John Edwin. *A Short History of Classical Scholarship*. Cambridge: Cambridge University Press, 1915.

Sansovino, F. *Historia di casa Orisina e degli huomini illustri della famiglia*. Venice: 1565.

Santi, B. "Bernardo Cennini." In *DBI*, http://www.treccani.it/enciclopedia/bernardo-cennini_%28Dizionario-Biografico%29/ (accessed November 15, 2011).

Santini, Emilio. *Firenze e i suoi "oratori" nel Quattrocento*. Milan: Remo Sandron, 1922.

Santini, Emilio. "La protestatio de iustitia nella Firenze medicea del Sec XV." *Rinascimento* 10, no. 1 (June 1959): 33–106.

Scala, Bartolomeo. *Humanistic and Political Writings*. Edited by Alison Brown. Tempe, AZ: Medieval & Renaissance Texts & Studies, 1997.

Schulz, Anne Markham. *The Sculpture of Bernardo Rossellino and His Workshop*. Princeton, NJ: Princeton University Press, 1977.

Schuyler, Jane. *Florentine Busts: Sculpted Portraiture in the Fifteenth Century*. New York: Garland, 1976.

Setton, Kenneth. *The Papacy and the Levant*. Philadelphia: American Philosophical Society, 1976–1984.

Shepherd, William. *The Life of Poggio Bracciolini*. Liverpool: J. M'Creery, 1802.

Simonetta, Marcello. *Rinascimento segreto: Il mondo del segretario da Petrarca a Machiavelli*. Milan: FrancoAngeli, 2004.

de Sismondi, J. C. L. *A History of the Italian Republics*. New York: Longmans, Green, 1901.

Smith, Christine and Joseph F. O'Connor. *Building the Kingdom: Giannozzo Manetti on the Material and Spiritual Edifice*. Tempe: Arizona Center for Medieval and Renaissance Studies, 2006.

Sozzi, Lionello. "Lettere inedite di Philippe de Commynes a Francesco Gaddi." In *Studi di bibliografia e di storia in onore di Tammaro de Marinis*, vol. 4, 205–262. Verona: Valdonega, 1964.

Spencer, John R. *Andrea del Castagno and His Patrons*. Durham, NC: Duke University Press, 1991.

Stinger, Charles L. *Humanism and the Church Fathers: Ambrogio Traversari (1386–1439) and Christian Antiquity in the Italian Renaissance*. Albany: State University of New York Press, 1977.

Strehlke, Carl Brandon. "Zanobi di Benedetto di Caroccio degli Strozzi, known as Zanobi Strozzi." In *Painting and Illumination in Early Renaissance Florence*, edited by Laurence B. Kanter, Barbara Drake Boehm, Carl Brandon Strehlke, Gaudenz Feuler, Christa C. Mayer Thurman, and Pia Palladino, 349–361. New York: Harry N. Abrams, 1994.

Strocchia, Sharon. *Death and Ritual in Renaissance Florence*. Baltimore: Johns Hopkins University Press, 1992.

Strocchia, Sharon. *Nuns and Nunneries in Renaissance Florence*. Baltimore: Johns Hopkins University Press, 2009.

Strozzi, Alessandra. *Selected Letters*. Edited by Heather Gregory. Los Angeles: University of California Press, 1997.

Swartz, David. *Culture and Power: The Sociology of Pierre Bourdieu*. Chicago: University of Chicago Press, 1997.

Tacconi, Maria S. *Cathedral and Civic Ritual in Late Medieval and Renaissance Florence*. Cambridge: Cambridge University Press, 2005.

Temple-Leader, John and Giuseppe Marcotti. *Sir John Hawkwood (L'Acuto)*. Translated by Leader Scott. London: T. Fisher Unwin, 1889.

Tognetti, Sergio. *Da Figline a Firenze: Ascesa economica a politica della famigilia Serristori (secoli XIV–XVI)*. Florence: Opus Libri, 2003.

Tognetti, Sergio. "Gli affari di Messer Palla Strozzi (e di suo padre Nofri): Imprenditoria e mecenatismo nella Firenze del primo Rinascimento." *Annali di Storia di Firenze* 4 (2009): 7–88.

della Torre, Arnaldo. *Storia dell' accademia platonica di Firenze*. Florence: G. Carnesecchi e Figli, 1902.

Traversari, Ambrogio. *Latinae epistolae*. Edited by Lorenzo Mehus. Florence: Caesareo, 1759.

Trexler, Richard C. *The Libro Cerimoniale of the Florentine Republic*. Geneva: Librairie Droz, 1978.

Trexler, Richard C. *Public Life in Renaissance Florence*. Ithaca, NY: Cornell University Press, 1991.

Trinkaus, Charles. In *Our Image and Likeness*. Constable: Garden City Press, 1970.

Trivellato, Francesca. "La missione diplomatica a Venezia del fiorentino Giannozzo Manetti a meta quattrocento." *Studi Veneziani* 28 (1994): 203–235.

Ullman, Berthold L. *The Humanism of Coluccio Salutati*. Padua: Editrice Antenore, 1963.

Ullman, Berthold L. "More Humanistic Manuscripts." In *Calligraphy and Palaeography*, edited by A. S. Osley, 47–53. New York: October House, 1965.

Ullman, Berthold L. and Philip A. Stadter. *The Public Library of Renaissance Florence: Niccolò Niccoli, Cosimo de' Medici and the Library of San Marco*. Padua: Editrice Antenore, 1972.

Vasari, Giorgio. *Lives of the Artists*, vol. 1. Translated by George Bull. London: Penguin, 1987.

Vasoli, C. "Iacopo Bracciolini." In *DBI*, http://www.treccani.it/enciclopedia/ iacopo-bracciolini_%28Dizionario-Biografico%29/ (accessed April 23, 2012).

Vedovato, Giuseppe. *Note sul diritto diplomatico della Repubblica Fiorentina*. Florence: G. C. Sansoni, 1946.

Verde, Armando. *Lo studio fiorentino, 1473–1503: Ricerche e documenti*. Florence: Leo S. Olschki, 1973–2010.

Viti, Paolo. "Il carteggio della seconda missione romana di Alessandro Braccesi." In *Forme letterarie umanistiche: Studi e ricerche*, 361–388. Lecce: Conte Editore, 1999.

Viti, Paolo. "Francesco Filelfo." In *DBI*, http://www.treccani.it/enciclopedia/ francesco-filelfo_%28Dizionario-Biografico%29/ (accessed April 13, 2012).

Viti, Paolo, ed. *Leonardo Bruni Cancelliere della Repubblica di Firenze*. Florence: Leo S. Olschki, 1990.

Viti, Paolo. *Leonardo Bruni e Firenze: Studi sulle lettere pubbliche e private*. Rome: Bulzoni, 1992.

Viti, Paolo. "Leonardo Dati." In *DBI*, http://www.treccani.it/enciclopedia/leonardo-dati_res-de29ae09–87eb-11dc-8e9d-0016357eee51_%28Dizionario-Biografico %29/ (accessed May 8, 2012).

Viti, Paolo. "Note su Niccolò Michelozzi." In *Forme letterarie umanistiche: Studi e ricerche*, 267–279. Lecce: Conte Editore, 1999.

Walser, Ernst. *Poggius Florentinus, Leben und Werke*. Leipzig: Teubner, 1914.

Walsh, R. J. *Charles the Bold and Italy (1467–1477): Politics and Personnel*. Liverpool: Liverpool University Press, 2005.

Watkins, Renée Neu, ed. *Humanism and Liberty: Writings on Freedom from Fifteenth-Century Florence*. Columbia: University of South Carolina Press, 1978.

Weddle, Saundra. "Saints in the City and Poets at the Gates: The Codex Rustici as a Devotional and Civic Chronicle." In *Florence and Beyond: Culture, Society and Politics in Renaissance Italy*, edited by David S. Peterson with Daniel Bornstein, 179–194. Toronto: Centre for Reformation and Renaissance Studies, 2008.

Weinstein, Donald. *Ambassador from Venice: Pietro Pasqualigo in Lisbon, 1501*. Minneapolis: University of Minnesota Press, 1960.

Weiss, Roberto. *Medieval and Humanist Greek*. Padua: Antenor, 1977.

Weissman, Ronald F. E. "The Importance of Being Ambiguous: Social Relations, Individuals, and Identity in Renaissance Florence." In *Urban Life in the Renaissance*, edited by Susan Zimmerman and Ronald Weissman, 269–380. Newark: University of Delaware Press, 1989.

Weissman, Ronald F. E. *Ritual Brotherhood in Renaissance Florence*. New York: Academic Press, 1982.

Winterbottom, Michael. "Fifteenth-Century Manuscripts of Quintilian." *Classical Quarterly* n.s. 17, no. 2 (November 1967): 339–369.

Witt, Ronald G. "Civic Humanism and the Rebirth of the Ciceronian Oration." *Modern Language Quarterly* 51, no. 2 (1990): 167–184.

Witt, Ronald G. *Coluccio Salutati and His Public Letters*. Geneva: Librairie Droz, 1976.

Witt, Ronald G. *Hercules at the Crossroads: The Life, Works, and Thought of Coluccio Salutati*. Durham, NC: Duke University Press, 1983.

Witt, Ronald G. *In the Footsteps of the Ancients: The Origins of Humanism from Lovato to Bruni*. Leiden: Brill, 2000.

Witthoft, Brucia. "Marriage Rituals and Marriage Chests in Quattrocento Florence." *Artibus et Historiae*, 3, no. 5 (1982): 43–59.

Wittschier, Heinz Willi. *Giannozzo Manetti, das Corpus der Orationes*. Cologne: Böhlau, 1968.

Yates, Francis Amelia. *Giordano Bruno and the Hermetic Tradition*. London: Routledge and Kegan Paul, 1964.

The Years of the Cupola: Digital Archive of the Sources of the Opera di Santa Maria del Fiore, 1417–1436. Edited by Margaret Haines. Florence: Opera di Santa Maria del Fiore, 2009, http://duomo.mpiwg-berlin.mpg.de/eng/IN/INlist21552So.HTM (accessed February 9, 2012).

Zaccaria, Raffaella Maria. "Bernardo Guadagni." In *DBI*, http://www.treccani.it/enciclopedia/bernardo-guadagni_%28Dizionario-Biografico%29/ (accessed May 8, 2012).

Zaccaria, Raffaella Maria. "Biagio Guasconi." In *DBI*, http://www.treccani.it/enciclopedia/biagio-guasconi_%28Dizionario-Biografico%29/ (accessed April 16, 2012).

Zaccaria, Raffaella Maria. "Documenti su Giannozzo Manetti." In *Dignitas et excellentia hominis*, edited by Stefano U. Baldassarri, 333–345. Florence: Le Lettere, 2008.

Zaccaria, Raffaella Maria. "Niccolò Guasconi." In *DBI*, http://www.treccani.it/enciclopedia/niccolo-guasconi_(Dizionario-Biografico)/ (accessed October 24, 2011).

Zaccaria, Raffaella Maria. "Nicola de' Medici." In *DBI*, http://www.treccani.it/enciclopedia/nicola-de-medici_(Dizionario-Biografico)/ (accessed June 21, 2011).

Zaccaria, Raffaella Maria. "Nicola di Vieri dei Medici." In *Alberti e la cultura del quattrocento*, edited by Roberto Cardini and Mariangela Regoliosi, vol. 1, 415–439. Florence: Edizioni Polistampa, 2007.

Zaccaria, Raffaella Maria. "Zenobi Guasconi." In *DBI*, http://www.treccani.it/enciclopedia/zenobi-guasconi_res-5d8c3d23–87ee-11dc-8e9d-0016357eee51_%28Dizionario-Biografico%29/ (accessed October 10, 2011).

Zippel, Giuseppe. *Carlo Marsuppini d'Arezzo: Notizie, biografiche, raccolte.* Trento: Giovanni Zippel, 1897.

Zippel, Giuseppe. *Niccolò Niccoli.* Florence: Bocca, 1890.

Zuraw, Shelley E. "The Public Commemorative Monument: Mino da Fiesole's Tombs in the Florentine Badia." *The Art Bulletin* 80, no. 3 (September 1998): 452–477.

Index